RESEARCH IN
SOCIAL MOVEMENTS,
CONFLICTS
AND CHANGE

Volume 4 • 1981

RESEARCH IN
SOCIAL MOVEMENTS,
CONFLICTS
AND CHANGE

A Research Annual

Editor: LOUIS KRIESBERG
Department of Sociology
Syracuse University

VOLUME 4 • 1981

 JAI PRESS INC.

Greenwich, Connecticut   *London, England*

CONTENTS

LIST OF CONTRIBUTORS

Judith Huggins Balfe   Department of Sociology
Douglass College, Rutgers University

David Bromley   Department of Sociology
University of Hartford

Bruce C. Busching   Department of Sociology
James Madison University

Lillian J. Christman   Resources for Evaluation, Analysis
and Planning, Washington, D. C.

James D. Cockcroft   Department of Sociology, Douglass
College, Rutgers University

Ted Davies   Department of Sociology
Indiana University, Bloomington

J. W. Frieberg   Harvard Law School and Centre
d'etude des movements sociaux,
Paris

Omer R. Galle   Department of Sociology
Population Research Center
University of Texas, Arlington

James A. Geschwender   Department of Sociology
State University of New York,
Binghamton

Joseph R. Gusfield   Department of Sociology
University of California,
San Diego

David Jaffee — Department of Sociology University of Massachusetts, Amherst

William R. Kelly — Department of Sociology Population Research Center University of Texas, Arlington

Robert A. Ladner — Behavioral Science Research Institute, Coral Gables, Florida

Rhonda Levine — Department of Sociology Bowdoin College

Gerald E. Markle — Department of Sociology Western Michigan University

Florence McCarthy — Ford Foundation and the Government of Bangledesh

Abu Hassan Othman — Dean of the Faculty of Social Sciences, Universiti Kebangsaan, Malaysia

James Peterson — Department of Sociology Indiana University, Bloomington

Richard E. Ratcliff — Department of Sociology Syracuse University

Sandra J. Roker — Behavioral Sciences Research Institute, Coral Gables, Florida

Barry J. Schwartz — Behavioral Sciences Research Institute, Coral Gables, Florida

Anson D. Shupe, Jr. — Department of Sociology University of Texas, Arlington

Loretta S. Titterud — Behavioral Sciences Research Institute, Coral Gables, Florida

Ralph Turner   Department of Sociology
                                 University of California, Los Angeles

John Useem   Department of Sociology
                                 Michigan State University

Ruth H. Useem   Departments of Sociology and
                                 Education, Michigan State University

INTRODUCTION

For many years, the sociological enterprise has been expanding in diverse directions. Theoretical and methodological approaches have proliferated and numerous schools of thought have emerged and been renewed. In such circumstances it is difficult to discern any dominant or even widely shared perspective; nevertheless, I think there are signs of convergence toward a paradigm that encompasses many contemporary ways of doing sociology. The core ideas in this paradigm can be simply stated. Persons, groups, or other units are viewed as purposive actors who collaborate, contend, and compete with each other. Although the actors are decidedly unequal in their abilities to shape developments, none of the actors is able to fully control events. Correspondingly, there are some regularities in the general outcomes of situations studied by sociologists and a problematic character to particular outcomes. Events and structures are the resultant of the complex interactions among many actors.

The central focus on interaction is obviously of fundamental significance for observers working in the often seemingly divergent traditions of symbolic interaction, exchange theory, and conflict sociology. Sometimes this view has been proposed as the essential character of the sociological perspective (Elias, 1980). Others have seen it as an alternative to the Marxist and to the functionalist approaches (Boudon, 1980). Others have synthesized aspects of the different traditions as they bear on a specific set of issues (Collins, 1975). The paradigm seems particularly relevant for studies of social movements, conflicts, and change. I believe that an approach emphasizing the centrality of interaction and the problematic character of outcomes with due attention to the unequal resources available to the many interacting parties provides the framework within which much contemporary work can be unified.

I think signs of convergence can be found in many contemporary works. Thus, many persons who are conducting research from a Marxist tradition have developed Marxism in ways which make their work congruent with this paradigm. The attention to the state as a somewhat autonomous actor is one indication of this (Skocpol, 1979; Evans, 1979). Neither objective conditions nor the dominant economic class are thought to determine the structure of a country nor the direction of events. Rather a struggle among varyingly powerful groupings produce outcomes that reflect a blend of the interests of the contending classes, recognizing the relative dominance of some classes and factions over others (McEachorn 1980; Clawson, 1980). In addition, current empirical analyses of many different spheres of social life develop interpretations that emphasize the mutual dependency of interacting organizations, world regions, and collectivity members engaged in decision making (Milner, 1980; Wallerstein, 1980; Zablocki, 1980; Mansbridge, 1980).

Since social analyses are based on different perspectives and address different substantive questions, the paradigm is manifested in many varieties. Before considering major variations, the basic components of the emerging paradigm need to be described more fully.

An essential element in the paradigm is that persons, groups, organizations, and other collectivities seek to advance their interests as they conceive them. This effort is made by persons in the name of various collectivities; and other persons varyingly support those efforts. Of course, the formulation of interests and of strategies to pursue them are not often carefully calculated and explicitly stated. There usually is no weighing of the costs and benefits of alternative policies. Cultural patterns and unreflecting assumptions about what appears to be self evident matters guide much conduct.

These various actors interact with each other through several social processes. People conflict, cooperate, compete, differentiate, merge and exchange with each other. The entities with which people identify themselves and by which they denote those with whom they are interacting are infinite. A particular set of such entities become relevant at a given time for a given issue. Within that set, as the interaction proceeds, the prominence of selected identifications and characterizations shifts. For example, a struggle between two groups of people develops with varying importance given to ethnic, religious, class, regional, or interpersonal networks. The boundaries of the system of interacting parties, consequently, are not clearly marked nor stable.

One resultant of these interactions are re-shaped entities as people modify the characteristics they use to define themselves and those with whom they interact. Indeed, the characteristics of each actually change in the course of the interaction. For example, as class relations change so do characteristics of the class members and then the class relations further change.

From these interactions new structures arise and are sustained and modified by the resultant consequences of all the processes. These structures include the institutional arrangements which characterize a society or a community or an organization. These structures are the background of constraints and opportunities for the continuing interaction of other entities. The structures appear as external realities for these other collectivities. In addition to social structures, material objects and technological systems are produced through the interaction and constitute a physical environment for further interactions.

The resources of each interacting entity help shape the resultant structures. The balance of resources among the actors affects the likelihood of cooperative, symbiotic, conflicting or other processes dominating the relationship. The balance also affects the resulting structure of domination, dependence, or collaborative patterns.

Since the paradigm gives attention to large as well as small actors, to structural consequences of interaction, and structural constraints of interaction, the phrase structural interaction might seem appropriate for the paradigm. But the term has been used in a different sense by Cohen (1955) and others and using it here would be confusing. Analysts working within the context of the paradigm also stress the complex and inter-related character of many simultaneous interactions. Consequently, I will refer to this emerging paradigm as a ''multiple interaction'' paradigm.

Different social scientists emphasize varying aspects of this paradigm. One major issue about which sociologists differ is the importance attributed to subjective orientations as opposed to objective conditions. That is, analysts may emphasize the way in which the interacting parties define themselves and each other, perceive their goals, and how to pursue them. Other analysts may stress the circumstances within which the parties are interacting; and how those circumstances constrain conduct.

Another issue about which analysts differ is the relative importance attributed to the processes of interaction. For example, either conflict or assimilation may be emphasized, depending on the importance given to issues of coercion and domination as opposed to issues of the content and degree of consensus about values and beliefs.

Analysts differ, finally, in the relative prominence given to parties in interaction. Individual persons, groups, large associations, or countries may be more or less emphasized. Varying significance is given to collectivities based on class, religion, ethnicity, gender, or kinship.

I will use this paradigm as a framework to briefly introduce each of the contributions in this volume. The contributions vary in theory, method and substantive content. Discussing them in the context of the multiple interaction paradigm will facilitate noting links and comparisons among the contributions. It will also reveal possible uses of the paradigm.

In the first paper, Ralph Turner critically examines the resource mobilization approach to the study of social movements and notes the continuities and discontinuities with the earlier collective behavior approach. He stresses the continuities, noting for example, the approaches' shared assumption of purposiveness among social movement leaders and most adherents. The approaches appear to be in disagreement only when restrictive assumptions are made in the resource mobilization approach. In practice, these assumptions are not generally made. The restrictive assumptions include the following: "to adhere to an optimizing rationality model of movement decision making, to assume that decision making is rather effectively centralized in most movements, (and) to treat goals as relatively stable and unproblematic" (p. 20).

The contributions he sees each approach making to the other indicates aspects of the convergence toward the structural multiple paradigm outlined earlier. Application of the paradigm would contribute to both. The paradigm calls attention to the multiplicity and interlocking character of the entities in interaction. As a result every entity in interaction becomes problematic. While leaders and adherents are together interacting with an opposing social movement or authority, they are interacting with each other. Attention to the interaction with other movements and organizations helps resolve some of the issues about the relationship between grievances and resources as the decisive factor in the emergence of a social movement. It suggests that what social movement leaders and adherents seek is affected by what others are willing to grant and the availability of resources may make what seemed an unattainable goal become accessible and hence worth striving for (Kriesberg, 1982).

Bromley, Shupe, and Busching in their contribution to the volume analyze the interactions between members of organizations affiliated with the Unification Church and their families and churches, particularly fundamentalist churches. The authors direct attention to the theological content of the Unification Church and fundamentalist churches to help account for the competing and basically conflicting relationships between them. The authors examine the emergence of the anti-cult movement as a coalition of parents of Unification Church members and of fundamentalist church members.

Within the context of the multiple interaction paradigm, we can discern that contending groups try to define each other and seek allies and hence seek definitions which will protect themselves and gain supporters in order to defeat adversaries. For the anti-cult coalition, the effort was a symbolic degradation and a kind of repression. The analysis helps elaborate the collective behavior and resource mobilization approaches by directing attention to the struggles among social movement organizations, established organizations, and small groups and individuals.

Freiberg analyzes the printers strike against the management of *Le Parisien Libre* as an instance of class struggle between workers and capitalists. In doing so, however, he pays detailed attention to the complexities of the several actors engaged in this longest French strike. He examines the strategies that each major adversary uses against the other in a long, shifting interactive series. Prospective technological changes were the source of the defensive struggle by the printers union and the outcome was an agreement which would lead to the modernization of the Parisian press and printing industry. The agreement reflected the interests of both management and the current printers, but it would transform the setting in which future contests would be waged between workers and managers. In this paper, like that of Bromley, Shupe, and Busching, the interactive character of the conflict is given attention. The issues of interaction and the corresponding uncertainties in outcome are too often neglected in analyses seeking only to account for the outbreak of a particular manifestation of a conflict. Freiberg also examines technology as the material condition upon which a conflict is based and as the resultant of the struggle among adversaries. The importance of technology is a point that Levine and Geschwender also make in their analysis of agricultural labor in Hawaii.

Christman, Kelly, and Galle undertake a comprehensive examination of industrial conflict, considering it as economic behavior and as collective behavior. They seek to specify the relative significance of each characterization by considering different structural contexts and repertoires of contention. They argue that saliance of economic versus political-collective action explanations depends upon several factors, particularly: elite strategies, definitions of labor struggle, the development of the labor movement, and the extent of government regulation of the worker-management relationship. The authors' specification and hence elaboration of the saliance of these approaches is a kind of synthesis. The synthesis indicates the usefulness of giving attention to the multiplicity of actors and how they affect, but do not determine, each other.

Ratcliff and Jaffee provide another analysis of an instance of the class struggle: a battle over the attempt by business interests to enact an antiunion ''right-to-work'' law in Missouri. In their analysis they reveal the multifaceted nature of what might seem a simple two-sided fight between capitalists and the unions. The primary adversaries compete for popular support and so try to define the struggle in terms which would have a general appeal. The fight shifted in level as past struggles were evoked and the current one was a fight in an interlocking series. Shifts in level also occurred as several conflicts converged when outside groups entered to mobilize possible constituencies. Ratcliff and Jaffee, as the other analysts of manager-labor struggles in this volume, also give detailed attention to the interacting strategies of the main adversaries. The aggressive antiunion campaign and its defeat in this instance have particular pertinence after the conservative electoral victories in 1980. Their analysis should also be compared to the successful campaign of workers in Hawaii to pass the "Little Wagner Act," as analyzed by Levine and Geschwender in the following contribution.

Levine and Geschwender examine the role of the state in relationship to the struggle between capitalists and agricultural workers in Hawaii. They conclude that "the state represents the balance of class forces in a particular historical conjuncture" (146). Their analysis traces the complex interaction among several major actors. The outcomes are the resultant of these generally conflicting interactions, and are not simply determined by the dominance of one party over another. The rationalization of labor can be viewed as one kind of outcome. Thus, workers react against their conditions of employment by organizing and struggling for increased wages. As workers raise the price for their labor, capitalists develop and use machinery to replace increasingly costly labor. Their analysis can be usefully compared to Freiberg's study of a labor aristocracy, the printers in France; it revealed a similar pattern, but with a different sequence. Two kinds of sequences can be distinguished, depending upon the time observed and the setting: (1) managerial and capitalist efforts to rationalize labor by increasing capital investment may be viewed as a response to workers' efforts to increase their share of the gains of production; and (2) worker efforts to maintain their working conditions may be seen as a response to ever increasing rationalizing efforts by managers and capitalists.

Petersen and Markle examine five controversies related to the treatment of cancer. Beginning as knowledge disputes among scientists, the disputes expand into public controversies when they become recast into value issues. When the controversy is waged in terms of value issues, it becomes more similar to the religious conflicts examined by Bromley, Shupe and Busching. Petersen and Markle utilize mobilization theory in their analysis and in doing so attend to the variations from case to case. The analysis of conflict escalation makes clear again that conflicts are interlocked and that conflicts are not simply between two, clearly-bounded adversaries. As with many other of the contributions in this volume, the analysis makes clear that social movements do not exist in isolation but are formed and transformed in interaction with many other movement organizations (Zald and McCarthy, 1980). The interaction is not only of competition and collaboration within the same movement, but also in conflict between organizations in different movements.

Ladner, Schwartz, Roker, and Titterud combine many different kinds of data to describe and account for the 1980 riots in Miami. The eruption of the riot after five policemen were found not gulty of killing Arthur McDuffie was explained to be the result of a covergence of many long run trends, recent developments, and the specific events of Saturday, May 17, 1980. The variations in riot activity in different neighborhoods in Miami with predominantly black populations makes it possible to relate differences in riot activity with objective conditions as well as individual and collective values and beliefs. Within the context of prevailing opinions of blacks in Miami, the conditions in different neighborhoods were found to be associated with variations in riot behavior. Attention to both objective conditions and subjective conceptions and the relations between them helps understand and predict riots. Studying the multiplicity of interactions helps account for the convergence which is essential for a major historical event, such as a riot.

Ragin and Davies seek to account for Welsh political distinctiveness. They compare the usefulness of a developmental and a reactive perspective. On the basis of their analysis, they conclude that a revised developmental perspective accords better with the findings. In one sense the reactive perspective, by emphasizing the relations between a dominant and dominated ethnic group, seems to stress interaction. But the revised developmental approach also gives attention to interaction among various groupings, stressing the context of the larger British policy. Which cleavages and which identifications are the salient ones is the bases of controversy among different theoretical approaches; mapping them out provides a way to understand major shifts.

Balfe offers an explanation for the emergence of a transforming art style in the United States: abstract expressionism. In her analysis, too, many different groupings interact; but in this case they do so in a mutually supporting way and over a few years to provide a base for a new art style. She analyzes how changes in self-recruited artists, distributors, critics, and art audiences mutually reaffirm each other and converge to sustain abstract expressionism. Her analysis illustrates some of the issues discussed in the concluding contribution by Gusfield: social change can appear to be quite diffuse but its manifestation typically has significant organizational aspects.

Cockcroft in his analysis of the relations between Mexico's economy and the transnational corporations (TNC) gives attention to impersonal struggling forces. But within such struggling forces, one can also discern particular persons and groups interacting and adopting strategies to counter the strategies pursued by other organizations. For example, the efforts of the Mexican government to control some of the dependency-producing effects of transnational corporate investments is countered by the TNC's development of new techniques to gain profit from their capital. Cockcroft's discussion of the class struggle in Mexico can be usefully compared to the analyses by Freiberg and by Levine and Geschwender. The multiple interaction paradigm contributes to our understanding of dependency between different national economies, as well as relations within societies. Using the paradigm encourages researchers to examine many interlocking systems or subsystems. That multiplicity facilitates various actors forming a variety of alliances and playing one adversary off against another. A world system approach that focuses only on one system, like the functional approach, tends to make the world seem more static and less open to shifts than it really is.

Useem, Useem, Othman, and McCarthy examine the professional networks in which scientists in two Southeast Asian developing countries are embedded. Their analysis of empirical data on academic scientists in the Philippines and Malaysia indicates that the world-wide movement to establish higher educational systems in thrid world countries to promote decolonization, nation building and development has generated new and constantly changing structures between scientists in core and peripheral countries. The meaning of such characteristics as country of citizenship, ethnic identity, scientific field, gender and generation shift in response to events over which the scientists have differential degrees of control and are modified by the scientists' redefinitions of themselves and others in interaction. This study is part of the newer research tradition in comparative sociology and cross-cultural studies which emphasises the utility of the multiple interaction paradigm.

In the last contribution, Gusfield discusses the diffuseness of many social movements and how they constitute change itself rather than causing it. This perspective is consistent with many aspects of the multiple interaction paradigm particularly in noting how the outcomes of various efforts by many different sets of people may be quite independent of the intentions of any of the striving people. Gusfield's discussion also provides a relatively concrete way of thinking about and analyzing what might otherwise be larger-scale impersonal forces.

The diversity and specificity of the many contributions in this volume indicate some of the limits as well as the uses of the paradigm sketched out at the beginning of this introduction. The generality of the multiple interaction paradigm does not provide a basis for determining when class, ethnic, national, or other cleavages will be the most salient ones for identification and organization. But many of the papers provide answers for specific conditions. The emergence of a shared framework within which research on social movements, conflicts, and change is increasingly conducted can make important contributions to the cumulative character of research and theory. We can increasingly specify the conditions in which one or another kind of interaction is salient and the conditions in which different kinds of resources affect particular outcomes.

Regardless of the utility of the paradigm, the contributions in this research annual can be read independently and located in a variety of contexts. The annual is not designed to provide a systematic, comprehensive approach to social movements, conflicts, and change. It is my intention as editor to bring together a set of papers which are diverse in approach and subject and which individually make useful contributions in providing information, insight, and theoretical ideas. In addition their juxtaposition should be stimulating for the reader.

In editing this volume, I have called upon colleagues here at Syracuse University, former contributors to the series, and others for help in reviewing the contributions. I wish to thank the following persons: John Agnew, J. David Edelstein, Allan Mazur, John D. McCarthy, Denton Morrison, Anthony Oberschall, and Charles Tilly.

REFERENCES

Boudon, Raymond
  1980   The Crisis in Sociology: Problems of Sociological Epistomology. Trans. by Howard H. Davis. New York: Columbia University Press. (Originally published in 1971).
Clawson, Dan
  1980   Bureaucracy and the Labor Process: The Transformation of U.S. Industry, 1860-1920. New York: Monthly Review Press.
Cohen, Albert
  1955   Delinquent Boys, Glencoe, Ill.: Free Press.
Collins, Randall
  1975   Conflict Sociology. New York: Academic Press.
Elias, Norbert
  1980   What is Sociology? Trns. by S. Mennell and G. Morrissey. New York: Columbia University Press. (Originally published in 1970).
Evans, Peter
  1979   Dependent Development: The Alliance of Multinational, State, and Local Capital in Brazil. Princeton, N.J.: Princeton University Press.
Kriesberg, Louis
  1982   Social Conflicts. Second Edition. Greenwich, Conn.: Prentice Hall.
McEachorn, Doug
  1980   A Class Against Itself: Power and Nationalization of the British Steel Industry. Cambridge: Cambridge University Press.
Mansbridge, Jane J.
  1980   Beyond Adversary Democracy. New York: Basic Books.
Milner, Murray Jr.
  1980   Unequal Care: A Case Study of Inter-organizational Relations in Health Care. New York: Columbia University Press.
Skocpol, Theda
  1979   States and Social Revolutions: A Comparative Analysis of France, Russia, and China. Cambridge: Cambridge University Press.
Wallerstein, Immanuel
  1980   The Modern World System II. New York: Academic Press.
Zablocki, Benjamin
  1980   Alienation and Charisma. New York: The Free Press.
Zald, Mayer and John D. McCarthy
  1980   "Social Movement Industries: Competition and Cooperation among Movement Organizations," Pp. 1-20 in Louis Kriesberg (Ed.) Research in Social Movements, Conflicts, and Change, Vol. 3. Greenwich, Conn.: JAI Press.

COLLECTIVE BEHAVIOR AND RESOURCE MOBILIZATION AS APPROACHES TO SOCIAL MOVEMENTS:
ISSUES AND CONTINUITIES

Ralph H. Turner

A social movement has been defined as:

> a collectivity acting with some continuity to promote or resist a change in the society or
> organization of which it is a part. As a collectivity a movement is a group with indefinite
> and shifting membership and with leadership whose position is determined more by
> informal response of the members than by formal procedures for legitimating authority.
> (Turner and Killian, 1972, p. 246)

Movements range from mobilizations of short duration around limited objectives, such as a movement of property owners to resist further development in adjacent areas or of citizens to prevent oil drilling or nuclear plant construction

Research in Social Movements, Conflict and Change, Volume 4, pages 1-24
Copyright © 1981 by JAI Press Inc.
All rights of reproduction in any form reserved.
ISBN: 0-89232-234-9

in a specific location, to large and enduring mobilizations such as the peace movement, the anti-nuclear power movement, and the ecumenical movement among religious organizations. They range from movements for self help and personal transformation to reform and revolutionary movements. They promote or resist change in such varied sectors of society as the polity, the economy, religion, education, the arts, recreation and secular morality.

Contributions to a theory of social movements have come from many disciplines. Yet when propositions from the traditional approaches are juxtaposed there are few instances in which they generate contradictory hypotheses. Most often, different approaches merely address different questions. But when they address the same questions, their propositions are often so vague as to be consistent with quite contradictory hypotheses. Review of the hypotheses that Hundley (1965) extracted from Turner and Killian (1957) and Smelser (1963) for empirical test reveals that most of the hypotheses had inductive rather than deductive origins. Their confirmation or refutation said little about the propositions central to each approach. The more clearly deductive and controversial hypotheses in the traditional literature either deal with a limited class of social movements, as in mass society theory of extremist political movements (Kornhauser, 1959), or treat specific behavioral manifestations such as collective violence (Gurr 1970).

Recently, however, *resource mobilization* theory has emerged with the promise of generating testable hypotheses. The most comprehensive statements are those of Oberschall (1973), MacCarthy and Zald (1973, 1977), Tilly (1978), and Zald and MacCarthy (1979). The aims of this paper are to examine the resource mobilization claim to generate testable hypotheses, to note continuities and discontinuities in relation to the collective behavior tradition, and to examine major differences between the approaches from the point of view of researchable issues. It is first necessary to clarify the assumptions underlying the traditional collective behavior approach for comparison with resource mobilization theory.

COLLECTIVE BEHAVIOR

The concept of collective behavior was given sociological currency by Robert Park and Ernest Burgess in 1921, elaborating on Park's (1904) earlier effort to delineate the crowd and public as distinctive social forms. They acknowledged —but were selective and skeptical in using—the efforts of earlier students to explain large gatherings engaged in unconventional behavior on the basis of a ''crowd mind'' (LeBon 1897), an atavistic herd instinct (Trotter 1916), psychopathology (Sighele 1901), and imitation (Tarde 1890). But their distinctive contribution was to identify a field of study in sociological terms without resort to judgmental or psychiatric concepts. Their groundwork of assumptions concerning essential processes and problems for investigation has guided elaborations of the field by such scholars as Edwards (1927), Dawson and Gettys (1929, 1948), Blumer (1939, 1943, 1957), Turner and Killian (1957,

1972), Kurt and Gladys Lang (1961), Gusfield (1963) and Klapp (1969, 1972). And their influence can be seen in the work of Smelser (1963), Heirich (1971), Wilson (1973), Lauer (1976), and Zurcher and Kirkpatrick (1976).

Park and Burgess described a heirarchy of social phenomena from social behavior to collective behavior to society. Behavior is social insofar as each interacting individual is more or less influenced by the action of every other. Society, at the other extreme, is "the social heritage of habit and sentiment, folkways and mores, technique and culture . . . " (1970, p. 81).

> The community and the natural order within the limits of the community, it appeared, are an effect of competition. Social control and the mutual subordination of individual members to the community have their origin in conflict, assume definite organized forms in the process of accommodation, and are consolidated and fixed in assimilation.
>
> Through the medium of these processes, a community assumes the form of a society (1970, p. 366).

We shall disregard the confusion created by Park and Burgess' use of the term collective behavior in both an inclusive and a restrictive sense, by adhering to the restrictive usage that constituted the foundation for the field of investigation.

> The term collective behavior, which has been used elsewhere to include all the facts of group life, has been limited for the purposes of this chapter to those phenomena which exhibit in the most obvious and elementary way the processes by which societies are disintegrated into their constituent elements and the processes by which these elements are brought together again into new relations to form new organizations and new societies. (1970, pp. 440-441)

In keeping with this conception, Park and Burgess treat *social unrest*—socially transmitted and mutually reinforcing unrest—as the most elementary form of collective behavior because "it represents at once the breaking up of the established routine and a preparation for new collective action." (1970, p. 382).

Themes

The collective behavior approach can be outlined by enumerating several themes that characterize most of the work in the Park and Burgess tradition. While elementary collective behavior has received considerable systematic attention, fewer efforts have been made to characterize social movements comprehensively as collective behavior. I shall draw principally on my own (Turner and Killian, 1957, 1972) and Killian's (1964) elaborations of the earlier work by Edwards (1927), Dawson and Gettys (1929, 1948), Blumer (1939, 1943, 1957) and Hopper (1950).

1. The primary focus of interest for students of collective behavior is the social movement as a sociological phenomenon and as a form of collective behavior. Interest in the movement in its own right contrasts to the orientation of investigators whose interest in movements is incidental to the study of social change, political change, collective violence, or revolution, or is a context

within which to study individuals. Conceptualization in broadly sociological terms means that theorizing about specific types of movements such as political reform movements, revolutionary movements, religious movements, secular self help movements, and expressive movements will be guided by a search for the features of collaboration that are common to all or several of these diverse realms of action. For example, any study of separatist tendencies would look first for characteristics common to religious, political and intellectual separatism (Turner and Killian, 1957, pp. 385-408). Studying the movement as collective behavior means paying careful attention to processes and principles linking social movements to other forms such as crowds and publics. But specifying common features has also meant *highlighting differences* for a balanced account of social movements.

2. From the collective behavior perspective social movements are instances of intentional collaboration to promote or resist change when the collaborators find established institutional direction and mechanisms inappropriate or insufficient for their purposes. It is no accident that Park chose the adjective *collective* since it is the very collaboration that is sociologically problematic. Collective behavior is distinguished from mass behavior (Blumer, 1935). The collective behavior approach contrasts to *convergence* (Turner, 1964) or *grass roots* approaches which assume that when enough people share the same interests, impulses, or dispositions to action with sufficient intensity, a movement will automatically develop. Individual and social unrest are firmly distinguished (Blumer, 1939). Collective behaviorists investigate how adherents are recruited to a movement, often for reasons bearing little relationship to the movement's goals and assumptions (Snow, 1976), and how commitment and solidarity are created and participation gratifications supplied. Patterns of internal decision making and organizational structure have received less attention, except in relation to leadership, perhaps because collective behaviorists underestimated the extent to which organizational dynamics in movements may differ from organizational dynamics in more institutional contexts.

Following Dawson and Gettys (1929, 1948) and Blumer (1939), collective behaviorists emphasize that sustaining collaboration over extended periods of time and among a dispersed body of adherents requires stabilizing organizational mechanisms not found in elementary forms. In practice, collective behaviorists have given more attention to the mechanisms than to the organizational framework through which the mechanisms are applied, though few would disagree that a more balanced attention would facilitate understanding of social movements.

3. Because of their relative freedom from constraint by the established institutional structure, social movements are changeable rather than stable phenomena. Patterns and determinants of change during movement careers have been major topics for investigation. Early work generally incorporated a search for typical life cycles (Edwards, 1927; Hopper, 1950). Later work increasingly dealt with changes of a more situational kind.

As collective behavior, social movements are not necessarily or typically coterminous with movement organizations. Although organizations carry out much of the movement work and frequently attempt to control and speak for movements, membership and leadership are defined by action and public definition rather than formalization. Thus John Brown, an unwelcome outsider to the American abolitionist establishment, had to be accepted as a movement spokesman and martyr symbol because he was overwhelmingly so regarded by the abolition public. The rise and fall of organizations and organizational contention and splintering within movements has attracted some attention from collective behaviorists.

A consequence of this view is ambiguity about the boundaries of specific movements. One thinks of movements within movements within movements, as with contemporary environmental movements and their component movements. The collective behavior emphasis on processes and mechanisms lessens the difficulty of working with this kind of conception.

A characteristic volatility of goals and ideology is likewise a prime topic for collective behavioral investigation. Many studies of social movements take goals as the givens from which the analysis proceeds. Collective behaviorists see goals arising, evolving, and constantly changing through the interplay of collective definition among movement adherents and public opinion. Evolution of the American temperance movement goal from temperance to prohibition, and recent evolution of the black lung movement from modest efforts to obtain state workman's compensation benefits for local victims of the disease to broader concerns with bureaucracy (Judkins, 1979) follow an often documented pattern. How busing came to be the accepted goal of a movement for racial integration cries out for investigation. Likewise, broad strategies are seen to shift along dimensions of reform-revolution and control-separatism.

Indeed the complex and volatile nature of movements makes assessments of success and failure difficult, and collective behaviorists often find it more meaningful to develop theory concerning process than concerning movement success. When Caesar Chavez achieved recognition for the United Farm Workers, thereby speeding up the loss of jobs for farm workers through the mechanization of California agriculture, is it meaningful to simplify the outcome as success or failure? One attempt to deal with this problem in collective behavior terms recognizes a constant tension within every movement among conceptions of success as the realization of movement values, the exercise of power by the movement, and the maintenance of a large and enthusiastic body of adherents (Turner and Killian, 1957, 1972).

4. The character and course of a social movement are shaped through continuous interaction between the movement on the one hand and the institutional regime, the community, and opposing or contending movements and interest groups on the other hand, mediated through publics. The treatment of collective behavior and the societal problem of social control are so intertwined as to be inseparable in Park's writing.

Collective behaviorists have generally rejected as unrealistic the view of society as a tightly integrated or harmonious system and simplified conceptions of society as polarized on a single dimension such as class. Park opted for a Durkheimian view of control through emergent collective sentiments and opinions, but he sharply contrasts this view to Tarde's and Giddings' assumptions of like-mindedness and LeBon's conception of group mind (Park and Burgess, 1970, pp. 27-43). The pivotal nature of accommodation in the face of ubiquitous competition and conflict indentifies a society marked by the loose coordination recently redescribed by Janowitz (1978).

5. Whether it is called psychological or not, every approach to social movements makes assumptions about human behavior. Collective behaviorists assume that human beings both in and out of movements are a *heterogeneous* lot of *social* beings. A movement grows in numbers because it attracts and holds adherents with diverse motives, goals and conceptions of the movement. The socialized actor mixes rational, irrational, and arational action, substantially oriented to group membership and role identitities, and assigning meanings to action both prospectively and retrospectively. Skepticism has been consistently expressed toward analyses that give central explanatory power to personality types such as the authoritarian and the true believer or to nonrational mechanisms such as the frustration-aggression linkage.

6. Although it is not evident in Park's writings, the developing collective behavior and symbolic interaction traditions have been closely linked. Because of this linkage, social movements are viewed as instrumentalities in the continuous construction and reconstruction of collective and individual views of reality. Altered ways of viewing both self and larger systems of social relationships are often more important products of social movements than any specific organizational or political accomplishment. Conditions that have long been viewed as misfortunes are reassessed as injustices (Edwards, 1927, pp.54ff.; Turner, 1969), and these redefinitions persist and are embedded in the transmitted culture. Niebuhr's (1929) thesis that altered self conceptions as a result of sectarian experience can facilitate improved material and social status, though now known to apply less universally than Niebuhr implied (B. Wilson, 1973), has long been of interest to collective behaviorists. Klapp's (1969, 1972) interpretation of social movements as "collective search for identity" builds on this tradition, though few collective behaviorists would emphasize this process so disproportionately. The theme of reality construction highlights an important commonality between political and religious and self-help movements, contributing to the justification for treating them together.

Contrasting Approaches

1. The adjective "collective" and attention to the problems of achieving collaboration distinguish the collective behavior view from a simplistic *grass roots* approach that is labeled the "classical approach" by some critics (e.g.,

Jenkins and Perrow, 1977). By a grass roots approach I mean the common-sense view that social movements crystallize spontaneously whenever enough people come to share appropriate attitudes, feelings of concern, or states of deprivation. In contrast to this view, collective behaviorists found one explanation for the early collapse of a California tax rebellion in the absence of preexisting communication channels linking residential property owners in different neighborhoods and suburbs (Jackson, et al, 1960). As an alternative to *status politics* theory, the usefulness of Senator Joseph McCarthy to an out-of-power Republican party was proposed as an explanation for the meteoric growth of his "anti-communist" following and its subsequent demise (Turner, 1958).

A prevalent effort to *use* instances of collective behavior in the guise of analysis is a frequent source of confusion. Alain Touraine's (1971) exciting account of the 1968 student uprisings in Paris is a masterful mixture of insightful analysis with heavy-handed imposition of particular meanings on events. Liberal Americans have been understandably more interested in using incidents of public disorder to draw attention to the legitimate grievances of the disadvantaged than in explaining why disorder occurred when and where it did. Sharing this liberal perspective, social scientists of diverse theoretical persuasions often restricted their analyses of 1960s and 1970s movements to an exposition of grievances. The liberal intellectual climate in juxtaposition with the recent prominence of movements of the disadvantaged is probably a more important explanation for the popularity of grass roots analysis than any specific theoretical tradition.

2. From Park's earliest writings, collective behavior explanations have been contrasted to *psychopathological* interpretations of social movements. Historically the rise of fascism, the post-war popularity of psychoanalysis, and the transformation of Marx's *alienation* into a psychiatric concept have given rise to a separate stream of interpretation, involving such figures as Fromm (1941), Adorno (1950), Hoffer (1951) and Feuer (1969). Although there has been limited borrowing in both directions, the streams have remained intellectually separate.

3. The collective behavior approach contrasts to the relatively desocialized versions of *self-interested rationality* theory. Historically the concern of collective behaviorists with purportedly altruistic movements such as religious and charitable reform enterprises and movements *for* the downtrodden has been distinguished from the more restricted concern of many political scientists and Marxists with movements of aggrieved classes to advance their own condition, which have also been studied by collective behaviorists. We shall comment further on this contrast when examining resource mobilization.

4. Collective behavior and *social system disruption* theories incorporate incompatible assumptions about the institutional order of society. Neil Smelser (1963) attempted to assimilate the collective behavior tradition into a structure-functionalist view of society. His concept of *structural strain* is only

meaningful if it can be identified independently of the individual strain it sometimes produces. The problems are well explained by Salert (1976) in her critique of Johnson (1966) on revolutionary movements. The view of a *short-circuited* decision process in collective behavior incorporates the untenable assumption that decision making in institutional settings is more logical. Smelser's account of the *generalized belief* is unacceptable in depicting movement imagery as more magic-laden than institutional imagery; as separating cognition from sentiment and action-orientation, which together constitute a flexible sense of value; and in failing to incorporate Park's (Park and Burgess, 1970, p. 34) distinction between likemindedness and the sense of being constrained or released through collective sentiment and opinion, which is crucial for an *emergent norm* conception of collective behavior.

The more fundamental issue, however, is the priority between microsociological and macrosociological analysis. The collective behaviorist image of movement dynamics makes substantial correlation between broad social structural indicators and movement characteristics seem improbable. In this respect there is also divergence from Kornhauser (1959) and from some of the work of Lipset (1955, 1970). Collective behaviorists are disposed to work from the inside out, while structuralists proceed in the opposite direction.

5. Finally, a collective behavior perspective is decreasingly applicable to movements as they become formalized and institutionalized. Except for understanding wild cat strikes and internal dissension, the collective behavior image does not facilitate study of established labor unions, religious denominations, professional associations and institutionalized interest group organizations.

Collective behavior is a perspective rather than a theory. By characterizing the social movement phenomenon and indicating what is problematic about it, the perspective supplies the framework within which *specific* theories can be applied to appropriate questions. For example, the proposition that emergent norms are crucial to the coordination of beliefs and actions in a movement points to the use of normative theory. Emphasis on the volatility of ideology signals the importance of applying reality-construction theory.

RESOURCE MOBILIZATION

Like collective behavior, resource mobilization is a loose cluster of ideas that exponents use selectively and interpret ideosyncratically. Hence, a generalized account cannot do justice to the views of any individual. Pioneering exponents were generally more interested in the political process than in movements *per se*. But the logic of resource mobilization is applicable to all movements, and will be presented in that way.

In practice resource mobilization ranges from a perspective to a theory. As a *perspective* it assigns greatest importance to research and theory that will assist social movement decision makers to resolve their strategic dilemmas with optimal results. Why movements develop in support of certain goals rather than others is regarded as a less significant problem than delineation of the most effective means for promoting whatever goals have been adopted. Strategies are conceived as plans for the acquisition of resources and for their utilization. Attention is focused on relatively highly organized units capable of centralized decision making in the control and use of resources. Movements are to a large extent created by an institutionalized movement "industry," led by professionals who make their careers in the movement industry, and funded by foundations, government, and other established organizations.

Thus far, resource mobilization *theory* has dealt more with the incidence of social movements than with the conditions for their effectiveness. Theories posit that movements are produced and shaped by organizations engaged in the rational selection of strategies and tactics for the mobilization of resources. Adherents are generally viewed as acting rationally within the movement. Whether the typical adherent is motivated by concern for movement goals as they are viewed by movement decision makers or toward promoting a more individualistic self interest is a matter on which there is less agreement, as we shall see later. Economic optimization models supply the prototypes for resource mobilization theory. The level and diversity of potential discontent in society are (nearly?) always above the threshold for movement formation, so it is variation in the availability of resources and in the level of organization to exploit those resources—rather than the level of grievance—that determines whether movements will develop or not. Whether this proposition can be extended to explain why movements develop around one goal rather than another does not appear to have been clearly stated. Likewise, the boundaries and the metrics of the concept *resource* are not yet agreed upon.

As a perspective, resource mobilization has substantially rearranged priorities among topics for investigation and stimulated many interesting hunches about movement dynamics. It has stimulated renewed interest in the detailed study of movement tactics and some attention to the tactics of successful and unsuccessful movements. It has refocused attention on the core of each movement and away from the mass of adherents. And it has produced important studies of the institutional sources for movement resources and direction. But it is in the effort to progress from a perspective to a theory of resource mobilization that issues between resource mobilization and collective behavior become clearest.

ISSUES

Four broad sets of issues distinguish the theoretically more distinctive versions of resource mobilization theory from the collective behavior tradition and suggest questions for further thought and research.

Rationality

Resource mobilization theory is distinguished by the prominence given the assumption of rational decision making. Collective behavior and resource mobilization exponents share the assumption that social movement leaders and the bulk of adherents are *purposive* and that the course of a social movement is a product of continuous monitoring and planning and not a mere succession of outbursts. Edwards (1927, p. 101) undoubtedly overstated the case:

> Mobs which intervene decisively at the crises of revolution are always raised and organized for the purpose by a small group of revolutionary leaders acting through subordinates. The mob's activities are carefully planned out beforehand and directed toward the end which the leaders have in view. The whole procedure, so far from being a spontaneous outburst of violence, is exactly the opposite.

The customary weak type of rationality assumption has been widely used in theorizing about power relations, strategies, and tactics in the traditional collective behavior literature. Nevertheless, collective behavior theorists are not surprised to see some movements become fixated on courses of action that are dramatically counterproductive or even self-destructive from a conventional perspective, like the Symbionese Liberation Movement and the People's Temple of Jonestown. The more partisan advocates of the resource mobilization approach have been unwilling to dilute the dominating rationality assumption except as it is limited by the prevailing awareness of alternatives and easy availability of resources.

In the theoretically more powerful sense associated with resource mobilization *theory*, the rational decision maker selects courses of action that will optimize the ratio of benefits to costs. Since the certainty of most benefits and costs is less than unity, the rational actor must also multiply each cost and benefit by a probability estimate. But most analyses conducted under the name of resource mobilization settle for the much weaker meaning of rationality as simply selecting courses of action that foster rather than impair the stated goals of the movement. This weak use makes rationality akin to mere purposiveness and does not ask whether gains could have been achieved with less cost or greater gains achieved by use of a different strategy. As Tilly (1978) has shown, movement strategists select from familiar and "legitimate" repertoires most of the time, rather than exploring all possible tactics. But if we settle for mere purposiveness we surrender much of what is unique about this aspect of the resource mobilization approach and find ourselves working more closely to the traditional collective behavior framework.

Having raised the issue of rationality, resource mobilization theorists have made surprisingly little use of alternate models already available. Because sociologists rarely observe anything approximating optimizing rationality in social behavior of any sort, Herbert Simon's (1957, 1966) models of *satisficing* rationality should have special interest. Simon observes that the demands for knowledge and for computational ability made upon the choosing organism by classical concepts of rationality are excessive. He proposes instead a model involving simplified pay-off functions, simplified information gathering, and partial ordering of payoffs. One important assumption is that information is processed sequentially rather than simultaneously and that the process often stops with the first alternative evaluated as satisfactory. Applying Simon's approach to human behavior in response to disaster warnings, Slovic, Kunreuther, and White (1974) and Kunreuther (1978) observe that people usually assess the imminent probability of disaster before evaluating risk, and only proceed with assessment of risk if the imminent probability exceeds a relatively high threshold. In weighing information they rely more on personal experience than on objective information sources.

As resource mobilization theorists observe, the more sophisticated movement organizations make use of specialists in the use of optimizing rationality. But in few movements is the specialist's rule unchallenged. And insofar as movement adherents must be satisfied that core decisions are correct, the impact of satisficing must dilute the purity of optimizing rationality. Simon proposed the satisficing model in order to describe decision making in the business firm; it is hardly plausible that an even more demanding model would fit social movements!

But even the concept of satisficing rationality does not incorporate the acknowledged need by people who are aroused over a cause to act, and to act conspicuously and dramatically for the cause. We call this *expressive* behavior because its importance to the actor is in expressing support for the cause, regardless of whether it produces the desired visible consequences. The question is not one of acting rationally or irrationally: the advocate wants to "do something," to "go on record," to "strike a blow" for the cause. Demonstrations, published manifestos, violence, and even terrorism are sometimes ways of expressing commitment. Even when sophisticated leaders are immune to this concern, which is probably rarely, they must satisfy adherents' demands for action.

Even models of satisficing rationality require that the decision maker have some experience with which to evaluate the probable effectiveness of a course of action. But the complex, opaque, and slowly evolving situations within which most social movements operate make assessment of any but the most immediate effects extremely difficult. Even today it would be hard to determine conclusively whether Viet Nam war demonstrations hastened or retarded American withdrawal. Consequently most action must be governed by the accepted symbolic significance attached to a course of action, which is the criterion for expressive rather than effect-rational behavior. Both successful and unsuccessful movements hold demonstrations and send computer-personalized letters to potential adherents. In the absence of credible grounds for assessing probable effectiveness, it is certainly not irrational to employ whatever techniques are currently in use by other movements. But if this constitutes rational decision making, it is in so weak a sense as to destroy the meaning of the term.

Assuming appropriate modifications in the model to allow for satisficing and expressive behavior, the investigator must still be able to distinguish between rational and irrational choices. This can be done by external or internal criteria. By *external* criteria a choice is rational when the resulting course of action contributes toward achieving a movement goal, if we use a weak or satisficing conception of rationality, or the most cost-effective course of action feasible, if we use an optimizing model. Unfortunately, long experience with such models demonstrates that costs and benefits can seldom be reduced to a common scale of measurement, except for the bureaucratic defense purpose which accounts for most of their use.

The limited knowledge of alternatives, costs, and consequences, and the occurrence of unexpected contingencies mean that observed consequences of a course of action provide only an imperfect guide to the rationality of the process by which it is selected. By *internal* criteria a choice is rational if the decision makers, acting with an unambiguous conception of their goal, systematically weigh the probable costs and benefits of alternative courses of action in making their eventual choice. A rational choice process may result in counterproductive action because of unforeseeable events.

If it is difficult to apply external criteria of rationality it is even more difficult to assess subjective rationality. Just as government agencies often hold open hearings and commission investigative reports without allowing the results to influence their decisions, movement leadership may practice ritual forms of information search and rational choice without ultimately making the decision on rational grounds. Investigators often resort to the dubious process of evaluation by projection—projecting self into the situation and considering whether the decision is the one that he or she would have taken.

Whether the criterion of rationality is external or internal, the judgment hinges on unambiguous designation of the goal of action. If collective behavior observations concerning the usual vagueness and changeability of goals are correct, the difficulties in applying rational models are escalated. But more particularly, they render any theory of movement dynamics that takes goals for granted quite incomplete. At least as significant as investigating the strategy and tactics of the early American temperance movement is a study of how the explicit goal evolved from temperance to abstinence. Tactics that were most appropriate for one goal could be less appropriate as the goal changed.

Any adequate approach to movement strategy and tactics must also take into account the universally noted tendency for means and tangents to become translated into goals that often compete with the value goals of a movement. Achievement of power and the attraction of a large and enthusiastic body of adherents come to be viewed as evidence of movement success. The autonomous goal of defeating the opposition that arises in every conflict relationship often displaces value goals.

If the assessment of subjective rationality, even in the weaker sense, requires some co-measurement of potential costs and benefits and a clear conception of goals, it also requires knowledge of the view of reality generated within the movement and in the external relations of the movement. The range of alternatives, anticipated costs and benefits, and associated probabilities must all be extracted from the reality conceptions in use. If the collective behavior hypothesis is correct, for example, that a solidaristic movement tends to become a microcosm through which the outside world is seen, then movement victories are likely to be accepted uncritically as evidence that the view from within the movement is widely shared outside. Some such misperception must have accounted for the disastrous effort by Caesar Chavez to enlarge recent dramatic gains for California farm workers through seeking popular enactment of Proposition 14 in the state election of 1976.

In practice, resource mobilization theorizing has dealt with rationality in rather unsophisticated terms. By casting theories in terms of fairly gross differentials of power and resources, a reasonable consensus about externally rational and irrational strategies facilitated hypothesis formulation. For example, one can specify the conditions under which guerilla tactics are most appropriate and conditions under which disciplined nonviolent resistence is the favored course of action. But such hypotheses have a long history of use by exponents of varied approaches to social movements, including collective behaviorists. Only by advancing beyond such formulations and making more discriminating use of rationality models can resource mobilization claim that its focus on rationality does more than extend existing directions in movement theorizing.

RELATIONSHIP BETWEEN CORE AND ADHERENTS IN DECISION MAKING

Resource mobilization theorists' favored image of social movements as governed by highly centralized decision making requires that special attention be given to the relationship between this centralized process and input from movement adherents at large. Because it is built on the assumption of rationality, Mancur Olson's (1965) classic work, *The Logic of Collective Action*, has been pivotal in formulating this aspect of resource mobilization theory. Olson challenged the common assumption that rational self interest would cause people to combine forces to correct a shared grievance. He pointed out that the benefits sought—such as clean air or better working conditions—accrue equally to those who pay the costs by fighting for improvement and those who do not (public goods). Since one individual's contribution is unlikely to affect the outcome decisively, a rationallly self-interested individual would not pay the cost, but would accept whatever benefits were gained through the sacrifices of others as a free rider. Only if the group were small enough or the individual's resources great enough that one individual's contribution could be decisive, or if the movement were able to provide incentives in the form of benefits available only to contributors (private goods) or to exercise coercion, would rational self interest induce participation. The illustration of Olson's conclusion is clear for labor unions, which negotiate for the coercive power accorded them by closed shop and union shop agreements, and provide shop stewards and grievance committees to assist individual union members. But recognized unions have already passed from social movements into institutionalized entities, and both their ability to coerce and their ability to offer selective incentives to members depend largely on their institutionalized character. How, then, are we to explain the early growth of movements?

One response to Olson's argument is to emphasize the less tangible benefits of membership, such as sociability and identity repair, and the emergence of norms and social control within the movement. This response brings the investigator back into the mainstream of collective behavior thought, with emphasis on participation gratifications and member commitment and control, but with self interest ''purified'' by the sense that one is fighting to promote an idealistic value. Furthermore, by making noncommensurable variables central to the model, it undermines the hope of formulating hypotheses in precise terms that can be assessed quantitatively (Fireman and Gamson 1979, pp. 20-21).

In contrast, other responses challenge Olson on either empirical or logical grounds. Tillock and Morrison (1979) failed to find the predicted relationships between reason for joining and perceived size of the movement or local chapter among Zero Population Growth members, though the test was hardly decisive. Bonacich, et.al. (1976) showed experimentally that investment in a public good is not necessarily reduced when group size is increased. Marwell and Ames (1979) found less free riding in an experimental situation than predicted. Others have questioned the applicability of Olson's conception of rationality to human behavior except in highly individualized situations. Normal socialization produces a conception of self made up largely of social identities so that pursuit of self interest is usually equated with enhancement of group interests (Fireman and Gamson, 1979).

Olson's logic has been attacked on the ground that a rational person would recognize that the outcome when everyone pursued individual self interest in this way would be the failure to produce *any* public good. By pragmatic test the rational person would be forced to reject this form of rationality as ultimately irrational. In its place would be some form of *exemplary* rationality, acting so that desired benefits would be reaped when enough other people followed the same rule of behavior (suggesting Kant's categorical imperative). Fireman and Gamson (1979) argue that by exalting selective inducements to the status of sole motivation, Olson renders the movement goal irrelevant and destroys all reason for supporting a movement. This argument may push Olson to a *reductio ad absurdem* not required by his logic.

It is important to distinguish between saying that Olson's exposition of the logical implications of attributing participation in collective action to individualized self-interested rationality is faulty, and saying that empirical evidence shows that this type of rationality is not the dominant form of motivation underlying participation in collective action. Olson himself proposes that participation in many social movements may have to be explained in other ways, for example, by irrational motivation. Accepting that exemplary rationality is more a normative than a rational solution, Olson's logic is impressive. The more effective attacks address the more empirical question of the model's applicability. But if the model is inapplicable, economic models that have generally been designed with the individualized self-interested rationality of the market place in mind should be used only with great caution. The assessment of rationality and the identification of goals become increasingly difficult as one attempts to work with more social forms of motivation.

Still another response to Olson by McCarthy and Zald (1973) is to argue that for the most significant recent movements the Olson argument, though possibly correct, is largely irrelevant. In movements controlled by professional social movement organizations, so little is demanded of most adherents that costs of support are trivial. A small annual contribution from an affluent middle class citizen is sufficient. While this observation may indeed describe the operation of an interest group (movement?) like Common Cause, most contemporary movements must be able to mobilize large demonstrations, massive letter campaigns, and similar evidence of widespread commitment in order to establish credibility. Or they depend in large part on the personal transformation of members, as in the self-assertion of women and minorities and boycotting of attractive consumer items such as lettuce and grapes. Hence, the McCarthy-Zald argument seems overdrawn.

The most theoretically significant response is based on acceptance of the general outlines of Olson's argument. Such leading exponents of resource mobilization as Oberschall (1973), McCarthy and Zald (1977), and the Tillys (1975) accept the hypothesis that movements seldom develop except out of existing organized groups that already possess the resources necessary for providing selective inducements and exercising coercion over potential adherents. This solution, which accepts both the primacy of rational self interested motivation and Olson's conception of rationality, has probably been associated with resource mobilization's most distinctive contributions to social movement theory. Both Obershcall (1973) and Fireman and Gamson (1979) employ this hypothesis while also substituting a more socialized conception of self interest for Olson's highly individualized view. We will come back to the paramount significance of existing groups later.

One of the important contributions of resource mobilization theory has been the attention focused on the relationship between core and adherents in wrestling with Olson's challenge. In some cases this discussion has brought investigators back to collective behaviorists' concerns with participation gratifications and member commitment and control. But theoretically, more distinctive contributions have been made by reconsidering the extent of investment required of the mass of adherents in most social movements, and by advancement of the hypothesis that movements are most often spawned by established organizations that already possess an adequate fund of resources.

GRIEVANCE, ORGANIZATION, AND RESOURCES

There is extensive agreement among leading exponents of resource mobilization that the time and place of a social movement are affected very little by the rise and fall of objective deprivation, subjective sense of grievance, relative deprivation, or the circulation of relevant beliefs and ideas. According to Oberschall (1973, p. 194):

> The central problem in creating an enduring movement is not the development of novel beliefs and of opposition ideas, but the cementing together of an organizational network, which is always easier when some group networks already exist. Ideas and beliefs that have a revolutionary potential are usually present and are available for use by a protest leadership. Sentiments of opposition, of being wronged, are also frequently present in the lower orders and can be easily linked with more elaborate ideologies and world views. (Cf. also McCarthy and Zald 1977, p. 1215).

The broader implications of this type of assertion seem obviously contradicted by the many instances in which movements have arisen or gained strength directly in response to a grievance-producing event. For example, a movement against channel oil drilling burgeoned in Santa Barbara, California, directly after the oil spill of 1969; the America First movement developed as the trend toward United States involvement in the second World War became increasingly evident; the movement for American withdrawal from Viet Nam grew as the war dragged on and became increasingly stalemated. The much touted success of Howard Jarvis in organizing the successful movement to limit California property taxes (Proposition Thirteen) in 1978 should not obscure his long career of unsuccessful efforts to organize tax revolts as an agent of organized apartment house owners. It would be difficult to explain his one success without reference to escalating inflation, particularly in property values. On the other hand, for many conditions of long standing it is difficult to explain the rise of movements at a particular time. For example, the recent physical fitness movement in the United States, the world wide growth of environmental movements, and resurgence of the women's movement all attack conditions that have existed for decades or centuries.

The problem is plainly much too complex to be defined as a simple contestation between the predictive power of grievance and organization. The Tilly's (1975) brilliant historical study, often cited by resource mobilization exponents, is not strictly relevant because the dependent variable is collective violence rather than movement activity, and because of the necessarily unsophisticated treatment of grievance. It would surely be naive to treat incidence of collective violence as a highly correlated indicator of the extent of social movement activity and support, depending as it does on both strategic and expressive considerations on the part of authorities as much as movement personnel and the discipline of both police and demonstrators. And the popularity of concepts like relative deprivation reflects a long standing dissatisfaction with any simple connections between deprivation and response without reference to the mediating context.

The resource mobilization argument about the critical place of formal organization in the creation of social movements is nontrivial when it can be demonstrated that a movement is the creature of an organization (a) whose principal formal aims focus on activities other than fostering the movement; (b) which existed as a powerful organization before it took up the movement cause, and that; (c) the decision to create a movement was based on organizational considerations and was not simply an effort to support or take control of an already burgeoning movement. If these conditions are not met, the importance of organization as a neglected component of social movements is not minimized, but the distinctive theoretical position of resource mobilization is weakened.

The Sierra Club of California, as one of the mainstays of recent environmental movements, constitutes one of the most promising examples for resource mobilization theory. The Sierra Club was, and continues to be, a highly respected organization for the primary purpose of providing organized outdoor recreational activities, and only recently in its long history has its environmental activity been of the scale and kind that could fuel a popular movement. The more difficult question to resolve is whether enlargement of the Club's environmental protection activities and its transformation from a politically conservative to a liberal activist stance preceded and provided the crucial resources for development of the movement or responded to an already growing movement. The question is whether the Sierra Club and organizations like it created and took control of the environmental movement, or whether the movement coopted the Sierra Club with its many resources. Just as long dormant grievances and protest ideas can suddenly become the focus for a social movement, so organizations of long standing can suddenly become movements for vehicle development. The fundamental question of why the movement occurred when it did rather than at some other time remains unanswered by resource mobilization theorists as well as by collective behavior theorists.

Followers of resource mobilization and collective behavior approaches have also expressed disagreement on what functions of organization to emphasize in the development of social movements. Prior organization and linking networks have been discussed from the collective behavior perspective as contributing to interpersonal sensitization, the emergence of suitable redefinitions of the situation, and the maintenance of communication and coordination among dispersed individuals and groups. Resource mobilization theorists stress the accumulation and deployment of resources.

In part this difference in emphasis reflects the resource mobilization image of movement initiative stemming disproportionately from the core, who must rely on mass media and other expensive means to create and maintain a movement. In part it also reflects more attention to the question of how the movement exercises influence over target groups. In these respects the resource mobilization perspective provides needed balance to the work of collective behaviorists.

From the point of view of formal theory this difference in emphasis points up the question of the relative merits of specifying various tasks or functions of organization versus defining the crucial task of organization as the mobilization of undifferentiated resources. Conceptualization as *resources* facilitates use of the analogy of an economic transaction in which the social movement is the buyer and the desired reforms are the goods to be purchased. The analogy has utility specifically when resources can be used interchangeably. For example, a relatively impecunious movement can compensate with committed adherents willing to withhold essential services in support of the movement. But the analogy weakens when the term *resource* is extended to include elements like a communication network that are indispensable and whose deficiencies cannot be offset by the availability of other resources. Some clarifying distinction between resources, interchangeable currency, and indispensable components and their mutual interaction, is a needed refinement of theory. This observation also reminds us of the continued use of *resource* as an impressionistic rather than precise and bounded concept. Until greater precision is introduced into use of the central concept, a *theory* of resource mobilization giving rise to testable propositions is not possible.

VALUES, REALITY, AND JUSTICE

Resource mobilization has both the advantage and disadvantage of being more narrowly focused than collective behavior in the variables it employs and the questions it addresses. The principal advantage is that by restricting the range of questions addressed the perspective enhances the possibilities for achieving a statement of testable theory. But unless work in the resource mobilization mode is coupled with studies in the collective behavior or other perspective, a bias against dealing with value and reality-construction aspects of social movements may impair even the central concern with movement effectiveness.

When the history of a social movement is written, advocate historians usually discover a retrospective continuity in the goals and ideology that would not have been found if history were being written as the movement developed. In the diverse assemblage of goals and ideological elements having currency in the movement, items constantly drop out, are added, and undergo change. Even when statements of goals and ideological slogans persist, their meanings and the behavior they signalize often change (Belin-Milleron, 1951). These component changes often signify a more inclusive transformation in value orientation, such as the change in the American temperance movement documented by Gusfield (1963). In part these changes can be explained through a rationale familiar to both resource mobilization and collective behavior theorists, as movement conceptions and goals are adjusted to the incidence of successes and setbacks. But a balanced account also requires attention to the ubiquitous processes of reconceiving reality and revising social norms.

Akin to creating goals is the continuous redefinition of reality associated with movement process. Active movement adherents typically refer to profound ''discovery'' experiences in the course of their participation—discoveries about the world with which the movement is engaged and discoveries about themselves. These reconstructed versions of reality are disseminated through the medium of movement publics and often outlive the movement and the specific reforms it effects. Changing conceptions of public versus family responsibility for support of the elderly were more profound in their effects than any of the specific pension programs enacted in response to old age pension movements. Thinking about movement success in the resource mobilization frame has emphasized tangible accomplishments and tangible recognition for movement organizations (Gamson 1975). This thinking should be balanced by attention to the manner in which public conceptions of reality and value undergo change as a result of the interplay of movement, countermovement, target institutions and publics.

Inseparable from reality construction are the establishment, disestablishment, and transformation of social norms. Of particular significance are conceptions of what is just and unjust, of what is legitimate and illegitimate. From Park's intertwined treatment of collective behavior and social control to the concept of emergent normative integration, these processes have commanded major attention among collective behavior theorists. It has also been striking how often investigators working in the resource mobilization mode have found the impact and transformation of such normative conceptions crucial in their own analysis.

DISCONTINUITY, CONTINUITY, AND THE VOLUNTARISTIC MODEL

If the foregoing characterization of issues between the two streams of thought is correct, resource mobilization is only sharply divergent from the earlier collective behavior tradition when advocates are prepared to adhere to an optimizing rationality model of movement decision making, to assume that decision making is rather effectively centralized in most movements, to treat goals as relatively stable and unproblematic, to find that levels of grievance and relative deprivation are generally irrelevant to the rise and decline of movements, to assess movement success strictly in terms of tangible accomplishments, and to conceive movement dynamics as the mobilization of measurable and exchangeable resources. When all of these restrictive assumptions are made, resource mobilization theory generates hypotheses that are crucially in conflict with hypotheses in the collective behavior tradition.

Most exponents seem reluctant to accept such restrictive assumptions, but work from a more balanced view that differs from a collective behavior approach more in terms of emphasis than underlying assumptions. There is less of the sharp discontinuity once asserted by Gamson (1975) and more of the continuity suggested by Oberschall (1973). We have already suggested how we think resource mobilization theory could benefit from giving more attention to this continuity. The encounter with resource mobilization can also enhance work in the collective behavior tradition by stimulating attention to the applicability of such models of decision making as Simon's *satisficing* rationality; highlighting the importance of empirical investigation of the interaction between the movement core and the mass of adherents in decision making and in the shaping of public action for the movement; emphasizing the need to integrate the study of movement organizations into the broader study of social movements; and renewing attention to the traditional topic of movement strategies and tactics (e.g. Lee, 1944) and responses to them.

Stripped of pretensions to precision and measurability, the concept of *resource* implies a voluntaristic conception of collective action that is shared by the collective behavior perspective and offers a contrast to popular deterministic conceptions. What some investigators treat as determinants are viewed from a voluntaristic standpoint as resources and constraints. As resources, a wide variety of potential assets are available to be used or ignored, and used effectively or ineffectively. Similarly, movements function within a set of constraints that may be confronted or accepted, effectively or counterproductively. While the nature and balance of resources and constraints are *predisposing*, outcomes are ultimately shaped by an idiosyncratic decision process and a series of more or less unpredictable events and response decisions.

ACKNOWLEDGMENT

The paper has benefitted from penetrating critiques by Clarence Lo and William Roy (though I have changed less than they advised), and from comments by my colleagues during an extended visit to Nuffield College, Oxford.

REFERENCES

Adorno, Theodore, E. Frenkel-Brunswick, D.J. Levinson, and R.N. Sanford
1950   The Authoritarian Personality, New York: Harper and Row.
Belin-Milleron, Jean
1951   "Les expressions symboliques dans la psychologie collective des crises politiques." Cahiers Internationaux de Sociologie 10: 158-167.
Blumer, Herbert
1935   "Moulding of mass behavior through the motion picture." Publications of the American Sociological Society 29: 115-127.
Blumer, Herbert
1939   "Collective behavior." Pp. 219-280 in Robert Park (ed.), An Outline of the Principles of Sociology. New York: Barnes and Noble.
Blumer, Herbert
1943   "Morale." Pp. 207-231 in William Ogburn (ed.), American Society in Wartime. Chicago, Il.: University of Chicago Press.
Blumer, Herbert
1957   "Collective behavior." Pp. 127-158 in Joseph B. Gittler (ed.), Review of Sociology. New York: Wiley.
Bonacich, Philip, Gerald H. Shure, James P. Kahan, and Robert J. Meeker
1976   "Cooperation and group size in the N-person prisoner's dilemma." Journal of Conflict Resolution 20:687-706.
Dawson, Carl A., and Warner E. Gettys
1929   An Introduction to Sociology. Third Edition. 600-714. New York: Ronald Press.
1948
Edwards, Lyford P.
1927   "The Natural History of Revolution." Chicago, Il.: University of Chicago Press.
1970   Reissued with a foreword by Morris Janowitz.
Feuer, Lewis S.
1969   The Conflict of Generation: The Character and Significance of Student Movements. New York: Basic Books.
Fireman, Bruce, and William A. Gamson
1979   "Utilitarian logic in the resource mobilization perspective." Pp. 8-44 in Mayer Zald and John McCarthy (eds.), The Dynamics of Social Movements. Cambridge, Mass: Winthrop Publishers.
Fromm, Erich
1941   Escape from Freedom, New York: Farrar and Rinehart.
Gamson, William A.
1975   The Strategy of Social Protest. Homewood, Il.: Dorsey Press.
Gurr, Ted Robert
1970   Why Men Rebel. Princeton, N.J.: Princeton University Press.
Gusfield, Joseph
1963   Symbolic Crusade: Status Politics and the American Temperance Movement, Urbana, Il.: University of Illinois Press.

Gusfield, Joseph
  1968   "The study of social movements." International Encyclopedia of the Social Sciences
           Vol. 14.
Heirich, Max
  1971   The Spiral of Conflict: Berkeley 1964. New York: Columbia University Press.
Hoffer, Eric
  1951   The True Believer: Thoughts on the Nature of Mass Movements. New York: Harper
           and Row.
Hopper, Rex D.
  1950   "The revolutionary process; A frame of reference for the study of revolutionary
           movement." Social Forces 28:270-279.
Hundley, Jr. James R.
  1965   "A test of theories in collective behavior: The National Farmers Organization."
           Unpublished Ph.D. dissertation in Sociology. Ohio State University.
Jackson, Maurice, Eleanora Peterson, James Bull, Sverre Monsen, and Patricia Richmond
  1960   "The failure of an incipient social movement." Pacific Sociological Review 3:35-
           40.
Janowitz, Morris
  1978   The Last Half-Century: Societal Change and Politics in America. Chicago, Il.:
           University of Chicago Press.
Jenkins, J. Craig, and Charles Perrow
  1977   "Insurgency of the powerless: Farm workers movements." American Sociological
           Review 42: 249-268.
Judkins, Bennett M.
  1979   "The black lung movement: social movements and social structure." Pp. 105-129 in
           Louis Kriesberg (ed.), Research in Social Movements, Conflict and change. Vol. 2.
           Greenwich, Conn.: J.A.I Press.
Killian, Lewis M.
  1964   "Social movements." Pp. 426-455 in Robert E.L. Faris (ed.), Handbook of Modern
           Sociology. Chicago, Il.: Rand McNally.
Killian, Lewis M.
  1968   The Impossible Revolution? Black Power and the American Dream. New York:
           Random House.
Killian, Lewis M.
  1972   "The significance of extremism in the black revolution." Social Problems 20:41-48.
Klapp, Orrin E.
  1969   Collective Search for Identity. New York: Holt, Rinehart and Winston.
Klapp, Orrin E.
  1972   Currents of Unrest: An Introduction to Collective Behavior. New York: Holt, Rine-
           hart and Winston.
Kornhauser, William
  1959   The Politics of Mass Society. New York: Free Press.
Kunreuther, Howard
  1978   Disaster Insurance Protection: Public Policy Lessons. New York: Wiley.
Lang, Kurt, and Gladys E. Lang
  1961   Collective Dynamics. New York: Thomas Y. Crowell.
Laver, Robert H. (ed.)
  1976   Social Movements and Social Change. Carbondale: Southern Illinois Press.
LeBon, Gustave
  [1896]   The Crowd: A Study of the Popular Mind. London: Ernest Benn
  1960   Reissued New York: Viking Press.

Lee, Alfred McClung
  1944   ''Techniques of social reform: an analysis of the New Prohibition Drive.'' American
            Sociological Review 9:65-77.
Lipset, Seymour M.
  1955   ''The source of the radical right.'' Pp. 166-233 in Daniel Bell (ed.), The New
            American Right. New York: Criterion Books.
Lipset, Seymour M., and Earl Raab
  1970   The Politics of Unreason: Right-wing Extremism in America: 1790-1970. New York:
            Harper and Row.
McCarthy, John D., and Mayer N. Zald
  1973   The Trend in Social Movements in America: Professionalism and Resource Mobiliza-
            tion. Morristown, N.J.: General Learning Press.
McCarthy, John D., and Mayer N. Zald
  1977   ''Resource mobilization and social movements: A partial theory.'' American Journal
            of Sociology 82:1212-1241.
Marwell, Gerald, and Ruth E. Ames
  1979   ''Experiments on the provision of public goods. I. resources, interest, group size and
            the free rider problem.'' American Journal of Sociology 84:1335-1360.
Niebuhr, Richard H.
  1929   The Social Sources of Denominationalism. New York: World Publishing Co.
Obershall, Anthony
  1973   Social Conflicts and Social Movements. Englewood Cliffs, N.J.: Prentice-Hall.
Olson, Mancur
  1965   The Logic of Collective Action: Public Goods and the Theory of Groups. Cambridge,
            Mass.: Harvard University Press.
Park, Robert E.
  1972   The Crowd and the Public and Other Essays. Edited with an introduction by Henry
            Elsner, Jr.: translated by Charlotte Elsner. Chicago, Ill.: Univeristy of Chicago Press.
  1904   Masse und Publikum. Bern: Lack und Grunaw.
Park, Robert E., and Ernest Burgess
  [1921]   Introduction to the Science of Sociology. Chicago, Il.: University of Chicago Press.
  1970   Student Edition, abridged and with a new preface by Morris Janowitz.
Perrow, Charles
  1979   ''The sixties observed.'' Pp. 192-211 in Mayer A. Zald and John D. McCarthy (eds.),
            The Dynamics of Social Movements. Cambridge, Mass.: Winthrop Publishers.
Salert, Barbara
  1976   Revolutions and Revolutionaries: Four Theories. New York: Elsevier.
Sighele, Scipio
  1901   La Foule Criminelle: Essai de Psychologie Criminelle. Paris.
Simon, Herbert A.
  1957   Models of Man. New York: John Wiley and Sons.
Simon, Herbert A.
  1966   ''Theories of decision-making in economics and behavioral science.'' American
            Economic Association and Royal Economic Association. Surveys of Economic
            Theory Volume III: Resource Allocation. New York: St. Martins Press.
Slovic, Paul, Howard Kunreuther, and Gilbert White
  1974   ''Decision processes, rationality and adjustment to natural hazards.'' In Gilbert
            White (ed.), Natural Hazards: Local, National, and Global. New York: Oxford
            University Press.
Smelser, Neil
  1963   Theory of Collective Behavior. New York: Free Press.

Snow, David
1976   ''The Nichiren Shoshu Buddhist Movement in America: A sociological examination
            of its value orientation, recruitment efforts and spread. Unpublished Ph.D. dissertation
            in Sociology. University of California, Los Angeles.
Tarde, Jean Gabriel
[1890]   Les Lois de l'Imitation: Etude Sociologique Paris.
1895
Tillock, Harriet, and Denton E. Morrison
1979   ''Group size and contributions to collective action: an examination of Olson's Theory
            using data from zero population growth, inc. Pp. 131-158 in Louis Kriesberg (ed.),
            Research in Social Movements, Conflict and Change. Vol. 2. Greenwich, Ct.: JAI
            Press.
Tilly, Charles
1978   From Mobilization to Revolution. Reading, Mass.: Addison-Wesley.
Tilly, Charles
1979   ''Repertoires of contention in America and Britain, 1750-1830.'' Mayer A. Zald and
            John D. McCarthy (eds.), The Dynamics of Social Movements. Cambridge, Mass.:
            Winthrop Publishers.
Tilly, Charles, Louise Tilly and Richard Tilly
1975   The Rebellious Century, 1830-1930. Cambridge, Mass.: Harvard University Press.
Touraine, Alain
1971   The May Movement: Revolt and Reform. Translated by Leonard F.X. Mayhew. New
            York: Random House.
Trotter, Wilfred
[1916]   Instincts of the Herd in Peace and War. London: T. Fisher Unwin.
1919
Turner, Ralph H.
1958   ''Needed research in collective behavior.'' Sociology and Social Research 42: 461-
            465.
Turner, Ralph H.
1964   ''Collective behavior.'' Pp. 382-425 in Robert E.L. Faris (ed.), Handbook of
            Modern Sociology. Chicago, Il.: Rand McNally.
Turner, Ralph H.
1969   ''The theme of contemporary social movements.'' British Journal of Sociology
            20:390-405.
Turner, Ralph H., and Lewis M. Killian
1957   Collective Behavior. Englewood Cliffs, N.J.: Prentice Hall.
1972
Wilson, Bryan
1973   Magic and the Millenium. New York: Harper and Row.
Wilson, John
1973   Introduction to Social Movements. New York: Basic Books.
Zald, Mayer N., and John McCarthy
1979   The Dynamics of Social Movements: Resource Mobilization, Social Control, and
            Tactics. Cambridge, Mass.: Winthrop Publ.
Zurcher, Louis A., and R. George Kirkpatrick
1976   Citizens for Decency: Antipornography Crusades as Status Defense. Austin:
            University of Texas Press.

REPRESSION OF
RELIGIOUS "CULTS"

David G. Bromley, Anson D. Shupe, Jr.,
and Bruce C. Busching

Early in the 1970's a number of new religious movements, which were subsequently labeled "cults" by their opponents, appeared in the United States and Europe. The best known among this diverse set of religious and quasi-religious groups were the Unification Church, Divine Light Mission, Scientology, Children of God, Transcendental Meditation and Hare Krishna. Virtually all of these new religious movements were charged with some combination of brainwashing and mind control, financial exploitation, political intrigue, ruthless and authoritarian leadership and sexual impropriety. These allegations stirred up enormous public hostility, making "cults" a source of controversy and conflict throughout the decade. Among the new religions the Unification Church was deemed the archetypical "cult" and became the focus of the "cult" controversy. In this paper we shall examine the sources of strain between the Unification Church and other major institutions

Research in Social Movements, Conflict and Change, Volume 4, pages 25-45
Copyright © 1981 by JAI Press Inc.
All rights of reproduction in any form reserved.
ISBN: 0-89232-234-9

25

in the United States, precipitating factors in the conflict which emerged and the process whereby repressive social control measures were invoked. Our broader objective will be to move toward a general statement of the conditions under which social movements come into conflict with the larger society, are labeled deviant and are repressed.[1]

The collection of organizations affiliated with the Unification Church,[2] hereafter referred to as the Unificationist Movement or UM, was characteristic of what we have termed "world transforming movements" (Bromley and Shupe, 1979a:27-9). Such movements incorporate the following qualities: (1) an ideology that forecasts total, imminent cataclysmic structural change; (2) charismatic leadership; (3) communal organization; (4) an intensive socialization process to build and sustain a high level of commitment; (5) reliance on a strategy of persuasion for inducing change; (6) emphasis on building both public visibility and legitimacy and; (7) rejection of conventional normative standards.

The UM closely approximated these characteristics. Its theology, the *Divine Principle* (HSA-UWC, 1977), contained predictions of the messiah's imminent return and the potential for man's full and final restoration to God if only mankind grasped the divinely proffered opportunity. Moon was viewed by UM members as either a prophet or the messiah himself and hence had enormous moral influence over his followers. The UM utilized its communal organization, built on a fictive kinship system, to create strong instrumental and affective ties to the movement. New members were enveloped in a totalistic community that attempted to provide for virtually all individual needs and to separate members from the "corrupted" outside world. In its relations with the outside world the UM sought to propound its "heretical" theological prophesy and also to locate itself within the purview of the Christian tradition so as to preserve its social legitimacy. As a result of its reliance on a strategy of persuasion, its rejection of the conventional social order and its need to draw upon resources controlled by conventional society (e.g., members, money), the UM manifested considerable tension and ambivalence in its relationships with the larger society.

We shall argue that, as a world transforming movement, the UM posed a major threat to both the interests and authority structures of established institutions. In the case of the UM it was the religious and familial institutions that were most directly threatened and that formed the nucleus of the Anti-Cult Movement (hereafter, ACM). Precisely because world transforming movements such as the UM as part of their own organizational requisites have aggressively sought radical, immediate social change, what might otherwise have been dismissed as empty threats quickly precipitated opposition to these movements. The outcome of this conflict was a function of both the degree of threat perceived by each side and the relative power balance between the two sides. Because world transforming movements have tended to antagonize a broad spectrum of established institutions and posed a more serious threat to some, the balance of power rarely has been favorable to such movements. In the UM's case we shall contend that it was the familial and religious institutions' alliances with other institutions that created the potential for systematic repression. The process of social repression involved a combination of symbolic construction of the opponents' motives and actions that located them outside the boundaries of public morality and the imposition of sanctions. The family/church led Anti-Cult Movement was successful in exercising significant repression as a result of its success in designating the UM and other new religions as "cults" and allying itself with other institutions that possessed sanctioning capacity. The process of social repression has forced social movements in the direction of either greater accommodation or radicalism; in the UM's case the former direction has apparently been chosen.

SOURCES OF STRAIN BETWEEN THE *UM* AND THE FAMILIAL AND RELIGIOUS INSTITUTIONS

Family

The major source of strain between the family and UM related to the family's goal of preparing sons and daughters for participation in the economic order. Much of the socialization process within families was directed at producing offspring prepared to pursue socially and economically successful personal careers/lifestyles. Parents, therefore, sought to rear children who would be able to play highly specialized roles, possess self-interested motivation, be free from ideological constraints, and hold instrumental (as opposed to affective) role orientations. By contrast, membership in the UM involved taking on a diffuse member role that required few specialized skills. The UM's communal organization was specifically designed to suppress self-interested motivation by forbidding the accumulation of more than nominal possessions, limiting individually controlled wealth and even discouraging personal grooming or clothing which might accentuate individuality. Novitiates in particular expended a great deal of time and energy in "freeing" themselves from ego contraints, learning to put the good of the group above their own personal needs and desires and pursuing spiritual rather than material ends. In addition, members were taught to reject the calculated reciprocity characteristic of instrumentally based role relationships for what they termed "heartistic" relationships. The latter referred to affectively based relations predicated upon the UM's fictive kinship system in which other members were quite literally treated as one's "brothers" and "sisters." These requisites of communal organization (Kanter, 1972) were strongly supported both by peers and by the movements' ideology which identified selfishness and pursuit of individual goals as the source of mankind's most serious problems. Thus communal solidarity, rather than developing the skills and attitudes necessary for conventional careers, was the predominant UM concern, and the movement's socialization process provided virtually no preparation for entry into the contemporary American economic system.

The other source of strain between parents and UM members related to the structure of authority within the family unit. While parents socialized their sons and daughters to become autonomous adults, they did not anticipate that adulthood was inconsistent with continued loyalty to the family or even their own titular leadership of the family. But UM novitiates usually were deeply involved in witnessing and fundraising activities that entailed constant geographical mobility and left minimal time for personal or familial concerns. As a result, visitation and even letter writing typically were sporadic which distraught parents took as evidence of diminished familial loyalty.

Even more disconcerting to parents than physical separation, however, was the feeling that their parental roles were being appropriated by Moon and his wife. Such fears were not totally unfounded as within the UM's fictive kinship system Moon and his wife were designated as "true" parents and clearly contrasted with members' "biological" parents. Because of the charismatic status accorded to Moon by UM members, this distinction was of more than symbolic importance. Members' recognition of Moon's superior moral status had the effect entitling Moon to make extraordinary personal claims on them and correspondingly they assumed the role of disciples, open and submissive to Moon's moral leadership. On one level it simply was galling to parents that their offspring willingly abandoned profanity, alcohol and drugs, long hair and sexual freedom for Moon while even parental advice on these issues produced conflict and resistance. What posed a greater threat to parental authority was UM members' willingness to grant Moon control over fundamental life decisions in which parents felt some rightful interest. Initially these decisions involved matters such as giving up possessions, taking up residence in a UM center, assuming a new public identity, postponing or disavowing former marital and career plans, and attenuating relationships with individuals outside the UM. Later even more basic and apparently irrevocable commitments were involved such as marriage, child rearing and career development within the confines of the movement.

Religion

While most established churches in the United States expressed some degree of rejection of the UM, the opposition was centered in the fundamentalist churches whose interests and authority structures were most directly threatened by the UM. In delineating the nature of this threat it is important to begin by observing that religious belief systems are inherently non-empirical in nature. Given their lack of an empirical referent, such belief systems depend upon consensus and consistency rather than independent verifiability for their status as knowledge. Because religious norms usually are universalistic in nature (ie., they are phrased so as to apply at all times, under all conditions, to all people) in order to maximize their authority, it is imperative that they retain the appearance of immutability. Religious belief systems are, therefore, subject to two fundamental sources of challenge: to the content of the beliefs themselves and to the essentially subjective experiences associated with the beliefs and their expression. Historically, Christian churches have sought to combat such threats by circumscribing the range of both legitimate theological doctrine and spiritual experience. The more closely and extensively church members' behaviors were guided by theological doctrines, the more importance their authoritative character assumed. It was for this reason that fundamentalist churches experienced a greater threat from UM doctrinal innovation than did mainline denominations. Substantively the UM's theology posed three distinct but interrelated challenges to the interests and authority structures of fundamentalist (and to a lesser degree other mainline) churches: (1) a reformulation of the orthodox interpretation of the Trinity; (2) revision of Biblical history and; (3) an emphasis on works rather than grace as the basis for salvation.

An understanding of the threat posed by the UM's reinterpretation of the Trinity must begin with the observation that, from a sociological perspective, the source of God's ultimate moral authority in Christianity lies in the reciprocal reduction of man's moral status (ie., doctrine of original sin) and the elevation of God's moral status (ie., through attribution of omniscience, omnipotence, omnipresence, etc.). The moral balance created in this fashion was so great that God was due total obedience from man. Given the enormous moral distance between man and God, Jesus became a bridge (ie., the "way-shower" and "redeemer") between the physical and spiritual worlds. Jesus, the God/man, was the founder of the Christian Church, the direct human link with deity and the referent for invocation of divinely ordained normative prescriptions. He was, therefore, a charismatic leader in the classic sense, an individual who was able to exercise diffuse, intense influence over the normative orientations of other actors (Etzioni, 1961:203 and Katz, 1975). Jesus' unique status had significant implications both for the formal authority structure of the churches and for the behavioral orientations of individual members *vis à vis* those churches. On the one hand, as the Son of God, Jesus was the link through which church leaders claimed spiritual authority; any redefinition of the messianic role thus constituted a direct challenge to the formal, explicit sources of churches' authority. On the other hand, Jesus was the source of authority through which individual church members oriented their own interpersonal behaviors. Regulation of a variety of behaviors (e.g., drug and alcohol use, sexual behavior and husband-wife role definitions) based upon religious norms was common among fundamentalist denominations.

Jesus' human qualities and the prediction of the messiah's return rendered Christianity particularly vulnerable to such theological innovations and made it impossible to dismiss *a priori* individuals claiming to be the returned messiah. UM theology posed precisely such a challenge. According to Moon's *Divine Principle* Jesus was merely the latest in a series of messianic figures who sought to restore fallen man to God, and like others before him Jesus was not successful in this effort (although he did succeed in achieving ''spiritual'' as opposed to ''physical'', restoration). Three elements of this formulation were particularly offensive to fundamentalist Christians. First, Jesus' ultimate moral authority was diminished because he was portrayed as having failed to complete his divinely ordained mission. Second, since the messianic role was defined as an achieved one, an individual with the proper credentials (ie., spiritual qualities *and* accomplishments) became a legitimate candidate for this role. Such an interpretation had the effect of obviating the unique, ascribed kinship-based role definition of Jesus as the only Son of God and raised the possibility of claiming messianic authority on the basis of achievements rather than spiritual authority vested in and transmitted through the church. Third, because Jesus failed to complete his mission it remained possible and indeed necessary for a new messiah to complete the divinely mandated task of restoration. Not surprisingly, Moon's own personal characteristics and life trajectory closely matched the criteria by which he claimed new messianic candidates were to be judged.

Through his reformulation of the Biblical doctrine concerning the Trinity Moon thus created and in himself constituted an alternative source of spiritual authority. His Unification Church literally sought to unify (ie., supplant) existing churches based upon the new spiritual authority offered by the Biblical reformulation offered in the Divine Principle and Moon's status as the messiah. The visible evidence of this challenge presented itself through a reformulated Bible, a new church which repudiated the spiritual authority of its established Christian counterparts and members who reoriented their lives and priorities as individuals would only for a leader with ultimate moral authority.

Another major but related source of strain between the UM and established churches emanated from the former's attempts to redefine the temporal structure shared by a broad range of Christian denominations. The churches symbolically constructed the past and the future in such a way as to locate themselves along a historic course that began with creation and would culminate in the erection of the kingdom of God on earth. This formulation had two important consequences. First, established churches were designated as the legitimate heirs to the legacy of Jesus Christ and the only pathway to the kingdom of God. Therefore legitimacy was accorded to the contemporary church by virtue of its relationship to the past and future. Second, ultimate charismatic authority was carefully segregated from the present and located in the past or future. Since the churches were the legitimate heirs to Christ, charismatic leadership was available to them in routinized form. However, the revolutionary implications of the messiah's return, his condemnation of a corrupted world, and a radical restructuring (or even disbanding) of human institutions were all simply relegated to the indeterminate future. This was somewhat less true of fundamentalist than of the dominant, mainline denominations, but the differences were not as great as those between both of these groups and the UM which sought total mobilization of its membership. Had established churches pursued any other course they would have found it requisite to develop an organizational structure involving the mobilization of greater social control over members than the latter would permit and one that was incompatible with the political accomodation (based on mutual support and noninterference) worked out with the state.

The UM challenged the churches' spiritual authority by reconstructing Biblical history and prophecies. According to the Biblical reinterpretation contained in the Divine Principle, the fall of man (which resulted from Eve's physical seduction by Lucifer) left all future human generations literally satanic in origin. It was to this source that mankind's current problems and historic failures were traced. Rather than the heirs to a sanctified spiritual tradition, then, Christians bore the stigma and corrupting influence of their satanic lineage. With respect to the future, the Divine Principle taught the redemption of mankind was at hand if only the opportunity revealed in the Divine Principle and made possible by Moon's personal presence was seized. This reinterpretation of past and future history contained in Christian theology both discredited contemporary churches as bearers of a corrupt tradition and dramatically increased the salience of current religious behavior since redemption was potentially imminent. UM theology therefore challenged the basis of church-state accommodation (and established denominations were compelled to disavow it) because the church was quite simply ceded authority over the state. Ultimately human problems could be resolved only if their spiritual sources were recognized and political actions were made consistent with them. In addition, of course, the Divine Principle's historical reconstructions simultaneously undermined the basis of established churches' control over their members.

The final source of conflict between the UM and fundamentalist churches grew out of the former's emphasis on salvation through works and the latter's assertion that salvation was attainable solely through grace. The churches' doctrine that faith in Jesus Christ as the only savior was the sole path to spiritual salvation had the effect of firmly locating spiritual salvation under the jurisdiction of the church. Even more importantly, the doctrine of salvation through grace served to divorce salvation from individuals' secular activities. As long as one acknowledged Christ (and, hence, tacitly the church), salvation was assured. This symbolic formulation was consistent both with the limited social control sought *vis à vis* their members and with their quest for a monopoly on spiritual authority. Further, since the effects of one's spiritual status were detached from one's secular behavior religious norms were less intrusive on economic and political behavior . Again, this doctrine permitted an accommodation with the political institution such that the church was relatively free from regulation so long as it did not challenge the political and economic priorities of the dominent institutions and interest groups within the society.

The UM threatened these arrangements by its emphasis on works as the basis of salvation. According to the Divine Principle, man's fall necessitated the payment of indemnity as a precondition for man's full and final restoration to God. UM members, therefore, were continuously engaged in theologically legitimated activities which were believed to help members purify themselves and to set the conditions necessary for the world's physical restoration. Such apparently secular activities as fund-raising, for example, were endowed with a virtually sacramental status. The capacity to gain donations was taken as an index of a member's spiritual growth (ie., their ability to love others brought donations which could be put to God's work) and the money so collected was defined as being "restored" to God's (rather than Satan's) purposes. Indeed virtually all of members' daily activities were imbued with spiritual relevance and were evaluated in terms of their contribution to restoration.

Further, the UM's communal organization and separation from the larger society as a result of the latter's perceived corruption took individuals out of conventional career networks. The fact that spiritual works became the individual's preeminent concern created the potential for conflict with the political and economic institutions since members were no longer influenced by the kind of incentives controlled by the dominant institutions. Churches therefore were threatened by a doctrine of works not only because of the implications for church authority but also because of the prospect of upsetting accommodation with the state. In fact Moon's theology went so far as to specify a role for the United States as the archangel in the cosmic struggle against the satanic forces of Godess communism. This archangel role mandated the military protection of the ''new Israel'' (South Korea) as well as defense of western democracies in general. Needless to say, this doctrine explicitly projected the religious institution back into the political domain in unacceptable fashion. While the UM itself did not pose any immediate political or economic challenge and political action against the UM *per se* was of little consequence to established churches, the precedent set by political sanctions against any church raised the highly threatening specter of state intrusion into religious matters.

EMERGENCE OF THE ANTI-CULT MOVEMENT

The Anti-Cult Movement was comprised primarily of family and fundamentalist Christian based groups which together formed a loose coalition. The two groups supported one another through sharing information, overlapping, memberships, churches' provision of facilities for parents' groups meetings and each group's defending the other's claims that the UM was fraudulent and dangerous. Both groups responded rapidly once they perceived that their respective interests were threatened by the UM's pursuit of its millenarian goals. The UM was in no position to compromise with either group since recruitment of new members, separation from the "corrupted" world and rejection of conventional beliefs and institutions were requisite to its organization as a world transforming movement. Thus, the UM routinely provoked antagonism with both groups in the course of seeking to achieve its own goals.

What sparked initial resistance from the fundamentalists was a series of nation-wide speaking tours in which Moon publically propounded his "heretical" theology as Christian, represented himself as a Christian evangelist and explicitly rejected orthodox doctrine as a sufficient basis for spiritual salvation. From the perspective of the Christians who opposed him, then, the issue was not merely that Moon had created his own theology and church but that he was resuming the cover of Christianity to attack its "truths" from within, to gain audiences for his "heretical" teachings and to recruit members from within their ranks. After warnings from fundamentalist groups about the "heretical" nature of its theology went unheeded by the UM, fundamentalists felt compelled to challenge the UM and warn Christians of the danger it posed to unsuspecting or naive Christians.

For the individual families from which the UM recruited members conflict was precipitated by the perceived "loss" of a son or daughter. In the event that parents accepted their offspring's participation in the UM a mutually supportive, if somewhat distant, relationship was possible. However, for parents who perceived that their offspring's often sudden decision to abandon conventional occupational and domestic careers in favor of the UM's millenarian goals was irrational and even self destructive, such acceptance was difficult to proffer. Because the UM's crisis orientation and communal lifestyle placed virtually limitless demands on members' time and energy, it was relatively easy for the UM member to deflect parental objections to family separation. Heightened parental resistance was met by assigning members to highly mobile witnessing/fundraising teams or distant locations that sharply reduced family contacts or even by warnings to members of satanic influence on their parents. As distance and tension between offspring and parents grew, the latter were likely to feel that they could no longer ignore the situation or compromise. They then began to consider more desperate measures to "rescue" their son or daughter who, they concluded, was no longer behaving responsibly or rationally.

Both fundamentalist churches and individual families quickly found that it was difficult to combat the well funded, nationally organized and geographically mobile components of the UM. As a result, parents whose offspring had joined the UM (or one of the other new religions) banded together after discovering that other families faced the same problem. Similarly fundamentalist churches formed coalitions to oppose UM organizations in their locale and to warn Christians of the danger posed by "cults." The churches more easily formed coalitions as they were highly visible to one another and contacts sometimes already existed among clergy. The task of organizing families was considerably more difficult; however local organizations sprang up rapidly as media accounts of "missing children" and contacts through churches facilitated communication among similarly situated parents.

The family and church based organizations sought to defend their respective interests, and the organization and ideology of each component of the ACM relfected the degree of social control it sought to exercise over the UM. Many parents were unwilling to accept their offspring's UM membership and, hence, created an organizational network to directly enforce their wills on their errant offspring. In addition, another set of organizations was created which was designed to attack the UM in order to discredit and undermine the movement itself. In either case the ultimate goal was the same. Because family based ACM groups sought to exert extreme social control measures, a radical ideology developed that sought to legitimate coercion. By contrast, the fundamentalist churches, although highly threatened did not possess the capacity nor face the necessity of exercising such extreme social control measures in order to preserve their interests. As a result the fundamentalist based component of the ACM developed organizations which merely sought to warn its own constituency of the spiritual danger posed by "cults." Correspondingly the ideology of this ACM component attempted to legitimate little direct social control over either the UM or its members.

Family

For many parents of UM members there was but one major objective-extrication of their son or daughter from the UM.[3] In seeking to realize this objective the family based component of the ACM created two different organizational networks: anti-cult associations and deprogrammers. The former consisted of local/regional groups that very much resembled conventional voluntary associations. These associations served several important functions for parents of UM members. They offered a group context in which parents could assuage one another's sense of responsibility for their offspring's "bizarre" behavior, mutually condemn the UM as a fraudulent religion, share information about the best strategy by which to deal with an individual under the influence of a "cult," monitor UM activities, socialize parents of new UM members into the ACM ideology, and "educate" the public about the danger posed by cults. Even more importantly these associations lobbied to gain the support of other organizations which possessed a greater sanctioning capacity.

The network of deprogrammers undertook direct action at the request of parents to "rescue" UM members and return them to their families. Many deprogrammers were ex-members or parents of ex-members of new religions who saw in "deprogramming" a lucrative career. In essence deprogrammers were moral entrepreneurs, acting as parental agents, who employed a series of ad hoc approaches in an effort to induce UM members to renounce the movement. After abducting and physically restraining UM members, deprogrammers relied on techniques such as Biblical refutation of the Divine Principle, emotional appeals from family members, threats of long term restraint and allegations of deceit in a wide range of UM activities to shake their commitment. Whatever combination of these approaches showed promise of success in a particular case was employed, and the individual was pronounced "deprogrammed" once the UM had been convincingly renounced.

The family based component of the ACM faced two major problems in developing an ideology that would legitimate the kind of social control which parents felt it was necessary to exert and creating organizations which were capable of imposing sanctions on the UM. First, parents were willing to physically constrain their offspring if all other means failed, a power strictly controlled by the political institution. Second, UM members were virtually all legally adults, which seriously undermined parental claims to the right to exercise control over them. The symbolic construct upon which the anti-cultists drew was that of "brainwashed children." In searching for an explanation for what they perceived as a sudden, inexplicable, self destructive change in beliefs and behavior, the anti-cultists rediscovered the Korean War era literature on brainwashing of American soldiers by their Korean and Chinese captors (e.g., Hunter, 1953; Lifton, 1953; Meerloo, 1956). Over time a number of behavioral scientists lent support to the ACM cause by offering an updated, cult-specific version of the brainwashing process (e.g., Clark, 1979; Conway and Siegelman, 1978; Verdier, 1977).

The brainwashing metaphor constituted the secular equivalent of "possession." UM members were portrayed as the helpless victims of mind control, variously attributed to drugging, hypnosis or physical/psychological manipulation. They bore no responsibility for their present behavior because they had been reduced to zombie-like slaves by UM leaders. These victims constituted a real danger to others, who they might "infect," and to themselves since their free will and capacity for autonomous action had been destroyed. Thus symbolic construction of UM members as "programmed" through coercive mind control techniques led naturally to the concept of "deprogramming," and exorcism like ritual which presumably restored an individual's former "natural" personality and free will (Shupe and Bromley, 1980c).

The brainwashing metaphor was buttressed by ACM references to UM members as "children." This presentation of UM members in their familial roles was intended to confer on parents not only the right but the responsibility to take whatever actions were necessary to "protect" their "children." It was on the basis of this combination of imagery which depicted UM members as "brainwashed" and as "children" that anti-cultists relied to legitimate the extreme social control they sought over UM members.

Religion

Fundamentalist churches had as their primary objective discrediting the UM's claim to membership in the Christian community and to special spiritual knowledge that superceded and supplanted orthodox theology. The UM posed no threat to fundamentalist churches' membership or financial bases as the overwhelming majority of UM members were drawn from mainline denominations (Bromley and Shupe, 1979b). Nor were fundamentalists as opposed to overt political activity as mainline denominations. Rather it was the challenge to these churches' legitimacy and authority that was at issue.

The emphasis by the fundamentalist churches on rebuffing UM assaults on their legitimacy and authority and the very real constraints on the churches' capacity to exert social control over the UM led to the development of defensively oriented organizations. Certainly the best known of these was the Spiritual Counterfeits Project based in Berkely, California. While such fundamentalist groups railed against "cults" in general and the UM as the archtypical "cult," the rhetoric was aimed predominantly at members of fundamentalist churches. A torrent of literature in the form of books, periodicals, reprinted sermons and religious tracts were published by small local and regional fundamentalist presses (for a comprehensive listing see Shupe and Bromley, 1981). The vast majority of this literature went unnoticed by the public at large, amid a substantial, popular/secular literature (e.g., Edwards, 1979; Patrick and Dulack, 1976; Stoner and Parke, 1977), since it was distributed almost exclusively through Christian bookstores. Nevertheless, these materials were widely circulated among the fundamentalist audience to which they were primarily directed.

Because fundamentalist churches sought greater authority over their members than did mainline denominations, the UM posed a more serious threat to the former. At the same time the fundamentalists neither possessed the capacity nor felt the necessity of exercising coercive control over the UM or its members. Had the fundamentalist church leaders attempted to "rescue" wayward Christians they would have exceeded their authority within their own churches and created internal divisions and conflict. Further, a wide spectrum of churches would have opposed any such effort due to the dangerous precedent set by any one church exerting force against another in what was at least nominally a pluralistic system.

The metaphor consistent with the kind of social control which the churches sought to exercise was "deception" (as opposed to "possession"). UM members were portrayed as idealistic, if gullible, youth whose immaturity, personal insecurities or lack of proper Christian education led to their seduction by UM leaders. In contrast to the "zombie" imagery employed by the family based component of the ACM (in which UM members were depicted as robots or automatons), the deception metaphor presented UM members as misguided ''zealots.'' According to this imagery the individual's personality and free will were essentially intact; indeed it was the individual's passionate idealism and humanitarian concerns which rendered him susceptible to the UM's millenarian quest. UM members therefore were not perceived as highly dangerous to themselves or others, and it was felt that they could be confronted with Christian truths and persuaded of the error of their ways. At the same time the fundamentalists made the costs of the UM's quixotic quest clear: to stray from the teachings of Christianity was to throw away the opportunity for real spiritual fulfillment and salvation.

THE DYNAMICS OF REPRESSION

Once the two components of the ACM had developed ideologies to legitimate the exercise of social control and organizational apparatus to mobilize their respective constituencies, the problem remained of imposing sanctions on the UM. However, neither the fundamentalist nor the family based component of the ACM possessed significant sanctioning capacity. The UM also lacked the resources to achieve its goals independently. Both sides, therefore, were reliant upon allies in the ensuing conflict. The UM was never able to marshal a significant number of allies and hence was at continuous disadvantage in its struggle with the ACM. With the exception of civil liberties organizations and some liberal academicians and clergy, the UM had few supporters. And even these groups were in essence defending religious liberty and not the UM itself. On occasion the UM did receive protection when other institutions viewed repression as threatening their own interests (e.g., the political and judicial institution's concern with the ACM's attempts to legitimate the use of force in achieving its goals).

The ACM possessed a significant advantage in the balance of power as a result of support from a number of major institutions. This support was critical to its success in repressing the UM because virtually all of the sanctions it sought to impose required at least the tacit approval of some other group. Each of the group's which provided support to the ACM, of course, had some interest of its own in opposing the UM. Among the most important of the ACM's allies were the mainline churches, various components of the political institution and the media.

Church Support for the ACM

Although the fundamentalist churches were able to discredit the UM among their own membership, they did not possess the capacity to exclude the UM from the Christian community. Mainline denominations supported fundamentalist efforts to discredit the UM for several reasons. First, UM witnessing and fundraising teams often identified themselves as Christian. It was in the interest of mainline churches to "expose" these claims because public suspicion began to affect their own local solicitation and proselytization activities. Second, the interdependence between the familial and religious institutions placed considerable pressure on major denominations (with which the families of most UM members were affiliated) to support those parents who were unalterably opposed to their offsprings' UM membership. Third, the UM engaged in overt political activity by lobbying for military/political support for South Korea (the "New Israel" from which the new messiah was to appear) and openly defended President Richard Nixon during the Watergate episode. The mainline denominations felt compelled to disavow these blatant violations of church-state boundaries.

Although the mainline churches were not immediately and dramatically threatened by the UM, they did have an interest in excluding the UM from specific legitimating organizations (such as the national, state and local councils of churches) and, more broadly, from the community of "legitimate" churches. The UM was affected in two ways by this exclusion. On the one hand, because the UM was reliant upon a strategy of persuasion to achieve its goals, exclusion from legitimating organizations seriously hindered its capacity to gain cooperation or even a hearing from important segments of the population it sought to reach. On the other hand, rejection of the UM as a legitimate church caused or enabled other institutions to suppress UM activities. For example, because of its marginal status among churches, the UM was regularly denied access to college campuses and prohibited from establishing affiliated student organizations. Such exclusion from college campuses was a major impediment to UM recruitment efforts. Similarly, it was in part the "questionable" status of the UM as a church that led the New York Regents to deny accreditation to the Unification Theological Seminary. The inability to gain accreditation had a number of negative consequences for the UM's capacity to educate its own leaders: inability to transfer credits earned at the seminary to other colleges and universities, ineligibility of seminary faculty for certain employee benefit and retirement programs, and ineligibility of students for certain categories of scholarship funds. In sum, then, established churches' rejection of the UM had the effect of encouraging or permitting other groups to deny crucial access or resources to the UM when such decisions were based on the UM's legitimacy as a church.

Political Support for the ACM

The ACM was relatively successful in winning support from various components of the political institution. In general, efforts to gain imposition of substantive sanctions against the UM were more successful at the local level than at the state and federal levels where support was primarily symbolic. For example, ACM leaders convinced local governmental officials in many communities to invoke solicitation statutes originally enacted to control peddlers and vagrants against UM fundraising teams. The anti-cult associations were successful at local level harassment, both because they were able to mount a more significant lobbying effort locally and because other local charities were concerned that UM solicitation was syphoning off local charitable dollars and increasing mistrust of all public fundraising. In numerous communities across the country local officials denied the UM solicitation licenses, set up complex application procedures and arrested UM fundraisers or escorted them out of town. These harassment campaigns had mixed effects. On the one hand, appellate court decisions unanimously overturned such ordinances as infringements on religious liberty. On the other hand, the UM was forced to divert time, energy and money away from movement goals in order to deal with literally hundreds of local conflicts. These disputes also were unfailingly reported in the media and frequently provided the occassion for the full range of ACM allegations against the UM.

The anti-cultists were less successful in mobilizing substantive sanctions at the state level, but they did manage to achieve some symbolic victories through which the UM was denigrated and discredited. Anti-cult leaders were able to exert influence on state legislative representatives in somewhat the same way they did on local officials. District representatives in a number of states responded to these lobbying efforts by establishing special committees to hold public hearings on "cults" (e.g. Vermont, 1977), and even introduced legislation stipulating a definition of "pseudo-religious" (e.g., New York, 1977). There were other instances where state agencies launched investigations of "cults" (e.g., New York, 1975; New York, 1979) and a few cases where legislation designed to hinder fundraising was passed (e.g., Minnesota, 1978).

These hearings and investigations usually represented a means of responding to constituency pressures without committing the government to substantive legislation. The problems of passing legislation that touched on the issue of religious freedom were formidable. Recognizing the questionable wisdom and legality of such bills, legislators opted for hearings both as a "cooling out" mechanism and as a means of lining the state up with the anti-cultists. For the UM these bills and hearings were damaging as each such hearing necessitated a defense. More importantly, however, these proceedings received extensive media coverage, and the allegations were incorporated in official reports which had the effect of discrediting the UM (e.g., New York, 1979).

On a federal level the anti-cultists were only occasionally successful at gaining governmental support, which was forthcoming primarily when governmental interests were threatened. For example, during the "Koreagate" scandal ex-UM members testified to their own lobbying activities on behalf of Korea (U.S. Government, 1978), and following the tragedy in Jonestown, Guyana the ACM made a concerted effort to label the UM "the suicide cult" (Carroll and Bauer, 1979). The only instance in which the ACM received direct support was in two sets of informal hearings conducted in the offices of Senator Robert Dole. A large group of parents, former UM members and ACM supporters testified and a transcript of the proceedings was published (CEFM,

1976). Again these reports were circulated to the public through the media and ACM organizations and had the effect of providing symbolic support for the ACM. Taken as a whole, this continuous flow of governmental activity, even though largely symbolic, had the effect of discrediting the UM. The mere fact that so many allegations were made and investigations initiated through governmental agencies at all levels enhanced the credibility of ACM allegations.

The deprogramming wing of the ACM received support in a variety of forms from the law enforcement and judicial systems. In numerous cases when police were present at or informed of a forcible abduction of a UM member by deprogrammers (usually accompanied by parents), they chose to regard the incident as a "family matter" and refrained from intervening (Bromley, Shupe and Ventimiglia, 1980; Patrick and Dulack, 1976). Parents and deprogrammers also were able to convince local judges to issue either writs of *habeus corpus*, so that UM members' mental incapacity could be demonstrated in court, or temporary conservatorships, which placed UM members in the custody of their parents so that deprogramming could take place. Literally hundreds of deprogrammings occurred in the 1970's with either the direct or indirect support of law enforcement and judicial officials who shared parental views of the UM. Even where deprogrammers were brought to trial judges and juries often either dismissed charges against them or issued only token penalties. As the decade wore on and local judicial decisions were reversed on appeal, police and judicial support became more difficult for the ACM to obtain. However, despite the risk involved, deprogrammings continued with devastating consequences for the UM.

Certainly the most important consequence of deprogramming for the UM was that its brainwashing ideology was bolstered by successful deprogrammings. Enough individuals who had been put through the deprogramming process eventually agreed to leave the UM to enhance ACM arguments that programmings had taken place. The UM was hard pressed to offer a convincing public explanation for why deprogrammed individuals left the movement. Even more damaging to the UM, however, were public statements by former UM members to the effect that they had indeed been brainwashed and that only deprogramming had allowed them to escape UM domination. These first person accounts were devestatingly effective in swaying public opinion (Edwards, 1979; Wood and Vitek, 1979; Underwood and Underwood, 1979) and may well have been the single most effective weapon in the ACM drive to discredit the UM. Of course, deprogrammings also created a siege mentality within the UM and increased members reservations about making visits home. Finally, deprogrammings created some morale problems within the movement as members, who often were in the process of building and testing their own faith, found it disheartening to hear former members reinforce their own doubts and publically impugn the movement.

Media Support for the ACM

The source of the ACM's greatest support was the media. Media representatives by and large shared the same cultural assumptions and biases as did UM family members and, hence, were readily sympathetic to ACM allegations. From journalists' perspectives ACM members appeared to be reputable but distraught middle-class citizens with no apparent axes to grind. It was difficult for media representatives to believe that such ordinary middle-class citizens would go to the lengths of jeopardizing their own careers, expending great amounts of time and money travelling around the country, and risking legal prosecution by having their offspring kidnapped and deprogrammed if their allegations were indeed groundless. Investigative reporters who chose to visit UM centers for themselves, as a number did, were prone to concur with parental assessments. Their suspicions about the UM were heightened further as a result of the range of charges against the UM proffered by church leaders, governmental officials and sympathetic behavioral scientists.

By the mid-1970's, the media had adopted a notably hostile posture toward the UM and media coverage was predominantly negative (Bromley, Shupe and Ventimiglia, 1980). ACM versions of the conflict were uncritically reported in television documentaries, newspaper and magazine articles, books by apostates and even "cult episodes" worked into regular television series. The ACM-UM conflict also had become a major "story" as it contained a complexing mix of dramatic themes (e.g., mind control, kidnapping, foreign conspiracy, meglomanic gurus, economic rip-off). Once the ACM-UM conflict gained prominence in the media, individual newspapers and magazines and television talk shows began competing with one another to produce the most sensational story. For example, virtually every magazine appealing to teenagers and homemakers ran at least one expose of "cults." Magazines such as McCalls (Rasmussen, 1976), Seventeen (Remsberg and Remsberg, 1976), and Good Housekeeping (Crittenden, 1976) ran articles with titles such as "How Sun Myung Moon Lures America's Children", "Why I left the Moon Cult" and "The Incredible Story of Ann Gordon."

Newspapers published similar stories, and local papers across the country reprinted one another's stories verbatim with no independent verification of reported events. These stories literally constituted a wave of events which left the impression that innocent children were being plucked off the streets and college campuses at an alarming, increasing rate. Of course such stories also created suspicion and opposition to the UM among a wide range of groups and individuals who accepted their face validity. Additional conflicts generated on this basis occasioned more negative media coverage. As a result of this self-feeding process, the UM lost the capacity to manage its public identity and was almost totally discredited publically.

CONCLUSIONS

In this paper we have attempted to move toward a preliminary statement of the process whereby social movements are repressed, using the response to the new religions in the United States as a case study. All social movements are emergent organizations which challenge the established social order; to the degree they are successful in achieving their goals the shape of the social structure would be altered. World transforming movements are particularly instructive cases because they are likely to antagonize a broad range of established groups within the larger society and generate social control responses. We have argued that the UM significantly reoriented members' behavior (that is, behavior was placed in a social context) which threatened the interests and authority structures of established groups. In the UM's case it was the family and fundamentalist churches which were so threatened.

A high level of threat typically is met initially by attempting to induce the challenging social movement to operate within established normative boundaries. Such efforts were made by both individual families and fundamentalist churches. If these efforts fail, as they did in the case at hand because the UM felt unable to compromise, the threatened group is likely to conclude that the norm violator is incapable (for whatever reason) of responding in an appropriate or acceptable fashion. It is at this point that attempts are made to move the violator into a deviant status. Both components of the ACM developed ideologies and organizations that served precisely this purpose: They attempted to define UM actions and motives as necessitating the exertion of social control because the UM had flagrantly violated the boundaries of public morality (i.e. Christian "truth" and family "sanctity").

Repression is dependent, however, upon a substantial imbalance of power between the parties to the conflict. Frequently no single group in the conflict possesses power sufficient in amount and scope to exercise repression. The ACM was in this precise position, and it was the alliances with other institutions which were the basis for the success it did achieve. The UM, by contrast, possessed virtually no allies and, hence, had a relatively low capacity to resist repressive sanctions. Once deviant status has been conferred and sanctions imposed, the deviant status tends to be self-sustaining. In this conflict society-wide acceptance of the ACM's depiction of the UM meant that a wide range of institutions engaged in direct or indirect exclusionary activity which only served to increase the UM's conflict with them. Much of this conflict was precipitated by the media, which accepted the ACM's ideology and played a major role in discrediting the UM.

One final word is in order regarding repression. The term repression frequently is used in a context that connotes the naked display of force. While such a connotation is not inapplicable to the UM-ACM conflict, it would camoflauge the more subtle aspects of repression. The ACM after all was a small, weak, poorly funded and often disorganized movement. Further, the campaign against the UM could hardly be deemed concerted or coordinated when compared with the repression of other social movements through history. Finally, even though the ACM possessed numerous allies most of these provided limited and usually symbolic assistance. Yet the impact of this relatively uncoordinated campaign provided graphic evidence of the awesome repressive capacity vested in the established order. It was also eloquent testimony to the effectiveness of symbolic degredation and nondecision-making in blocking unwanted social change. The analysis presented in this paper suggests that as the study of social movement moves away from a social psychological perspective toward an organizational perspective, the role of repression presents itself as an increasingly salient concern.

ACKNOWLEDGMENT

This paper is the product of a joint effort. The order of authorship is random and does not imply any difference in the importance of contribution.

NOTES

1. This paper is based on a several year study of the Unificationist Movement (Bromley and Shupe, 1979) and the Anti-Cult Movement (Shupe and Bromley, 1980a). Both monographs contain discussions of data gathering procedures. For additional information see Bromley and Shupe (1980) and Shupe and Bromley (1980b).

2. Among the organizations comprising the Unificationist Movement were the Unification Church (with numerous international branches), the Unification Theological Seminary, the *News World* (a New York daily newspaper), the Freedom Leadership Foundation (an anti-communist "education" organization) and International Cultural Foundation. In addition, there were a myriad of ad hoc groups, witnessing and fundraising teams, and businesses owned or affiliated with the movement.

3. The term deprogramming actually incorporated a range of activities from pastoral counseling to forcible abduction and detention. We refer here primarily to the latter since the more extreme activities gave deprogramming its unique character and were central to the ACM's organizational and ideological development.

REFERENCES

Bromley, David, and Anson Shupe
 1979a Moonies in America: Cult Church and Crusade. Beverly Hills, CA.: Sage Publications.
Bromley, David, and Anson Shupe
 1979b "Just a few years seem like a lifetime: a role theory approach to participation in religious movement. Louis Kriesberg (ed.), Research in Social Movements, Conflict and Change. Vol. 3: Greenwich, CT.: JAI Press.
Bromley, David and Anson Shupe
 1980 "Evolving foci in participant observation: research as an emergent process."

William Shaffer, Robert Stebbins and Allan Turowetz (eds.) in Fieldwork Experience. New York: St. Martin's Press.

Bromley, David, Anson Shupe, and Joseph Ventimiglia
1980   "The role of anecdotal atrocities in the social construction of evil." James
          Richardson (ed.), in the Deprogramming Controversy: Sociological, Psychological
          Legal and Historical Perspectives. New Brunswick, N.J.: Transaction Press.

Carroll, Jerry and Bernard Bauer
1979   Suicide training in the Moon cult. New West.

CEFM (National Ad Hoc Committee Engaged in Freeing Minds)
1976   A Special Report. The Unification Church: Its Activities and Practices. Vols. I and II.
          Arlington, Texas: National Ad Hoc Committee, A Day of Affirmation and Protest.

Clark, John
1979   "Cults" Journal of the American Medical Association 242 (July 20).

Conway, Flo and Jim Siegelman
1978   Snapping. New York: Lippincott.

Crittenden, Ann
1976   "The incredible story of Ann Gordon and Sun Myung Moon". Good Housekeeping.
          October:86ff.

Edwards, Christopher
1979   Crazy for God. Englewood Cliffs, N.J.: Prentice Hall.

Holy Spirit Association for the Unification of World Christianity (HSA-UWC)
1977   Divine Principle. Condensed Version. Washington, D.C.

Hunter, Edward
1953   Brainwashing in Red China: The Calculated Destruction of Men's Minds. New York:
          Vanguard.

Kanter, Rosabeth
1972   Commitment and Community. Cambridge: Harvard University Press.

Katz, Jack
1975   "Essences as moral identities: verifiabilably and responsibility in imputations of
          deviance and charisma." American Journal of Sociology 80 (May).

Lifton, Robert
1957   "Thought reform of Chinese intellectuals: a psychiatric evaluation." Journal of
          Social Issues 13: (3).

Meerloo, Jost
1956   The Rape of the Mind. New York: World.

Minnesota
1978   Section 309.50, Subdivision 10 of Minnesota Statutes, 1976. Amendment.

New York
1975   Final Report of the Activities of the Children of God to Hon. Louis Lefkowitz,
          Attorney General of the State of New York. Albany, New York: Charity Frauds
          Bureau.

New York
1977   Proposed Bill AB9566-A (Section 240.46 "Promoting a Pseudo-Religious Cult") to
          the New York Assembly. Albany, New York: October 5.

New York
1979   Public Hearing on Treatment of Children by Cults. The State Assembly of New York.
          New York: August 9-10. Reprinted by American Family Foundation, Inc.

Patrick, Ted and Tom Dulack
1976   Let Our Children Go! New York: E.P. Dutton.

Rasmussen, M.
1976   How Sun Myung Moon lures America's children. McCalls. September:102, ff.

Remsberg, C., and B. Remsberg
1976   Why I left the Moon cult. Seventeen. Pp. 107, 117, 127. July.
Shupe, Anson, and David Bromley
1980a   The New Vigilantes: Deprogrammers, Anti-Cultists and the New Religion. Beverly Hills, Cal.: Sage Publications.
Shupe, Anson and David Bromley
1980b   ''Walking a tightrope: dilemmas of participant observation of groups in conflict.'' Qualitive Sociology 2: January.
Shupe, Anson and David Bromley
1980c   ''Witches, moonies and evil''. Thomas Robbins and Dick Anthony (eds.), In God We Trust: Patterns in American Religious Pluralism. New Brunswick, N.J.: Tranaction Books.
Shupe, Anson and David Bromley
1982   The Anti-Cult Movement: An Annotated History, New York: Garland Publishers.
Stoner, Carol, and Jo Ann Parke
1977   All God's Children. Radnor, Pa.: Chilton.
U.S. Government
1978   Investigation of Korean-American Relations. (Report of the Subcommittee on Internatonal Organizations of the Committee on International Relations, U.S. House of Representatives) Washington, D.C.: U.S. Government Printing Office.
Underwood, Barbara and Betty Underwood
1979   Hostage to Heaven, New York: Clarkson Potter, Inc.
Verdier, Paul
1977   Brainwashing and the Cults. Hollywood, Calif.: Institute of Behavioral Conditioning.
Vermont
1977   Report of the Senate Committee for the Investigation of Alleged Deceptive, Fraudulent and Criminal Practices of Various Organizations in the state. Montpelier, Vt.: January.
Wood, Allan, and J. Vitek
1979   Moonstruck. New York: William Morrow and Co.

DEFENSIVE STRIKES OF A DOOMED LABOR ARISTOCRACY:
THE CASE OF THE PRINTERS IN FRANCE

J.W. Freiberg

You start working at 20 and you think you'll work until you're 65. Then halfway through
they give you the boot. Now the market is different. There is no typesetter. The typesetter is
like a Do-do bird, they don't exist anymore. Now they disguise our job as clerical work,
calling it technical typist or word processor. This way they push it on women so they can
make them take lower wages. We were getting union pay. The jobs out there are non-union
and half the pay.

Charles MacIsaac, typesetter
The Tab (Boston), August 6, 1980

The above analysis of the plight of the modern day printer is from a local
Boston newspaper, but it could have been expressed in New York (where
printers at the *Times*, went out on strike for 89 days in 1978 and 114 days in
1962-63), or in London, or in Copenhagen, or in practically any other city in

Research in Social Movements, Conflict and Change, Volume 4, pages 47-66
Copyright © 1981 by JAI Press Inc.
All rights of reproduction in any form reserved.
ISBN: 0-89232-234-9

the Western world. Printers, like many other elements of the traditional labor aristocracy, are under severe pressure from the concentration process and the ever increasing organic composition of capital with which it is associated. This essay is a case study of the printers and their unions in France, and more particularly about their recent efforts to defend their privileged position in the face of counterveiling historical trends. After a brief analysis of the political-economy of the printing sector which determines the field of action in which the printers find themselves, I want to look at the anarcho-syndicalism typical of their union organization, and at how this contributed to at least the short term success of recent defensive strike actions. The latter task involves a somewhat detailed analysis of the longest strike in French labor history—that of the Parisian daily, *Parisien Libéré*.

PART ONE: THE PRINTING SECTOR (THE FIELD OF ACTION)

Harry Braverman (1974), Stephen Marglin (1976) and numerous others have addressed the relationship between the concentration process and its effect on labor and labor relations. Their general thesis is that the constant search for increased productivity (that is, a higher rate of profit than the average enterprise in a given sector) leads to progressively more reinvestment in fixed capital equipment capable of diminishing wage costs. In order to remain competitive, other enterprises in the sector are forced to follow suit, and the decrease in job slots soon becomes generalized throughout the sector. Of course, only the larger firms have the capital to purchase the new productivity-raising equipment; hence, the productivity of these corporate firms is soon far superior to that of the smaller enterprises, which further fuels the concentration process, since the relatively high prices the smaller firms must charge soon make them noncompetitive.

Braverman and Marglin argue that the industrial reorganization in the technologically upgraded enterprises has serious consequences for those workers fortunate enough to maintain their jobs. First, there is a rapid "de-skilling" of this personnel as their work functions become progressively fractionated and their once highly skilled crafts become reduced to machine tending. This de-skilling allows highly trained and well-paid craftsmen to be replaced by less-skilled labor. It leads (as Marglin stresses) to a progressive elimination of the control functions of the worker over his production activities and their transfer to management. This transfer in turn exacerbates the separation of "mental" from "manual" labor, that is, it divorces the conceptualization of work processes from their execution, rendering the work force increasingly dependent upon both technical expertise and management. Since the working class is excluded from the former category by the selective education system and from the latter by its lack of capital, the process operates to increase both the immediate control of management over the work site and the long-term structural inability of labor to run an industrial sector without the technical and organizational skills monopolized by management. In almost every industrial sector, workers themselves are today far less capable of operating that industry than they were 50 or 100 years ago.

This set of hypotheses is examined in the material which follows. There is, however, a great absence in Braverman's analysis. As several of his critics have noted (Ehrenreich and Ehrenreich 1976; Johnson 1978), Braverman does not trace the effects of these altered labor relations on the unions and union activities of the workers involved. He views the entire process more in terms of structure than of struggle. As Johnson (1978, p. 42) states, ''The heart of the labor process is the struggle between capital and labor . . . The relations of classes, as they work themselves out in historical settings, dialectically inter-relate with the structural determinations that Braverman analyzes.'' Braverman does not see that the capitalist has a second motivation behind increasing machinery and decreasing living labor: the quantitative and qualitative reduction of labor eliminates the effective strike threat in the work place. It is to the credit of Marglin (1976) that he underscores this important point. The present essay will examine this issue in detail. Labor does not passively accept these structural changes, as even Braverman (1974, p. 197) knows: in a footnote he quotes a vice president of General Motors who ''pointed out that in 10 plant reorganizations conducted by the G.M. Assembly Division after 1968, 8 of them produced strikes.'' But he does not follow this up and, hence, fails to assess the counter strategies available to labor, or the politicization of unions and union federations to which the progressive displacement and de-skilling of labor leads.

It is in fact essential in industrial sociology to study a given economic sector in light of its internal interplay of structure and struggle. It follows that before we can observe the demise of the printers as an element of the labor aristocracy (and their defensive struggles to prevent this slippage), we must first observe, if only briefly given the space limitations of this essay, the current structural transformations characteristic of the printing sector in France.

As fixed capital investment has risen progressively in the larger enterprises of the sector, printers have been progressively displaced with new generations of photo electronic equipment. The amount of fixed capital in the average print shop increases by roughly 10 percent per year; in 1961 the average fixed capital per printer was about NF 29 million, while by 1972 it was about NF 57 million (INSEE 1974, p. 13). The total fixed capital of the press and book publishing sub-sectors as a whole has risen from NF 4.8 billion in 1959 to 14.5 billion in 1972, while hundreds of enterprises have closed during this period (*ibid.*, p. 14). The consequent increased productivity of the ever enlargening corporate units of the sector has given them an increased cash flow which has been used in two principal fashions: first, to buy out smaller enterprises to further reduce competition, and second, to reinvest in still more labor-reducing equipment (especially facsimile communication of fully composed pages to regional printing plants) to better compete with other large corporate units. The entire process is therefore a spiral, which continually decreases the number of units in the sector, rendering ever larger firms as no longer competitive compared with the very largest.

The concentration process has important ramifications on an international level as well, especially insofar as it is accompanied by an overall reduction in productive capacity in the sector. This is clear in the case of both printing and paper production, where the decrease in French capacity has been part of a process of internationalization of production.

By 1972, 30 percent of all periodicals and 40 percent of all magazines edited in France were printed outside of the country. (Lecat government report, p. 21). Fully 203 periodicals were printed abroad: 125 in Italy, 60 in Belgium, and others in Holland, Spain and Luxembourg (*Presse Actualité*, September 1976). Two-thirds of all mail order catalogues, and many state publications (the Renault catalogues, autmobile registration forms, Air France magazines, etc.) were also printed abroad (*Le Monde*, September 6, 1977). Just how serious this externalization of French printing was, is evident when one looks at some figures for the importation and exportation of printed materials:

The Growth in the Importation of Printed Materials
(in millions of NF)

material	1962	1972
Journals and magazines	−10	−36
Books	102	−557
Catalogues	18	−200
Photographic	0	−30
Total	+110	−323

(*Source:* INSEE, 1974 *Industries Polygraphiques, press-édition*, p. 23)

By 1975 the yearly balance of payments deficit (in printed material) was NF 396 million, and in 1976 it jumped to 617 million (*Presse Actualité*, May 1977). This represents a considerable amount of printing: the printer's union estimates that the return to France of all of this printing would create about 10,000 printing jobs and restore the industry (in 1977 at a drastically elevated 14% unemployment rate) to full health. The trend, however, is going in the other direction, with imports rising 18 percent annually since 1962 (Communist Party, 1976). The effects of this process are highly visible; throughout France dozens of perfectly serviceable printing plants lie idle—quite a few occuped by the laid-off printers (*Le Monde*, September 6, 1977).

The same story is true in the related paper industry, where production is dominated by two monopolistic corporations, each organized by a major bank, (Banque Paribas and Banque Suez). The production of newsprint in France fell from 436,000 metric tons in 1960 to 260,000 metric tons in 1976 (Communist Party, 1976). During the same period, imports of newsprint rose froɪn 170,000 to 320,000 metric tons (Mattelart 1976, p. 272). This increased dependency on multinational paper corporations has had two concomitant effects: first, serious consequences for the French balance of payments (paper is second to oil, *Presse Actualité*, May 1977), and second, a meteoric rise in price (in 1974 the price of newsprint climbed fully 84%).

Taken together, the increasing investment in labor-eliminating equipment and the partial dismantling of productive capacity in the printing sector have led to a radically changed situation for workers in the sector. Besides the inordinantly high unemployment rate, many of those remaining are threatened with de-skilling when the highly skilled craft specialties of traditional printing are replaced with the meager tasks of the automated print shop. Where lino-typists and typesetters (who had to be able to read in mirror image) once took 3 to 5 years to train, today's press employees need merely typing skills to feed texts into the photocomposition equipment. There are of course, important class differentials in this transformation of the work process in printing: printers were invariably from traditional working class origins, although their early ability to read and write helped catapulted them into the "aristocratic" strata of this class. In contrast to this, today's typists, besides often being women, are from lower middle-strata backgrounds, typically having learned their typing not for printing, but for school work. This shift from "manual" to "mental" labor radically alters the situational ideology of the print shop, for although highly skilled manual labor is in fact far more "mental" than lowly skilled mental labor, the traditional workers saw themselves in craft terms, and hence as essentially opposed to management. The new mental workers wear the same white collars as management, and are probably less likely to union-ize, and certainly far less likely to form the combat-ready anarcho-syndicalist type of unions typical of printers throughout the Western world. It is of course possible that the new white collar workers of the sector will create new forms of activism and new labor demands. On the other hand, they are fewer in number and more easily replaced given their lower skill level.

Now that the field of action in the printing sector has been briefly analyzed, we can pass to an introduction of the actors who must operate in respect to the structural topography of this field. Only then can we finally assess the struggles between these actors.

PART TWO: THE PRINTERS AND THE PRINTING BOURGEOISIE (THE ACTORS)

A. *The Printers: Last Days of a Labor Aristocracy*

One of the major traits which characterizes the printers unions is its jealously guarded automomy with respect to union federations. The central organizations are structured more to coordinate and negotiate than to determine policy for the member unions. This autonomy is found at multiple levels: the five trade unions (proofreaders, typographers, linotypists, mold-pressers and press operators, and technical cadres) each have an operational autonomy while coordinating on both the shop level in a given enterprise and nationally in the printers federation (Fédération française des travailleurs du livre). Similarly, the printers federation—although one of the founding members in 1895 of France's largest union confederation, the (Communist Party linked) GGT—maintains its distance from this powerful organization. Although the printers federation is glad to have CGT cooperation during its strikes, it maintains a one-way relationship; seldom does it heed CGT calls for strikes eminating from other sectors or general political events. It is also interesting to note the independence of the printers federation—and even of the CGT itself—from the positions of the French Communist Party. The practical need for this became obvious during a study of printers at *Le Monde*, which was typical of the Parisian press: whereas 30 percent of the press operators were Communist Party members, only 5 percent of the typographers and linotypists, and no proof readers were members. Here we see that Party membership varied directly with the degree of ''manual'' labor: the more mental the labor, the less likely was membership. This finding underscores the political significance of the shift from the traditional print shop to its modern equivalent, which eliminates many of the manual labor positions.

With considerable pride, the typographers, linotypists, and proof readers refered to their union—and to the FFTL—as ''anarcho-syndicalist.'' They used this term not with reference to a notion of a revolutionary general strike, but to express a deep sentiment which seemed to be composed of three elements. First, they referred to the autonomy of each union from the FFTL and of the FFTL from the CGT, as discussed above. Second, they spoke at length about the 150 year tradition of internal solidarity in their unions (printers were among the very first craft organizations to form, long before it was legal; *see* Chauvet, 1971). Third, they have in mind their tradition of a widespread rank and file involvement in militant activism during strikes. More about this later.

In many ways, the mid-1970s was a turning point for the nearly one-hundred-year old printers unions. With the concentration, decrease in productive capacity and unemployment typical of the sector, the printers can only fight a defensive battle; most of their demands are aimed at saving the employment of those individuals currently working. There is no hope of preserving these positions for future generations of printers. Some efforts, of course, are being made to ensure the printers are retrained to function as the operators of the new photocomposition material in the future. But regardless of the class origins of the technical and clerical personnel who will work in tomorrow's print shops, these workers will not be unionizable in the same way as the traditional printers have been.

At the height of its power, the CGT affiliated printer's union enjoyed an (extremely rare) absolute monopoly in Paris, which provided the union with the structural possibility of demanding and winning "aristocratic" advantages. First, the union was able to bargain with the newspaper owners syndicate for all Parisian papers at once. This prevented the idiosyncracies of particular owners and print shops from entering into consideration, and allowed the union to bargain from a position of unity and strength. Second, the union not only supplied the men to each print shop (i.e., the printers were not hired by the enterprise, but by the union, which then distributed them as per the needs of particular enterprises, hence eliminating paternalism and cross cutting loyalties), but also supplied their foremen (cadres techniques). These formen were initially elected by fellow printers. They provided a shield between the printers and management at each print shop; management communicated any complaints or directions to these union foremen, not directly to the printers. This also helped (perhaps even guaranteed) union solidarity.

Third, the monopoly in Paris allowed the union to negotiate some extremely favorable work norms, which held down the intensity of labor quite considerably. Strict definitions of overtime (including any work on a second publication put out by the same enterprise) have insured an increased average income for the printers. Because of the strength of their bargaining position, the printers have been able to demand a salary almost totally out of proportion to their working class origins. A recent government study showed the 20 percent of printers earned between NF 30,000 and 50,000, with 80 percent earning more than NF 50,000 annually. (Toussant 1976, p. 41) An executive of Hachette, the largest corporate printing company in the world, recently noted that the average salary of printers at its Parisian daily, *France-Soir*, in 1976 was NF 63,000 (INA 1976, p. 10). The approximately NF 5,000 monthly salary for Parisian printers compares favorably with the already high salary of non-Parisian printers of NF 3,800. The only way to put these figures in perspective, however, is by comparing them with the following average incomes in France:

Average Incomes of Full Time Male Workers, 1976

occupation	net monthly salary, NF	
UPPER MANAGEMENT		
administrative	9,600	
technical (engineers)	7,520	
MIDDLE MANAGEMENT		Parisian printers
administrative	5,369 ←	(5,250)
technical	4,035	
LABOR		
foremen	3,965	
clericals	2,870	
skilled manual	2,570	
unskilled manual	1,780	

Source: Le Monde 1976. L'Année économique et sociale. p. 55

As the above makes clear, the average printer's salary in 1976 ranked well within the average salaries received by management. It was out of all proportion to other salaries in the traditional working class. In 1976 only 10.8% of *all* monthly French salaries were higher than NF 5,060. (*Le Monde.* 1976. "*L'Année économique et social.* p. 54)

B. The Printing Bourgeoisie: Concentration, Centralization, and Control

The owners of the printing enterprises are not free to produce *any* set of strategies and tactics; they must conform, to be successful, to the structural tranformations which characterize late capitalism, and which underlie and determine the possibilities within the printing sector. The concentration, centralization, internationalization of production and associated trends referred to above were not initiated by the relatively small scale bourgeoisie of the economically minor printing sector, but it is they who have willingly imported these trends into their sector. As such we can trace their strategies and analyze their intent.

The printing bourgeoisie has set out to increase its productivity through the introduction of new labor-eliminating equipment. The larger the enterprise, the more likely one is to find this trend (partly for reasons of available capital). It is particularly the newspaper chains and major press groups which have emphasized this strategy, particularly the press chain of Robert Hersant, who by 1979 controlled three of the six major Parisian newspapers. The social wastefulness of this increased capacity of the larger shops become evident when one realizes that there is actually a surplus of many types of new equipment. Among offset printing presses this surplus runs to 30 percent, while 2-color offset presses are underused by 44 percent, at the same time that 15 percent are being added per year (Interview with Roger Coquelin of the printers union, June 1, 1977). Such statistics, however, involve a societal viewpoint, which contradicts the reality that in capitalism, for all practical planning purposes, the only operative level is that of the individual enterprise. It may be advantageous for an individual corporate firm to add a certain press, even though the business attracted is taken away from another (typically smaller) firm whose presses thereafter sit idle.

To understand the idling of serviceable equipment, one needs to employ the concept of "devaluing" (dévalorization) of capital. This is accomplished by forcing smaller, less competitive firms out of business and by favoring such a rapid turnover of new generations of equipment that the equipment of the closing firms cannot (profitably) be reused, and must be sold for scrap. (At the closed Chaix printing plant, for example, NF 50 million worth of relatively modern equipment was sold as scrap for NF 3 per kilo (*Le Monde*, September 6, 1977). This devaluing of capital, or, in plain terms, this destruction of perfectly serviceable and extremely valuable equipment, is a serious drain on socially productive labor. It serves the interests of individual monopolistic firms by counterveiling the tendency of the falling rate of profit (by decreasing competition), but for the society as a whole it is purely destructive and wasteful.

The printing bourgeoisie has a double interest in introducing the new labor-eliminating equipment; above and beyond the question of raising productivity, they see the possibility of breaking, once and for all, the powerful hold on the Parisian printing industry of the CGT-linked printers federation. Between 1969 and 1974, more than 13,000 printers were laid off permanently (*Presse Actualité*, March 1976). This sudden, massive unemployment and the reaction it provoked among the printers led to the appointment of an *ad hoc* government commission, the Lecat Commission, which concluded that 3,000 more printers would have to be laid off each year between 1974 and 1980 to bring employment in the sector into line with the needs of the new equipment. In sum, the report supported the future firing of fully 25 percent of all printers then working. It also called for an increase in printing capacity of 25 percent this same period, a capacity to be met by the introduction of more photocomposition and offset equipment. The report, in brief, all but openly called for increased concentration in the sector.

The printing bourgeoisie is perfectly aware that the quantitative reduction in the labor force which undermines the strength of the printers union is complemented by the qualitative reduction accomplished through the de-skilling process. The principal thrust of the effect of the displacement of the skilled craftsmen needed in a traditional printing shop was evident in the successful elimination of unions in the Canadian press; as one researcher writes, ''The introduction of photocomposition in Toronto dailies in Canada led to the breaking of the printers union and the assigning of the work to non-trained and non-union secretaries'' (Dumas 1972, p. 30).

We have now looked at the political-economy of the printing sector (the field of action), the printers and their union, and the press bourgeoisie (the actors). The remainder of the essay traces out what happened recently when these combatants met in an all-out conflict.

PART THREE: THE LONGEST STRIKE IN FRENCH LABOR HISTORY: *Parisien Libéré*

A. The Combatants

Le Parisien Libéré is a sensationalist newspaper, where soft news overwhelms hard news; the paper has principally a working class readership, which implies that its conservative editorializing has little direct impact on its left-voting clientelle. Before looking in detail at the strategies and counter-strategies used by both management and the printers, I want to spend a moment discussing the combatants. In any specific instance of class struggle, the many levels of life become confused. In the case of the *Parisien Libéré* strike, for example, the specific personality of its owner, Emilien Amaury, played as big a role in determining the flow of events as did the general structural transformations discussed earlier.

The printers union was introduced in the preceding section; here I want to examine the concrete methods used by the union in its defensive struggle. The keystone of its capacity to struggle was the funding it was able to gather: all Parisian printers gave 10 percent of their salary every month for 29 months, which was enough to provide roughly 80 percent of the usual salary of the more than 500 *Parisian Libéré* printers out on strike. This internal support totaled more than NF 60 million, and was supplemented by other funds raised through benefits, demonstrations, sales of posters, and sales of the printers federation's publication of a fascinating book on the strike, *Amaury's Putsch*.

But besides this financial underwriting which allowed the federation to carry out such a protracted strike, great use was made of another aspect of the printer's anarcho-syndicalism, namely, the high percentage of activist involvement during a strike. About 30 percent of all printers in Paris consistently participated in an endless series of demonstrations, occupations, break-ins, sit-ins, commando raids, and the like.[2]

Furthermore, the printers union could count on both CGT and Communist Party support. The highly independent anarcho-syndicalist position of the union toward the CGT was quickly overcome by the material and political help the powerful labor confederation was able to provide during the lengthy strike. The same is true to a lesser extent for the CP, whose dependable militants were extremely valuable to the union during the two and one-half years of action. In some ways, the heat of the confrontation united the printers union and the CGT, and some printers expressed fears that the union might become permanently overly politicized and have difficulty returning to its corporatist patterns. On the other hand, officers of the union federation claimed that the union had gone through a self-critique and had rejected its past corporatism (Interview with Emilien Spaziro, September 11, 1976). In any case, in view of the structural developments affecting the printing industry, the politicization of union members will probably continue to grow.

Opposing the printers was Emilien Amaury, owner of the *Parisien Libéré* and of the press group of which it was a part. Amaury had had no formal education to speak of; before he entered the advertising business at age 25, the only thing he had really done well was amateur boxing. The printers were taking on a man who, as a boxer, was known for lasting out the entire fight; he had never been knocked out (*Echo de la Presse*, December 4, 1967).

Amaury had led a double life during the war. On the one hand, he had worked comfortably enough under the Vichy regime, in which he held the position of director of the Office of Family Budgets from 1940 to 1944. Before the war he had been in advertising, and the contacts he had made helped him to found the Office of General Advertising, which was in charge of distributing the advertising budget for both the minister for the family and the under-minister for youth under Vichy. The office did more than NF 50 million worth of business from 1941 to 1944, and there is little question but that Amaury made handsome profits (FFTL 1976, p. 24; Faucier 1964, p. 290). On the other hand, Amaury loaned his apartment to the Comité National de la Résistance for its clandestine meetings during the war, and he gave money to the clandestine newspapers (*Presse Actualité*, June 1975). So while he was successfully doing business as usual, he was also building up a dossier to document his involvement in the Resistance.

From the liberation until 1947, Amaury served as director of the state-owned Havas Advertising Agency. In 1947, he left this position to devote full time to his principal newspaper, *Parisien Libéré*, and soon succeeded in changing the statutes of the enterprise from a worker-controlled corporation (S.A.R.L.) to a formal stock corporation (S.A.). Once Amaury took direct control, *Parisien Libéré* changed quickly from its liberation format to a progressively more sensationalist and overtly depoliticized, while implicitly reactionary newspaper. During this period, he was able to clear his name of collaborationist charges.

Amaury's press group consisted of a second Parisian daily, *L'Equipe* (which covers sports exclusively), and daily papers in Anger and Le Mans, as well as numerous magazines, including his reactionary, openly racist (anti-Algerian) political monthly, *Carrefour*. This was the third largest press group in France in 1976, grossing NF 350 million, and employment 1,500 (*La Croix*, August 18, 1976).

Amaury enjoyed struggling with unions, which he condemned continuously, along with Algerians, drugs, Communists, birth control pills, and other assorted evils in the headlines of *Parisien Libéré*. He consistently refused to bow to union demands, which occassionally led to short strikes at his plants (*Le Monde*, May 21, 23, 1969).

B. Strategies and Tactics of the Great Strike

The "strategic confrontations" of this struggle are outlined in the following table. Each party had a small set of central strategies, and the other produced counterstrategies to offset these. There is much to learn about the inevitably concrete nature of class struggle in particular confrontations by examining the development of these efforts at initiative and defense.

The struggle began in early 1974 when Amaury quit the Parisian Press Owners Syndicate and joined the Regional Press Owners Syndicate to escape the CGT monopoly in Paris. His logic was based on the fact that he had fought off a decrease in his circulation (due to the "deproletarianization" of Paris) by purchasing small press enterprises in bedroom communities around Paris

Principal Strategies in the Great Parisien *Libéré* Strike

PRINTERS UNION (F.F.T.L.)	moments of strategic confrontation	AMAURY/PARISIEN LIBERE	COMMENTS
Principal Strategies		*Principal Counter-Strategies*	
1) Block production and sale of *Parisien Libéré* to force Amaury to negotiate the lay-offs he had made		–1) Avoid the blockade by closing the *Parisien* print shops and "regionalizing" the paper by opening print shops just outside of Paris	Amaury's surprise opening of the new shops in 2 weeks is a stunning victory. In the long run, however, the strike cuts his circulation 61% and his advertising income 31%
2) Use spectacular actions to attract public attention to a) pressure for negotiation and b) lessen state/police intervention		–2) Use the "Tour de France", the new *Parisien Libere*, and handouts to put across the management perspective.	F.F.T.L. victory: a series of remarkably innovative tactics catches the imagination of the population. Large solidarity developed for the printers.
3) Strike the entire press to a) force the isolation of Amaury, b) push for the industry-wide Accords at the same time c) structure the eventual inclusion of the *Parisien* in the Accords.		–3) Be the only paper in Paris and one of only 5 in France to appear on the 15 total-strike days called by the printers. Claim it is the printers who are the cause of concentration and monopolization	F.F.T.L. victory. The *Parisien Libéré* strike helps put through the general accords, which in turn guarantee the future employment of the *Parisien Libéré* printers. Except at the *Parisien Libéré* the monopoly stands intact.

Principal Counter-Strategies

–1) Block the "scab" paper through calling a strike in the CGT affiliated newspaper distribution corporation. Publicize the illegal 49-person "mini-companies," and the fanatical anti-unionism of Amaury

–2) Neutralize state intervention through general CGT and C.P. and S.P. solidarity

Principal Strategies

1) Break the C.G.T. monopoly among printers and the S.N.J. majority among journalists by hiring Force Ouvriere printers, and starting a house journalist union. Create multiple 49-person companies to avoid representation and committees

2) Rely on state help for
1) ideological support; 2) police protection; and 3) court decisions

Does lead to union pluralism at the *Parisien*, but does not effect the CGT monopoly elsewhere. Agreement later bans the 49-person structure. Amaury forced to create his own distribution company at great expense; commandos attack & destroy.

The state intervened with police and ideology for Amaury, but in the end with "early retirement" funds, to make the negotiations possible

Note: Arrows indicate relation of strategies and counterstrategies.

where the Parisian working class (his readership) had been forced to move. All of these editions were typeset and printed in Paris; nonetheless, Amaury claimed that since a great part of his circulation was ''regional'' (that is neither Parisian nor provincial), and since he now belonged to the Regional Press Owners Syndicate, he was no longer bound to the contract of the Parisian printers federation.

In June several strikes broke out at the *Parisian Libéré* when negotiations were stalled. Then, in May 1975, Amaury laid off 200 typesetters, while simultaneously attempting to launch a house union to overthrow the CGT linked printers union. A major strike broke out at once.

From the 7th to the 20th of May, no *Parisien Libéré* appeared. This was standard printers union strategy: block the production and appearance of the paper and the owner must eventually negotiate since newspaper sales and advertising income lost on a particular day are sales lost forever. But, completely unbeknownst to the printers, Amaury had a brilliant double-edged counterstrategy prepared. And since the second and major thrust of his counterattack necessitated perfect secrecy, he made the first campaign particularly visible. This involved arranging to have the *Parisien Libéré* printed in Belgium and trucked into France. On May 21, the first Belgium-printed edition appeared. The printers, taken totally by surprise, turned all of their attention to stopping this Belgium edition. Besides attacking the delivery trucks and destroying their contents, commando raids were carried out on several of the Belgium printing plants (*Parisien Libéré* 1976, p. 100; FFTL 1976, p. 57). At the same time, negotiations were undertaken by the French printers with their Belgian equivalents towards producing an international policy on the matter; eventually these proved successful.

But while the printers union was committing its entire attention to the anti-Belgium operation, Amaury was carrying out his principal counterattack on the printers strike and occupation of his plant. In late May he purchased two building sites—large existing warehouses—and had new cement floors and other basic construction work begun at once. At the same time he began two other processes that normally would take the better part of several years. First, he applied to the cities of Saint-Ouen and Chartres for permits to construct printing plants. Given the rococo bureaucratic extremes of French municipal authorities, even individuals applying for the most mundane of requests need months to accomplish their objectives. Since Amaury obtained his permits in a matter of weeks, and especially since Saint-Ourn initially turned down his request, it is probable that he enjoyed governmental help at the highest levels.

Secondly, the equipment necessary for a complete press printing shop is not quickly obtained as a rule. It is extremely costly to produce and so is typically made to order. It is also massive and only shipped and installed with serious long-term planning and usually lengthy delays. It can take up to two years, and yet Amaury hoped to accomplish it—in secret—in three weeks. He was fortunate: two Marinoni offset printing complexes were for sale; one was still at the manufacturer in the U.S., the second was in Sweden. How to get them to Paris in anything less than a delay of half-a-year? Airmail. Amaury actually had several hundred meric tons of equipment shipped to him airmail; one estimation of the cost of this air-freight alone is put at NF 30 million (FFTL 1976, p. 59). It was no problem for him to arrange for Force Ouvriere printers to provide the scab labor (they too were out to break the CGT monopoly), and the state agreed to provide the security policy Amaury would need to protect his new printing plants. He was back in business.

Imagine the surprise and dismay of the printers: they were occupying the print shops of the paper, they had successfully cut off the Belgium production of the paper, and suddenly one morning the paper appeared in full quantity at all the newstands! A brilliant strategic move for Amaury, which allowed him *ipso facto*, to modernize his printing operation without any negotiations with the union. It is not so clear however, that he could ever hope to make back the NF 75 to 100 million the secret manoeuvre had cost him.

The printers had a tactic in reserve, however. Almost all distribution of the French press is handled by the state regulated distribution company, NMPP. It so happened that the CGT had a strong majority in the NMPP, and thus it was not difficult to arrange a solidarity strike. While carrying on distribution as normal for the other papers, the NMPP workers refused to handle the *Parisien Libéré*. Amaury had a newspaper, but no way to deliver it.

Amaury countered this tactic by hiring delivery trucks, while quickly purchasing a fleet of his own. This tactic, however, called up one of the quintessential facets of the anarcho-syndicalist printers: direct action. The formation, *at the base*, of independent actions units was immediate. These guerrilla-like commando units set out each night to locate and destroy Amaury's delivery trucks. Some of the trucks were escorted by police vans, and those of course could not be touched. But it was not possible to provide protection for each of the hundreds of trucks needed for both the Parisian and regional deliveries. Amaury's unmarked delivery trucks turned to tactics of constant route changing and high speed driving. This proved only partially successful: many were intercepted by the commandos, and they destroyed not only the papers but often the truck as well. One militant "colonel" with whom I spoke had personally set more than a dozen trucks on fire and dumped others into the Seine. Several times the printers brought a night's catch of delivery trucks to the Champs Elysées, which they left literally knee-deep in torn-up copies of what they considered to be scab editions of their paper.

Another principal strategy of the printers was to keep the strike highly visible to the general public. There were two reasons for doing this. First, a supportive public opinion would help pressure the state to push Amaury to arbitrate. Second, and more immediately important, repressive state intervention in favor of Amaury was hampered by the highly public nature of the strike. Given that both the Socialist and Communist parties were strongly opposed to the then recent maneuvers of the press bourgeoisie (especially Hersant's purchase of the important Parisian dailies *Le Figaro* and *France-Soir*) and given that the united left was polling about 50 percent of the French vote leading up to the important legislative elections in 1978, the state could not legitimate a violent suppression of workers in the press sector. High visibility can be an effective defense.

It is difficult to convey adequately the highly innovative tactics employed by the printers to keep the strike before the public eye. The following list illustrates some of the wide range of actions undertaken by the rank and file of the printers union, often without any communication to the central printers federation, and just as often to the total chagrin of the tactically conservative CGT:

The Parisian stock exchange was invaded by about 200 printers who disturbed trading for haf an hour. The action received national coverage, as press photographers had been forewarned. Two employees of the stock exchange died of heart attacks as a result of the chaos. Police cleared the exchange with considerable violence.

Amaury was the organizer of a major sporting event, the "Tour de France", a series of bicycle races to which the French are addicted. The television coverage is extensive, and the printers managed to borrow a fully equipped camera truck and make a five minute appeal for their cause.

Several hundred printers climbed the thousands of steps to the top of Notre Dame Cathedral and from the principal balcony unfurled a banner reading NEGOTIATIONS AT *PARISIEN LIBÉRÉ*! It was a simple matter to close to the doors behind them; the cathedral is as impregnable today as in Quasimodo's time.

The oceanliner S.S. France, in mothballs in the north of France, was occupied for five days, with appropriate banners draped over her sides.

In early 1977 Raymond Barre, prime minister, attended a secret dinner held at *France-Soir* by Jacques Hersant of the Hersant press group. Several other personalities of the press bourgeoisie and governmental circles were present as well. The printers learned of it, and a commando of 100 filed quietly up the back stairs and burst into the room, disarming Barre's bodyguard. Barre, a forthright and persuasive man, immediately gave in to their desire to debate the *Parisien Libéré* situation. A one-hour argument ensued in which the prime minister defended his position of noninterference, and the printers held theirs.

Another major strategy of the printers was to strike the entire Parisian press, including socialistic *Le Monde*, which was openly on the printers' side, and even the Communist Party's *L'Humanité*, which, of course, was totally pro-printers. The idea behind these strikes was that the press bourgeoisie would help pressure the state to bring Amaury to the bargaining table. In 1975 there were seven strike days, in 1976 there were six, and in 1977 there were two more before the strike was finally negotiated. This total of 15 strike days was financially difficult for many papers, as a good deal of their expenses had to be paid (journalists' salaries, rent, and so on), despite the forgone income that could never be recouped. The strategy pressured the press bourgeoisie in another, far more important way as well: it served as a general threat and helped bring the press owners' syndicates to sign a general agreement regulating the transition of the remaining enterprises to the highly automated equipment of the future (the General Accords of July, 1976).

The final component of Amaury's strategy was based on the consistent support he received from the state, which took several forms. First, Amaury was conspicuously successful in the courts. As early as June, 1975 a superior court (Tribunal de Grande Instance) ruled that the occupied print shops be evacuated immediately. However, due to the pressures put on the state by the CGT and the left political parties, it was not cleared by the police until after a later court decision in 1977. Amaury was equally successful in avoiding court-ordered sanctions; his numerous convictions for violations of labor codes, for example, were never pressed.

Secondly, the police were particularly visible in their role of guarding Amaury's new print shops. They also provided guards for the delivery trucks, and could be seen in front of his home. In all, the state spent a small fortune protecting Amaury's private interests.

Thirdly, friends in high places proved valuable to Amaury. As previously mentioned, the licenses he obtained in two weeks to build his major print shops in Saint-Ouen and Chartres would have required many exasperating months of battle without support at the highest levels. Sometimes this intimacy was plain; news photographs from the annual Tour de France showed Amaury seated between Giscard d'Estaing, President of the French Republic, and Michael Poniatowski, Minister of the Interior.

Fourthly, there was heavy-handed, pro-Amaury state intervention in the so-called "Mottin Report," which was issued by a government-appointed mediator who for several weeks had met with representatives of both sides. His report was so biased in favor of management that it bore little resemblance to the final negotiations that were at long last worked out between the printers and the management of *Parisien Libéré* in 1977.

Who won this colossal struggle? According to the printers federation, it was a "victory of exceptional importance" (*Le Monde*, August 18, 1977). *L'Humanité* was headlined the next day, August 17, 1977, VICTORY AT LE PARISIEN. The management of *Parisien Libéré*, (which had changed due to the accidental death of Amaury), claimed that the day was "a great date in the history of the press" and noted that "yesterday's accord was a result of a compromise" (*Correspondence de la Presse*, August 17, 1977). The minister of labor called it a tie, "a compromise without victor or vanquished" (*Le Monde*, August 18, 1977).

Although the *Parisien Libéré* indeed won several of the rights for which it had struggled (the right to hire its own printers, union pluralism in the print shop, and recognition as a regional paper), management cannot possibly claim this an outright victory. Consider the following statistics. Besides a 30 percent drop in advertising income between 1974 and 1976 (CESP 1976), the circulation of the paper fell from 786,000 in 1974, to only 310,000 in 1976 (*Presse Actualité*, May 1977). This sustained loss of 30 percent of its advertising income and 60 percent of sales income coupled with the immense expenditures referred to earlier must have made the strike financially devastating for the enterprise. No doubt it survived only on the strength of other publications in the group and on outside money and collateral derived from Amaury's real estate holdings. Furthermore, given the decline in circulation of sensationalist papers in Paris, it is highly doubtful that the circulation of the paper will ever reach even 350,000 again. The great strike was over, and if the printers had survived it with relatively minimal losses restricted to one paper, the *Parisien Libéré* would take decades to recover financially from the direct and indirect effects of the longest strike ever waged in French labor history.

CONCLUSION: THE PRINTER'S OMINOUS FUTURE

There is no better way to assess the relations of force between the press bourgeoisie and the printers union than to look at the negotiated accords signed in 1976. In entering into the negotiations, the printers hoped to provide a future plan to reduce the wild effects of the unemployment that would be created by the introduction of the new photocomposition, facsimile, and computerized equipment. This consideration is missing from the Braverman (1974) analysis. At least in the case of the printers, labor is highly aware of the "degradation" process he describes, and attempts to do what can be done about it. In the present case this amounted to a creative admixture of negotiating and striking; one lent credence to the other, and the printers saw them (correctly) as complementary. On one hand, the strike served as a warning to the press bourgeoisie of the need to negotiate transitional labor codes for their transformation from traditional to automated printing shops. On the other, the negotiations served to outflank the *Parisien Libéré* management; the printers knew that if a general agreement could be reached with the press owners syndicates in general, the particulars of the *Parisien Libéré* strike would have a limited effect.

The printers saw very clearly that their profession was undergoing profound changes and that their union would be structurally deprived of the position of force from which it had previously bargained with the press bourgeoisie, especially in Paris. The time for negotiation, they knew, was while they were still in a reasonably strong bargaining position.

As the printers union clearly told all members in the material distributed to them on the accords, "an accord is always the result of a compromise." Certainly the agreement reached, which became the actual guiding document for the modernization of the Parisian press and printing industry, reflected the interests of both management and the printers. In brief summation, the agreement planned for a reduction in labor hours but assured those printers currently working that they would not have to pay personally for the eliminations of their functions. On the other hand, the agreement did not, in fact could not, safeguard the role of the union in the years ahead. When the current generation of printers has retired and been replaced by the technicians of tomorrow— regardless of whether this personel has been derived in part from reconverted printers—unionization in the sector will have been significantly altered.

Clearly, given the above, we can predict that in the modern print shops of tomorrow, the personnel will not be unionized in the anarcho-syndicalist, fiercely proud and self-respecting trade groups which have been characteristic of the sector for the past century. In addition, with the higher organic composition of capital in the average enterprise, it will be harder to strike effectively, even if tomorrow's white collar employees organize into new types of unions with new types of demands. Skeleton crews of management personnel will most likely be able to run the electronic equipment to put out minimal editions and, hence, unions will decline in importance with the replacement of living labor with automated equipment. Workers who cannot strike effectively will certainly not maintain the work site privileges accumulated by the printers, nor will they earn the same high wages. Clearly the days of the printers as an element of the aristocracy of labor are coming rapidly to an end.

NOTES

1. For further analyses of the French press, see Freiberg, J.W. *The French Press: Class, State and Ideology*. Praeger, 1981.

2. Given the sensative nature of some of the information to follow, I will occasionally refer to an interview without disclosing the name of my informant(s). I have attempted to confirm reports by checking with independent informants.

REFERENCES

Braverman, Harry
    1974   Labor and Monopoly Capital. New York: Monthly Review Press.
CESP (Centre d'études des supports de publicité)
    1975   Etudes du Centre d'études des supports de publicité: La presse quotidienne." Paris: Photocopy of Bound Report.
Chauvet, Paul
    1971   Les ouvriers du livre et du journal. Paris: Les Editions Ourriers.
Communist Party
    1976   "Livre: les travilleus luttent contre la crise, les gâchis, les monopoles, l'autoritarianisme." Paris: CP Press.
Dumas, Evelyn
    1972   "La crise de la presse en France." Ottawa: Editions Lemeac.
Ehrenreich, John, and Barbara Ehrenreich
    1976   Work and Consciousness. Monthly Review. (July-August).

Faucier, Nicolas
   1964   "La presse quotidienne." Paris: Les Editions Syndicalistes.
FFTL (Fédération Française des Travailleurs du Livre)
   1976   "Le Putsch d'Amaury." Paris: Editions Sociales.
INA (Institute Nationale de L'Audiovisual)
   1976   "Cinque monopoles de l'information." Paris: mimeograph (November 18-20).
INSEE (Institute National de la Statistique)
   1974   "Industries polygraphiques, press-edition." Status dossier prepared for the Commis-
             sariat General au Plan. Paris: INSEE.
Johnson, Dale L.
   1978   "Strategic implications of recent social class theory." The Insurgent Sociologist 8:
             No.1.
Lecat Report (Rapport du groups de travail sur la situation et les perspectives de l'imprimérie
             française, presenté par Lecat, J.-Ph.)
   1975   Paris: Ministère de l'Industrie et de la Recherche.
Marglin, Stephen
   1976   "Value and price in the labor surplus economy." Oxford University Press, New
             York.
Mattelart, Armand
   1976   "Multinationales et systèmes de communication: Les appareils ideologiques de
             l'impérialism. Paris: Anthropos.
Parisien Libéré
   1976   Livre blanc de journal Le Parisien Libéré. Paris: Le Parisien Libéré.
Toussaint, Nadine (Ed).
   1976   "La presse quotidienne." Cahiers Francais (October-December).

COMPARATIVE PERSPECTIVES
ON INDUSTRIAL CONFLICT

Lillian J. Christman, William R. Kelly,
and Omer R. Galle

The expression of discontent in the work place is embodied in an assortment of actions covering a whole "range of behavior and attitudes that express opposition and divergent orientations between industrial owners and managers on the one hand and working people and their organizations on the other" (Kornhauser, et al, 1954, p. 13). Included are actions such as grievance filings, production slow-downs, absenteeism, organized "sick-ins", quitting, sabotage, political activity, lockouts, boycotts and strikes.

Worker discontent can be expressed either through the behavior of unorganized individuals (e.g., quitting) or through the coordinated activity of a group (e.g., strikes), and, depending on the circumstances of the particular work situation, individual and collective actions can serve as alternative forms of protest (Udy, 1965; Hyman, 1972). For instance, Turner, et al (1967) noted that the dismissal of certain shop stewards employed in a strike prone auto-

Research in Social Movements, Conflict and Change, Volume 4, pages 67-93
Copyright © 1981 by JAI Press Inc.
All rights of reproduction in any form reserved.
ISBN: 0-89232-234-9

mobile company reduced the frequency of strikes but increased the occurence of such individual acts of protest as absenteeism, accidents and quitting. Circumstances can dictate not only the substitution of individual for collective acts (and vice versa) but, also, the type of collective action employed by workers (see Hyman, 1972). These types of collective action can be thought of as strategies for resolving discontent or addressing grievances.

While recognizing that industrial conflict is manifested in a variety of actions, we focus on one particular strategy, the strike. Primarily as a consequence of a number of relatively recent studies of the strike, the present state of research in this area offers an opportunity for integrating two rather divergent schools of thought on the determinants of strike activity: the economic and collective action models. Taking into consideration certain environmental-contextual influences, called throughout the structural context of conflict, we delineate the conditions under which either the economic or the collective action models is most appropriate, plus examine the ways in which these models are complimentary rather than strictly competitive. We also make use of Tilly's concept of repertoires of contention as an analytic tool for understanding the form (collective versus individual, violent versus nonviolent) industrial conflict takes.

In the following pages, we will discuss the economic and collective action models and the research which has been aimed at establishing the relative import of those explanations of the occurrence and changing levels of industrial conflict. After outlining their basic elements, we discuss the societal structural conditions (contexts) under which one model or the other might be expected to provide the better explanation of strike activity, which in turn has implications for the sources of discontent (e.g., economic issues, political contention). We suggest four contextual features of a nation which could be examined to provide clues as to which model might provide a better explanation of the frequency of strikes and the breadth of their impact as well as the types of conflict which should be salient. We then discuss several methodological issues including choices of units of analysis and strategies for measuring industrial conflict. Finally, we discuss a research agenda for the future investigation of industrial conflict.

INDUSTRIAL CONFLICT AS ECONOMIC BEHAVIOR

All economic explanations of industrial conflict assume that strikes are sparked by economic issues (wages, fringe benefits, etc.) and that the decision to call a strike over a particular labor-management dispute (or, in the case of management, the decision to risk a work stoppage) is heavily influenced by general economic conditions, as well as by the economic health of the particular plant or firm involved. Further, it is typically assumed that the actors in the dispute strive to maximize their utilities (i.e., well-being) while, at the same time, minimizing their disutilities. For the workers, this means going on the offensive when their real income begins to decline, or when the economy is expanding. For the employer, this means avoiding strikes during periods of good economic conditions when he stands to lose the most in potential profits, and being more demanding at the bargaining table during bad times when his productivity is at a low level. Also, when union leaders are considered as a group separate from workers, they are assumed to act in a utility-maximizing manner. Their activities are aimed at enhancing both their own careers and the well-being of their unions.

The career of the economic explanation of industrial conflict has passed through three distinct phases. Early work on the conformity of strike cycles to business fluctuations left theoretical explanations implicit. Beginning with the work of Rees (1952) a coherent theory of industrial conflict began to emerge. Most recently, work on bargaining theory (Ashenfelter and Johnson, 1969) has moved the development of this explanation in some new directions.

The earliest works investigating the economic correlates of strike activity typically demonstrated a fairly close positive correspondence between strike activity and some measure of the business cycle. The various economic correlates which were considered in these studies included employment (and unemployment), profits, consumer expenditures, real wages, and prices (Hansen, 1921; Douty, 1932; Wolman, 1936; Yoder, 1940; Jurkat and Jurkat, 1949; Goldberg and Yabroff, 1951; Knowles, 1952).

Although these earliest studies repeatedly demonstrated the conformity of business and strike cycles, none of the studies produced a systematic explanation of industrial conflict as economic behavior. Such an explanation was first offered by Rees (1952). Rees argued that strikes result from the economic calculations of the parties involved in the bargaining situation (i.e., labor on one side and management on the other) in an attempt to maximize their utilities from their relationship with the other party. Employers cannot be as adamant in their opposition to workers' demands during prosperity as during depression, otherwise they lose their share of the expanding market; labor can weather strikes better during prosperity than it can during depression since its financial position is more secure during prosperity. This argument implies a positive correlation between strike activity and the business cycle. Consistent with his argument, Rees demonstrates that the empirical relationship between strike activity and economic conditions is positive. Later studies reconfirmed Rees' findings (O'Brien, 1965; Weintraub, 1966; Skeels, 1971; Sapsford, 1975).[1]

The work of Ashenfelter and Johnson (1969) represents a new direction for the economic explanation of industrial conflict. It combines "certain received theories of the firm, trade union behavior, and bargaining in order to derive testable implications under which labor disputes are more likely to occur" (Ashenfelter and Johnson, 1969, p. 35). The resultant combination is a bargaining theory which differs fundamentally from earlier bargaining explanations and from the type of research discussed above.[2] Previous work in the area of bargaining theory has focused on determining the agreement which is reached prior to a strike. The Ashenfelter and Johnson theory presents the strike as one of the possible outcomes of the bargaining situation. Also, unlike earlier work, this theory supposedly offers a determinate solution (as opposed to a possible range of solutions) to the bargaining situation. Ashenfelter and Johnson claim that a determinate solution is possible once the objectives of the union leadership are taken into account. They treat the leadership as the third party in the bargaining situation, a party whose most salient objectives include 1) the promotion of the union's well-being; and 2) the advancement of its own career within the union (Ross, 1948 in Ashenfelter and Johnson, 1969).[3] These objectives can be satisfied through the leadership's attempts to meet the rank and file expectations which must be dealt with during the contract negotiation process.

The bargaining process is described as follows: 1) the rank and file membership has certain expectations concerning an acceptable wage increase; (this theory is developed explicitly in terms of wage increases; other nonmonetary benefits are considered to be part of the contracted wage;) 2) if management offers a lower than expected wage increase, the union leaders try to lower the expectations of the rank and file; 3) if they are unable to do this, the best alternative for the leadership is to call a strike; 4) the occurrence of a strike lowers the membership's expectations; 5) as time passes, the rank and file expectations lower to a level acceptable to management so the union leaders can safely sign an agreement.

The following expression is a simplified verbal representation of the Ashenfelter and Johnson model.

strike activity = function (acceptable wage increase at time of contract expiration, ration of profits to total wage compensation)

The acceptable wage increase is not observable but can be thought of as a function of the unemployment rate, a moving average of previous changes in real wages and profit level. The unemployment rate is negatively associated with the acceptable wage increase since during periods of low unemployment, there are alternative sources of jobs to help workers bear the economic costs of striking. Ashenfelter and Johnson specify a negative effect of a moving average of real wages on strike activity by reasoning that the larger the recent wage increases have been, the more satisfied labor is and, thus, the less militant it is in its dealing with management. They also reason that high profits produce a situation in which management is most likely to give in to wage demands. At the same time, they raise the workers' expectations about future wage increases, and, so, encourage the union leadership to press for large wage increases. Due to the complexity of this situation, they do not make an assertion about the net impact of profits on strikes.

Ashenfelter and Johnson tested their model with data for the U.S. from 1952 to 1967. The results of their analysis provide substantial support for their argument. Except for the profits variable, the coefficients for all of the independent variables are significant (the total explained variance is 94%). Pencavel (1970) replicated their analysis using post World War II data for Britain and arrived at similar results (87% of the variance in strike activity is explained). Using Canadian data, Walsh (1975) also finds convincing support (95% explained variance) for the Ashenfelter and Johnson model.[4] Although the Ashenfelter and Johnson model provides a good fit to the data for which it has been tested, we argue later that important differences in economic models may emerge in different spatial or temporal contexts. We suggest therefore that one should withhold judgement on such models until the influence of different contexts can be assessed.

As an economic behavior theory, the Ashenfelter and Johnson model of industrial conflict is necessarily limited. First, it applies only to those strikes which result from contract negotiations. To use this model to understand strike activity, one must *assume* that virtually all strikes arise from the contract negotiation process and that the issues over which there is disagreement are *strictly economic* in nature. These assumptions are problematic even when one is considering industrial conflict in the most highly industrialized countries.[5] Secondly, the model does not acknowledge the strike as collective action on the part of workers, which might be influenced by sociopolitical factors. There is an implicit assumption in this model that the social/political environment is constant. However, it is reasonable to argue that the mobilization strength and the political power of labor fluctuate over time in even the most economically advanced nations. These factors may be important determinants of strike activity but they have not received much attention among those who consider industrial conflict to be strictly economic behavior.[6]

INDUSTRIAL CONFLICT AS COLLECTIVE BEHAVIOR

When industrial conflict is analyzed as collective behavior, the most salient feature of the strike situation becomes the power struggle between the opposing groups. Collective action theorists, while taking into consideration economic factors as predisposing conditions of strike activity, have emphasized the mobilization of resources and the influence of political factors on the mobilization process.

A major resource of labor is the organizational strength of the union. Among others, Britt and Galle (1972; 1974) have noted the influence of unionization on industrial conflict. Starting with the assumption that groups do *not* necessarily act in their own interests simply because the members of the groups have these interests in common, Britt and Galle use the ideas of Mancur Olson (1968) to demonstrate that union organization is important for understanding collective action. Olson contends that for large groups collective action is difficult to initiate and orchestrate.[7] This is so for three reasons: 1) the larger the group, the smaller the portion of the collective good obtained goes to each member; 2) the larger the group, the smaller the likelihood that individuals or subgroups will be willing to bear the burden of obtaining the collective good; and, 3) the larger the group, the higher the initial organizational costs.

Britt and Galle (1974, p. 650) point out that:

> (i) industrial work forces are so large that the incentives for individual strike action are minimal. Under such conditions, before effective collective action can be taken, some capacity for organization must be present. Unions serve this function.

Pre-existing union organization facilitates mobilization for striking because it mitigates a good portion of the costs of the second and third factors listed above. An operating union organization already has the machinery necessary to stage a strike, including strike funds, and a functioning organization to coordinate strike activities and impose discipline upon the workers. Also, the initial costs of organizing have already been incurred so the union and its members can launch a strike without first having to go through a period of recruitment during which union organizers would need to convince workers to join a new and untried organization.[8]

Other collective action theorists have used the work of Oberschall (1973) to underline the importance of pre-existing union organization for the efficient mobilization of workers (Shorter and Tilly, 1974; Tilly, 1978). Oberschall argues that conflict groups, in the process of mobilizing, take advantage of existing organizational structures in order to reduce the cost of organizing. Specifically, then, in terms of worker militancy:

> (the) effects of prior organization will show up, among other places, in a tendency for surges of strike activity to come disproportionately from increased involvement on the part of sectors of the labor force which were *already* involved, rather than from the drawing in of aggrieved but previously unorganized workers (Shorter and Tilly, 1974, p. 9).

The model of collective action, then, can be drawn from the theoretical arguments of Shorter and Tilly (1974) and Britt and Galle (1972; 1974). Simply conceived, this model can be expressed in the following manner:

strike activity = function (labor organization, political position of labor)

Labor organization can be specified as degree of unionization. Degree of previous organization is relevant since organizational efforts take some time to pay off. Labor organization is positively associated with strike activity. The political position of labor can be specified as a function of the party affiliation of the political head of a country, the strength of the official labor party (or any party generally sympathetic to labor) in the national legislative body, and the occurrence of a national election campaign (Shorter and Tilly, 1974). These are all positively associated with strike activity.

In addition to the effects of pre-existing organization, the outcomes of strikes can influence worker mobilization efforts (Snyder and Kelly, 1976, 1979). The attainment of strike goals can be considered a resource which feeds back into mobilization activities. For example, a group of workers may strike over both wages and working conditions. If management concedes even one of these issues, the partial success of the work stoppage may encourage those workers who did not participate in the strike to join future strikes. In this way, strike outcomes can be determinants of worker mobilization.

Opportunity, in addition to organization, is an integral part of any collective action (Tilly, 1978). Political crises or change (e.g., national elections) present labor with the opportunity to pursue potentially high payoffs (Shorter and Tilly, 1974). Through the intentional use of the strike during periods of political change, workers attempt to force government to take labor's interests into account when making policy decisions. Shorter and Tilly constructed a model of industrial conflict containing indicators of economic activity, mobilization of resources and political change. Using data for France, they tested the adequacy of this model for various time periods and industrial sectors. Labor organizations (the measure of resource mobilization) has the largest and most consistent (positive) relationship with strike activity. Political change, in terms of cabinet changes and elections, shows a smaller, less systematic association with strike activity. Lastly, the economic variables of business fluctuations and wages prove to be of little importance as explanatory variables.[9]

Along with organizational capability, political resources play a role in industrial conflict. Korpi and Shalev (1979) have argued that an integrated labor movement is one in which labor is not only highly organized in centrally controlled unions, but is also represented in the political arena by a relatively powerful political party. As the organizational strength of labor increases, the political, rather than the industrial arena, becomes an increasingly important stage on which to play out the class struggle. "To the extent that labour is successful in acquiring control over political institutions, it can exercise its power through these means and will not be limited to the industrial arena" (1979, p. 170).

Korpi and Shalev trace the history of industrial conflict in Sweden and note that as the union-based strength of labor increased, so did strike activity. However, this activity sharply declined and remained at relatively low levels after the Social Democrats came into power in the early 1930's. So, although the mobilization of labor's union-based resources generally increased industrial conflict, the expansion of labor's power into the political arena was accompanied by the increased use of its polity based resources, thereby reducing the amount of industrial conflict.

Hibbs (1976), like Korpi and Shalev, argues that as labor becomes more politically powerful, through Labor or Socialist parties, it will resort less frequently to the strike weapon. Utilizing time-series data on ten highly industrialized nations, Hibbs tests a model of industrial conflict which combines economic factors identical to those of Ashenfelter and Johnson (1969), with a specification of political factors which include the "relative status in the political system of labor-oriented parties on the non-Communist left, the presence of governments controlled outright by Labor or Socialist parties, and the extent of Communist party influence in the labor force" (1976: p. 1051). He hypothesizes that the strength of Labor and Socialist parties will dampen industrial conflict. This combined model explains about 60 percent of the variation of strike activity in the ten countries. The economic variables prove to be highly significant, however, the only political variable with a significant effect is the organizational strength of the Communist party.

Considered separately, one might conclude that economic explanations are rather powerful, (for example, in terms of variance explained, cf., Ashenfelter and Johnson, 1969; Pencavel, 1970; Walsh, 1975) and, thus, the addition of political factors would probably be inconsequential. However, goodness of fit is only one criterion for assessing the explanatory power of a theoretical model.

The collective action model suggests that although purely economic considerations are a vital component of an explanation of industrial conflict, a more comprehensive approach must not ignore factors related to the *capacity* to strike (organizational considerations), but, perhaps, more importantly, it must include those political factors which influence the *necessity* for industrial conflict. Political factors related to the necessity for conflict are of two kinds: 1) political change as an opportunity to contend for power and, 2) the use of polity based resources as an alternative to the strike. Essentially, this latter consideration involves a shift in the strategies of contention or in Tilly's (1979) words, a change in the repertoire of contention. Considering empirical criteria, the results reported by Shorter and Tilly (1974) suggest that political factors may be more important than economic ones. Although the results reported by Hibbs (1976) indicate that the influence of political factors may be problematic, research by Korpi and Shalev (1979) emphasizes the salience of political resources.

A logical extension of the preceeding discussion is some kind of synthetic explanation which includes both economic considerations and political factors. However we argue that the salience of economic or political factors for explaining industrial conflict, as well as the aims of conflict (economic or political) are contingent upon certain structural-contextual features which are specific to particular times and/or ecological areas. The following section develops the idea of the structural context of conflict and attempts to link it to the applicability of economic versus political explanations.

STRUCTURAL CONTEXT AND REPERTOIRES OF CONTENTION

The locus and distribution of power both within the industrial relations system and within the larger society are structural features which figure most prominently in discussion of the determinants of strike activity. We will first consider the lasting impact of historical elite groups on the industrial relations system.

Dunlop (1958) argues that one of the most decisive influences on the development of a national industrial relations system is the type of strategy used by the elite in directing the initial industrial development of their country. Two of the elite groups Dunlop describes are relevant to this discussion. The first of these, the "dynastic-feudal" elite, is rooted in the landed or commercial aristocracy; the second, the "middle-class" elite, arose from the merchant middle class.

Elite strategies affect both the manager's relationship with the worker as well as the worker's relationship with the manager. A "dynastic-feudal" elite produces a system in which managers behave in a paternalistic manner toward their workers. The workers, in turn, become accustomed to relying on their employers for a wide range of needs. The "middle-class" elite extend the market concept to the employment situation: managers are buyers, workers are sellers. This, in turn, produces a work force which expects to have to protect its own interests.

It logically follows from these types of worker-manager relationships that one would find active discouragement of independent worker organizations in the "dynastic-feudal" system. In this case, plant level organization is usually heavily influenced by management. Whatever industry level organization exists exercises limited powers. On the other hand, the "middle-class" elite are more receptive to independent labor organization. These organizations closely monitor management activities that affect the workers. One also finds that competition among labor confederations in "dynastic-feudal" societies are fueled by social, religious, and political differences causing deep divisions within the labor movement. "Middle-class" societies tend to suffer less competition with such highly emotional overtones. Extensive regulation of jurisdiction and representation rights further reduces conflict within the labor movement itself. Conflict resolution is also affected by elite strategies. In the "dynastic-feudal" system, extensive use is made of government machinery. Direct resolution procedures involving discussions between workers and managers is discouraged. On the other hand, these direct procedures are encouraged in the "middle-class" system. Public intervention is generally the course of last resort.

Table 1 is a summary of the above discussion concerning elite strategies. This table is modified from Dunlop (1958: pp. 331-33).

Table 1.   Impact of Elite Industrializing Strategies on Industrial Relations Systems

Issue	Dynastic-Feudal Elite	Middle-Class Elite
What is the relation of plant managers to workers?	Paternal on a personal basis.	A market transaction.
What is the relation of workers to plant managers?	Personally dependent industrial worker.	The independent worker.
What is the function of workers' organizations?	Social functions at the plant level; little constraint on management.	Regulate management at the local and industry level.
How much competition takes place among workers' organizations?	Multiple unions vie for representation at plant level; unions represent deep ideological differences among workers.	Exclusive jurisdiction tends to produce keen competition at the plant level; however deep ideological issues do not keep the labor movement divided.
What shall be the structure of the labor movement?	Large number of industrial unions. A centralized confederation often limited by rivals. Unions perform a narrow range of functions.	Variety of structural forms. The confederation is not highly centralized. Unions perform broad range of functions.
What attitudes are adopted toward industrial conflict?	Industrial conflict is regarded as a moral challenge to the paternal view of industrial society. Conflicts often take the form of demonstrations.	Industrial conflict is an extension of the market; some conflict has affirmative value.
How are disputes settled, and who holds the the balance of power?	Government decisions are extensive and substantive.	Great effort is made to secure settlement by workers and managers directly. Government intervention is often procedural, and substantive decisions are infrequent.

Japan is one of the few highly industrialized nations which entered the modern era under the tutelage of a feudal leadership (Dunlop, 1958; Christman and Maguire, 1979). The system of management that emerged in Japan is exceedingly paternalistic. Enterprise unionism is the predominant form of labor organization while the highly competitive union federations are politically active but do not have a role in collective bargaining. Government often intervenes in disputes between labor and management (Christman and Maguire, 1979).

On the other hand, the U.S. is an example of a country which underwent industrialization dominated by a "middle-class" elite (Dunlop, 1958; Kerr, et al, 1960). In the U.S., union organization takes a variety of forms (craft, industrial, and general); competition between unions and between federations can be intense but is generally not ideological, and government regulates some aspects of the bargaining process but does not impose compulsory settlement of disputes (Reynolds, 1979).

With respect to industrial conflict itself, the two leadership styles generate different national attitudes. "Industrial conflict is abhorrent to the dynastic-feudal elite; it shatters the paternalistic view of manager-worker relations; it involves a moral crisis in which the workers are held to be ungrateful, stubborn, and rebellious or the managers to be insensitive or unjust" (Dunlop, 1958: p. 327). Industrial conflict embodies a questioning of the entire system. Many strikes take the form of public demonstrations. In contrast, the "middle-class" elite takes a more relaxed view of conflict. It is usually considered the result of the failure of a buyer and a seller to reach an agreement.

At this point, we can specify the first feature of the national structural context which can have an impact on industrial conflict.

Feature 1. Societies which were led by "dynastic-feudal" elites should tend to experience strikes as political phenomena. Industrial conflict is considered a form of challenge to the established social order. For these countries, the collective action model should be the best predictor of strike activity. Conversely, in societies which were led by "middle-class" elites, the strike is primarily an economic tool, and, thus, the economic model of strike activity should prove to be the best predictor of strike activity.

Consistent with these predictions, available evidence on post-war Japan and the U.S. suggests that the collective action explanation is more appropriate for Japan, while the economic model is the better predictor of strike activity in the U.S. (Snyder, 1975, 1977; Christman and Maguire, 1979). However, for earlier periods in the U.S., the collective action explanation is more appropriate (Snyder, 1975, 1977).

These results only partially support the significance of elite strategies. However, this is not the only structural feature used to determine how industrial conflict is generated. Another equally important feature is whether the labor struggle is defined in political or economic terms. The existence and support of Labor and other Socialist parties indicate that labor defines its problems in political terms and attempts to find political solutions. So, in those countries where Left parties not only exist, but also receive popular support, we expect that the collective action model is the best predictor of strike activity. Where there are no Left parties, or where these parties receive only nominal support at the polls, problems faced by labor are defined in economic terms and solutions are sought in the industrial arena. The economic model is the salient one under these conditions.

These predictions can further be refined by reconsidering the power structure. Nations can be distinguished according to how much power labor wields in the political arena. From the historical experience of the industrialized West and Japan, it is apparent that labor must become powerful within the industrial sphere before it can build an effective political organizaion. However, if labor has developed considerable political strength, it has a continuing and direct access to the policy making process. With this alternative open to labor, many problems can be solved through the workings of the political rather than the industrial relations machinery. By siphoning off potential collective bargaining issues, the number of both minor and major irritants which could escalate into strikes is reduced (Ross and Hartman, 1960; Korpi and Shalev, 1979). So, in those countries where labor is very strong in both the industrial and political spheres, the total level of industrial conflict will be low. The political variables of union organization, political change and labor party support will operate to suppress strikes. Problems arising from economic conditions will be frequently solved through political means so the type of strike activity explained by the economic model will not be a frequent occurrence in such countries.

There is some evidence which supports this prediction. Korpi and Shalev (1979) developed several indicators of working class organization and power resources of Left parties. In those industrialized countries for which these indicators are highest (e.g., postwar Sweden, Norway, and Austria) industrial conflict is much lower than in other highly industrialized nations.

There are also nations in which labor's interests are defined politically, but, despite this, labor has little or no access to the polity. These are parliamentary democracies with popularly supported Left parties which have generally been excluded from government participation. In these countries, the political arena is not open to labor so the industrial arena is of necessity the stage for labor's activities. The variables in the collective action model will exert a positive influence on strikes. The economic model will not be salient in these countries.

Countries which fit this explanation are postwar Italy, France and Japan (Korpi and Shalev, 1979). Snyder (1975) found that the collective action model is a better explanation than is the economic model for both Italy and France and that the political variables in this model exert a positive influence on strike activity. The evidence on Japan is equivocal because the picture there is complicated by the presence of enterprise unionism (Christman and Maguire, 1979).

Finally, in those countries where labor's struggle is defined as an economic rather than a political one, labor has fewer ties to the polity. In these countries "the working class *per se* has never played a significant role in national politics . . . conflicts between buyers and sellers of labour power continue to be manifested primarily within the employment context" (Korpi and Shalev, 1979 p. 181). So, under these conditions, the economic model will be of more importance in explaining strike activity than will the collective action model (Tilly, 1979).

Countries which display this last set of characteristics include the postwar U.S., Canada and Ireland (Korpi and Shalev, 1979). Snyder (1975, 1977) finds that the economic model is the best predictor for the U.S. while for Canada some elements of both models are important. [10]

The second structural feature can be summarized as follows:

> *Feature 2*. For those countries where labor defines its goals in political terms, the collective action model is more appropriate. Where labor has regular access to or control over the polity, the political variables in the model will act to suppress strikes. Where labor is excluded from the polity, these variables will exert a positive influence. For those countries where labor defines its problems in economic terms, the economic model is most appropriate.

Snyder (1975) has incorporated labor's access to political resources into a structural context schema which also includes aspects of unionization and collective bargaining. He argues that a certain combination of structural features molds the strike into an economic tool; another shapes it into a political tool.

> Where union membership is large and relatively stable, the political position of labor firmly established and collective bargaining well institutionalized, assumptions under-lying the economic model hold well (1975: p. 265).

The converse of these conditions which validate the economic model—small, unstable union membership, lack of legitimate political status of labor, and resistance of employers to the institutionalization of collective bargaining machinery—compose an institutional setting in which the strike functions primarily as a political weapon. Snyder offers this explanation for the prediction that, for countries exhibiting this latter type of institutional setting, the collective action model of strike activity is appropriate.

> Within these arrangements, labor's organizational strength is problematic and (longer run) political ends such as polity membership are more salient to labor than are short term, strictly economic costs and benefits. We, therefore, expect that, under *these* conditions, strikes fluctuate with organizational and political currents, as Shorter and Tilly find for France (1975: p. 266).

Snyder tested his predictions concerning institutional setting using data from three countries: the U.S., France and Italy. He divides the data for each country into two time intervals. The first interval begins around the turn of the century and lasts until World War II, while the second interval runs from the war until the present. Snyder argues that the only country for which the economic model holds is the U.S. Further, the economic explanation holds for the U.S. only after World War II. [11]

Snyder's results generally support his predictions. The economic model holds only for the postwar U.S. The collective action model holds quite well for the prewar U.S. and for Italy during both time periods. Surprisingly, the collective action model holds least well, but still much better than does the economic model for France.

From Snyder's work, we can propose two additional structural features.

Feature 3. In countries where the labor movement organization is large with a stabilized membership, economic issues are of primary importance. For this reason, the economic model is appropriately applied to these countries. Conversely, where labor is still in the process of organizing, political issues are still of importance to labor. The collective action model applies to such countries.

The importance of the organizational capacity of labor, i.e., the ability to strike, underlies this prediction. If the organizational issue is resolved, labor is left with primarily economic issues. Where labor is still in the process of organizing, organizational issues must be resolved before labor can mobilize an economic strike. Thus, political conflict may function to challenge impediments to worker organization.

One further aspect of structural context to be considered is that of government regulation of the relationship between manager and worker. Dunlop (1958) and Ross and Hartman (1960) indicate that governmental regulation is influential in shaping industrial conflict. Dunlop points out that the "dynastic-feudal" elite tend to favor government intervention and regulation. "Middle-class" elites, on the other hand, encourage direct communication between employer and employee, actively shunning government regulation. If one follows Dunlop's argument to its logical conclusion, government regulation should reduce the efficacy of the economic model for explaining strike activity. As Shorter and Tilly (1974) suggest, the government official and not the individual employer can be the target of strikes started in countries where the strike is used as a political tool.

Feature 4. Countries which extensively regulate the relationship between employer and employee necessarily reduce the type of strike activity the economic model attempts to explain. So, for these countries, the collective action model should be applied. The economic model should be an adequate explanation of strikes in countries which engage in little governmental regulation of the worker-manager relationship.

In Japan there is extensive government regulation of collective bargaining and industrial disputes. As has been stated before, the collective action model is the better explanation of strike activity in this country (Christman & Maguire, 1979). On the other hand, in the U.S. government, legislation covers only some conditions of work so the scope of collective bargaining is quite wide. There is no government machinery to provide for compulsory settlement of disputes, but there is some regulation of collective bargaining procedures

(Reynolds, 1970). As Snyder (1975) demonstrates, the economic model holds well for the U.S.

By introducing the idea of structural context, it becomes clear that the salience of economic versus political/collective action explanations is dependent or conditional upon particular social structural factors. We have identified four factors which should influence the relation between strike activity and economic or political determinants: 1) elite strategies for directing industrial development; 2) the manner in which the labor struggle is defined; 3) the degree of development of labor movement; and 4) the extent to which the government regulates the worker-management relationship. Table 2 provides a summary statement of how these contextual features may affect industrial conflict.

Table 2. Expected Impact of Contextual Factors on Salience of Economic and Political/Collective Action Explanations of Industrial Strike Activity

Contextual factor	Salient Explanation
1) "Dynastic-Feudal" elite	Political
"Middle-Class" elite	Economic
2) Open access of labor to political decision-making	Economic
Closed access of labor to political decision-making	Political
3) Mature labor movement	Economic
Undeveloped labor movement	Political
4) High governmental regulation of worker-manager relation	Political
Low governmental regulation of worker-manager relation	Economic

An issue related to the idea of structural context involves alternatives to the strike, i.e., other forms of redressing grievances. We have argued above that certain structural factors may influence the salience of models of conflict and thus the type of strike (economic or political). It is equally reasonable to think that the availability and effectiveness of alternative means or strategies will influence the frequency of strikes as well as their duration, breadth, and degree of violence. What we have in mind is what Tilly (1979: p. 131) refers to as repertoires of contention.

> Within any particular time and place, the array of collective actions that people employ is 1) well defined and 2) quite limited in comparison to the range of actions that are theoretically available to them ... at a given point in time, it (the existing repertoire) significantly constrains the strategy and tactics of collective actors.

The point is relatively straightforward. In a given time and place, is the strike a legitimate and/or effective manifestation of industrial conflict? Or is collective action repressed by authorities or otherwise rendered ineffective? The form of industrial conflict (i.e., the strategies) will depend upon the degree to which the repretoires are composed of alternatives to the strike. Factors such as the effectiveness of strikes and alternatives, the repressive action of authorities, the past experiences of collective actors and the legitimacy of collective action likely influence the content of repertoires (Tilly, 1979). These factors might be considered in the same light as structural context variables since they emphasize that the relation between forms of industrial conflict and its determinants is conditional on other mediating factors.

An illustrative example may help clarify the relation between industrial conflict, repertoires of contention and the determinants of repertoires. Tilly (1979: pp. 134-135) discusses the impact authorities have in shaping strikes.

During the nineteenth century workers, employers and governments engaged in a continuing struggle; its general outcome was not only the legalization of some sort of strike activity but also the creation of shared understandings concerning the actions that constituted a strike. By no means all concerted withholding of labor qualified: the parties hammered out detailed rules excluding individual absenteeism, occupation of the premises, refusal to do particular jobs, and so forth. It is not simply that legislators made some forms of the strike legal and other forms of the strike illegal. That happened, too. But in the process, the antagonists created—in practice as well as in theory—a sharper distinction between the strike and other forms of action with which it had previously often been associated: sabotage, slowdown, absenteeism, the demonstration. A narrowed, contained strike entered the repertoire of workers' collective action. Pressure from the authorities shaped the particular contours of the nineteenth-century strike.

The content of the repertoire at a given point in time will determine not only *whether* strikes occur but, also, the form they take, e.g., violent. Thus authorities might restrict rights of assemblage or otherwise render collective actions ineffective or highly costly. When these types of conditions exist, conflict may emerge in the form of individual activity, such as absenteeism, sabotage or more subtle forms of collective action, such as slow-downs or ''sick-ins.'' Alternatively, not only may strikes be permitted, but prevailing norms may legitimize violence as a strategy in conflict. Under these circumstances, conflict may from time to time be violent.

We have attempted to emphasize that the relation between industrial conflict, its forms and determinants is *conditional* upon certain structural features of the social, economic and political environment. Our discussion of the influence of structural context on strikes has limited the effect to the nation-state or national level. However, certain structural influences could conceivably operate at different levels, such as the extent of labor organization within various industries, or differential government regulation by industry or occupation. Our discussion has been designed to suggest possible structural influences on industrial conflict, and thus should be considered illustrative rather than exhaustive.

Finally, we want to again emphasize the relation between structural context and repertoires of contention. The economic and collective action models of industrial conflict attempt to explain the level of strike activity. Structural contexts modify the relation between conflict and its antecedents and in part determine the type of strike (economic versus political). Repertoires specify the strategies which are available to contenders. Thus knowledge of the repressive capacity or actions of authorities or the success rate of violent strikes (both of which should influence available repertoires) should help explain levels and forms of industrial conflict. Thus combining the ideas of structural context and repertoires into one analytic framework, researchers should be better able to address the various dimensions of level, form and type of conflict.

METHODOLOGICAL CONSIDERATIONS

This section addresses some major methodological issues related to research on industrial conflict. We discuss issues of measurement, the heterogeneity of conflict and units of analysis.

Issues surrounding the measurement of industrial conflict have been raised by various writers including Britt and Galle (1972), Shorter and Tilly (1974), Shalev (1978) and Stern (1978). Stern (1978) notes the implications that measures of different dimensions of strikes have for explanatory models of industrial conflict. As dependent indicators of conflict, frequency, breadth, and duration can be expected to be related to different underlying structural conditions. Frequency should be primarily associated with economic conditions, and breadth should be related to the organization of the labor force and the structure of collective bargaining. Since the different dimensions of strike activity appear to have different structural antecedents, past research, including many of the studies cited earlier, may not have properly tested competing models of industrial conflict. If the choice of a particular dependent measure can determine which explanation is more salient, a necessary analytic strategy is to employ multiple dependent variables (i.e., indicators of various dimensions of conflict) when testing alternative explanations.[12] This approach takes into account the potentially confounding influence of being differentially influenced by economic or organizational determinants. In addition to methodological advantages, this strategy has theoretical importance. Conflict is not a unidimensional phenomenon; thus assessing the impact of various determinants on several aspects of strikes should lend a much broader understanding to industrial conflict.

A similar issue surrounding the measurement of industrial conflict involves the heterogeneity of strike activity. The assumption underlying the use of an indicator like strike frequency is that all events are homogeneous. Obviously, this is not necessarily the case since strikes can differ in terms of duration, number of participants, economic loss and a commonly overlooked aspect, the degree of violence. The heterogeneity of industrial conflict is important in two respects. First is the question of what causes some strikes to be longer, violent, and involve more participants. A second question, and one which has only recently emerged in the collective action literature, (Shorter and Tilly, 1974; Snyder and Kelly, 1976; Kelly and Snyder, 1980) is what effect does the heterogeneity of industrial conflict have for the *consequences* of work stoppages. In terms of the resource management framework (e.g., Gamson, 1968), the dimensions of duration, breadth, and violence can be conceptualized as constraint resources. Constraint resources add some disadvantage to the position of, in this case, management. Such resources are employed in a bargaining process and thus can influence the success or failure of work stoppages, i.e., in most instances, a broader, longer, and more violent strike may serve as a more powerful bargaining resource, implying ceteris paribus, a higher probability of success. One might also hypothesize that constraint resources influence the organization of collective action. For example, violence against nonstriking fellow workers may persuade them to join the strike, thus further enhancing the bargaining position of workers.

The study of the consequences of industrial conflict is important in two respects. First is the question of what aspects or dimensions of conflict affect the probability of strike success. (Work by Forcheimer, 1948; Goetz-Girely, 1965; Shorter and Tilly, 1974; and Snyder and Kelly, 1976, among others, addresses this question.) Secondly, Snyder and Kelly (1976) argue that analyses of strikes facilitate the study of the relation between violence and change. Snyder and Kelly (1976: 133) state:

> Strikes avoid many of these difficulties (ambiguity concerning relevant outcomes and difficulty in measuring the consequences of violence) because they have fairly clear spatial, temporal and conceptual boundaries . . . moreover, strike outcomes are regularly recorded in most countries . . .

Briefly, then, we are suggesting that the measurement of industrial conflict should be multidimensional so that the salience of one set of determinants is not contingent upon the choice of a particular indicator of conflict and so that it is possible to trace the set of causal antecedents of the different strike dimensions. Further, the use of multiple indicators will allow the study of the impact of the various dimensions on outcomes. Also, incorporating outcomes into the study of strikes will illuminate the more general issue of the relation between conflict (violence) and its consequences.

An additional methodological consideration involves the appropriate unit of analysis. The notion of structural context lends itself most readily to cross-section analysis since in one sense it is easier to identify and link contextual factors to ecological units. Thus, the four contextual factors, as well as factors influencing repertoires of contention may be considered characteristic of a whole economy or society or of smaller ecological units, such as cities, industries, market sectors, etc. For example, earlier we briefly mentioned that labor organization or government regulation may vary across industries. Within the same economy, one industry may be highly organized while another may be essentially unorganized. In the first case, we would expect conflict to be economic; in the latter industry, we would expect primarily political conflict. The point is that the analysis of contextual factors probably should not be restricted to cross-national data since variation within a nation (e.g. across industries) may be equally or more important than differences across nations. [13]

The choice of the level of analysis, i.e., nation, industry, city, etc., depends in part on how one expects the contextual factors to vary across units. For example, if development of the labor movement, or governmental regulation differs by industry as well as nations, one should opt for the industry level of analysis. This is desirable for two reasons. One is that the lower the level of aggregation the closer one is to the actual conflict process (see Stern, 1978). The second consideration is the relation between the dimensions of conflict and structural characteristics, e.g., duration of conflict could be, in part, influenced by specific local conditions such as characteristics of the industry, community, etc. At higher levels of aggregation such influences could be obscured.

Ecological units such as nations, industries, cities, etc., are probably best suited for determining the impact of contextual factors. However, a cross-sectional framework may not be the most appropriate design for testing economic versus collective action arguments. Past research aimed at testing the economic or collective action perspectives has relied heavily on time series data. Strikes, in a specified ecological unit, usually a nation, are aggregated on an annual basis. Fluctuations in industrial conflict are then related to fluctuations in the economy or power relations in the political arena. According to the economic argument, strike activity rises and falls with fluctuations in the economy—generally, a dynamic argument. Similarly, the collective action perspective links the waxing and waning of strike activity to changes in power relations in the polity—again, generally a dynamic explanation. In principle, then, time series data are best suited for testing the economic and collective action arguments. This follows since these explanations are constructed in terms of change over time. However, time series data may be less useful for incorporating contextual effects, unless one is able to 1) link time periods with particular contextual factors; and 2) identify shifts in those factors over time (see Snyder, 1975; Smith, 1979).

Different units of analysis are designed to address different aspects or dimensions of industrial conflict. If time series data are most appropriate for testing economic and mobilization theories, and, cross-sectional data are most useful for analyzing the effect of contextual factors, a relevent question at this point is, since the theoretical approach to industrial conflict has been modified, i.e., the addition of contextual factors, is there some means of altering the research design to analyze contextual factors, as well as the salience of political or economic determinants? The pooling of cross-sectional and time series data provides a design which allows the analysis of temporal as well as cross-sectional variation, thus bringing as much information as possible to bear in one research design. The unit of analysis in such an approach is the ecological-time unit or, for example, the country-year. Methods of analyzing pooled cross section, time series data, are fairly straightforward. (See, for example, Kmenta, 1971.)

To summarize, we argue that no single design strategy is sufficient to address empirically the modified model of industrial conflict. Although all analytic methods provide unique views of the conflict process, the two most relevant for addressing the major issues raised earlier are the cross-sectional and time series designs. Combining these in a vary real sense constitutes a "best of both worlds" analytic strategy.

A final unit of analysis we will consider is the individual event case study. A case study approach allows a wealth of detailed information to be collected, as well as providing the opportunity to study the strike as an ongoing process. This latter characteristic allows one to test the revised mobilization model discussed earlier (Snyder and Kelly, 1979) i.e., the idea that outcomes of contention feed back on the mobilization process. The detail of information and time series designs. Combining these in a very real sense constitutes a approach.[14] However, the costs involved in conducting comparative case studies, as well as the inability to generalize to other spatial and temporal contexts might be viewed as major drawbacks.

AN AGENDA FOR FUTURE RESEARCH

Although some evidence can be brought to bear on the importance of particular structural contexts, the influence of these factors needs further empirical verification. In addition to testing for effects of contextual factors as specified, i.e., at the national level, research might profitably be aimed at industries, cities, occupations or other units which may mediate the antecedent-strike relation. In short, the theoretical importance of structural contextual factors warrants the explicit incorporation of such influences.

Our earlier discussion indicated that past research has provided strong support for both the economic and collective action models, although neither has been consistantly empirically superior. One likely reason why one of these models has not emerged as the most important is that in actuality the models are complimentary rather than competing explanations of strike activity. As complimentary explanations, they emphasize different dimensions of the same underlying phenomenon. The product of a theoretical synthesis of these models is a much more comprehensive explanation of strike activity. The specification of structural contexts not only facilitates the synthesis of explanations but also specifies under what conditions a particular dimension (political or economic) will be salient.

The major point is that given the probable impact of contextual factors it is misleading to try to empirically establish the superiority of one model over another. Rather researchers should begin with a more comprehensive explanation and attempt to determine the conditions under which particular aspects are more important than others.

In a given time and place, the strategies available to contenders should be an important determinant of levels and forms of conflict. This knowledge of the repertoires of contention should add substantially to an understanding of strike activity. But how does one obtain information about repertoires? One way is by looking at the forms of conflict already being used. If strikes are not frequent there are two plausible reasons. One is that labor has no or few grievances thus labor disputes are not common. The other is that although disputes are common, strikes are not an acceptable or legitimate manifestation of conflict. It would be important to be able to discriminate between these explanations, since they have very different implications for models of the determinants of strikes. Repertoires are important as well when dimensions other than frequency of strikes are addressed. Obviously at this point it is an empirical question as to the extent to which repertoires can influence the intensity, breadth, collectiveness or other aspects of conflict. Thus further effort might be fruitfully spent on this question, both in terms of empirically testing relations and in developing further the concept of repertoires and devising more direct measures.

Methodologically, a major point is the use of multiple measures of strike activity. This serves a dual function of first treating conflict as a multidimensional phenomenon and secondly allowing the researcher to determine whether in a given situation, the relation between strike activity and its antecedents is context or measure dependent (cf Stern, 1978). Sorting out this question should help illuminate when and under what conditions economic and/or political/collective action variables are most important.

ACKNOWLEDGMENTS

An earlier version of this paper was read at the First International Conference on Industrial Sociology at the University of Monterrey, Mexico, on February 11, 1979. The authors gratefully acknowledge the criticisms of Louis Kriesberg and three anonymous referees on an earlier version of this paper.

NOTES

1. Skeels (1971) also analyzes the relationship between political variables and public attitudes and strikes. However, GNP is the only predictor that is significantly related to all eight measures of strike activity used in this study. Skeels does not attempt to clarify the role of the noneconomic variables that are included in his analysis.

2. There has been some controversy over whether or not they have succeeded in creating an

actual bargaining theory. Objections to the Ashenfelter and Johnson formulation revolve around their description of the bargaining process. Critics of the theory contend that the effective control of the strike decision rests with the union so there is no meaningful give and take which is the heart of a true bargaining situation.

3. Ashenfelter and Johnson do not address the very real possibility that these two goals may be at odds.

4. In contrast to the Walsh study, Vanderkamp (1970) finds the model to be a poor explanation of strike activity in Canada. However, his analysis tends to cloud the issue rather than clarify it because he uses a measure of strike activity—time lost as a percentage of estimated total working time—which is rarely used in studies of this sort. Also, his specification of the independent variables is slightly different from that in the Ashenfelter and Johnson model.

5. Even in the most highly industrialized nations, a large number of strikes may occur outside of the contract negotiation, and over other than economic issues—shop floor conditions, safety factors (a major factor in wildcat strikes among coal miners), and other working conditions (the speed of the assembly line for example) are some of these factors.

6. In several early studies the impact of social events on strike activity was discussed but statistical analysis of the social/political correlates of industrial conflict was minimal (Douglas, 1923; Douty, 1932; Peterson, 1937; Griffin, 1939; Goldberg and Yabroff, 1951; Goldner, 1951; Knowles, 1952; Rees, 1952; Ross, 1954). More recently, Skeels (1971) has done some analysis of social variables while maintaining an emphasis on the economic motivations behind strike behavior.

7. Olson introduces his theory of collective behavior with the declaration that:

it is *not*, in fact, true that the idea that groups will act in their self-interests follows logically from the premise of rational and self-interested behavior. It does *not* follow, because all of the individuals in a group would gain if they achieved their group objective, that they would act to achieve that objective even if they were all rational and self-interested. (1968: 1-2)

He goes on to argue that, in fact, group and individual interests often diverge, and, even when they do not, any individual can profit the most by letting others take care of the group's interests.

8. Using cross-sectional data for the U.S., Britt and Galle (1972, 1974) find a moderately high positive relationship between degree of unionization and various measures of strike activity.

9. Since Shorter and Tilly do not report the residuals for their various path models, it is not possible to assess how well this model works for France. In a later study, Snyder (1975) found that the Shorter and Tilly model works much better than the economic model for France during two time periods.

10. Snyder has incorporated labor's access to political resources into a structural context schema which also includes aspects of unionization and collective bargaining. He argues that a certain combination of structural features molds the strike into an economic tool, another shapes it into a political one.

Where union membership is large and relatively stable, the political position of labor firmly established and collective bargaining well institutionalized, assumptions underlying the economic model hold well. (1975: 265).

The converse of these conditions validates the collective action model. Snyder predicts that the economic model will hold well for the U.S. because its union membership is large and stable, the political position of labor is strong and collective bargaining is well institutionalized. His reasoning behind this predicton is somewhat questionable. Compared to many highly industrialized countries, the density of unionization in the U.S. is quite low. Furthermore, employment in traditionally unionized industries (e.g., manufacturing) is decreasing while employment in industries with historically low levels of unionization (e.g., services) is increasing (Browning and Singelmann, 1975). Also, his assertion that U.S. labor is strong politically is equally questionable. There is no official labor party in the U.S. and, although labor generally supports the Democratic party, it frequently does not have much influence on relevant policy decisions. We reach the same conclusion about the U.S. that Snyder does—that the economic model is most appropriate for the U.S.—but we reach this conclusion by using a different set of assumptions. We argue that strong worker organizations coupled with regular access to the polity should depress strikes but that the collective action model is still the salient one under these conditions.

11. In many instances, the theoretical formulations guiding empirical studies are aimed, either explicitly or implicitly, at the explanation of strike frequency. This poses interpretive problems in those studies which employ more than one measure of conflict since there is often no explanation of how the variables in the proposed causal scheme differentially affect the various strike dimensions.

12. Stern also suggests that standardizing, in terms of the population at risk, measures of the three basic dimensions of conflict—frequency, breadth, and duration—in order to facilitate comparison of findings among studies.

13. Also, the use of only nationally aggregated data can obscure the diversity of strike activity within a nation. For example, see Stern (1977) and Smith (1978) for a discussion of how structural features of Canadian provinces affect the generation of industrial conflict within these political subdivisions. Stern (1976), Stern and Galle (1978), and Lincoln (1978) demonstrate how the characteristics of large U.S. cities influence the strike activity of these cities. Also, Pencavel (1970), Shorter and Tilly (1974), and Christman and Maguire (1979) show how the causal antecedents of strike activity differ among industries and industrial sectors in Britain, France and Japan.

14. The hypotheses which we discussed earlier are structural in nature and consequently require a rather high level of aggregation in order to empirically test. This structural orientation necessarily ignores other relevant kinds of questions. Thus although the economic model is based on very specific assumptions of how the bargaining process operates, the model is specified using variables which are aggregate level reflections of the bargaining process. The bargaining process is assumed to work in a certain way and given that these assumptions are correct, certain observable relationship should hold. However, it is possible that different sets of assumptions could lead to the same predictions as the economic model. For instance, contrary to Ashenfelter and Johnson's contentions, a theory which simply ignores the behavior of union leaders and concentrates on the rational calculations of workers could be specified in a manner similar to the Ashenfelter and Johnson model. It would be premature to uncritically accept as valid a particular set of assumptions. It is important to know more about the strategies used by management, the relationships between management and the union leadership, the dynamics of union operations, the relationship between the leadership and the rank and file.

The collective action model focuses heavily on the power relationships between the various groups involved (workers, management, government) without consideration of the internal dynamics of these groups. How can a group of workers sustain a wildcat strike? To what degree is the rank and file involved in the running of the strike? How is rank and file involvement obtained? Does this involvement make any difference in terms of strike outcomes or future strike effortrs? How does labor use its political resources? How does this affect conflict? How and why does government intervene in the industrial arena? How do management policies and strategies affect conflict? None of these questions can be answered by aggregate models since their focus is on the actions of groups in relation to other groups rather than on the internal workings of the groups involved.

Case study designs are appropriate for addressing these kinds of issues. Our emphasis on structural features of conflict tends to de-emphasize these kinds of questions but that should not imply that they are any less important.

REFERENCES

Ashenfelter, Orley, and George E. Johnson
1969   "Bargaining theory, trade unions and industrial strike activity." American Economic Review 59: 35-49.
Britt, David, and Omer Galle
1972   "Industrial conflict and unionization." American Sociological Review 37: 46-57.
Britt, David, and Omer Galle
1974   "Structural antecedents of the shape of strikes: a comparative analysis." American Sociological Review 39: 642-51.
Browning, Harley, and Joachin Singelmann
1975   "The emergence of a service society: demographic and sociological aspects of the sectorial transformation of the labor force in the U.S.A." Mimeographed. Manpower Administration Report.
Christman, Lillian, and Mary Ann Maguire
1979   "Industrial conflict in postwar Japan." Paper presented at the annual meetings of the American Sociological Association. Boston.
Douglas, Paul H.
1923   "Analysis of strike statistics, 1881-1921." Journal of the American Statistical Association 18: 866-877.
Douty, H.M.
1923   "The trend of industrial dispute, 1922-1930." Journal of the American Statistical Association 27: 168-172.
Dunlop, John T.
1958   Industrial Relations Systems. New York: Holt.
Forcheimer, K.
1948   "Some international aspects of the strike movement." Bulletin of the Oxford University Institute of Statistics 10: 9-24.
Gamson, William
1968   Power and Discontent. Homewood, Ill.: Dorsey Press.
Geotz-Girely, Robert
1965   Le Mouvement des Greves en France, 1919-1962. Paris: Sirey.
Goldberg, Joseph P. and Bernard Yabroff
1951   Analysis of Strikes, 1927-1949. Monthly Labor Review 72: 1-7.
Goldner, William
1951   Strikes. Institute of Industrial Relations, Berkeley, Ca.: University of California.
Goldner, William
1954   "Strikes and prosperity: a comment." Industrial and Labor Relations Review 6: 579-581.
Griffin, John I.
1939   Strikes: a study in quantitative economics. New York: Columbia University Press.
Hansen, Alvin
1921   "Cycles of strikes." American Economic Review 11: 616-21.
Hibbs, Douglas A., Jr.
1974   "Industrial conflict in advanced industrial societies." Cambridge: Center for Political Studies, Massachusetts Institute of Technology.
Hibbs, Douglas A., Jr.
1976   "Industrial conflict in advanced societies." American Political Science Review 70: 1033-58.
Hirschman, Albert O.
1970   Exit, Voice and Loyalty. Cambridge, Mass.: Harvard University Press.

Hyman, Richard
    1972   Strikes. London: Fontana/Collins
Johnston, J.
    1972   Econometric Methods. New York: McGraw-Hill.
Jurkat, Ernest H., and Dorothy B. Jurkat
    1949   ''Economic functions of strikes.'' Industrial and Labor Relations Review 2: 527-45.
Kelly, William R., and David Snyder
    1980   ''Racial violence and socioeconomic changes among Blacks in the United States.''
            Social Forces, 58: 739-60.
Kerr, Clark, and Abraham Siegel
    1954   ''The interindustry propensity to strike: an international comparison.'' Industrial
            Conflict, Kornhauser et al. (eds.) 182-212. New York: McGraw-Hill.
Kerr, Clark, John T. Dunlop, Frederick M. Harbison, and Charles A. Myers
    1960   Industrialism and Industrial Man. Cambridge, Mass.: Harvard University Press.
Kmenta, Jr.
    1971   Elements of Econometrics. New York: MacMillan
Knowles, K.G.J.C.
    1952   Strikes: A Study in Industrial Conflict. Oxford: Blackwell.
Kornhauser, A., P. Dubin, and A.H. Ross (eds.)
    1954   Industrial Conflict. New York: McGraw-Hill.
Korpi, Walter, and Michael Shalev
    1979   ''Strikes, industrial relations and class conflict in capitalist societies.'' British
            Journal of Sociology 30: 164-87.
Lincoln, James R.
    1978   ''Community structure and industrial conflict: an analysis of strike activity in
            SMSA's.'' American Sociological Review 43: 199-220.
Mallet, Serge
    1963   La Nouvelle Classe Ouvriere. Paris: Scuil.
Oberschall, Anthony
    1973   Social Conflict and Social Movement. Englewood Cliffs, N.J.: Prentice-Hall.
O'Brien, Francis
    1965   ''Industrial conflict and business fluctuations: a comment.'' Journal of Political
            Economy 73: 650-54.
Olson, Mancur
    1968   The Logic of Collective Action. New York: Schocken Books.
Pencavel, John H.
    1970   ''An investigation into industrial strike activity in Britain.'' Economica 37: 239-56.
Peterson, Florence
    1937   ''Strikes in the United States, 1880-1936.'' U.S. Department of Labor, Bureau of
            Labor Statistics Bulletin No. 651. Washington, D.C.: U.S. Government Printing
            Office.
Rees, Albert
    1952   ''Industrial conflict and business fluctuations.'' Journal of Political Economy 60:
            371-82.
Reynolds, Lloyd G.
    1970   Labor Economics and Labor Relations: Englewood Cliffs, N.J.: Prentice—Hall.
Ross, Arthur M.
    1948   Trade Union Wage Policy. Berkeley, Ca.: University of California Press.
Ross, Arthur M.
    1954   ''The natural history of the strike.'' pp. 23-36 in A. Kornhauser et al. (Ed.) Industrial
            Conflict. New York: McGraw-Hill.

Ross, Arthur, and Paul Hartman
   1960   Changing Patterns of Industrial Conflict. New York: Wiley.
Sapsford, D.
   1975   "A time series analysis of industrial disputes." Industrial Relations 14: 242-49.
Shalev, Michael
   1978   "Lies, damned lies and strike statistics: the measurement of trends in industrial
             conflict." Pp. 1-19 in Colin Crouch and Alessandro Pizzorno (eds.), The Resurgence
             of Class Conflict in Western Europe Since 1968.
Shorter, Edward, and Charles Tilly
   1971   "The shape of strikes in France, 1830-1960." Comparative Studies in Society and
             History 13: 60-86.
Shorter, Edward, and Charles Tilly
   1974   Strikes in France, 1830-1968. Cambridge University Press.
Skeels, Jack W.
   1971   "Measures of U.S. strike activity." Industrial and Labor Relations Review 24:
             515-25.
Smith, Michael R.
   1979   "Institutional setting and industrial conflict in Quebec." American Journal of Soci-
             ology 85: 109-34.
Snyder, David
   1975   "Institutional setting and industrial conflict." American Sociological Review 40:
             259-78.
Snyder, David
   1977   "Early North American strikes: a reinterpretation." Industrial and Labor Relations
             Review 30: 325-41.
Snyder, David, and William R. Kelly
   1979   "Strategies for investigating violence and social change: illustrations from analyses
             of racial disorders and implications for mobilization research." In M. Zald and J.
             McCarthy (eds.) Dynamics of Social Movements. Cambridge, Mass.: Winthrop.
Snyder, David, and William R. Kelly
   1976   "Industrial violence in Italy: 1878-1903." American Journal of Sociology 82: 131-
             162.
Stern, Robert N.
   1978   "Intermetropolitan patterns of strike frequency." Industrial and Labor Relations
             Review 29: 218-235.
Stern, Robert N., and Omer R. Galle
   1978   "Industrial conflict and the intermetropolitan structure of production." Social
             Science Quarterly 59: 257-73.
Stern, Robert N., and John C. Anderson
   1977   "Canadian strike activity: union centralization and national diversity." Industrial
             Relations Research Association, Proceedings of the 30th Annual Winter Meeting,
             New York.
Stern, Robert
   1978   "Methodological issues in quantitative strike analysis." Industrial Relations 17:
             32-42.
Tilly, Charles
   1978   From Mobilization to Revolution. Reading, Mass.: Adisson-Wesley.
Tilly, Charles
   1979   "Repertoires of contention in America and Britain, 1750-1830." In M. Zald and J.
             McCarthy (eds.), The Dynamics of Social Movements. Cambridge: Winthrop.
Touraine, Alain
   1955   L'Evolution du Travail Ouvrier Aux Usines Renault. Paris: CNRS.

Turner, H.A., G. Clark, and G. Roberts
   1967   Labor Relations in the Motor Industry. London: Allen and Unwin.
Udy, Stanley
   1965   ''The comparative analysis of organizations.'' Pp. 678-709 in J.G. March (ed.),
           Handbook of Organizations. Chicago: Rand McNally.
Vanderkamp, John
   1970   ''Economic activity and strikes in Canada.'' Industrial Relations 9: 215-230.
Walsh, William
   1975   ''Economic activity and strike activity in Canada.'' Industrial Relations 14: 45-54.
Weintraub, Andrew
   1966   ''Prosperity versus strikes: an empirical approach.'' Industrial and Labor Relations
           Review 19: 231-38.
Wolman, Leo
   1936   Ebb and Flow in Trade Unionism. New York: National Bureau of Economic Re-
           search.
Yoder, Dale
   1940   ''Economic changes and industrial unrest in the United States.'' Journal of Political
           Economy 48: 222-37.

CAPITALISTS VS. THE UNIONS:

AN ANALYSIS OF ANTIUNION POLITICAL

MOBILIZATION AMONG BUSINESS LEADERS

Richard E. Ratcliff and David Jaffee

The classic conflict portrayed in modern political theory is that between labor and capital. For Marx and many of those who followed him, the ongoing struggles between the proletariat and the capitalist class embody the fundamental dynamic shaping industrial societies. In recent decades the importance of such struggles has often been questioned. Many contemporary political analysts have argued that the development of modern industrial societies has led not only to the amelioration of the conditions that promoted such open class conflicts, but even to the elimination of struggles between labor and capital as an important social force. According to these analysts, clearly defined class confrontations rarely occur and when they do the antagonists are seldom of central importance within their own class groups.

The present research examines a recent episode of antiunion political mobilization among capitalists in order to reevaluate certain prevailing assumptions

Research in Social Movements, Conflict and Change, Volume 4, pages 95-121
Copyright © 1981 by JAI Press Inc.
All rights of reproduction in any form reserved.
ISBN: 0-89232-234-9

regarding the relationships that capitalists see as existing between corporations and unions in the United States. The current character of these relationships is decidedly problematic, especially because of contrasting indications of acceptance and accommodation and of hostility and confrontation on the part of business groups in their dealings with unions. In general, over the last several decades a range of observers have portrayed capitalists as having accepted the legitimacy and permanence of organized labor and, accordingly, as having worked out practices of accommodation with labor unions. These basic accommodations are typically said to be most characteristic of large corporations and the dominant capitalist groups that control them. After labor unions won the major organizing drives in the 1930s and 1940s, these centrally important economic groups supposedly not only accepted the inevitability of having an organized work force but also came to see strong labor unions as important supporters of their own interests. In contrast, small corporations and more marginal capitalist groups have been seen as bases of continuing antiunion sentiments.

Due to their growing economic dominance, the key issue regarding any thesis that capitalists have accepted the role of unions concerns the behavior of the largest corporations and their leaders. However, the view of dominant capitalists having accepted unions has been challenged in recent years by many indications of an apparent regrowth of antiunion activism among leading capitalists. Large corporations, as well as smaller ones, have shown an increasing willingness, and at times even an eagerness, to engage in open struggles with unions. These struggles have emerged in political arenas as well as in organizing drives and strike situations (Forbes, 1978; von Hoffman, 1978; Gall and Hoerr, 1978; Cameron, 1978).

Our research considers an instance in recent history where the character of conflict between capital and labor, and in particular of the new aggressiveness of business interests towards unions, is open for examination. The focus here is on a 1978 election in the state of Missouri to add a ''right-to-work'' amendment of the state's constitution. This campaign provides a unique opportunity to study the bases of antiunion mobilization within the capitalist class. The central concern is with understanding both the nature and the sources of the support that business interests provided in behalf of this campaign. More specifically, this study attempts to identify from where within the capitalist structure the support came. Of particular interest to us is the issue of whether the principal financial backing for the amendment came from within, or from outside, the central networks of economic power and upper class prominence that exist among business interests in Missouri. Our purpose is to determine whether the current growth of antiunion political mobilization is based among the largest and most important corporations or whether it represents more a reassertion of the more typical antiunion sentiments among more marginal capitalist groups.

"RIGHT-TO-WORK" AS AN ANTIUNION ISSUE

The Missouri "right-to-work" amendment would have made it illegal for employees to be required to belong to a union or to pay union dues as a condition of employment. The precise purpose of the amendment would have been to forbid "union security clauses" in collective bargaining agreements. Union security clauses typically require that all employees covered by a union contract must join the union within thirty days of employment. "Right-to-work" laws are allowed on a state by state basis under the provisions of the federal Taft-Hartley law enacted in 1947 (Sultan, 1958; Skinner, 1958; Mills, 1978: 288). Twenty states, mostly in the South and West, currently have "right-to-work" laws.

In the 1940s and 1950s "right-to-work" was a major political issue, and numerous attempts were made in almost all states to enact such laws. Almost all of the currently existing state laws were passed in that period. The mobilization in behalf of "right-to-work" peaked in 1958 when the issue was on the ballot in six different states. After voters in only one of these states (Kansas) passed the measure, backers of such proposals turned away from electoral strategies and in recent years "right-to-work" proponents have relied primarily on efforts to win adoption by state legislatures (U.S. News and World Report, 1979).

Since 1947 the "right-to-work" issue has generated a tremendous amount of controversy between supporters of organized labor and its critics (Warshal, 1966; Congressional Digest, 1965; Bradley, 1956; Mossberg, 1975). Union suporters argue that union security clauses are legitimate work rules which must be agreed to by a majority of the affected workers. In contrast, the "right-to-work" advocates decry the "compulsion" and loss of individual freedom that comes with required union membership. While such rather philosophical arguments often are central to public debates over "right-to-work" laws, they are hardly the key questions involved. The basic issues concern the strength of unions and efforts by business interests to weaken unions. All of the studies of "right-to-work" campaigns that have been done show clearly that the backers are overwhelmingly business groups motivated by antiunion economic concerns rather than by any commitments to workers' individual freedoms (Miller and Ware, 1963; Meyers, 1955; Witney, 1958). As Meyers has noted, " . . . the proponents of "right-to-work" laws hope by their enactment to make unions more insecure—to slow down or halt the rate at which unions are organized, and to destroy existing unions" (Meyers, 1955; 78). In Texas these sentiments were implied in the preamble to the law which stated the goal of curbing the "excessive" demands made by labor unions (Meyers, 1959: 5). Labor unions, perceiving "right-to-work" laws as decidedly antiunion, have always led the fights against these proposals. No evidence exists in any of the studies of state campaigns that sizable numbers of wage workers opposed to compulsory union membership have ever been leading supporters of a "right-to-work" law.

Despite the intended purpose of these laws to weaken labor unions, the existing research concerning the actual impact of "right-to-work" laws presents a rather mixed picture. While "right-to-work" states are generally less unionized than states without such laws, these states also share a number of other social and economic characteristics, such as lower levels of industrialization, less urbanization and less unionization prior to the Taft-Hartley law, which are associated with less current unionization, regardless of the presence of a "right-to-work" law. The specific added impact of a "right-to-work" law is difficult to determine. In fact, it has been argued that "right-to-work" laws are mainly of symbolic importance, signifying that the state is generally unsympathetic towards unions and that unions in the state are relatively weak (Meyers, 1959). In contrast, union leaders, as well as a number of labor relations experts, argue strongly that "right-to-work" laws do weaken unions. They point to the sizable number of nonmembers in unionized plants who limit dues collections as well as impede negotiating and strike decisions and to important constraints on organizing specific to "right-to-work" states (Kuhn, 1961; Shirk, 1978).

Regardless of the actual impact of the laws, "right-to-work" has become the single issue that has been most central to continuing antiunion mobilization among capitalists. The importance of this issue has been reflected in the establishment and growth of the National Right To Work Committee. This organization collects millions of dollars each year, primarily from business contributors, to carry out its mission to promote "right-to-work" and other antiunion laws. The continuing popularity of the issue among businessmen, despite the scarcity of victories in the last two decades, and the corresponding widely held beliefs that "right-to-work" laws do weaken unions makes the Missouri campaign all the more significant as an opportunity to study the contemporary bases of capitalist antiunion activity.

CAPITALISTS AND ORGANIZED LABOR

The attempt to enact a "right-to-work" law in Missouri resulted in an old-fashioned battle between business and labor of the sort that supposedly no longer occurs, especially in Northern industrialized areas. Looking beyond the specific question of "right-to-work", the Missouri campaign poses some important issues regarding class conflict in modern American society. Of particular interest are questions concerning the kinds of struggles that can be expected to occur between business and organized labor.

Few observers retain any expectation that American unions represent a potential revolutionary challenge to the capitalist system. However, there is considerable disagreement over the extent to which business and unions have continued to be antagonists in any fundamental sense. Major ambiguities in the relationship between capitalists and organized labor became evident as soon as industrial unions were well established in many of the largest corporations. For example, C. Wright Mills, writing in the late 1940s, described the new leader as a former rebel against business who had become a "manager of discontent" (Mills, 1948: 9). Increasingly, his task had become perhaps more one of ensuring the workers' discipline and observance of contract than one of confrontation with the employers (Mills, 1948: 224). The corporation was seen as coming to depend on the union to maintain orderly control over the work force.

Other observers have gone much further than Mills to claim that capitalists and established labor union leaders have come to realize that each depends on the other for its survival and prosperity. Accordingly, despite occasional adversarial posturing during contract negotiations, business and labor unions are seen as having reached an accommodation whereby each side recognized the importance of each other and neither side attempts to challenge the basic interests of the other.

This viewpoint is certainly imbedded in much of the modern field of industrial labor relations where the acceptance of the legitimacy of unions on the part of responsible business interests is assumed. A similar assumption has also been central to the arguments of some on the political left who criticize American labor unions for having abandoned the interests of most workers. Aronowitz, for example, described unions as "an appendage of the corporations and as "a vital institution in the corporate capitalist complex" and states that the modern union has "evolved into a force for integrating the workers into the corporate capitalist system." He also suggests that " . . . employers regard labor leaders as their allies against the ignorant and undisciplined rank and file" (Aronowitz, 1973: 217, 219). Another writer states that:

> The function of the labor bureaucracy is to guarantee the stability of the nations' labor force. In return the labor bureaucrats are afforded by government and management a more or less free hand in running their unions as they choose (Parenti, 1978: 156).

This image of a basic accommodation having been established between business and labor unions parallels the more historically focused "corporate liberalism" thesis. According to this thesis, the most important groups within the capitalist class came to recognize during class struggles in the early decades of this century that the labor movement needed to be made legitimate and institutionalized in order to neutralize working class radicalism and to help stabilize capitalist economic relationships (Weinstein, 1968; Scheinberg, 1966). Federal labor legislation, and especially the Wagner Act in the 1930s, is seen as having been promoted by leading "corporate liberals" in the capitalist class as a means for ensuring the development of reasonably strong, but nonradical, labor unions.

Few proponents of the corporate liberalism thesis claim that capitalists in general have such fairly sophisticated attitudes towards labor relations. Hostility towards unions is seen as being very common in the business community. However, it is argued that such views, or at least the associated practices, are embedded in the policies of the largest corporations. Given their ability and willingness to pay the price, in terms of higher wages and benefits, for more manageable and predictable labor relations, the large corporations are seen as having established a basic accommodation with labor unions (Aronowitz, 1973: 217).

Certainly there is evidence that some business leaders recognize the supportive roles played by unions. For example, a recent article on current labor struggles in a leading business publication stated:

> Organized labor is now so interwoven into the fabric of the U.S. economy, especially in basic industry, that any sudden and serious loss of its authority would probably distress management more than please it (Forbes, 1978: 44).

According to this view, the modern manager of big business would seem unlikely to become involved in a campaign to destroy or even to seriously weaken labor unions.

The issue that is seldom clearly addressed in these arguments is whether this recognition of the contributions unions supposedly make to the interests of management is in fact widespread among modern business leaders and whether such leaders are correspondingly oriented to maintaining good relations with labor unions. Such orientations, if they do exist at all as a commonality, have certainly been put to a test in the past several years.

A related issue concerns the question of whether the apparent accommodation between large capitalists and organized labor represents a firm policy commitment on the part of capitalists or whether it is based more on a belief that such accommodation is simply a pragmatic necessity in light of the power of unions. If the policy has more than just a pragmatic basis, then we would expect large corporations to avoid involvement in antiunion activities even if serious weaknesses in the labor movement were perceived. In contrast, if the practices of accommodation only represent compromises due to a recognition of union strength, and if actual attitudes embody enduring antiunion orientations, then we would expect leading capitalists to strike out at unions where the prospects of success seemed good and the likelihood of union retaliation seemed slight.

In the 1970s two major trends have raised important questions regarding the course of relations between labor and capital in coming years. First, there have been continuing signs of growing weaknesses with organized labor. Second, there have been numerous indications of a sharp increase in antiunion activities on the part of businesses. It is worthwhile to consider briefly both of these trends.

A number of factors indicate a fundamental weakening of the American labor movement. Most notable is the overall decline in union membership. In the mid 1950s the proportion of workers who belonged to unions climbed to over a third of all those with private, nonfarm employment. By 1976 the share of union members in the nonfarm labor force had dropped to under 25 percent (Business Week, 1978b). Correspondingly, union organizing drives have increasingly been failing and a growing number of union members have been lost due to decertification elections. Involved in these membership trends has been the failure of the labor movement to respond effectively to changes in the American economy. There has been a major shift of jobs to the South and the Southwest and a shrinkage, certainly in relative terms and to some extent in absolute terms, of industrial jobs in the Midwest and Northeast where unions have traditionally been strongest. Many union members have been lost simply because unionized plants in the North closed, only to be replaced directly or indirectly by non-unionized plants in the South (Kistler and MacDonald, 1976). The South in particular, of course, has been much less receptive to unions than the North (Marshall, 1967). The antiunion tendencies of Southern employers have been strengthened by the active cooperation of state and local public officials. Moreover, while there are indications of recent advances by unions in the South, workers in that region—especially white workers—have traditionally been skeptical of the benefits of union membership.

The power of unions has also been affected by the rapidly changing techno-logical base of the American economy that often has made obsolete particular skills upon which strong unions were based. Advances in technology and automation have also made strikes in many industries difficult to win since businesses can continue to operate despite union walkouts (Lhotka, 1980). In addition to such unfavorable economic trends, social surveys in which re-spondents are asked to evaluate different institutions in the society have indicated that public confidence in the labor movement has been dropping.

The current aggressiveness of business in its dealings with labor is certainly not unrelated to the perceptions of weaknesses in the labor movement. In any case, regardless of the appearances of accommodation between labor and capital in American society in the 1950s and 1960s, there has been increasing evidence in the late 1970s and early 1980s of a re-emergence of hostile conflict between labor and capital on a broad range of fronts (von Hoffman, 1978). In legislative arenas business interests have done a notably militant and effective job of opposing the legislative programs of unions and of championing their own (Business Week, 1977; Merry, 1979). Since 1976 a newly mobilized coalition of probusiness groups defeated a package of proposed federal laws governing union organizing that was a top priority for organized labor and that had been expected to pass and also beat down a number of other prounion and proconsumer proposals supported by unions (Cameron, 1978).

In the work place many corporations have been actively resisting organizing drives by unions. A new element in these fights has been the use of a new cadre of antiunion lawyers and other consultants who are experts in legal issues relating to union organizing and in techniques for resisting organizing drives. With these new allies many corporations have been successful in defeating union drives (Martin, 1979; Business Week, 1979a and 1979b; Lhotka and Matthews, 1978b). The newly aggressive activity of businesses in these areas is reflected in the sharp increase in the number of accusations the National Labor Relations Board has received of illegal antiunion actions by businesses (Business Week, 1978b). Antiunion activities by businesses have been particularly common in the South where new plants have been opening at a high rate, but struggles have also appeared in northern highly industrialized areas (Lhotka and Matthews, 1978b). Moreover, there have been numerous instances where corporations have stood firm in the face of strikes and hired strike breaking workers as permanent replacements and even have cooperated with dissident groups of workers to cause unions to be decertified (Martin, 1979). These efforts have received support from the National Association of Manufacturers which recently formed a "Council on a Union-Free Environment" to advise companies on techniques for resisting, or eliminating, union representation (Gall and Hoerr, 1978).

Despite the expectations of some that overt antiunion activity would be concentrated among corporations that are smaller, in largely nonunionized industries or in some other way marginal to the dominant centers of business power, there have been numerous instances in recent years where major unionized corporations, such as General Motors and McDonnell Douglas, have suddenly begun to act more aggressively in their dealing with unions (Forbes, 1978). Similarly, in 1977 the Business Roundtable, a group representative of the chief executives of the nation's largest corporations, voted to fight against the labor law changes sought by organized labor (Guzzardi, 1978).

It would be misleading, nevertheless, to suggest that the largest corporations have clearly taken the lead in the new struggles between business and labor. The picture is considerably more ambiguous. For example, some spokesmen for major business interests, noting the evidence of increased antiunion aggressiveness among leading corporations, have made nervous statements which suggest attitudes consistent with the corporate liberalism model (Business Week, 1977; Gall and Hoerr, 1978; Forbes, 1978). These leaders have cautioned that by being too militant in their antiunion actions large businesses could seriously disrupt vital cooperative relationships they have with the labor movement. Moreover, it does not appear that the largest national corporations have become the central leaders in the major antiunion political campaigns. Central leadership roles have been eagerly handled by such groups as the U.S. Chamber of Commerce, the National Association of Manufacturers and the National Right to Work Committee, most of which are more representative of medium sized regional corporations (Cameron, 1978).

The contradictory character of the evidence regarding which business groups are most involved in the modern upsurge of antiunion activities helps to focus the concerns of our research on the Missouri "right-to-work" campaign. Our purpose is to examine this campaign carefully in order to determine which capitalists chose to join in this one campaign of overt opposition to unions. As the following report of our findings will make clear, the relative clarity of this research focus was not matched by any ease of gathering the data necessary to provide answers. We will now describe the research approaches we used.

THE RESEARCH STRATEGY

Our research on the Missouri "right-to-work" campaign had three main components. First, a review was conducted of news accounts of the campaign in the major St. Louis and Kansas City newspapers for the several months preceding and a short period following the election. Several national publications, including the *Wall Street Journal* and *Business Week*, were also reviewed for coverage of the Missouri campaign. Campaign materials and post-election analyses, published and unpublished, by both opponents and supporters have been obtained whenever possible. Second, all available quantitative data on financial contributions to both sides of the campaign have been collected. Limitations in these data will be discussed below. Third, lengthy interviews were conducted with key supporters and opponents of the amendment.

Initially it was planned to focus the research primarily on the quantitative data on campaign contributions. Missouri has a reasonably strong campaign disclosure law requiring both supporters and opponents of the amendment to make public lists of their contributors. From these lists we identified all corporate and individual contributors with St. Louis area addresses to the three principal committees that supported the "right-to-work" amendment. We also reviewed the main lists submitted by the opponents to identify any St. Louis businesses or business leaders who supported the campaign against the amendment. Ideally, these lists would have provided a complete record of all money that flowed into the campaign. Unfortunately, the disclosure reports suffer from several important deficiencies which made them quite incomplete. The most important defect is that due to a successful court challenge to an earlier law and delays in the enactment of a replacement, the operating campaign law in Missouri only came into effect in August of 1978, less than three months before the election. As a consequence, all contributions made prior to that time did not have to be disclosed. Since most of the money given to the amendment's backers came in 1977 and early 1978, we found that the records they submitted covered only about ten percent of the money contributed. A secondary problem is that the law does not require contributions of $50 or less to be reported. This problem is less significant since our interest is primarily in big contributions. An additional limitation of unknown importance is that the supporters of the amendment used a private foundation that operated as a tax exempt organization, free of any obligation to disclose the identify of donors or the amount of donations received, as a vehicle for distributing pro–"right to work" literature and for producing and broadcasting some "public education" television programs that supported the amendment. The amount of money contributed to this foundation for the campaign is not known. The legality of its operations are still being examined and, in fact, in 1980 several of the key supporters of the amendment still faced possible indictments for violations of the Missouri campaign disclosure law related to the operation of this foundation.[1]

The interviews were conducted in the fall of 1980 in St. Louis, Kansas City and Jefferson City. The primary interviews were conducted with five individuals and lasted from two to four hours each. In order to encourage openness, the subjects were assured of complete confidentiality. Additional shorter interviews were conducted with six other individuals knowledgeable about particular aspects of the campaign.

This research is related to a larger study of networks of power and prominence among leading corporations and banks in the St. Louis metropolitan area (Ratcliff, 1980 a, b, c; Ratcliff, et al., 1979). For the larger study extensive materials have been gathered on the several hundred largest corporations and financial institutions in the St. Louis metropolitan area and on all of the directors and top officers associated with them. These data provide us with a context for evaluating the more specific information on the contributors to the "right-to-work" campaign.

In the following analysis we will present the results of our research in three parts. First, the history of the campaign will be detailed. Second, the data available from the campaign disclosure lists will be examined. Third, the question of the sources of contributions will be considered more qualitatively, using the interview data as well as other available information.

THE HISTORY OF THE "RIGHT-TO-WORK" CAMPAIGN IN MISSOURI

The Missouri "right-to-work" campaign was regarded as highly significant by those interested in labor-management relations. One distinctive feature was the attempt to win approval for "right-to-work" directly from the voters. In this respect the vote involved an open test of how eroded popular support for unions had actually become. Also, in contrast to the existing "right-to-work" states, Missouri is a heavily industrialized and heavily unionized state. It ranks tenth among all states in union membership with 31.9 percent of its workers belonging to unions. The St. Louis area in particular has been regarded as a union stronghold. The Missouri election was thus seen as a test of whether after two decades in which few battles had been won by "right-to-work" advocates, the issue could be raised again in the industrialized states of the Midwest and Northeast.

The origins of the Missouri "right-to-work" campaign are found in an alliance between longtime Missouri antiunion activists and the newer, and more aggressive, conservative Republican politics that emerged in the state during the last decade. In the early and mid 1970s, conservative businessmen and their legislative supporters initiated a series of attempts to get legislative approval for ''right-to-work'' and to oppose increases in the levels of payments for workmen's compensation and unemployment insurance. While the ''right-to-work'' proposals were quickly killed, the latter campaigns were relatively successful. One result of these efforts was that working political relationships were established between some militantly conservative businessmen tied to the Chamber of Commerce and young conservatives in the legislature. In 1975 and 1976 a small group of businessmen with longstanding ties to the National Right To Work Committee, legislative lobbyists and legislators held a series of meetings in which the possibility of such a campaign was explored.

After preliminary discussions were held with the National Right To Work Committee, the Missouri group came away feeling encouraged. They believed that they had been promised up to $500,000 in assistance if they could initiate a serious campaign, and raise $750,000 in Missouri. The Missouri activists, having no formal organization and calling themselves the ''Freedom of Choice Group'' proceeded to plan a campaign and in two or three months succeeded in gathering solid pledges for $1,250,000. The money collected was placed in a special account of the Missouri Chamber of Commerce.

Despite this impressive beginning, the group soon ran into one major, and unexpected, problem. The National Right To Work Committee began backing away from its earlier promises and in early 1977 quietly announced that it would not provide any financial support—ostensibly on the grounds that an electoral approach was not wise. At this point, however, the Missouri group was sufficiently committed and well financed, and they decided to carry on, regardless.

With over one million dollars in hand, the group decided to invest in a massive survey effort to reach *all* residential telephones in Missouri. On one level, the aim was to determine popular sentiments on the issue but the more basic purpose was to identify as fully as possible all supporters and activists on the ''right-to-work'' issue throughout Missouri. In the survey calls, those yielding responses neutral or opposed to the ''right-to-work'' position were quickly terminated. However, those indicating support were asked how much time they would be willing to spend working in support of a ''right-to-work'' amendment. With the responses to this one question the planners hoped to establish a vast network of supporters throughout the state.

While the questions were hardly written in an objective form, the scale of this survey would humble most academic researchers. Beginning with 800 employees and lists of all household names in Missouri obtained from the company that prints telephone books, they claimed to have completed over

1,100,000 calls. They reported that from these calls they identified "over 700,000" who supported "right-to-work" and among those "over 100,000" who were also willing to work to support a campaign.

At this point they believed they had solid grounds for thinking they could win an electoral campaign. In addition to the support for "right-to-work" revealed in the large survey, a more conventional poll conducted late in 1977 showed over 70 percent favoring a "right-to-work" law. While some of this support reflected biases in the surveys, it is notable that polls done privately for unions during the fall of 1977 and early in 1978, and never released, showed that nearly 60 percent of the respondents agreed to the statement that "a person has the right to get and keep a job without having to join a union or pay union dues where he works." While the unions felt that this particular language was biased against them, their polls also showed that even if the issue were re-phrased in the language they preferred to state that "a majority of workers in a particular business should have the right to vote to make union membership a requirement for all workers in that business" the responses were split evenly (Worley, 1979: 9). Union leaders subsequently acknowledged that these polls and their own perceptions of weaknesses in their ranks made them very fearful in 1977 and early 1978 that if the amendment made it onto the ballot, they could easily lose.

In addition to conducting parallel surveys that yielded similar results, labor union leaders and the "right-to-work" advocates shared a number of other perceptions about the situation in Missouri. In interviews labor union leaders spoke frankly of internal weaknesses. They stressed the declining union memberships, the awareness among union members as well as other citizens that industrial jobs were leaving the state, the skepticism young union members often had of union officials, the support the polls had found for "right-to-work" even among union members and the low level of political activity among union members. On this last point, one estimate indicated that less than half of the labor union members in Missouri were even registered to vote (Worley, 1979: 11).

While the various surveys focused on the issue of compulsory union membership, that particular issue was not the dominant concern of the amendment's backers. Based on the materials prepared for potential donors and other supporters and on the information gained from interviews, two other issues appear to have been most central. Both of these issues reflect the presumption that the key purpose of the "right-to-work" amendment was to substantially weaken unions in relation to the power of employers. The first issue centered on the claim that economic growth in Missouri was lagging, and that the lack of a "right-to-work" law was a major cause. The backers stressed the substantially higher rates of growth that could be found in the five "right-to-work" states bordering Missouri and argued in effect that with a "right-to-work" law Missouri's growth would become similar to that of the fast-growing Sunbelt states (cf. Stark, 1978). This argument was apparently especially important for the business leaders in Kansas City who had seen the rapid expansion just across the border in Kansas, a "right-to-work" state.

The second issue dealt with questions of the presumed "flexibility" or "reasonableness" of unions. Business backers of the amendment argued that with a "right-to-work" law it would become easier for employers to win concessions on work rules, strikes would occur less often and unions would generally be less militant and extreme in their demands. In effect, it was argued, though this point was seldom made publicly, that unions in "right-to-work" states are "softer" and generally weaker than in states without such laws. While the primary leaders in the amendment campaign claimed that they did not want, nor expect, unions to disappear with a "right-to-work" law, it is clear that many nonunionized employers believed that the measure would help them stay that way. In this regard it is notable that interview responses indicated that the principal "right-to-work" supporters were strongly committed to the benefits of weaker unions as opposed to no unions and that at least some of them were disturbed that some business supporters clearly wanted to drive unions out of their plants. Some of these comments paralleled the images central to the corporate liberalism thesis by acknowledging the importance of unions for the efficient functioning of the corporate system through their roles in disciplining and helping control the work force, especially in regard to their functions in grievance processing and related contract enforcement.

In addition to these two issues, supporters also noted the beliefs held by many businessmen that too many union officials were corrupt and that such corruption was encouraged by compulsory membership. It was argued that with a "right-to-work" law there would be fewer corrupt union officials.

In early 1978 the backers of the "right-to-work" amendment made a calculated effort to get the legislature to put the measure on the ballot, knowing that labor's allies would defeat them, in order to gain further publicity. They also continued to raise money and work earnestly, especially through the Missouri Council for Economic Development, the tax exempt foundation that had been created, to disseminate materials supportive of the amendment.

In April, 1978, after the legislature had killed the proposal, the petition drive was launched. According to Missouri law a certain proportion of signatures had to be obtained within each of seven congressional districts out of the ten in the state. In more rural districts the campaign received substantial help from the Farm Bureau. The Farm Bureau is a major political force in outstate Missouri, as in other agricultural areas, due to its combination of a militant conservative orientation with an extensive network of agents and commercial operations.

In urban areas the petition drive encountered major problems. The unions were by this time fully aware of the group's plans and had begun to mount its own attacks. One effective tactic involved following the "right-to-work" petition gatherers and having union activists stand beside them urging people not to sign. The amendment backers have acknowledged that these aggressive union efforts created serious problems for them. Volunteer petition gatherers were quickly driven off and the "right-to-work" forces had to rely on paid workers. Even these people seldom could take the pressure for more than a few days. One "right-to-work" activist reported that in order to get the final signatures needed in St. Louis they were having to pay gatherers up to $10 per hour. They were ultimately forced to spend several hundred thousand dollars more than expected in order to get the amendment on the ballot.

The proponents were further hampered by a series of court challenges initiated by the unions. Based on charges of procedural irregularities in the petition gathering process and on questions concerning the legality of the wording of the amendment, the unions demanded that the courts throw the amendment off the ballot. These challenges were not finally resolved until late in October, just weeks before the election. In retrospect the amendment's backers acknowledged that these highly publicized court battles both disrupted the momentum of their campaign and raised doubts in voters' minds regarding the legality of the proposal (Laner, 1980).[2]

By the early fall, the labor unions had become mobilized in an aggressive campaign against the amendment. This union campaign is distinctive in that while it was thoroughly modern in its use of consultants, computers and pollsters, and was quite expensive, it was decidedly "grass roots" in its focus. The union expenditure on television, radio and newspaper ads was only about $250,000, an amount considerably less than ten percent of its total budget (Worley, 1979: 14). Based on a strategy designed and coordinated by a Washington, D.C. campaign consulting firm, the basic plan was to mobilize the largest possible number of prolabor voters without carrying on a noisy public media oriented campaign that would also motivate potential "right-to-work" supporters to go to the polls. As one part of this plan an expensive voter registration campaign produced an estimated 100,000 union members newly eligible to vote, out of just about 500,000 in the state. The consultants also merged a complex bank of computerized census data with polling data on the "right-to-work" issue to enable them to target blocks according to whether the residents were likely to be "leaning toward" opposition to the amendment or at least were "persuadable" (Worley, 1979: 13). Using these data the unions mobilized a campaign of mail, phone and door to door canvas contacts that focused on those areas where they felt they were most likely to find opponents to the amendment. There is evidence that the union efforts substantially increased voter turnout. Overall, Missouri had a record voter turnout rate for an offyear election and the turnout was highest in those areas that voted heavily against the amendment (Worley, 1979: 21).

In the fall the "right-to-work" forces began to receive indications that their campaign was in trouble. A poll done by the unions in late September still showed that the ''right-to-work'' advocates were ahead but their lead was falling. The amendments' supporters had become hampered, moreover, by a shortage of money. Due to the costs of the statewide survey and the petition drive as well as the other activities in their three years of work, they had by the summer of 1978 already spent $1,400,000 before any real public campaign was begun. Their original plans had called for an extensive—and expensive— mail and telephone campaign directed at the hundred of thousands of supposed ''right-to-work'' sympathizers identified in the survey done a year earlier. However, they found that they lacked the necessary money and a large part of this strategy was set aside. Similarly they had to abandon much of the television and radio advertising that had been planned.

The sudden scarcity of funds is striking, especially given the financial success the activists had initially experienced. However, they had apparently not anticipated the effect of public disclosure of contributions on the willingness of business interests to give money. This effect was reportedly increased by the aggressive actions of the unions at the time the new campaign disclosure law took effect. The first lists were made public in the middle of September. One bank whose name appeared on the first contributor list was immediately approached by union representatives with the message that certain funds would be withdrawn from the bank. Word of this ''message,'' and other similar threats, moved rapidly through the Missouri business community and, according to one of our interview sources, ''almost overnight'' contributions for the amendment largely ceased. The ''right-to-work'' backers reported that they had expected a pattern of contributions that is normal in political campaigns, with a large share pouring in during the final few weeks of the campaign. Instead they received relatively little at the end.

It is impossible to determine accurately how much money was raised and spent in the struggle by both sides. As noted, most of the money raised in behalf of the amendment was given prior to the date when disclosure was required. According to the sources we interviewed, the total budget of the advocates of the amendment for the entire three years was about $2,700,000. Of this amount only about $1 million remained to be spent on the election campaign itself after the measure had been placed on the ballot. The total amount of contributions reported by the major labor union committees was between $2.5 and $3 million. Almost all of this money came from unions, both in and out of Missouri. These figures probably understate the amount spent by opponents because some union financed activities from outside the state were apparently never reported. In any case, it is clear that the prolabor forces spent considerably more on the actual campaign than did the amendment's supporters.

In the last weeks of the campaign public opinion polls began to show voter sentiments shifting against the amendment (Huckler, 1978). The election itself confirmed the strength of the trend against the amendment. Across the state it lost by a 60 percent to 40 percent margin. Even though the backers had counted on strong support in those areas of Missouri outside of St. Louis and Kansas City, the amendment lost not only in the urban areas, but also in all but a few of the rural counties as well.

Despite the prospect of broad support indicated by the early evidence of popular disaffection with organized labor, most of the strong support for the amendment, at least in urban areas, was limited to affluent and traditionally Republican areas. In fact, the vote followed social class lines to a remarkable extent. For example, the election results in St. Louis showed that the union opponents to the measure were particularly successful in working class neighborhoods, while support for the amendment was concentrated in upper middle class and other affluent areas where Republican candidates run strongest. In the most affluent area in St. Louis County (Clayton Township), the amendment was supported by 76 percent of the voters. In contrast, in one working class township where the residents are predominantly moderate income families (Airport), the amendment received only 15 percent of the votes; and in another similar township that has a few more middle income families (Ferguson) only 25 percent of the voters supported the amendment. In the largely black areas of St. Louis City, the defeat was even more pronounced, with as few as six percent (Ward 26) of the voters supporting "right-to-work." As these figures indicate, the election thus not only revealed a very striking amount of polarity depending on the different characteristics of voting districts but also demonstrated the ultimate failure of the amendment's backers to capitalize on the supposed popular disaffection with organized labor.

PUBLICLY DISCLOSED CONTRIBUTIONS IN BEHALF OF THE "RIGHT-TO-WORK" AMENDMENT

Despite the obvious problems with the publicly disclosed contributions, it is worthwhile to carry through with our original purpose of analyzing the patterns that exist among such donations. In addition to our interest in determining what patterns do exist in these data, this part of the analysis helps establish a context for our interview data on the sources of contributions. Our purpose here is to determine how the contributions relate to the structures of economic power and upper class prominence that prevail in St. Louis. In this regard, our primary interest is in determining whether contributors tend to come from more centralized positions within these structures or whether the antiunion financial supporters tend to be found in relatively marginal locations.

In examining these contributions we looked initially at those which came from 434 large, St. Louis based, nonfinancial corporations identified in our other St. Louis research. This group of corporations includes all large locally based corporations, ranging from such well-known national firms as Monsanto, McDonnell–Douglas and Anheuser–Busch to numerous firms of only local or regional importance. Most firms in this group have at least 100 employees.

The data in Table 1 allow for a general overview of the results of our examination. Here we only look at contributions from corporations or from individuals who could be identified as the top officers of a corporation. While these contributions are listed separately as well as in combination, the actual unit of analysis we are most interested in is the corporation itself. Thus, if an individual top officer makes a contribution, it is assumed that it can be viewed as coming from the corporation. Missouri law allows corporations to make political contributions in state and local elections.

We find that only 48 (or 11 percent) of the 434 large St. Louis corporations either gave directly or had top officers who gave contributions in support of the "right-to-work" campaign that were publicly disclosed. The contributions amounted to a total of $13,025 with about two thirds ($8,600) being made by the corporations themselves and one third ($4,425) coming from top officers.

We began this analysis with a particular interest in the involvement of the largest local corporations in relation to smaller, more marginal, firms. When only the 434 largest corporations are considered, no tendency is found for the smaller corporations to be more likely to contribute. However, this pattern should not divert our attention from the more important finding that the largest corporations, despite their unambiguous dominance over the local economy, contributed only a tiny share of the money reported here. The fifteen firms with 10,000 or more employees contributed a total of only $500 and most of that amount came as individual gifts from top officers.

The dominance of smaller firms as contributors in behalf of the amendment in the disclosed lists is revealed even more clearly when we consider all money received from St. Louis area firms and their top officers. We were able to identify 150 other firms which either made contributions directly or had top officers who gave money. While some of these firms could not clearly be ranked by size, most were found to be firms that were not large enough to be included on the list of 434 major firms. These firms provided most of the disclosed local contributions: of the total of $49,243 that came from St. Louis businesses and their officers, these firms accounted for nearly three fourths (36,218). The bulk of this money came directly from the corporations ($30,958) rather than from top officers. Thus, the major conclusion that emerges from the data in Table 1 is that the great bulk of disclosed contributions came from smaller, and presumably marginal, corporations.

The issue of a possible relationship between the class centrality or marginality of corporations and "right-to-work" contributions was also examined from a number of different perspectives. The results of these examinations, which yield no clear patterns, are not reported in Table 1. The closeness of corporations to centers of economic power and upper class social prominence through the board interlocks and upper class club ties of their top officers

Table 1. Distribution of Publicly Disclosed Contributions in Favor of the ''Right-to-Work'' Amendment Among St. Louis Area Corporations By the Number of Employees of the Corporations

Total Number of Employees of Corporations	Total Contributions Given By the Corporations	% of Corporations Contributing	Total Contributions By Top Executives of Corporations	% of Corporations With Executives Contributing	Total Contributions by Corporations and Their Top Executives	% of Corporations Giving Directly or With Top Executives Who Gave	Total Number of Corporations Giving Directly or With Top Executives Who Gave	Number of Corporations in Category
Among 434 of the Largest St. Louis Based Corporations[1]								
10,000 or More Employees	$ 100	6.7%	$ 400	13.3%	$ 500	20.0%	3	15
1000-999 Employees	450	4.3%	1,050	17.0%	1,500	21.3%	10	47
500-999 Employees	800	3.8%	800	9.4%	1,600	11.3%	6	53
Under 500 Employees	7,250	6.0%	2,175	4.7%	9,425	9.1%	29	319
Total for 434 Contributions	8,600	5.5%	4,425	6.9%	13,025	11.1%	48	434
Other St. Louis Corporations[1] That Contributed	30,958	N.A.	5,260	N.A.	36,218	N.A.	150	N.A.
TOTAL FROM ST. LOUIS CORPORATIONS	$39,558		9,685		49,243			

[1]Banks and Savings and Loan Associations excluded.

Note: The contributions included here are only those reported in campaign disclosure statements from the three primary committees that supported the amendment. See the text for a discussion of the limitations of these reports.

proved to be unrelated to the level of contributions. Firms were further classified according to the ''core'' or ''peripheral'' character of, and the extent of unionization within, the particular industry to which they were most closely tied in order to determine if ''right-to-work'' contributions were more concentrated among firms in relatively marginal industries. Again, no meaningful relationships emerged.

While the clearest conclusion that emerges from the study of the campaign disclosure records is that the largest corporations appear to have played a minor role in the ''right-to-work'' campaign, it is critically important to remember that these data are very incomplete due to the limitations in the reporting requirements. The question that must be addressed is whether the same conclusion would be drawn if data on all contributions were available.

In fact, based on the information we gathered through interviews a markedly different picture of the sources of ''right-to-work'' contributions appears. We will now turn to these more qualitative findings.

BIG MONEY SOURCES FOR THE MISSOURI "RIGHT-TO-WORK" CAMPAIGN

Surprisingly little information on the identities of the actual funding sources behind the ''right-to-work'' campaign, other than the publicly disclosed lists, has become public. Newspaper accounts typically categorized the backers in a general fashion, for example referring to the campaign as being ''financed by contributions from businesses, businessmen and business groups'' (Lyman, 1978a) To the extent observers tried to be more specific, the one point made most consistently was that the primary backers did not come from among the largest corporations in Missouri. For example, one reporter, relying primarily on the disclosure records, observed that there were ''few donations from major Missouri corporations'' and that ''most of the proponents' funds come from individuals or small businesses'' (Lhotka, 1978b). A report in the *Wall Street Journal* described an effort late in the campaign to raise funds in St. Louis from ''some of the corporate elite from this city's prominent medium-sized companies'' (Merry, 1978). Similarly, another national publication stated shortly after the election that ''the RTW forces at least matched the unions in total spending, but they received virtually no support from major corporations'' (Business Week, 1978a).

This view that large corporations were not centrally involved seems also to have been held by many of the labor union leaders who fought to kill the ''right-to-work'' proposal. One union leader wrote following the election that ''major unionized corporations such as McDonnell-Douglas, Anheuser-Busch and the Big Three automakers assumed a neutral stance throughout the campaign. In St. Louis, where labor and management have unusually good relations, most big businesses kept their distance from the RTW fight'' (Worley,

1979:5). Similarly, a labor spokesman in Kansas City was quoted as saying "a lot of these companies [major corporations in Missouri] have a good relationship going with their unions and they don't want to blow it by giving money to some antiunion campaign (Lyman, 1978a).

Parallel conclusions were offered by the union leaders we interviewed. Union leaders in both St. Louis and Kansas City stated the view that, seen in retrospect, the 1978 campaign, despite the concerns they had felt at the time, was something of an anachronism. They suggested that the key individuals behind the amendment were "old time" antiunion activists who had decided to make a big attempt to win a "right-to-work" law before they simply got too old. It was claimed that these activists never won a broad following among important business leaders. The union leaders did not suggest that corporate leaders harbored many prounion sentiments. For example, one St. Louis union official stated his own belief that few St. Louis businessmen liked unions but rather simply accepted them as organizations that were here to stay. In his view, most businesses might actually like to do without unions but given the important beneficial ties with labor that existed there was a "great reluctance to risk it all" on the "right-to-work" fight. While they might be tempted by their antiunion sentiments, they recognized that they could get hurt in any fight with the unions and they were simply "unwilling to pay the price."

Despite the pervasiveness of the views that contributions had come largely from individuals and from small and medium-sized businesses, there were some indications during the campaign of a quite different reality. Most significantly, discoveries were made during the campaign of three major contributions that came from large Missouri corporations. First, in the course of regulatory proceedings regarding a request by the St. Louis electrical utility for a rate increase it was discovered that this company had made a contribution of $50,000 to the Missouri Council for Economic Development, the tax exempt foundation already discussed that played a central role in the campaign (Lhotka, 1978a). Second, as the result of a copy of a cancelled check being leaked to the news media by a unionized employee, it was disclosed that the leading Kansas City utility had pledged $10,000 for each of three years to the special account run for the "right-to-work" backers through the Missouri Chamber of Commerce. Third, the company that publishes the two Kansas City daily newspapers acknowledged that it had contributed $10,000 through the Chamber of Commerce account in 1977 (Lyman, 1978a).

The size of these three contributions, and the fact that all three were disclosed inadvertently, suggested a flow of donations from large corporations that clearly contradicted the beliefs of many observers that major Missouri firms had been relatively uninvolved in the campaign. In this regard, it is notable that the single contribution from the St. Louis electrical utility was equal in size to the entire amount of contributions from St. Louis donors revealed in the publicly disclosed lists from the three "right-to-work" committees that were analyzed in the preceding section.

In the context of the contradictory evidence regarding the source of contributions, the data gathered from interviews become all the more significant. It should be noted, of course, that the information gained from interviews could not always be fully checked and confirmed against hard data due to the still secret status of the full list of donors. However, the checks that were possible supported the accuracy of the interview responses.

The picture that emerges from the interview data from within the core group of "right-to-work" backers is strikingly different from that suggested by the publicly disclosed contribution lists. Instead of being supported by smaller businesses, the bulk of the support for the "right-to-work" campaign apparently came from many of the largest corporations in Missouri. In the three years preceding the brief period when the new campaign disclosure law was in effect, the "right-to-work" backers raised over $2 million, of which we were told about 85 percent came from large corporations and their top executives. The average contribution during this period was said to be between $3000 and $4000. The size of these contributions contrasts markedly with the average of about $250 that existed for the contributions from St. Louis corporations included on the disclosure reports.

This money was raised as the result of an aggressive effort led by the three or four prominent Kansas City business leaders and the one or two in St. Louis who were involved in the campaign from the start. We were told that due to the extensive contacts of these men in both Kansas City and St. Louis, and to their unquestioned upper class standing, they were able to approach directly their peers at the heads of major Missouri corporations. For example, one of the leading Kansas City fund raisers not only sat on the boards of several large Kansas City corporations but also was on the board of Southwestern Bell Telephone, one of the largest firms based in St. Louis. The importance of these personal contacts was reflected in a statement made during the campaign by the president of the Kansas City electric utility when his company was criticized for pledging the $30,000 to the backers of the amendment. He stated that he had made the pledge based largely on his own personal trust in the judgement of one of the prominent fund raisers.

In the interviews we sought to determine whether the "right-to-work" fund raisers had encountered corporate leaders in Missouri who seemed to embody the approach of corporate accomodation with unions. Such individuals would presumably have not only refused to contribute but also would have indicated their own opposition to any overt challenge to the position of unions on the grounds that they believed in reasonably strong unions, and good relations with unions, as a necessary feature of a strong corporate system. In fact, we were told that the fund raisers found universal agreement among corporate leaders that a "right-to-work" law would be a major benefit to Missouri. Moreover, they were reportedly enthusiastic about the idea of weakening unions in Missouri.

It is not true, however, that all large Missouri corporations approached were willing to contribute. Some declined. The willingness or unwillingness to support an antiunion campaign did not appear, nevertheless, to be related to a firm's acceptance of unions or to any beliefs regarding the legitimacy of unions and the positive contributions they supposedly make to the corporate system. Instead, we find evidence of pervasive antiunionism among leading capitalists that is held in check only in those instances where unions are seen as having the potential for retaliating against attacks. This conclusion is supported by the reports that the major shared characteristic among those major corporations refusing to give to the ''right-to-work'' campaign was their status as identified sellers of brand name products to mass markets. The chief officers of such corporations told the ''right-to-work'' fund raisers that even though they agreed, typically strongly, with the proposed amendment, they were not willing to risk union boycotts or other union campaigns of retribution directed at their sales if their contributions were to be discovered. In St. Louis, corporations that refused to contribute on these grounds reportedly included Anheuser-Busch, Pet and Ralston Purina. In contrast, the largest St. Louis contributors were the major manufacturers who do not sell many products directly to the public. For example, among the leading contributors in St. Louis were said to be Emerson Electric and McDonnell Douglas.

The interview responses also indicated that the unionization of a company's work force was not related to the willingness of a firm to contribute. In fact, it was stated that most of the large manufacturers who were the largest contributors were unionized and had been so for many years.

While the campaign was overwhelmingly financed by large corporations, supporters received little aid from corporations based outside of Missouri. The contributors were primarily headquartered within the state. No sizable role was attributed even to those national corporations, with headquarters elsewhere, which have large plants in Missouri. The lack of involvement by such firms is significant because this group includes many of the largest employers in the state. There were some exceptions, including the Coors family (the Colorado beer brewers who have long supported conservative causes) and Bunker Hunt of Texas, owner of the Kansas City professional football team. Nevertheless, these contributions accounted for a small share of the money received. While the backers used the lack of outside contributions to justify their criticisms that they opponents received massive support from national unions, they were apparently disappointed, and even surprised, that leading national capitalists had not seen their campaign as having enough importance in the struggle with unions to warrant sizable contributions.

As a final point regarding contributions, it is worthwhile to consider whether any business contributions were made by businesses *against* the ''right-to-work'' amendment. In our review of the disclosure reports filed by the major union committees we found no contributions from the 434 largest that went to the opposition to the amendment. Apparently none of the large St. Louis corporations supported a strong union movement enough to make even a symbolic cash donation to the union efforts to defeat the amendment. One press account of a union sponsored parade against the amendment did report that Anheuser-Busch sent the "Budweiser Car," a racing car used by the company for promotional purposes and also a young female representative known as "Miss Budweiser," and that several other companies, mostly ones headed by big contributors to Democratic candidates, allowed some company identified trucks to participate (St. Louis Post-Dispatch, 1978). These gestures however, were hardly substantive.

Thus, in contrast to contributions to political candidates where businessmen in Missouri typically divide their gifts between Republicans and Democrats, in the "right-to-work" campaign there were no public rebels to defined business interests. A notable kind of uniform class loyalty prevailed, even among those who were not willing to provide any open support for the amendment. This pattern suggests a degree of class cohesion that is consistent with the interview reports of general business support for the amendment, even among those refusing to take a public stand.

CONCLUSION

While the 1978 "right-to-work" campaign in Missouri was a significant example of the growing aggressiveness of business interests in their struggles with organized labor, it also clearly represented a fundamental miscalculation. The business interests behind it thought they could win a majority of the voters to their cause. Given the relative numbers of businessmen as compared to workers in the electorate, the backers of "right-to-work" were making a bold gamble. In this instance organized labor proved itself quite able to meet the challenge. Given the size of the majority won by the opponents of the amendment, political observers predicted after the election that the issue would not appear again in Missouri for at least a decade. The statements of "right-to-work" supporters following the election did not indicate that subsequent attempts in behalf of that measure or related ones in other states would focus on legislatures rather than on proposals submitted directly to the voters. Businesses have a much better record winning support from legislators than from voters.

The research demonstrated the precariousness of using public disclosure data unless the adequacy of the particular data is carefully examined. The disclosure reports considered here were not only incomplete, but taken literally they conveyed the fundamentally incorrect picture that the funding sources of the "right-to-work" campaign had been largely small businesses and individuals. Only through our interviews were we able to reveal the large corporate origins of the bulk of the contributions.

It is similarly significant that the perceptions of the funding sources held by important labor union officials, including ones who had been centrally involved in the campaign, were very inaccurate. The union leaders appeared to believe, or at least want to believe, that the "right-to-work" campaign was carried out primarily by a somewhat isolated small group of right-wing businessmen. They were, of course, not alone in this assessment. Most newspaper accounts and other analyses of the campaign offered similar views. Given the disparity between these images and the actual reality, it is clear that the "right-to-work" backers did an impressive job of protecting their contributors.

Of course, the central role played by large corporations in the campaign is not without its ambiguities. Despite the emphasis we have placed on the discoveries regarding the centrality of financial support from the largest Missouri corporations, it is significant that in public most corporate leaders kept themselves and their firms on the side lines. The public image that they carefully projected during the amendment battles was one of neutrality.

Given these patterns of covert antiunion aggressiveness that are represented in the "right-to-work" contributions of the large corporations, the actual character of the amendment campaign is difficult to describe. Without the large corporate financial support, the campaign would have had only a small fraction of the resources it was actually able to obtain. In fact, it is unlikely that the backers would have even carried through with their plans. Thus, the campaign was fundamentally a project on behalf of the large corporate interests. Still, because most corporate leaders refused to acknowledge their support, the campaign appeared to be a somewhat marginal and isolated effort.

Certainly, one conclusion is that in Missouri at least there is no general support for strong labor unions among top corporate leaders, or stated more accurately, for unions as strong as the ones that currently exist. Whatever accommodations corporate leaders have made with the labor movement would appear to be primarily based on a recognition that unions are strong enough to retalitate when attacked.

It is not clear what the Missouri campaign tells us about the future of antiunion political mobilization among business interests in the near future. Quite possibly the defeat of business in this instance is less significant than are the indications of the willingness of important capitalists to back such an effort. Given the conservative victories on both the federal and state levels in 1980, and the likelihood that the perceptions of growing weaknesses in the labor movement will become even more widely held, it is reasonable to expect that support for aggressive antiunion campaigns in the business community will increase.

ACKNOWLEDGMENT

We would like to thank Kathryn Strother Ratcliff, Maynard Seider and Susan Mizruchi for their helpful comments and assistance.

NOTES

1. Indictments had been recommended by the Missouri Campaign Finance Commission but the local prosecutor had in the fall of 1980 not yet decided whether to file charges.

2. When these "right-to-work" activists were asked in 1980 to advise a utility industry group on how to fight a petition campaign for antinuclear legislation initiated by environmental groups, they advised that a legal challenge should be made, even if the issues were largely spurious. In 1980 this tactic proved to be highly successful for business interests, with the underfinanced environmentalists being forced to spend time and money until the Missouri Supreme Court unanimously threw out the challenge barely two weeks before the election. The proposal lost.

REFERENCES

Aronowitz, Stanley
    1973   False Promises: The Shaping of American Working Class Consciousness. New York: McGraw-Hill.
Bradley, Philip D.
    1956   Involuntary Participation in Unionism. Washington, D.C.: American Enterprise Association.
Business Week
    1977   "The new chill in labor relations." October 24:32-33.
    1978a   "A big defeat in Missouri for the right-to-workers." November 20:41
    1978b   "Embattled unions strike back at management." December 4:54-69.
    1979a   "The antiunion grievance ploy." February 12:117-120.
    1979b   "Taking aim at 'union-busters'." November 12:98-99.
Cameron, Juan
    1978   "Small business trips big labor." Fortune. July 31:80-2.
Congressional Digest
    1965   "U.S. policy on labor-management relations." Aug.-Sept.:193-215.
Forbes
    1978   "Labor on the defensive." February 20:44-48.
Gall, Peter, and John Hoerr
    1978   "The growing schism between business and labor." Business Week. August 14:78-80.
Guzzardi, Walter Jr.
    1978   "Business is learning how to win in Washington." Fortune. March 27:56-57.
Huckler, Robert J.
    1978   "Labor winning open shop battle, poll shows." Kansas City Times. October 28:1.
Kistler, Alan, and Charles McDonald
    1976   "The continuing challenge of organizing." AFL-CIO American Federationist. November: 8-13.
Kuhn, James W.
    1961   "Right-to-work laws—symbols or substance." Industrial and Labor Relations Review 14:587-594.
Laner, Joel
    1980   "How Missouri business lost the right to work." Kansas City Outlook. July:34-39.
Lhotka, William C.
    1978a   "Amendment opponents spend most." St. Louis Post-Dispatch, November 1:1.
    1978b   " 'Right-to-work' group got $50,000 from UE." St. Louis Post-Dispatch. November 3.

1980   "New technology weakens position of labor unions." St. Louis Post-Dispatch.
          February 17.
Lhotka, William, and Curt Matthews
    1978a   "Foreign plague on U.S. industry." St. Louis Post-Dispatch, August 15:3B.
    1978b   "Firms counterattack". St. Louis Post-Dispatch, August 16:3G.
Lyman, Rick
    1978a   "Business, labor back their words with money in 'right-to-work' fight." Kansas City
             Times, October 27:1.
    1978b   "Business group's status in question." Kansas City Star, November 1:1.
Marshall, F. Ray
    1967   Labor in the South. Cambridge: Harvard University Press.
Martin, Douglas
    1979   "Labor nemesis: when the boss calls in this expert, the union may be in real trouble."
             Wall Street Journal. November 19:1.
Merry, Robert W.
    1978   "Right-to-work turning point?" Wall Street Journal, October 27:15.
    1979   "This year's hot labor issue." Wall Street Journal. May 24:13.
Meyers, Frederic
    1955   "Effects of 'right-to-work' laws: a study of the Texas act." Industrial and Labor
             Relations Review 9:77-84.
    1959   Right to work in Practice. New York: The Fund for the Republic.
Miliband, Ralph
    1969   The State in Capitalist Society. New York: Basic Books
Miller, Glenn W., and Stephen B. Ware
    1963   "Organized labor in the political process: a case study of the right-to-work campaign
             in Ohio." Labor History 4:51-67.
Mills, C. Wright
    1948   New Men of Power: America's Labor Leaders. New York: Harcourt, Brace and
             Company.
Mills, Daniel Q.
    1978   Labor-Management Relations. New York: McGraw-Hill.
Mossberg, Walter
    1975   "Right-to-work drive: a friend to workers or a menace to them?" Wall Street Journal.
             April 22:1.
Parenti, Michael
    1978   Power and the Powerless. New York: St. Martin's Press.
Pfeffer, Richard M.
    1979   Working For Capitalism. New York: Columbia University Press.
Ratcliff, Richard E.
    1980a   "Banks and the command of capital flows: an analysis of capitalist class structure and
             mortgage desinvestment in a metropolitan area." Pp. 107-32 in Maurice Zeitlin
             (ed.), Classes, Class Conflict and the State. Cambridge, Mass.: Winthrop.
    1980b   "Declining cities and capitalist class structure." Pp. 115-38 in G. William Domhoff
             (ed.), Power Structure Research. Beverly Hills: Sage Press.
    1980c   "Banks and corporate lending: an analysis of the impact of the internal structure of
             the capitalist class on the lending behavior of banks." American Sociological Review
             45:553-570.
Ratcliff, Richard E., Mary Elizabeth Gallagher, and Kathryn Strother Ratcliff
    1979   "The civic involvement of bankers: an analysis of the influence of economic power
             and social prominence in the command of civil policy positions." Social Problems
             26:298-313.

Scheinberg, Stephen
 1966   "The Development of Corporation Labor Policy 1900-1940" Unpublished Ph.D.
         dissertation. Madison: University of Wisconsin.
St. Louis Post-Dispatch
 1978   "Labor on parade opposing 'right-to-work' proposal." September 10:2G.
Shirk, Martha
 1978   " 'Right-to-work' in Iowa: gets the credit, takes the blame." St. Louis Post-
         Dispatch. November 1:1.
Skinner, Gordon S.
 1958   "Legal and historical background of the right-to-work dispute." Labor Law Journal
         9:411-420.
Stark, Jerrold L.
 1978   The Stalled Missouri Economy. Jefferson City, Mo.: Missouri Council for Economic
         Development.
Sultan, Paul E.
 1958   "Historical antecedents to the right-to-work controversy." Southern California Law
         Review 31:221-245.
U.S. News, and World Report
 1979   "Will dissension slow 'right-to-work' drive?" April 23:93-94.
von Hoffman, Nicholas
 1978   "The last days of the labor movement." Harper's, December: 22-28.
Warshal, Bruce S.
 1966   " 'Right-to-work', pro and con." Labor Law Journal 17:131-137.
Weinstein, James
 1968   The Corporate Ideal in the Liberal State. Boston: Beacon Press.
Witney, Fred
 1958   "The Indiana right-to-work law." Industrial and Labor Relations Review, 11:507-
         517.
Worley, Ken
 1979   Beating 'Right-to-work': A Report on the 1978 Missouri Campaign. St. Louis: UAW.

CLASS STRUGGLE, STATE POLICY, AND THE RATIONALIZATION OF PRODUCTION:

THE ORGANIZATION OF AGRICULTURE IN HAWAII

Rhonda F. Levine and James A. Geschwender

INTRODUCTION

The class struggle is an ongoing dynamic which takes place on many levels and at many locations. The class struggle is manifested both at the point of production and at the level of the state. State policy both in its formulation and implementation, is shaped through class struggle. This chapter will examine the class struggle in Hawaii which led to the passage of the Hawaii Employment Relations Act (Little Wagner Act) and to the ultimate consequences of its passage. This act, passed in 1945, extended to agricultural workers in Hawaii

Research in Social Movements, Conflict and Change, Volume 4, pages 123-150
Copyright © 1981 by JAI Press Inc.
ISBN: 0-89232-234-9

all rights and privileges granted to industrial workers by the National Labor Relations Act of 1935 (Wagner Act). Our analysis includes an examination of federal labor policy and its implementation in Hawaii, the relationship between the organization of Hawaii's economy and the struggle between labor and capital in Hawaii.

CONCEPTUAL FRAMEWORK

Within the past ten years, there has been a renewed intellectual interest in the study of the state apparatus. Much of this scholarship has been carried out by theorists operating within a Marxist framework. Instrumentalist conceptualizations of the state apparatus are based on a critique of pluralism, arguing that the state is an object used by a relatively small number of groups who possess a disproportionate share of the power to set forth policies which would be to their benefit (see Miliband, 1969). Structuralist perspectives of the state apparatus are based on a critique of orthodox Marxism and reject the notion that that state can be understood as a simple tool or instrument in the hands of the ruling class. The structuralist conceptualization of the state apparatus argues that certain state policies cannot be reduced to political domination alone (see Poulantzas, 1978).

Pluralist models of the state have traditionally argued that the state functions more or less to arbitrate between competing interest groups. Shifting coalitions of political participants make demands for state policies and are rewarded according to relative need (Truman, 1951; Dahl, 1967, 1968; Rose, 1967). According to Truman (1951), government activity is the result of interest group pressure which, in turn, is composed of organized as well as unorganized groups with overlapping concerns. However, organized groups are never "solid or monolithic," acording to Truman (1951:510). Truman agrees with Lasswell's definition of the state as "a time-space manifold of similar subjective events . . . That subjective event which is the unique mark of the state is the recognition that one belongs to a community with a system of paramount claims and expectations" (Lasswell, 1966:240-261). The pluralist model conceives of the state as a subject, adjudicating neutrally between competing interests. It asserts the neutrality of the state as the representative of the general interest in contrast to the divergent interests of "civil society". Hence, the state functions as an impartial referee (Polsby, 1963). Pluralists argue that "government is the focal point for group pressure and its task is to effect a policy which reflects the highest common factor of group demands" (Parry, 1969:65-66). Pluralists tend to focus on the immediate activities of politicians and self-defined interest groups and the pressure they bring to bear individually and collectively on legislative bodies. As such, scholars operating within a pluralist framework fail to examine the complexities of macro-historical change and the impact of extra-parliamentary struggles on the activity of legislative bodies. The state is perceived as a subject, outside of economic relationships. Moreover, the transformations within the state apparatus itself, and the changing structure of the state is explained in terms of broad evolutionary changes. No attempt is made to explain and examine the manner in which conflict and struggles both at the level of the state and at the point of production both shape ''institutional change,'' and is shaped by it.

Instrumentalist conceptualizations of the state apparatus argue that the state is not neutral, but rather is an object used by a ruling class. State policies are understood in terms of the instrumental exercise of power by economic elites (the monolithic capitalist class), either directly or indirectly through the exercise of pressure on state administrators. Most analyses of the state apparatus by an instrumentalist model document the coincidence of interests and of individuals in government and business. This interrelationship is generally couched in terms of criterion of an individual's relative share of a similar attribute (for example, power, authority, or configurations of social indices such as educational background, social milieu, and wealth). The state apparatus does not appear to have a relationship to the process of capital accumulation independent of the conscious intentions of the individuals who control it. The instrumentalist model fails to distinguish between intentions, interests, values, and behavior of members of the state apparatus and recognizable objective relations between the state apparatus and the process of capital accumulation. Working from the framework of this model, scholars focus on the definitions of a ruling elite without first asserting the primacy of state economic activity independent of its controlling managers.

Structuralist models of the state locate the state apparatus and state activity within the social relations of production. The state is neither an object or a subject, but rather is a relation between classes and class forces. Structuralist models of the state maintain the class character of the state and state activity while not reducing state activity to the need of a monolithic capitalist class. Structuralists resemble some pluralist conceptualizations of state policy formation in maintaining that conflicts arise within the state and that class conflicts shape state policy (Bachrach and Baratz, 1963). However, unlike those pluralists who stress conflict arising from interest groups, structuralists locate these conflicts within the contradictions of capitalist social relations of production. It is class struggle and class contradictions which shape state policy, not merely competing interests.

Structuralist conceptualization of the capitalist state provide the framework for analyzing the complexities surrounding class struggle and state policy. While not reducing state policy to the conscious desires of a ruling elite, structuralist conceptualizations of state policy recognize the importance of struggle and the divisions within the capitalist class. At the same time, structuralist conceptualizations of the state and state activity do not merely examine conflicts within the state and among state officials, but rather locate these conflicts and struggles within the context of the specifically *capitalist* social relations of production.

The capitalist state apparatus aids in the reproduction of social relations of production through state policies which help maintain and/or create conditions for private capital accumulation and which sanction and legitimize class domination. The capitalist class itself is divided by fissures and competing interests. Hence, the state apparatus serves as the political organizer and unifier of the capitalist class. Moreover, the state apparatus serves to disorganize the working class in order to maintain class divisions and therefore, reproduce capitalist social relations of production. The state apparatus is a condensation of a relationship of forces between classes and class fractions. The capitalist state apparatus is thus constituted and divided by class contradictions, and is thereby divided by conflicts between various state agencies, branches, and boards within the state. In the words of Poulantzas (1978:132):

> Contrary to conceptions that treat it as a Thing or a Subject, the State is itself divided. It is not enough simply to say that contradictions and struggles traverse the State—as if it were a matter of penetrating an already constituted substance or of passing through an empty site that is already there. Class contradictions are the very stuff of the State: they are present in its material framework and pattern its organization; while the State's policy is the result of their functioning within the State.

The fact that state policy is shaped by class contradictions and class struggle does not deny that capitalists and state administrators attempt to formulate coherent political projects and to orient state policy. However, policies advocated by representatives of the capitalist class or state agents may come into conflict with policies advocated within other state agencies, boards, and departments. Final policy outcomes are then implemented in a particular conjunctural context. Working class struggles also leave their imprint on the development and execution of state policy. This was the case in the formulation and final passage of the National Labor Relations Act and was even more striking with regard to the Little Wagner Act. The state apparatus granted through the NLRA limited concessions to some segments of the working class in order to incorporate them within the political process of the state and hence polarize the working class and short-circuit its political organization. In general, state policy seeks to resolve working class struggle and class contradictions by channelling such struggle within limits that are compatible with the overall relations of production and division of labor. Because the state apparatus is itself divided by conflicts, state policy may temporarily resolve the conflicts of a particular historical conjuncture, but in so doing, create new contradictions and conflicts. The ultimate consequence of state policy is contingent upon the nature and character of the class struggle.

Class struggle on the mainland helped to create the context for the class struggle in Hawaii examined herein (see Levine, 1980). The depression of the 1930s stimulated unrest and demonstrations among the employed and unemployed alike. The National Industrial Recovery Act was passed to help solve the problems of industrial capital and included Section 7a to simultaneously sidetrack the AFL-sponsored Black Thirty Hour Bill and to calm the unrest. This section gave workers the right to join unions and bargain collectively but did not prevent management subversion through the creation of company unions nor did it carry adequate sanctions against noncompliance. Nevertheless, it helped stimulate a wave of organizational activity among industrial workers. This newly developed strength and militancy of industrial labor led to the passage of the stronger National Labor Relations Act (Wagner Act) in 1935 after the NIRA had been declared unconstitutional. Agricultural labor did not possess the organizational strength of industrial labor and, consequently, was excluded from coverage under the act. Hawaii labor fell under the purview of the act but the strength of Hawaii's capitalist class kept labor organization to an absolute minimum prior to World War Two.

THE STRUCTURE OF HAWAIIAN CAPITAL

For the most part, the events which provide the data for this chapter took place in the decades of the forties and the fifties. Hawaii, at the outset of the forties, was virtually run by a small group of tightly knit capitalists. Consider, for example, the following statements abstracted from the Report of E. J. Egan, former representative of the NLRB to Hawaii, which was presented before the House Committee on Labor Board and Wagner Act, May 3, 1940:

> Virtually every business of any importance is owned or controlled by the so-called "Big Five", that is, American Factors, C. Brewer and Company, Ltd., Alexander and Baldwin, Castle and Cooke, Ltd., and T. H. Davies and Company, Ltd. These companies have interlocking directorships. This method of obtaining joint action extends not only to the companies named but also to various subsidiary corporations. . . . Most of the land in the Islands is owned or controlled by the same group which manage the affairs of the "Big Five.". . . There are no independent banks on the Islands. All . . . are controlled by . . . the same people who are interested in the "Big Five." . . . The Matson Navigation Company, which is . . . closely connected with the "Big Five" interests . . . . Practically every item purchased or sold in the Islands is handled by the "Big Five" who act as factors or agents. . . .

Eagen continued his analysis to show that economic domination led to political control. He noted that the police, the legislature, the Governor, the judiciary, the bar and the university were all under the direct control of the "Big Five." They also owned and controlled all communications media through which they could largely determine the outcome of elections and create a general climate of opinion. This was probably an important aid in their ability to influence the military. All of these factors were arrayed to control labor by any means necessary. Eagen stated in his report that:

> Judging from the testimony produced at the hearing, the sugar interests believe that anyone who engages in union activities is an undesireable person and they very cautiously impart their information to the army and navy intelligence units. If there is any truer picture of facism anywhere in the world than in the Hawaiian Islands, then I do not know the definition of it.

Eagen was not an alarmist. All available evidence is consistent with the picture that he paints. Thus we see that pre-war Hawaii was economically, politically, and socially under the hegemonic control of capital embodied in the ''Big Five'' agencies which tended to act as a single coordinated entity. There was little in the way of conflict between fractions of capital and overt conflict between capital, and labor was repressed by the smothering effect of the sugar agencies. As such, the relative autonomy of the state was constricted by virtue that the power bloc and the ''Big Five'' were one and the same.

The Agency System

This situation did not develop accidentally (Smith, 1942; Fuchs, 1961:241-259; Weaver, 1959:171-184; Kurita, 1953; Taylor, 1935:1-29; Slate, 1961:195-238; Morgan, 1948:173-194; Brooks, 1952:249-250; Lind, 1938:162-186). Hawaii, located in the middle of the Pacific, was not discovered by Europeans until 1778. However, once discovered, it attracted merchants because of its strategic location with regard to the whale hunting grounds and the developing Pacific trade. Profits were quite high and the merchants proved to be the only ready source of capital when the commercial production of sugar began in the middle of the nineteenth century. Plantation owners were strapped for funds. Their customers were far away, travel took a long time, and customer payments were a long time coming. At the same time, the plantations had to pay for supplies purchased at a great distance. Consequently, the merchant houses were in an excellent position to assume control over the sugar industry once they were convinced that sugar represented a potentially profitable investment.

The merchant houses used their monopoly over available capital to acquire stock in the sugar plantations, decision-making influence beyond the level of their stock ownership, and profitable contracts to serve as the agents of the planters. The sugar agencies received three commissions on every ton of sugar sold—a sales commission, a freight forwarders' commission, and an insurance commission. They also received a commission on all goods purchased for the plantations. Thus, the agencies could reap rich profits even when the plantations lost money. Profits so produced were too great to be consumed through reinvestments in sugar so they were used to start up a whole host of subsidiary enterprises which, in turn, often sold their product to the plantations.

The sugar agencies coordinated the activities of the plantations with which they worked. In turn, they coordinated their activities with each other through the Planter's Labor and Supply Company (later the Hawaiian Sugar Producers' Association). The industry developed a system of interlocking directorships and officers which insured unified action. This was reinforced by a pattern of intermarriage between agency families. In 1904 the planters collectively acquired a sugar refinery in California which gave them complete control over the industry from planting to market. It would be surprising if this degree of oligopolic control over the economy of Hawaii did not also manifest itself in the type of hegemonic control over the state described by Eagen.

The Plantations

Hawaiian sugar plantations may not have the characteristics normally conjured up by the use of the term (Taylor, 1935:34-39; Lind, 1938:162-186). The plantation as it developed in Hawaii became a system of large-scale corporate agriculture with absentee owners living in Honolulu and other urban centers with resident managers attempting to maximize profits. They incorporated a blend of what is normally considered to be agricultural, and what is normally considered to be industrial enterprises. This is what was to prove so difficult in later years in determining what, if any, portion of the plantation labor force fell under the purview of the Wagner Act. Taylor (1935) describes Hawaii's sugar plantations in the following manner:

> The sugar plantations of Hawaii are more than simple agricultural enterprises. The modern cane sugar industry, the world over, comprises four distinct phases: (1) the production of cane, an agricultural process; (2) the extraction of raw sugar from the cane, a factory process; (3) the refining of the raw sugar into various commercial grades, also a factory process; (4) the marketing of the finished product, a commercial process. The first two stages are closely associated. . . . It is not profitable to transport sugarcane long distances, since it is bulky in comparison to its value and ferments unless ground quickly. Raw sugar . . . will keep indefinately . . . and is of high value in comparison to its bulk. Sugar factories for the manufacture of raw sugar . . . are to be found where cane is grown. . . . In Hawaii the plantations and mills are generally operated under the same management.

> Of the 42 sugar plantations in operation in 1932, 39 were complete entities from field to factory, cultivating and harvesting their own crops and extracting the raw sugar at their own mills. The other three were small plantations whose crop was ground by neighboring sugar mill companies. In addition, there were some 1,500 more or less independent growers . . . from whom the mills purchased cane. The status of these outside planters is one of complete economic subjugation to the sugar corporation. . . . Over seven-eights of all the sugar cane ground by the mills is produced by the same companies which own and operate the mills (35-37).

Because the mills and the fields were owned and operated by the same companies, the labor force could be, and usually was, used interchangeably between factories and fields, as work loads dictated. This caused further difficulties in distinguishing between agricultural and industrial workers for the purpose of NLRB representational elections. The work force on Hawaiian sugar plantations was normally employed year round.

ORGANIZED LABOR IN HAWAII BEFORE THE WAGNER ACT

The plantation labor supply was recruited primarily from China, the Portuguese Azores, Japan and the Philippines, although Hawaiians'had provided the major portion of the labor force early. Management exerted strict legal and extralegal controls over labor. Working conditions were harsh, compensation was poor and opportunities for protest were limited. The early years saw many small-scale sporadic protests, but these were usually short-lived and normally involved workers of a single ethnic identity and from a single plantation. Organized labor activities extending beyond a single plantation were rare and those involving members of more than one ethnic group were virtually non-existent.

Prior to the mid- to late-1930's, there was little labor organization in Hawaii. A few craft unions had existed since annexation in 1898. The craft unions primarily consisted of white workers in the building and metal trades who came to Hawaii from mainland United States to work as civilian employees at the Pearl Harbor naval base and Schofield military barracks. These craft unions, like the AFL on the mainland, were unwilling to embark upon an organizing drive for the unorganized and native and oriental workers in Hawaii. The major organization efforts of plantation workers prior to the 1930's occurred outside of any mainland labor organization. Moreover, these labor unions were national (racial) in membership. The racial divisions within the Hawaiian working class were a major deterent in organizing workers. Capitalists were able to pit one race against another (i.e., Japanese were used as strikebreakers for Filipino strikes, and vice-versa).

Class oriented worker activities began to appear in Hawaii by the middle of the 1930s. Following the upsurge of labor militancy on the mainland and the development of industrial unionization, left-oriented maritime workers published the *Voice of Labor*, a militant class-conscious paper, between 1935 and 1939. Most of the serious labor organizing took place on the docks and among maritime workers, although it gradually spread into the urban areas of Honolulu and Hilo. Most of these activities were under the leadership of the left-dominated ILWU.

By late 1937, ILWU representatives in Hawaii were asking for support from the International and from the CIO to organize unorganized workers in Hawaii including the massive numbers of plantation workers. This call came after it became clear that capitalists were attempting to subvert unionization drives and to prevent the CIO from coming to Hawaii. Capitalists in sugar and pineapple attempted to undermine industrial unionism by encouraging nationalist divisions among different nationalities employed in the same industry. Capitalists were willing to allow the formation of an all-Filipino union in order to breed racial hatred and animosity and dividing workers against themselves.

The ILWU representatives in Hawaii argued that only the CIO, with a program of publicity and education printed in the language of the workers affected, would be able to overcome these divisions. Moreover, it was argued that Hawaii was an integral part of the United States and that the organization of Hawaiian workers of all nationalities was essential to the program of the

West Coast CIO. ILWU representatives in Hawaii asked for materials and equipment in order to start a plantation organization drive. These representatives argued that unorganized workers in Hawaii were ripe for organizing and that the 65,000 agricultural workers all desired industrial unionization. It was further believed that the sugar interests would not again resort to violence as they had in the 1920's because the labor unrest might damage the growing tourist trade (Berman, 1937b).

In late 1937, Jack Hall and the ILWU moved to organize plantation workers across national barriers. This drive was intensified after a multi-national union won the 1938 Inter-Island Strike of longshoremen and seamen. The outbreak of World War Two brought unionization attempts to a screeching halt.

THE DRIVE TO ORGANIZE PLANTATION WORKERS

The first significant move toward the organization of plantation workers came through the efforts of longshoremen from Port Allen (Hartung, 1948:32-33; Marutani, 1970:57; Aller, 1957:52; Brooks, 1952:83-86). The Wagner Act had guaranteed the right to collective bargaining to all nonagricultural workers. Sugar plantations appeared to employ both agricultural and nonagricultural employees, so some of the plantation workers should have the right to form unions. However, it was uncertain exactly which and how many plantation employees fell into each of the two categories. The unionization drive was directed by Jack Hall and conducted under the auspices of the United Cannery, Agricultural, Packing, and Allied Workers of America (UCAPAWA). While plantation workers were signed up in many locations, the focal point of the struggle was McBryde Plantation.

The battle was long and drawn out. McBryde agreed to hold a consent election under a stipulated definition of agricultural and nonagricultural labor, providing that it was clearly understood that McBryde reserved the right to argue later that all of its employees were exempt from the Wagner Act, as they were really agricultural laborers. The definitions agreed to for the purpose of the election classified as nonagricultural all workers who spent 51 percent of their working time in 1939 in the mills, the hydroelectric plants, or transporting raw sugar from the mills to the point of embarkation. All other employees were defined as agricultural laborers. Using this definition, the larger part of McBryde's labor force was classified as agricultural laborers and excluded from the election. UCAPAWA won the consent election on October 24, 1940, by a vote of 200 to 40.

It was not until August, 1941, that a contract was finally signed. The contract included provisions in which the company agreed not to reduce wages and to continue to pay the current rate for overtime work. It also allowed the company to continue to negotiate with individual workers and to make individual wage and/or fringe benefit adjustments. The union agreed not to strike for the term of the contract. The workers did make some gains in that they got seniority rights and some company purchase of needed tools and equipment. The major labor victory came simply from the fact that they had won an NLRB supervised consent election and they had negotiated a contract. The troublesome problem as to which plantation workers came under the scope of the Wagner Act was not settled but there was at least an implied precedent for establishing that some were covered. This was seen as the opening wedge for a plantation organizing drive but war intervened.

LABOR UNDER MARTIAL LAW

The attack on Pearl Harbor on December 7, 1941, brought labor's organizational efforts to a screeching halt (Anthony, 155:41-45; Marutani, 1970:58-60; Aller, 1957:52-55; Allen, 1950:305-326; Larrowe, 1972:262-264; Van Zwalenburg, 1961). Shortly after the attack on Pearl Harbor, Governor Poindexter proclaimed martial law and transferred all power to Lieutenent General Walter D. Short for the duration of the emergency. There is reason to believe that Governor Poindexter thought that this would be a relatively short term transfer and that civilian government would return as soon as the imminent threat of Japanese invasion was removed. This expectation was proved wrong as martial law lasted from December 7, 1941, to October, 1944. The war brought with it a labor shortage and the planters feared that their labor force would desert them for higher paid civilian defense work. They pressured the military into issuing a series of orders which protected their labor supply. Philip Brooks, a former director of research for the Hawaii Employers' Council, states:

> During World War Two there had been a shortage of labor and the plantations could not have held their employees if it had not been for the governmental controls over labor and transportation (1952:82).

On December 20, 1941, General Order 38 was issued which gave the military governor formal control over all matters, froze wages as of their December 7 level, froze workers into their December 7 position, and required unemployed persons to accept employment ordered by the military governor. This was modified by later orders, some of which required all able-bodied men and women to register with the United States employment service and required employers to notify the service when persons left their payroll. Legal holidays and overtime pay for them were abolished. Overtime was to begin at 44 hours in some occupations and 48 in others, rather than at the federally required 40 hours. Absenteeism was punishable by law, and many persons were sent to jail upon being found guilty. Plantation labor was especially hard hit by these controls. The military orders, in essence, froze them in their positions at fixed wages on all islands other than Oahu, and on Oahu informal agreements served the same purpose. Large numbers of civilian workers were imported from the mainland to work at defense-related jobs. These jobs did not come under any wage controls. Defense workers worked long hours and had much money to spend. Prices shot up rapidly and the plantation workers had to pay these higher prices despite their fixed incomes. The fact that plantation employees could not leave their employer to take defense jobs did not prevent them from doing defense work. The military worked out a system by which plantation labor could be "borrowed" as needed for defense-related work. Thus, plantation workers often worked on defense projects side by side with mainland imports who were being paid much more for doing the same job. It was only "just" that the employers should be compensated for the loan of their labor force (Aller, 1957:310). For example, the United States Engineers paid the plantations 62 cents per hour for borrowed workers who were paid at the level of 41 cents per hour plus fringes valued at nine cents per hour. Thus the planters made a net profit of 12 cents per hour minus administrative costs on each hour worked by those employees that they "lent out." It is not too surprising that the lifting of martial law found plantation workers receptive to unionization.

Martial law did not explicitly outlaw unions, but various general orders declared as void any and all contracts which contradicted the terms of the general orders. Thus, the unions might continue to exist but they were relatively powerless. The military established the Office of the Military Governor, peopled it with people from business who were overtly hostile to organized labor, and gave it authority to control labor. The extent to which the military actively interferred with union activities varied from island to island. There is clear evidence that military officials had one union bargaining agent arrested and confined to jail for six months without placing charges or bringing him to trial. Union officers on Kauai were prohibited from collecting dues or engaging in union activities. Van Zwalenburg concludes:

> The conclusion is inescapable, however, that in the labor field it [Ofice of the Military Governor] has adopted the employer's point of view that labor unions are by nature troublesome, and feels that friction can best be avoided by discouraging unions, or at least ignoring them, rather than by utilizing their cooperation with Hawaiian industry (1961: 60).

POST-WAR UNIONIZATION EFFORTS

As the war drew to a close, both labor and capital began to make preparations for the coming struggle (Aller, 1957:52-61); Brooks, 1952:88-98; Van Zwalenburg, 1961:70-71; Larrowe, 1972:263-266; Marutani, 1970:59-62). Hawaiian capitalists differed as to the appropriate position to take. Some recognized that a certain amount of unionization was inevitable under the Wagner Act but believed that the amount could be held to a minimum. Others believed that unionization was inevitable and that, properly controlled, could be adapted to with minimal difficulties. Still others urged an all-out resistance to organized labor. All saw the value of a united front on the part of capital. A series of discussions and meetings culminated in 1943 with the formation of the Hawaii Employers' Council (HEC) and the hiring of James P. Blaisdell as president. Blaisdell was the former president of the San Francisco Distributor's Association. Under Blaisdell's leadership, the HEC formed a policy under which all members of the Council agreed to clear through the council all actions with respect to labor (e.g., wages, hours, working conditions, responses to unionization attempts, etc.). Blaisdell convinced the members of the Council that their best strategy was to accept the dictates of the Wagner Act gracefully, extend recognition to organized labor with a minimum of struggle, to seek favorable definitions of the scope of the bargaining unit, and to attempt to negotiate the best possible contract terms. The ILWU began gearing up for the organizational campaign in early 1943. It spent a great deal of time in planning strategy and began making testing probes among plantation workers, with the partial lifting of martial law restrictions in 1943. In January, 1944, longshoremen in Honolulu voted to spend $5,000 to send a dozen of their members to other islands as part of the campaign. Other groups of longshoremen also promised aid. In June, 1944, Jack Hall was appointed regional director for the ILWU and Frank Thompson, an accomplished and experienced organizer, was sent from the West Coast. Thus the ILWU launched its two-pronged attack to change the face of Hawaii: organization at the point of production and struggle at the level of the state.

Capital may have been moving toward a gradual acceptance of the fact that they would have to deal with organized labor at some level, but they were not enthralled with the prospect of being confronted by the ILWU. The entire history of the ILWU convinced capital that it was too radical, too militant, too strong, and, in brief, simply too difficult to deal with. This may account for their relative lack of resistance when the AFL moved to organize Waiakea plantation. Jack Owens wrote to the Waiakea plantation on January 8, 1944, asking that Sugar Workers' Local 23587 be recognized as a bargaining agent. Discussions were conducted over the scope of the bargaining unit and Arnold Wills, Director of the Honolulu Office of the NLRB was consulted. The union and management reached agreement without the necessity of NLRB hearings and a contract was signed on July 1, 1944, without a representational election having been held. The bargaining unit was restricted to nonagricultural and nonsupervisory employees using a rather liberal definition as to who was a supervisory or an agricultural employee.

Meanwhile, the ILWU made representational requests for eleven plantations on the Island of Hawaii between April and August, 1944. Arnold Wills, after the filing of the first five representational claims in April, sent a questionnaire to the plantations involved, seeking their thoughts as to the proper definition of the bargaining unit. Direct negotiations accomplished nothing, and it became necessary to hold hearings to determine the scope of the unit. In direct negotiations the sugar companies had argued for a definition of agricultural labor which would have allowed for a maximum of between 15 and 20 percent of the work force to be included in the bargaining unit. The AFL-union agreed to management's definition but the ILWU challenged it, hoping to expand the bargaining unit up to between 20 and 30 percent of the work force. When hearings began, management took the position that all employees were agricultural inasmuch as the plantations dealt solely with an agricultural product. The ILWU in turn argued that all employees other than field workers were nonagricultural and belonged in the bargaining unit. The mainland precedent had been to define as nonagricultural all employees in processing sheds, packing houses and warehouses, but all involved in cultivating the soil or harvesting the crop were defined as agricultural workers (Larrowe, 1972:264). This would have set the size of the bargaining unit as roughly between ten and 20 percent of plantation employees. All sides were shocked by the eventual NLRB decision.

On January 12, 1945, the NLRB, through Arnold Wills, ruled that all plantation employees except those engaged in field work were covered by the Wagner Act. Thus any worker dealing with cane after it was cut and loaded into trucks was an industrial worker and must be allowed to organize and bargain collectively. In addition, the NLRB ruled that a number of occupations claimed by management to be supervisory were in fact not supervisory and should be part of the bargaining unit. This ruling placed beween 50 and 60 percent of the plantation labor force under the purview of the Wagner Act and gave the ILWU a tremendous boost in its struggle against agricultural capital. The ILWU won all eleven subsequent representational elections by a combined vote of 2,496 for the ILWU to 132 for either no union or the AFL.

The ILWU had continued its organizational drive during the period of NLRB deliberations and soon thereafter sought representational elections on 19 other plantations throughout the state. Capital saw no further point in insisting on NLRB hearings, so they agreed to consent elections. The ILWU won all 19 consent elections by a combined vote of 5,568 to 222. The ILWU sweep continued when the McBride Plantation contract was shifted from UCAPAWA to the ILWU and the Waialua Plantation was organized through a cross check procedure which did not require an election. Thus, by the end of 1945, the ILWU had organized the nonagricultural employees on 32 out of the 35 sugar plantations in Hawaii. All that remained outside their scope was the one plantation organized by the AFL (this plantation folded in 1948) and two other very small plantations which remained unorganized. Agricultural workers were the next organizational target of the ILWU and their successful organization was dependent upon the second prong of the ILWU drive: struggle at the level of the state.

CLASS STRUGGLE AT THE LEVEL OF THE STATE

The ILWU launched a political campaign in 1944 as the second prong of their drive to transform Hawaii. Their chances for success were enhanced by the almost simultaneous drive of Japanese-Americans, led by World War Two veterans, to make Hawaii into a more democratic society (see Geschwender, 1981). The two groups had different objectives. The ILWU and its allies, including many Japanese-Americans, were more concerned with achieving economic justice and economic equality than political democracy. Political democracy was seen more as a means to the achievement of other objectives than as a primary objective in itself. The Japanese-American veterans were more concerned with opening up Hawaiian society to provide access to groups other than the small Caucasian elite. Thus, the creation of a more democratic political structure was both a primary objective and a means toward the achievement of other ends. There was enough similarity of goals to allow for cooperation between the ILWU leadership and the Japanese-American veterans and enough points of difference to stimulate a continuing tension and competition. Cooperation and conflict continued as both groups recognized the necessity to revive the Democratic party in order to break the domination by sugar.

A small group of agricultural capitalists had hegemonic control over all aspects of life in pre-war Hawaii. They utilized the Republican party as the political embodiment of their collective interests. This was weakened only slightly by the election of Roosevelt and a Democratic Administration in Washington. When Roosevelt appointed Judge Ingram Stainbeck as Governor of the Territory in 1942, it marked the fourth consecutive time that a Democratic President appointed a Territorial Governor that was closely allied to the sugar interests (Wright, 1972:117). Stainbeck appointed more Republicans than Democrats to major political offices in the Territory.

The ILWU joined together with other labor unions in July, 1944, to form a Political Action Committee (PAC) in order to elect progressive persons to the Territorial Legislature. ILWU local unions spent most of that autumn raising funds for the campaign (*The Dispatcher*, July 17, 1944). The PAC endorsed candidates in both primary and general elections and, unlike mainland labor unions, ran a number of ILWU officials for office. PAC and the ILWU carried on a voter registration drive, as well as actively campaigning for endorsed candidates. Hawaiian music and Hulas were features, along with the sale of stamps carrying slogans such as ''Win with Labor'' and ''A Little Wagner Act for Hawaii'' (Frank Thompson, 1977a). More than $1,500 was raised in Hilo alone to pay for the campaign of three local candidates. Similar successes were reported throughout Hawaii.

The key objective in the legislative program of PAC was the passage of an act which they referred to as the "Little Wagner Act." This was somewhat inaccurate as a name in that the desired legislation would be much broader than the federal Wagner Act. PAC sought to have all rights granted to industrial workers under the Wagner Act extended to agricultural workers in Hawaii. This would eliminate the very difficult problem of distinguishing between agricultural and industrial plantation workers (n.b., the campaign was launched prior to the historic NLRB decision in this area), and it would pave the way for organizing plantation workers excluded from Wagner Act coverage. PAC also sought legislation against racial discrimination, to establish a "sheltered workshop" for disabled veterans, free public education for all children, and significant reform of state income tax laws (Hawaii: ILWU Conference minutes, Sept. 16-17, 1944).

The 1944 Territorial elections established labor as a political force to be reckoned with as ILWU and PAC endorsed candidates achieved a stunning victory. PAC endorsed 19 candidates for the 30 positions in the House up for contention, 15 of the endorsed candidates were elected. Two were elected officers in ILWU locals. Six of the eight persons elected to the 15 member Territorial Senate were endorsed by PAC. They joined at least one other carry-over Democratic Senator with pro-labor leanings. Labor had a great deal of political influence in the new legislature, although Republicans retained a majority in both houses (Frank Thompson, 1944b).

The growing degree of labor's political power was further illustrated by the appointment of Jack Hall to the Honolulu Police Commission in 1945 (Larrowe, 1972:265-266). However, this was not directly achieved through local political action. It followed a communication from Secretary of the Interior Ickes to Governor Stainbeck directing him to appoint more representatives from labor to boards and commissions in the territory. The ILWU formed its own PAC for the 1946 elections without the cooperation of other labor unions and were even more successful than they had been in 1944. The extent to which their endorsement was sought by politicians may be seen in their action in demanding an undated resignation before agreeing to endorse an incumbent senator seeking reelection (Thompson, 1946). The implication was that the ILWU would fill in the date and submit the senator's resignation whenever the ILWU leadership felt that he no longer represented their interests. It is unclear whether this was standard practice before awarding endorsements or simply was a device designed for one particular legislator with an anti-labor record.

Labor Legislation

Labor influence, particularly that of the ILWU, was the major factor bringing about the passage of the Hawaii Employment Relations Act in May, 1945.

However, it should be noted that capital did not fight very hard against it. They confined their efforts to getting "union responsibility" clauses incorporated along with "union rights" provisions. It would appear that the NLRB ruling which classified between 50 and 60 percent of plantation employees as industrial workers made it less meaningful for capital to resist the incorporation of agricultural workers into labor unions. They appeared to prefer the strategy of limiting the scope of union activities and preventing inroads on their flexibility to manage and run the industry as they saw fit. The growing strength of labor, both at the point of production and at the polls, made this course of action preferable to one which would lead agricultural capital to repeat the type of mistakes that brought on the wave of mainland strikes between 1935 and 1938 and which eventuated in indictments for unfair labor practices.

The "Little Wagner Act" extended to agricultural workers in Hawaii all rights granted to industrial workers by the Wagner Act. It also provided for the establishment of an Employment Relations Board which was charged with enforcing the provisions of the Act. This Act was the first state or federal legislation granting agricultural workers the legal right to bargain collectively and join unions of their own choosing. The legislature also passed other legislation favorable to organized labor, including that which brought agricultural workers under the purview of the provisions of the wage and hours law (Hartung, 1948:35). The legislature established a minimum wage of 40 cents which more than doubled the lowest wage previously paid to plantation employees (19 cents per hour).

This sequence of events demonstrates the wisdom of Hawaiian labor's decision, unlike that of mainland unions, to wage a simultaneous struggle at the point of production and at the level of the state. The ILWU involved its membership in electoral politics, cooperated with dissident Democrats, was able to uproot the hegemonic political rule of the agricultural capitalists, and get legislation passed which aided their struggle at the point of production. Agricultural capital did not resist these legislative gains as intransigently as capital had resisted the passage of the NIRA, partially because of the tremendous growth in the strength of American labor between 1934 and 1945 and partially because of labor's organizational strength in Hawaii. The demonstrated ability of labor to punish recalcitrant capitalists eased the way for the ILWU in Hawaii. Hawaii's capitalists concluded that they could retain more of their wealth and privilege by gracefully accepting unionization when it was no longer possible to exclude organized labor. The ILWU was more able than unions on the mainland to retain its radical, leftist, leadership throughout the war and the immediate post-war years. Consequently, they were better prepared to conduct a well-designed and effective political struggle. Victory over capital at the level of the state was soon translated into additional labor victories at the point of production, but this did not mean that capital was defeated and the class struggle over. Capital simply turned to different weapons and waged the battle in an intensified manner.

The political victory of the ILWU altered the nature of the political bargaining process in Hawaii. In some ways, the political victory of the ILWU was made possible because of the total hegemony of agricultural capital as the *only* fraction within the power bloc. Racial and class contradictions peaked during World War Two. The state apparatus was reorganized during the 1940s in such a way as to represent the changing balance of class forces in Hawaii. The ILWU's political campaign and the concommitant struggle of Japanese war veterans within the Democratic Party served to dismantle the political hegemony of the sugar interests. Consequently, the state was *able* to represent the balance of class forces thereby temporarily resolving racial and class contradictions.

Victory for the ILWU

The passage of the Little Wagner Act solved most of the remaining organizational problems for the ILWU (Aller, 1957:60-61, 77-80; Marutani, 1970:61-63; Brooks, 1952:99-100). Agricultural capital, through the Hawaiian Employers' Council, determined that there was no point in dragging their heels with regard to the recognition of unionization for agricultural employees. Meanwhile, the ILWU intensified its activities among agricultural workers. By August, 1945, they claimed to represent the agricultural employees on 30 plantations. In September negotiations began on an industry-wide contract. Agricultural capital was willing to trade union recognition and some wage increases for the acceptance by the ILWU of certain traditional management prerogatives. The contract was written to apply to nonagricultural employees. It called for a seven cent hourly wage increase, a grievance procedure, annual vacations, a definition of working conditions, the joint development of an industry-wide job classification system, and the extension of contract coverage to agricultural employees when and wherever cross checks confirmed that a majority of such employees were members of the ILWU.

These cross checks brought into the ILWU agricultural employees on every plantation on which the ILWU had succeeded in organizing the non-agricultural workers plus those at Waiakea where the AFL had organized the nonagricultural workers. Thus the ILWU had a power base on 32 of the 34 plantations. Only those workers at Waiamea and Gay and Robinson—two very small plantations—remained outside the fold. At the same time, the ILWU used the Fair Labor Standards Act as a basis for a court suit asking that the sugar industry be compelled to pay workers approximately $1,000,000 in unpaid overtime wages for the period between 1938 and 1945, inclusive. The ILWU managed to get $1,800,000 as settlement of their claim. Aller assesses the net impact of these gains for labor as follows:

> These dramatic events, coming suddenly after a century of employer controls, shook the community to its roots. Viewed from island eyes, a revolution had occurred—a revolution that had greatly weakened the power of the ''Big Five'' and raised a new power to the fore.

In a sense, it was an enduring revolution, since the union was a new power center that
remained powerful. But it was not as revolutionary as first appeared. No major battles had
yet been fought, and the respective strengths could not be appraised. The employers as a
group had seen the handwriting on the wall, made the necessary minimum concessions,
thereby riding out the first full tide of popular discontent, and in retreating, conserved
their forces for battles on issues they considered essential to survival. (1957:61).

It is hardly surprising, in light of the social context, that the 1946 sugar
negotiations would prove to be a test of strength between agricultural capital
and the ILWU (Brooks, 1952:133-162; Brissenden, 1956:9-15; Aller, 1957:
81-90; Marutani, 1970:65-70). The climate of opinion did not favor the
conclusion of the contract without a strike. Many segments of agricultural
capital did not believe that the ILWU could maintain its strength throughout a
prolonged strike. This belief was partially based upon the multi-racial composition of the ILWU and the historically demonstrated fragility of such
alliances in Hawaii. They also believed that they had a powerful threat to use
against labor in that a large portion of ILWU's membership resided in
company-owned homes which provided for the possibility of eviction. At the
same time, a wave of strikes on the mainland combined with some dissatisfaction over the modest level of gains made in 1945 created a strike propensity
among the workers.

Negotiations began on July 11, 1946. Agricultural capital presented a united
front despite some internal disagreements. Some elements in the industry
opposed an industry-wide job classification system, but the majority favored it
as a rationalization of the wage structure. The union which had initially
supported the notion began to have second thoughts. They questioned whether
it was enough to simply revise the existing structure, as opposed to scrapping it
and starting from scratch. Sugar interests also disagreed over the desirability of
eliminating the perquisite system. The union was adamant in its insistence that
it be scrapped to free labor of any and all vestiges of paternalism. Some
elements of capital wished to retain it for control purposes, others for humanitarian reasons, but the majority accepted the necessity to give way on the
matter. The most persuasive argument being provided by the federal enactment
of the Fair Labor Standards Act in November, 1945, which would have
required that the value of perquisites be included in all calculations of
overtime. The sheer complexity of that suggested that the rational course of
action for capital was to make a one-time determination of the value of
perquisites, eliminate them, and eliminate the continuing necessity to determine the value of perquisites time and time again in the future. Management,
through the HEC, determined that its best course of action was to abandon the
perquisite system, but to do so as cheaply as possible.

Negotiations over these issues were prolonged and difficult and were made
more complex by ILWU's demand for a union shop and management's unwillingness to consider establishing one. The strike began on September 1, 1946.

Some 28,000 workers on 32 of the 34 plantations walked out. Negotiations were conducted both privately and through the press in an attempt to sway public opinion. Capital publicly fought against the tyranny of the union shop, but the union had privately agreed to compromise on the union shop issue within two weeks after the strike began. The union publicly "exposed" the horrible conditions of plantation housing and tried to gain public support for the elimination of the perquisite system. However, management had already come to the conclusion that the system must go and had communicated this to the union. The ILWU also had publicly charged capital with attempting to break the union. This charge received support in the statement made by Federal Conciliator Stanley V. White when he withdrew from participation in the negotiations:

> I would have to conclude that no matter how costly it might be, the goal upon which you [agricultural capital] had fixed was the extermination of unionism on these islands (quoted in Johannessen, 1956:121).

It is probable that White overstated the case. It appears that the real fight was more of a straightline battle over wage costs, distribution of wage increases, and other economic issues, although a small segment of agricultural capital held out some hope of destroying the ILWU. As the strike wore on, labor remained relatively united, while cracks began to appear in the solidarity of capital. Plantations on the Island of Hawaii did not need irrigation and could therefore withstand the loss of labor, especially as the strike came during a slack work period. They were willing to hold out indefinitely. Other plantations used supervisory personnel, protected by labor injunctions, to irrigate their cane. They were experiencing some losses, but they could hold out for an extended period. However, Castle and Cooke wished to avoid giving any provocations which might cause violence. Their losses were heavy and they pushed for an early settlement. Finally, Castle and Cooke threatened to make its own private settlement if the industry could not agree on an industry-wide contract. A contract was signed and the strike ended on all except one of the plantations on November 19 after a duration of 79 days. A job classification system was agreed to, perquisites were eliminated, and their cash value was translated into a wage increase. An additional general wage increase was granted. It was generally conceded that the ILWU had won a resounding victory.

> Though the union conceded many issues—the union shop and representation of the supervisors were of importance to management—the end of the strike represented a remarkable union victory. In its first test of strength, the union emerged as the winner with its ranks intact. This display of strength not only frightened the industry, but it also made the union seem invulnerable in the eyes of other workers and the general public. For a time it appeared not only to the union leaders but to virtually everyone else in the community that the "Big Five" had been replaced by the "Big One," the ILWU. (Aller, 1957:89).

Rationalization of Production

Labor had waged a successful simultaneous struggle at the level of the state and at the point of production. They achieved favorable legislation, unionization, higher wages, and better working conditions. However, this should not be taken to mean that capital was helpless or that it abandoned the class struggle. It still could strike back through a reorganization of the labor process. Agricultural capital had always had an abundant supply of cheap, controllable labor. Thus agricultural capital had little incentive to rationalize production. All technological progress was aimed at increasing per acre yields through improved fertilizers, rodent control, improved varieties of cane, and improved techniques of cultivation and harvest (Sullivan, 1970:77-78; Mollet, 1961:62, 65). There was very little in the way of labor-saving equipment used prior to the depression-cause labor shortage in the late thirties. Even then, there were only very modest experiments along these lines. Labor now had ceased to be either cheap or controllable. It was in capital's best interests to change from a labor-intensive to a capital-intensive industry and they did so in a remarkably short period of time. Table 1 illustrates the dramatic increases which took place in the amount of total capital invested per worker, the amount of capital invested in equipment and power per field worker, the amount of net output per worker, and the amount of sugar handled per field worker.

Table 1.   Comparison of Rates of Increase in Level of Capital Investment and Worker Output: Hawaiian Sugar Plantations, 1900-1957

Years	Total Physical Capital per Worker[a]	Net Output per Worker[a]	Equipment and Power per Field per Worker[a]	Sugar Handled per Field per Worker[b]
1900-1940[c]	1.0	1.0	1.0	1.0
1940-1945	0.9	1.8	—	—
1945-1950	13.7	11.9	19.8[d]	6.3[d]
1950-1957	12.4	10.3	19.6	14.7

[a]adjusted to a constant work year of 2,000 hours and computed in terms of 1910-1914 dollars.

[b]adjusted to a constant work year of 2,000 hours and computed in terms of tons per year.

[c]all computations use 1900 to 1940 changes as index number of 1.0.

[d]1940 to 1950 change, mid-decade data not available.

Source: Adopted from Geschwender and Levine (1980; Table 1).

These changes were accompanied by a dramatic decrease in the number of persons employed in the sugar industry, a significant increase in the proportion of employees engaged in supervisory or other salaried positions, a dramatic decrease in the proportion of workers engaged in the least skilled and most degrading types of work activities, and a concommitant increase in the production of workers engaged in more skilled and more satisfying work activities

(Marutani, 1970:130; Beaumont, 1956:95-96). These Hawaiian experiences correspond to two general tendencies. The first is for plantation agriculture to be slow to mechanize so long as cheap labor is available but to do so rapidly when labor becomes scarce and/or expensive (Mandle, 1978:52-70; Rosenberg, 1968). The second is the general tendency for capital to offset the hard-won gains achieved through the struggles of organized labor by mechanization and otherwise rationalizing production (see Kriesberg, 1973:283).

CONCLUSION

What we have attempted to do in this paper is to explore the nature of class struggle and to examine its relation to rationalization of production. Class struggle takes place at many levels simultaneously. We have concentrated upon two of these: class struggle at the point of production and class struggle at the level of the state. We have demonstrated that the two are intrinsically linked. Working class victories at the point of production give added impetus and strength to working class struggles at the level of the state and working class gains at the level of the state in turn feed back upon and reinforce struggles at the point of production.

Levine (1980) has documented the manner in which struggles of the mainland unemployed stimulated the Black "Thirty Hour Bill" and made it possible to gain the inclusion of section 7a in the National Industrial Recovery Act (NIRA). These successes fed back upon and intensified the CIO organizational drives and other struggles at the point of production. The growing strength of labor and capital's fear of intensified violence combined to bring about the passage of the National Labor Relations Act (the Wagner Act) and the establishment of the National Labor Relations Board. This insured industrial workers the right to freely organize and to bargain collectively. Capital may have acquiesced in the passage of this act in an attempt to circumscribe the growing strength of labor, but its passage was, nevertheless, a victory for organized labor. It provided the contest for expanded organizational work and significant gains by labor.

The growing strength of labor on the mainland and the protection provided by the Wagner Act formed the context within which working class struggle in the Territory of Hawaii could take place. The hegemonic control of capital and the unified nature of Hawaiian capital created an obstacle to working class gains which was much more formidable than that faced by labor on the mainland. It is highly improbable that labor could have been successful in its struggle in Hawaii if the way had not been paved by labor on the mainland. The working class struggle in Hawaii was a two-pronged effort—simultaneous struggle at the point of production and at the level of the state. Each effort lent strength to the other, much in accordance with the mainland experience. Gains were made in organizing plantation workers who could be classified as industrial and who fell under the purview of the Wagner Act. These organizational gains facilitated the struggle at the level of the state and eventuated in the passage of the Little Wagner Act, which made possible the total organization of agricultural labor, regardless of the nature of the job performed.

Capital appeared to be defeated at both the point of production and at the level of the state. However, this was more appearance than reality. The working class made tremendous gains but capital had its fallback position. They shifted their attention to a speedup of the process of rationalizing production. Production, previously labor-intensive, rapidly became capital-intensive and the size of the work force was reduced. Labor continued to struggle in the context of contract negotiations and strikes to improve wages, working conditions and job security. But they also struggled to minimize the degree of negative impact that capital's response to labor's collective gains might have upon individual workers.

Class Struggle and the State

We have demonstrated that class struggle is a continuing process that takes place at many levels and which changes in form and content over time. In addition, our analysis has implications regarding the most useful conception of the nature of the state and the most useful manner of viewing rationalization of production.

In the pre-World War Two years, the Hawaiian Territorial State was firmly under the control of the ''Big Five.'' The dismantling of the hegemonic control of sugar interests and the consequent transformations within the state in the years following World War Two can best be analyzed within a structuralist conceptualization of the state apparatus. In short, the transformation of the Hawaiian state was shaped by the class struggle. The state, through state policy, did not represent the interests of a single class or fraction, but rather represented the changing balance of class forces in post-World War Two Hawaii.

Our analysis of the class struggle in Hawaii, which eventually led to the passage of the Little Wagner Act, implicitly provides a critique of the pluralist and instrumentalist conceptualizations of the nature of the state apparatus. Prior to World War Two, the state apparatus was firmly controlled by agricultural capital through the political apparatus of the Republican Party. The Republican party at this time was the political arm of the power bloc. The experience of Japanese-Americans in the United States armed forces and the experience of workers during the war period served to heighten both class and racial contradictions within the political terrain. The combination of the political struggle of the ILWU and Japanese-American war veterans within the Democratic Party served to undermine the political hegemony of agricultural capital and effectively displace the Republican Party. The challenge to the political hegemony of agricultural capital was made possible because racial and class contradictions could no longer be resolved, even temporarily, under the total political domination of one fraction of capital. Because the capitalist state apparatus reflects the balance of class forces at a particular historical conjuncture, the Republican Party could no longer, in the years following World War Two, solely disperse class and racial contradictions into conflicts between political parties.

Pluralist conceptualizations of the state argue that policies are the outcome of competing interest groups that place pressure on state officials to enact policy in their favor. While one could argue that the Little Wagner was a result of pressure brought to bear on state legislators by organized labor, the passage of the Little Wagner Act can not solely be understood in the context of a neutral state mediating between labor and capital in the "interest" of labor. Clearly, the state did not mediate neutrally prior to 1945! To argue that organized labor became a political interest group in the post-War period in Hawaii and was able to push through policy in its favor because the state ruled in neutral form, ignores both the manner in which *economic* struggles of labor in Hawaii reinforced *political* struggles, and the manner in which working class struggles on the mainland during the 1930's created the context for working class struggle in Hawaii.

Put briefly, the decline of the hegemonic political control of agricultural capital through the Republican Party did not occur because state officials realized that agricultural labor needed protection from agricultural capital. Rather, the enactment of the Little Wagner Act was the consequence of a strong labor movement which potentially threatened both political stability and continued capital accumulation in the Hawaiian Islands. Agricultural capital, through its agents in the state administration, realized the growing strength of labor at the polls and in the fields, did not wish to repeat the mistakes of mainland capitalist which brought on a wave of strikes between 1935 and 1938, and sought to limit the scope of union activities rather than to prevent unionization altogether. The passage of the Little Wagner Act was brought about both by the demands of a strong, politically anti-capitalist labor movement which took advantage of victories gained by labor on the mainland and the response of an oligopolistic capitalist class which wished to retain conditions favorable to continued capital accumulation.

Moreover the alliance of the Japanese-American veterans and the ILWU in reviving the Democratic Party would have been inconceivable if it were not for the experience of World War II. By arguing that the state is a subject, which adjudicates neutrally between competing interest groups, pluralist conceptualizations of the state lead to a failure to examine the complexities of the larger historical scene and to analyze the relationship between *economic* struggles and *political* struggles. By ignoring the class character of the state apparatus and the specifically *capitalist* class relations of capitalist society, pluralist modes of the state obscure the manner in which opposition political groups come into being, and the manner in which the balance of class forces change and are changed.

Instrumentalist conceptualizations of the state argue that state policies are understood in terms of the instrumental exercise of power by economic elites, either directly or indirectly through the exercise of pressures on the state administration (Miliband, 1969). While it is true that this model may be able to explain Hawaiian economic and social policy *prior* to World War II, instrumentalist conceptualizations of the state are incapable of generating adequate explorations of the events in Hawaii during the post-war years. To argue that the economic elite designed the Little Wagner Act to channel working class struggle within limits compatible with capitalist political domination, ignores the crucial fact that capital experienced serious setbacks. These political setbacks for the Republican Party resulted in Democratic control of the Hawaiian state administration which still continues to this day. Moreover, the political hegemony of agricultural capital was *challenged and defeated*. Since the state continued to function as a capitalist state (i.e., maintain conditions for profitable accumulation of capital and maintain capitalist relations of production), state policies must be a result of more than the conscious intentions of its controlling managers.

The instrumentalist model of the state is based on a critique of pluralism. As such, it does not adequately conceptualize the nature of the state. The state cannot be understood as a simple tool or instrument in the hand of the ruling class. Our analysis bears this out. Rather, the state represents the balance of class forces in a particular historical conjuncture. State activity is not simply explained as the amount of political pressure capitalists place on state administrators. State activity is located in the *total field of class struggle* and within the confines of the *social relations of production*. The state is not an object or a subject to be used by, or act in, the interest of a ruling elite. Rather, the state "is the *specific material condensation* of a relationship of forces among classes and class fractions" (Poulantzas, 1978:12-14).

We have argued in this chapter that the nature of the state can best be conceptualized within the framework of a structuralist perspective. In order for it to aid in the reproduction of a capitalist social relations of production, the state apparatus must maintain social peace and harmony. Through state labor policies, it attempts to prevent the political organization of the working class. State policies attempt to structure working class political practices so as to acccommodate them within existing political structures and within channels that are compatible with existing relations of production and class domination. The state apparatus is able to aid in the reproduction of capitalist social relations of production by managing through a variety of institutional mechanisms to *convey the image* of an organization of power which pursues the common and general interests of "society" as a whole, allows equal access to power and is responsive to "justified" demands (Offe, 1974). However, state policies are not implemented according to any pre-established functional harmony, but in and through the struggle of antagonistic classes (Therborn, 1978:144-148).

The political struggle of the ILWU in Hawaii led to the passage of the Little Wagner Act. Wages and working conditions improved and the dominance of the state apparatus by a single fraction of capital was ended. The transformation within the Hawaiian state structure resulted in the incorporation of the working class into the political bargaining process. The struggle of the ILWU changed the *political* character of the state, although it never was able to challenge its *class* nature. The gains made by the working class on the political terrain resulted in improved wages and working conditions. Capital responded to working class political gains by rationalizing production and transforming the labor process on the plantation. One phase of class struggle ended— another began.

This chapter has argued that we must bring class struggle back into our analysis and give it its deserved central place. The class struggle is an ongoing dynamic which takes place on many levels and at many places. We must pay as close attention to class struggle at the level of the state as we do at the point of production. The case study described herein illustrates the importance of examining class struggle waged by labor as part of the dynamic precipitating management rationalization of production rather than as a simple product thereof. This case study also illustrates the importance of taking the socio-historical context into explicit account. Our findings suggest that it is an open question as to whether rationalization leads to deskilling and degradation of labor. It may under some circumstances and may not under others, depending upon the socio-historical context.

ACKNOWLEDGMENT

We are deeply indebted to Charles P. Larrowe, who so generously shared with us his own research notes, and to Carol Schwartz, Librarian at the ILWU Archives in San Francisco, who was generous with her time and energy in providing valuable help in our research endeavors. The data upon which this paper is based was gathered as part of a larger project that was supported by Grant No. 18479 awarded by the Center for the Studies of Metropolitan Problems, National Institute of Mental Health. An early draft of a portion of this paper was presented before a seminar of the Institutional Racism Project at the University of Hawaii. The authors greatly benefited from comments made by seminar participants—most notably those of Ed Beechert and Kiyoshi Ikeda.

REFERENCES

Allen, Gwenfread
   1950   Hawaii's War Years, 1941-1945. Honolulu: University of Hawaii.
Aller, Curtis
   1957   Labor Relations in the Hawaiian Sugar Industry. Berkeley: University of California.

Anthony, J. Garner
   1955   Hawaii Under Army Rule. Stanford: Stanford University.
Bachrach, Peter, and Morton Baratz
   1963   "Decisions and non-decisions." American Political Science Review 57 (September): 632-642.
Beaumont, Richard Austin
   1956   Productivity and Causes of Productivity Change, Honolulu: University of Hawaii, unpublished Ph.D. dissertation.
Berman, Edward
   1937a   "Report on Hawaiian labor movement." August 30. ILWU Files, ILWU Organization, Hawaii Correspondence, Reports, etc., 1937-43. ILWU Archives, San Francisco.
   1937b   "The situation at present in the Hawaiian Islands." October 4. ILWU Files, ILWU Organization, Hawaii Correspondence, Reports, etc., 1937-43. ILWU Archives, San Francisco.
Bouslog, Harriet, and Meyer C. Symonds
   1948   "Memorandum on history of labor and the law in the territory of Hawaii." Brief submitted in ILWU vs. Walter D. Ackerman, Jr. in United States District Court for the Territory of Hawaii, August 24.
Brissenden, Paul
   1956   The Labor Injunction in Hawaii. Washington: Annals of American Economics.
Brooks, Philip
   1952   Multiple Industry Unionism in Hawaii. New York: Columbia University, unpublished Ph.D. dissertation.
Dahl, Robert
   1967   Pluralist Democracy in the United States. Chicago: Rand McNally.
   1968   Preface to Democratic Theory. Chicago: University of Chicago Press.
The Dispatcher
   1944   July 17
Egan, E.J.
   1937   Report to Bertram Edises. Twentieth Region National Labor Relations Board.
Fuchs, Lawrence H.
   1961   Hawaii Pono. New York: Harcourt, Brace and World.
Geschwender, James A.
   1981   "The interplay between class and national consciousness: Hawaii 1850-1950," In Richard L. Simpson and Ida Harper Simpson (Eds.), Research in the Sociology of Work, Vol. I. Greenwich, Ct.: JAI Press.
Geschwender, James A., and Rhonda Levine
   1980   "State policy and rationalization of the labor process: the case of the Hawaiian sugar industry." Paper presented at the Labor Process Conference, Santa Cruz, March 14-16.
Goldblatt, Louis
   1944   Letter to Frank Thompson, November 14. Frank Thompson Files, ILWU Local 15 Archives, Honolulu, Hawaii.
Hall, Jack
   144   Letter to Louis Goldblatt, October 23. ILWU Archives, San Francisco.
Hartung, Bruno J.
   1948   A Study of Changes in Employment Conditions Among the Sugar Workers of Hawaii. Washington, D.C.: Catholic University of America, unpublished Ph.D. dissertation.
Hawaii ILWU Conference Minutes
   1944   September 16-17. ILWU Archives, San Francisco.

Johannessen, Edward
  1956   The Hawaiian Labor Movement: A Brief History. Boston: Bruce Humphries.
Kriesberg, Louis
  1973   Sociology of Social Conflicts. Englewood Cliffs, N.J.: Prentice Hall.
Kurita, Yayoi
  1953   ''Employer's organization in Hawaii.'' Labor Law Journal 4 (April): 280-284.
Larrowe, Charles P.
  1972   Harry Bridges: The Rise and Fall of Radical Labor in the United States. New York:
           Lawrence Hill.
Lasswell, Harold
  1966   The Analysis of Political Behavior. Hamden, Ct.: Anchor Books.
Levine, Rhonda
  1980   Class Struggle and the Capitalist State: The National Industrial Recovery Act and the
           New Deal. Binghamton: State University of New York, Binghamton, unpublished
           Ph.D. dissertation.
Lind, Andrew
  1938   An Island Community: Ecological Succession in Hawaii. Chicago: University of
           Hawaii Press.
Mandle, Jay R.
  1978   The Roots of Black Poverty: The Southern Plantation Economy After the Civil War.
           Durham: Duke University Press.
Marglin, Steve
  1974   ''What do bosses do? the origins and functions of hierarchy.'' The Review of Radical
           Political Economy 6 (Summer):60-112.
Marutani, Herbert K.
  1970   Labor-Management Relations in Agriculture: A Study of the Hawaiian Sugar In-
           dustry. Honolulu: University of Hawaii, unpublished Ph.D. dissertation.
Miliband, Ralph
  1969   The State in Capitalist Society. New York: Basic Books.
Millis, Harry A., and Emily Clark Brown
  1950   From the Wagner Act to Taft-Hartley. Chicago: University of Chicago.
Mollett, J.A.
  1961   ''Capital in Hawaiian sugar: its formation and relation to labor and output, 1870-
           1957.'' Agricultural Economics Bulletin, No. 21, Hawaii Agricultural Experiment
           Station. University of Hawaii.
  1962   ''Capital and labor in the Hawaiian sugar industry since 1870: a study of economic
           development.'' Journal of Farm Economics 44 (May): 381-88.
  1965   ''The sugar plantations in Hawaii: a study of changing patterns of management and
           organization.'' Agricultural Economics Bulletin, No. 22, Hawaii Agricultural Ex-
           periment Station, University of Hawaii.
Morgan, Theodore
  1948   Hawaii: A Century of Economic Change. Cambridge: Harvard University.
Offe, Claus
  1974   ''Structural problems of the capitalist state.'' Pp. 31-57 in Von Beyme (Ed.), German
           Political Studies Beverly Hills: Sage.
Parry, Geraint
  1969   Political Elites. New York: Praeger.
Polsby, Nelson
  1963   Community Power and Political Theory. New Haven: Yale University Press.
Poulantzas, Nicos
  1978   State, Power, Socialism. London: New Left Books.

Rose, Arnold
  1967   The Power Structure: Political Process in American Society. New York: Oxford
          University Press.
Rosenberg, Nathan
  1969   "The direction of technological change: inducement mechanisms and focusing
          devices." Economic Development and Cultural Change 18 (October):1-24.
Slate, Daniel M.
  1961   Monopsony in the Labor Market: A Case Study of the Hawaiian Sugar Industry.
          Seattle: University of Washington, unpublished Ph.D. dissertation.
Smith, Jared Gage
  1942   The Big Five. Honolulu: Honolulu Advertiser.
Sullivan, Michael
  1970   Economic productivity, Urbanization and Technological Development in Hawaii,
          1900 to 1970. Honolulu: University of Hawaii, unpublished M.A. thesis.
Taylor, William H.
  1935   The Hawaiian Sugar Industry. Berkeley: University of California, unpublished Ph.D.
          dissertation.
Therborn, Goran
  1978   What Does the Ruling Class Do When It Rules? London: New Left Books.
Thompson, David E.
  1964   "The ILWU mechanization and modernization agreements" Pp. 4-7 in Harold S.
          Roberts (Ed.), Automation: Some of Its Effects on the Economy and Labor.
          Honolulu: University of Hawaii, Industrial Relations Center.
  1966   "Agricultural workers made it in Hawaii." Labor Today 5 (October-November):24-
          29.
Thompson, Frank
  1944a   Letter to Louis Goldblatt, September 30. ILWU Archives, San Francisco.
  1944b   Letter to Louis Goldblatt, November 13. ILWU Archives, San Francisco.
  1946   Letter to Louis Goldblatt, July 29. Frank Thompson Files, ILWU Local 142 Ar-
          chives, Honolulu.
Truman, David
  1951   The Governmental Process: Political Interests and Public Opinion. New York: Alfred
          Knopf.
Van Zwalenburg, Paul R.
  1961   Hawaiian Labor Unions Under Military Government. Honolulu: University of
          Hawaii, unpublished M.A. thesis.
Wason, James R.
  1966   Legislative History of the Exclusion of Agricultural Employees from the National
          Labor Relations Act 1935 and the Fair Labor Standards Act of 1938. Washington,
          D.C.: The Library of Congress Legislative Reference Service, May 19.
Weaver, Samuel
  1959   Hawaii, U.S.A.: A Unique National Heritage. New York: Pageant.
Weiner, Merle
  1978   "Cheap food, cheap labor: California agriculture in the 1930's." Insurgent Sociol-
          ogist 8 (Fall): 181-190.
Wright, Theon
  1972   The Disenchanted Isles: The Story of the Second Revolution in Hawaii. New York:
          Dial.

EXPANSION OF CONFLICT
IN CANCER CONTROVERSIES

James C. Petersen and Gerald E. Markle

Disputes in medicine have a political character much as do disputes over the distribution of tax dollars or other valued goods. Nowhere is this clearer than in controversies over cancer etiology or cancer therapy. Only recently, however, have scholars begun to explore the political aspects of cancer and cancer policy (e.g., Strickland, 1972; Rettig, 1977; Epstein, 1978, and Studer and Chubin, 1980). In this paper we examine five cancer-related conflicts in order to explore the processes by which such disputes become politicized. In considering and assessing the ongoing history of each dispute we focus on the role of vested interests, social movements, organizational participation, governmental involvement, as well as the role of knowledge claims and value claims. We then show how the case studies illustrate and strengthen various themes in the social movements literature, focusing particularly on recent studies in resource mobilization. We thus view this paper as an intermediate step toward the development of a theory of conflicts in medicine.

Research in Social Movements, Conflict and Change, Volume 4, pages 151-169
Copyright © 1981 by JAI Press Inc.
ISBN: 0-89232-234-9

It should not be surprising that cancer-related disputes—both those over possible carcinogens and those over therapies—are frequently more prominent in the public arena than are other medical disputes. While cancer is now the second leading cause of death in the United States, it is the most feared disease by a wide margin. The widespread concern over cancer has led to political action. In his 1971 State of the Union address, President Richard M. Nixon declared ''war'' on cancer and proclaimed:

> The time has come in America when the same kind of concentrated effort that split the atom and took man to the moon should be turned toward conquering this dread disease. Let us make a total commitment to achieve this goal (quoted in Rettig, 1977).

This commitment to cure cancer, now embodied in the National Cancer Act, led to great optimism (or ''overpromising'' [Kennedy, 1978] in the words of the former FDA Commissioner) in the professional and lay literature. For example, the American Cancer Society claims that: ''Cancer is one of the most curable of the major diseases in this country'' (Greenberg, 1975a). Throughout the early 1970s, however, five-year survival rates did not improve; in fact, with a few exceptions, they remained constant (Greenberg, 1975a; Enstrom and Austin, 1977). By the mid 1970s, the National Cancer Act and the bureaucracy which administered it had come under attack (Rettig, 1977). J.D. Watson, the Nobel laureate, has assailed the war on cancer as scientifically bankrupt, therapeutically ineffective and wasteful (cited in Greenberg, 1975b). ''By comparison with the fight against polio,'' asserts the former FDA Commissioner, ''the war on cancer is a medical Vietnam'' (Kennedy, 1978).

It seems today that there is disagreement among cancer specialists on almost everything from theory to therapy. To cite only a few examples, recent debate has taken place on the efficacy of surgery for early breast (Atkins, et al., 1972) and prostate (Byar, 1972) cancer, combined radiation therapy for cancer of the bile duct (Ingis and Farmer, 1975), and chemotherapy for a variety of gastrointestinal cancers. Even programs for the early detection of cancer have come under attack with the charge that x-ray screening procedures may increase the likelihood of cancer (Greenberg, 1977).

RESOURCE MOBILIZATION

In recent literature on social movements a resource mobilization theory has been developed. This framework begins with the assumption that society is composed of competing groups. Group conflict and the emergence of social movements are analyzed in terms of the abilities of the groups to create and mobilize resources. While medicine-related conflicts have not previously been studied within this framework, we feel an examination of resources and mobilization strategies will illuminate important features of the cancer conflicts. Further, an examination of this previously neglected form of social conflict may point out resources previously ignored by resource mobilization theorists.

Resources have been defined as " . . . anything from material resources—jobs, income, and the right to materials, goods and services—to nonmaterial resources—authority, moral commitment, trust, friendship, skills, habits of industry, and so on" (Oberschall, 1973:28). Some resources such as money are especially valuable since they are liquid (easily converted to other resources) while other resources such as task skills are much less liquid. Resources, while necessary, remain but a potential until mobilized in conflict.

In arguments predating resource mobilization theory, Schattschneider (1960) asserted that the main struggle in politics is over the scope of the conflict because the outcome of every conflict is established by the extent to which the audience participates in it. He further asserted that the likely winners of a dispute will try to limit the scope of the conflict while the likely losers will try to expand the dispute. Thus many ideas and arguments which emerge in conflicts are best understood as attempts to manipulate the scope of the conflict and thus determine the outcome of the dispute. Political history is made by the struggle between forces urging the privitization of conflict and those pushing for its socialization. Victory, however, is not automatic; nor is defeat inevitable. Rather each side attempts to convert available resources into tactical or strategic gain.

The resource mobilization literature (e.g., McCarthy and Zald, 1973 and 1977; Oberschall, 1973; and Barkan, 1979) has reached similar conclusions. This body of work stresses that movements which pose little threat of disruption and/or have a low level of internal resources have the greatest need for external support. Movements with a need for external support can be expected to try to form coalitions, seek sponsorship, and appeal to a wider audience (thus expanding the conflict) as a means of increasing their movement resources. The resource mobilization literature also emphasizes the role of strategy and tactics in effectively allocating movement resources (Barkan, 1979:19). A dynamic element is introduced into the analysis since the focus is on resources mobilized by groups in response to the employment of resources by the opposition group. Authorities as well as challengers possess resources; deployment by one side requires some kind of response (mobilization of additional resources) from the other side, lest the cause be defaulted.

Kriesberg's (1973) work on the sociology of social conflicts provides further detail about mechanisms involved in the escalation and de-escalation of conflict. Though Kriesberg considers both the social psychological and social organizational mechanisms which produce escalation, his discussion of social organizational factors is most relevant to our analysis. Within conflicts, he notes, issues often expand from the specific to the more general; moreover subgoals of the antagonists lead to the emergence of additional issues in the conflict. Another dynamic of conflict is polarization, wherein adversaries become isolated from another and neutrality becomes more problematic.

Finally escalation may produce intervention, drawing third parties into the conflict, and thus altering the balance of resources.

New work on technology disputes has recognized the importance of expansion of conflict. Mazur (1981) argues that technology protest movements, such as the anti-fluoridation and anti-nuclear protest, may go through a series of three successive steps. First, some warning about a technology is brought to the attention of the public, frequently through the mass media. Second, the warning becomes a cause for a limited group of activists. Finally, the conflict expands into a mass protest movement.

The foregoing literature should provide a framework for examining conflicts in medicine. How is the availability of resources, and the mobilization of such resources, related to the expansion of conflict? How are scientific findings (knowledge claims) and socio-political ideologies (value claims) related to the shape and scope of the controversy? By examining a type of social conflict previously ignored by resource mobilization theorists, we hope to discover additional resources and strategies relevant to understanding social conflict.

SELECTION OF THE CASES

Some disputes about cancer-related problems originate in the lay community; others arise as disputes among experts within the cancer-related professions. Conflicts which emerge at one locus may be expanded toward the other by appealing to various interests—economic, moral, occupation, political, or scientific. Thus some cancer-related conflicts move from the medical community into the public arena, while in others scientists are latecomers to expanding disputes that emerged among nonmedical specialists.

Five controversies—5 fluorouracil (FU), ascorbic acid (Vitamin C), estro.-en replacement therapy (ERT), saccharin and Laetrile—were selected to represent different types of conflict. In brief, FU is routinely used as a chemotherapeutic agent for colorectal cancer; recently, however, its efficacy has been questioned. Vitamin C has been used in the treatment and palliation of cancer; the orthodox medical community opposes this treatment. ERT is commonly used to treat postmenopausal symptoms, but many now argue that the treatment increases the risk of cancer. Saccharin is an artificial sweetener which, some charge, also increases the risk of cancer. Finally Laetrile, a derivative of apricot kernels, is said to prevent and control cancer; few medical experts or authorities support this claim.

We chose these particular controversies to study for several reasons. All are contemporary, on-going social disputes. Though we lack a historical perspective and can only speculate on the final outcome of each case, there are advantages in focusing on contemporary controversies which override these limitations. The archival and documentary sources, particularly fugitive materials, have not eroded. Moreover, access to key actors is possible.

In an analytic sense, the five cases considered here seem to vary independently on the three dimensions shown in Table 1. Three of these controversies— FU, Vitamin C and Laetrile—though different in so many ways, are substances which are used to treat cancer. In the remaining two disputes—ERT and saccharin—the substance purportedly causes cancer.

FU and ERT are similar in that both substances are generally used and endorsed by the medical community. On the other hand, medical orthodoxy opposes the use of Laetrile and Vitamin C in cancer therapy. The status of saccharin in this categorization is ambiguous. Though opposed by some authorities, it is—perhaps because it is an additive and not a drug—ignored by most.

Table 1. Selected Characteristics of the Cases

Case Study	Treatment/Cause	Medical Community: Endorsed/Opposed	Challenge: Innovative/Revisionist
FU	Treatment	Endorsed	Revisionist
Vitamin C	Treatment	Opposed	Innovative
ERT	Cause	Endorsed	Revisionist
Saccharin	Cause	?	Revisionist
Laetrile	Treatment	Opposed	Innovative

Finally we want to draw a distinction between "innovative" and "revisionist" controversy. In the former, exemplified by Vitamin C and Laetrile, proponents want to introduce something new into the system. In the latter, such as with FU, ERT and saccharin, proponents want to revise the system by expunging an element already in use. This basic inertial criteria, the difference between introducing innovations and opposing that which exists, as with our other two analytic dimensions, is bound to shape the socialization, expansion and politicization of controversy in science and technology.

Our most compelling reason for choosing these controversies is that they all show different degrees of politicization. FU is not, at this time, politicized; rather the dispute is between experts and there is no public involvement. The Vitamin C controversy is also one between experts, though the expert proponent is from outside the medical community. As of 1980 the dispute, though not confined solely to the medical community, is minimally politicized. The ERT controversy is being played out in the feminist, as well as the medical community and has thus become moderately politicized. With congressional action exempting saccharin from regulatory control, that controversy has become highly politicized. And finally the Laetrile controversy, with the substance now legal in 22 states, has been described as "the unorthodox brand-name health promotion generating the largest amount of public furor in the nation's history" (Young, 1980:11).

THE CASE STUDIES

Most analyses of social conflict have focused on the import of value claims. However, in scientific and technical conflicts, knowledge claims, as well as value claims, appear to play an important role. In previous work (Petersen and Markle, 1979a; Markle and Petersen, 1980), we have found it useful to focus on both value claims and knowledge claims as mechanisms for politicizing conflict. Table 2 presents quotations illustrating knowledge and value disputes for each of our five controversies.

Fluorouracil

5-fluorouracil, a fluorinated pyramidine which acts as an antimetabolite in inhibiting DNA synthesis, is commonly used to treat colorectal cancer (for a pharmacological review, see Goodman and Gillman, 1970:1365-1369). Developed in 1957, the drug was reviewed by the National Academy of Science in

Table 2.   Knowledge and value claims for the cases: selected quotations

Fluorouracil

Knowledge controversy

> The evidence is overwhelming that flourouracil and its nucleoside, floxuridine, are worthless as surgical adjuvants for colorectal cancer (Moertel, 1976).

> The present data indicate that flourouracil chemo-prophylaxis offers a significant improvement of five-year cure rates of patients with stage II and III [colorectal cancer] (Li and Ross, 1976).

Value controversy

> Patients with advanced gastrointestinal cancer and their families have a compelling need for a basis of hope. If such hope is not offered, they will quickly seek it from the hands of quacks or charlatans (Moertel, 1978:1051).

> We should stop deceiving the patients and face up to reality. To do less is to be a charlatan or a quack (Fitzgerald, 1979:436).

Vitamin C

Knowledge controversy

> There is little doubt, in our opinion, that treatment with ascorbate in amounts of 10g/day or more is of real value in extending the life of patients with advanced cancer (Cameron and Pauling, 1978).

> [We] cannot recommend the use of high-dose vitamin C in patients with advanced cancer . . . (Creagan et. al., 1979).

Value controversy

> Why does the government permit the drug industry to further toxic chemotherapy, when a natural and nontoxic form of chemotherapy, Vitamin C, is promising, readily available and cheap. (Stein and Day, publishers of *Vitamin C Against Cancer*.)

> It seemed quite ludicrous to suggest that this simple, cheap, harmless powder, which could be bought in any drugstore, could possibly have any value against such a bafflingly complex and resistant disease such as cancer (Cameron and Pauling, 1979:129).

Saccharin

Table 2 (*continued*)

Knowledge controversy

> Based on human data, we do not believe saccharin is a potent carcinogen for humans, if it is one at all (Guy Newell, Deputy Director of NCI, 1977).

> I think the data are pretty convincing that saccharin is carcinogenic (David Rall, Director of the National Institute of Environmental Health Sciences, 1977).

Value controversy

> I believe that, because of the division in the scientific community, . . . because of the genuine uncertainty on each side of the risk/benefit equation, the individual ought to be fully informed and than allowed to make a personal decision (Senator Edward Kennedy, 1978).

> By delaying a regulatory restriction on the use of saccharin in the food supply, Congress is risking the public health for the benefit of large economic interests (Senator Gaylord Nelson, 1978).

Estrogen

Knowledge controversy

> Women who take estrogen for relief of menopausal symptoms are several times more likely to develop cancer of the uterine lining than are comparable women not using the drugs (Kolata, 1976).

> Nobody has shown a cause-and-effect relationship between Premarin and cancer. It does not cause cancer. It just accelerates it (Ayerst Laboratory Vice President, 1977).

Value controversy

> Estrogen: The hormone that makes women more curvy, more female, and more responsive to men (Cosmopolitan, 1979).

> Estrogen pills are not a sexual godsend, helping menopausal "eunichs" satisfy their husbands (Solomon, 1972).

Laetrile

Knowledge controversy

> We generally say that a patient who has clinical cancer will be regulated or controlled with 50 grams of Laetrile. That is about 17 to 20 injections of three grams each (John Richardson, MD, n.d.).

> The use of Laetrile rather than known, effective cancer treatments is the cruelest of all frauds (Robert Eyerly, MD, Chairman, the Committee on Unproven Methods of Cancer Management. The American Cancer Society, 1976).

Value controversy

> These are bad times for reason, all around. Suddenly, all of the major ills are being coped with by acupuncture. If not acupuncture, it is apricot pits (Lewis Thomas, President, Memorial Sloan-Kettering Cancer Center, 1977).

> You people in authority consider all the rest of us a bunch of dummies . . . You set yourself up as God and Jesus Christ all rolled up into one. And we don't have any rights . . . as Patrick Henry said, "Give me liberty, or give me death." Glenn Rutherford says let me choose the way I want to die. It is not your prerogative to tell me how. Only God can do that (Rutherford, 1977).

158 JAMES C. PETERSEN and GERALD E. MARKLE

1970 and found to be "effective" for the palliative management of carcinoma of the colon or rectum. On 12 January 1978, the FDA approved an injectable form of FU, concluding that the drug was "safe and effective".

FU is an extremely toxic substance. Hoffman LaRoche, one manufacturer, issues the following "warning": "Although severe toxicity is more likely in poor risk patients, fatalities may be encountered occasionally even in patients in relatively good condition." Both Hoffman LaRoche and Adria Laboratories list common adverse reactions to FU which should induce extreme caution toward its use.

Recently doubt has been cast on the efficacy of FU, principally by Charles C. Moertel, Director of the Mayo Comprehensive Cancer Center. According to Moertel (1978:1049), "There is no solid evidence that treatment with fluorinated pyrimidines contributes to the overall survival of patients with gastrointestinal cancer regardless of the stage of the disease at which they are applied." Over and above reporting such negative findings, Moertel has, for several years, delivered anti-FU sermons to the medical community. Thus:

> To insist on 5-FU as standard therapy . . . offers precious little to today's patient and is a distinct disservice to tomorrow's patient (Moertel, et al., 1974).

And, in summarizing five studies which show no efficacy for FU, Moertel concludes that:

> . . . one can only hope that the good judgment of the American physician will dissuade him from treating thousands of postoperative colon cancer patients with this toxic drug in the misinformed belief that it will provide them with therapeutic benefit (Moertel, 1976: 1936).

Thus has Moertel argued against FU. But the dispute has, so far, been confined to pages of technical journals such as *The New England Journal of Medicine*, the *Journal of the American Medical Association* and *Cancer Chemotherapy Reports*. We do not read about the FU debate in newspapers or news magazines; no congressional hearings have been held on the issue. Religious or political opposition has not developed. No social movement organizations are not involved, and there seem to be no ties to social movements in American society. In short, the dispute has remained within the medical community.

The FU controversy remains a dispute among experts because Moertel has explicitly attempted to frame the dispute in the narrowest terms. After concluding, in 1978, that all chemotherapy, including FU, was worthless against gastrointestinal cancer, Moertel remarkably concluded that:

> By no means, however, should this conclusion imply that these efforts should be abandoned. Patients . . . and their families have a compelling need for a basis of hope. If such hope is not offered, they will quickly seek it from the hands of quacks or charlatans (Moertel, 1978:1051).

That statement, nor surprisingly, has engendered ethical objection, as quoted in Table 2. Whether this debate will move from the pages of medical journals to the pages of newspapers cannot be predicted with certainty. In considering the available resources; however, we suggest that Moertel who possesses considerable personal and institutional prestige, as well as strong empirical evidence, may expect to win this dispute without expanding the conflict. Those lacking such impressive resources might be more likely to broaden the conflict by appealing to possible allies among opponents of orthodox medicine.

Vitamin C

Though vitamins have been used to treat cancer for several decades, the current controversy over Vitamin C has its roots in a 1966 book written by Ewan Cameron, a Scottish physician. Entitled *Hyaluronidase and Cancer*, the monograph presented, ''a new theory on the causation of cancer . . . concerned with the relationships which exist between cells and their immediate environment'' (1966:1). Cancer cells, he wrote, release the enzyme Hyaluronidase which destroys the substances which hold normal cells together. Cameron suggested that reducing hyaluronidase production or strengthening cellular cement would greatly inhibit the growth of malignancies. Some years later Linus Pauling suggested that Vitamin C might strengthen this cellular cement, chiefly composed of collagen, ''in the same way as . . . steel rods in reinforced concrete'' (Cameron, 1979a:118). Cameron read about Pauling's thesis in a newspaper and initiated a correspondence which resulted in a collaboration between the two men.

Throughout the 1970s Cameron and Pauling conducted clinical studies in Scotland. In the most widely quoted study one hundred terminal cancer patients were given 10 grams of ascorbic acid per day, and matched with 1,000 patients who had received no Vitamin C. The researchers now claim that:

> The ascrobate treated patients were found to have a mean survival time about 300 days greater than that of the controls. Survival times greater than one year after the date of untreatability were observed for 22% of the ascorbate-treated patients and for 0.4% of the controls (Cameron and Pauling, 1978:4538).

Moreover eight of the patients treated with Vitamin C are still alive, some 3.5 years after untreatability.

In 1973, Linus Pauling asked the National Cancer Institute to carry out a double-blind clinical trial of Vitamin C. NCI declined to sponsor such a study but, in 1978 reversed itself and arranged for a clinical trial under the direction of Charles Moertel (see Cameron and Pauling, 1979b:133-134). Whereas the Cameron-Pauling study had used historical controls—comparing patients currently receiving treatment matched with survivorships of patients from an earlier period—the Moertel group used concurrent controls. This latter design is more expensive and ambitious, but also more trustworthy than an historical design. Comparing 60 ascorbate-treated patients with 63 control patients, the authors conclude that they "cannot recommend the use of high-dose Vitamin C in patients with advanced cancer who have previously received irradiation or chemotherapy" (Creagan, et al., 1979).

Cameron and Pauling (1979b:143) have criticized the Mayo study. Whereas most Mayo patients had previously received chemotherapy, such drugs, the authors claim, are rarely used in Scotland. Such differences are crucial, they claim, because chemotherapy may depress the body's ability to utilize ascorbic acid.

The Vitamin C controversy has to some degree become politicized. As an off-shoot of the controversy over Vitamin C and the common cold, this controversy moves into a pre-existing public arena. Perhaps because of the widespread interest in Pauling's previous book, *Vitamin C and the Common Cold*, there has been substantial popular media coverage of the newer Vitamin C controversy. In addition, key actors and voluntary association involved in orthomolecular medicine and the holistic health movement have lent support to Pauling. Also some organizations from the "cancer underground" (Markle, et al., 1978) have advocated the use of Vitamin C along with other alternative cancer treatments. However no organizations exist which are solely devoted to the promotion of Vitamin C in cancer therapy.

It is instructive to compare and contrast the FU and Vitamin C controversies. Both are led by one man; each is well known: Moertel as a respected oncologist and Pauling is winner of two Nobel prizes. In our terms Moertel is a revisionist. As an "insider" in the medical community he has attacked the use of FU, but at the same time has made no effort to expand the debate beyond the medical community. Pauling holds an intermediate position: though a distinguished scientist, he has no credentials in medicine or clinical oncology. An innovator in our terms, he has begun to expand the controversy. In November of 1979, for example, the Linus Pauling Institute of Medicine published a book, *Cancer and Vitamin C*, written for the general public. This book may lead to the further politicization of the controversy.

Estrogen Replacement Therapy

Though estrogen replacement has been prescribed by physicians for more than thirty years, routine therapy with conjugated estrogens dates from about 1965. By 1975 an estimated 5 million women, or 13 percent of all women between the ages of 45 and 64, were on estrogen replacement therapy (Pfeffer, 1977). Used for the relief of menopausal symptoms and related problems such as osteoporesis, ERT has become big business. By 1975 sales were some $80 million, 80 percent of which comes from sales of Premarin by Ayerst Laboratory.

The general association between any estrogen therapy and uterine cancer has long been noted (Gusberg, 1947 and see Goodman and Gillman, 1975 for a review). Recent work has claimed that the relationship is quite strong. In 1975 independent studies at Washington Medical School, Kaiser Permanente Medical Center and University of California, Irvine Medical School found that women on ERT are 4 to 14 times more likely to develop cancer of the uterine lining than are comparable women not using the drug (for a review see Kolata, 1976).

These studies have been attacked for a variety of methodological reasons (Hulka, et al., 1978; Feinstein and Horowitz, 1979). Among the criticisms are that women who receive estrogen come under greater diagnostic surveillance from their physicians so that a cancer is more likely to be found. Moreover sloppy method and misdiagnosis are also charged. Finally, as noted in the preceding controversies, all research protocols have used historical controls. However one recent study, though using historical controls, has attempted to address the methodological limitations of previous studies. In this research, Antunes, et al. conclude that "endometrial carcinoma was sixfold for estrogen users as compared with nonusers" (1979:9). As might be imagined, however, this latest study has not satisfied critics.

Unlike the FU debate, and to some extent the Vitamin C issue, the ERT controversy has been widely publicized, particularly in traditional women's magazines. In 1977, for example, Vogue Magazine printed a special Consumers Union Report on the dangers of ERT. Sometimes such magazines show ambivalence toward the dispute. A Cosmopolitan article, for example, called estrogen "The hormone that makes women more curvy" on its November, 1979, cover; the article inside, however, was subtitled: "The estrogen crisis."

The ERT controversy has become politicized over ideological as well as medical conflicts. Feminists have never been comfortable with Robert A. Wilson's initial justification of ERT. In his 1966 book, *Feminine Forever*, Wilson claimed that menopause is a malfunction which threatens the feminine essence. ERT, he claimed, could save women from being "condemned to witness the death of their womanhood" (1966:66).

A 1972 *Ms* article, written before the current medical evidence against ERT was uncovered, maintained that menopause was not a traumatic experience for most women, but rather a sexually liberating one. ERT, as indicated by the Solomon quote in Table 2, is seen as a male misunderstanding and even exploitation, of female sexuality. In more recent years, with both medical and ideological reasons for opposing ERT, feminist criticism has become widespread. The controversy receives a 70-page analysis titled "Promise Her Anything But Give Her . . . Cancer," in a 1977 book, *Women and the Crisis in Sex Hormones*, by Barbara and Gideon Seamon. And two articles in *Majority Report* entitled "New Discovery: Public Relations Cures Cancer" and "But You'll Make Such a Feminine Corpse," make the same point.

In our scheme, the ERT controversy holds an intermediate position in that it has expanded in both directions: from the medical to the lay community, and from voluntary associations to experts. Whether or not estrogen replacement causes cancer, a technical dispute, has been widely debated and publicized in the media, particularly within traditional women's magazines. At the same time the controversy seems to have grown independently out of feminist ideology. Such books as *Our Bodies, Ourselves*, published by the Boston Women's Health Collective, played a role in focusing medical attention toward the problems of ERT. Thus the ERT controversy, unlike the dispute over FU and to a greater degree than the Vitamin C debate, has been moderately politicized. A coalition of voluntary action groups, mostly feminist, have become active ideological opponents of the use of estrogen for menopausal relief.

Saccharin

Saccharin is a nonnutritive and noncaloric artificial sweetener which packs considerable economic wallop. In 1976 an estimated 70 million Americans, including a high proportion of teen-agers, consumed saccharin products with a value of some $2 billion. Each year about 7 million pounds of saccharin are used in foods, 75 percent of which goes in diet soft drinks (each bottle contains about 150 mg. of saccharin). In 1978 some 883 million cases of diet soda were sold, up 10 percent from 1977. Moreover the proportion of soft drinks which are dietetic has risen throughout the late 1970s, from 12.1 percent in 1974 to 16.6 percent in 1978 (Frazzano, 1978). The drug is used in a wide variety of other products. A 1977 survey by the Pharmaceutical Manufacturers Association shows that 619 products, ranging from chewable aspirin to oral antibiotics, contain saccharin (Chemical Week, 1977). Finally an estimated $53 million in television and $20 million in radio advertising would be lost in the event of a ban on saccharin products (Broadcasting, 1977). From these data it is obvious that a controversy over saccharin would have an impact on the political economy.

The controversy over saccharin is an old one. Saccharin and benzoate of soda were the first two substances proposed for a ban under the provisions of the first Pure Food and Drug Act, passed in 1906. As a response to this proposal, Theodore Roosevelt asserted that "Anyone who says saccharin is injurious to your health is an idiot" (quoted in Levine, 1977). As early as 1948 a study sonsored by the FDA implicated saccharin as a cause of lymphosarcoma in rats. And several studies from the 1950s to the early 1970s indicated that saccharin intake was related to a wide variety of tumors, particularly of the bladder, in rodents. Even as early as 1971, some prominent scientists were asking: 'Should Saccharin Be Banned?'' (American Druggist, 1971). In fact in 1972 the FDA removed saccharin from its GRAS (generally recognized as safe) list.

In spite of these earlier studies and warnings, the contemporary controversy broke with a March 1977 Canadian study which purported that large doses of saccharin caused bladder tumors in rats. The FDA then invoked the ''Delaney Clause'' which mandated that after a 60 day waiting period, saccharin would be banned. To explore the politics of saccharin during early 1977 would require a separate paper. Suffice it to say that, after hearings in the U.S. House and Senate, Congress postponed the FDA ban for 18 months. When the moratorium expired in 1979, the FDA announced that it would take no action on saccharin for at least one year.

The saccharin dispute has become highly politicized through a broad coalition of the soft drink industry, representatives of diet clubs, diabetics, and wide public activity. The controversy has received much attention in the mass media as well as trade journals. This coalition has been encouraged by disputes among experts. The strongest claim against saccharin is that it is a weak carcinogen. This had led Congressman Andrew Jacobs to facetiously ''warn'' that ''the Canadians have determined that saccharin is dangerous to your rat's health.'' Some experts, including officials of the National Cancer Institute maintain that saccharin's carcinogenicity is unproven. In fact studies by the National Academy of Sciences in 1955, 1969 and 1975 have concluded that saccharin use is not a health problem in the United States. And in 1977 the American Cancer Society stated that ''Banning saccharin may cause great harm to many citizens while protecting a theoretical few'' (Culliton, 1977). A new NAS study, however, has concluded that saccharin is a weak carcinogen in animals and a potential carcinogen in humans.

An important part of the political and medical debate over saccharin centers on ethical questions (see Lepkowski, 1977 and Havender, 1979). The issue is ''freedom of choice.'' Should a well informed adult, the argument goes, be allowed to assess his or her own risk in product consumption? Or does the government, as part of its mission to protect the citizenry, assume that responsibility? Unlike a controversy over, say, air pollution, where the consumer has no choice over which air to breathe, saccharin is said to be a ''user-risk'' situation. This argument, which touches strongly held values in America, is likely to be effective in the political and scientific struggle over saccharin. Havender (1979:23) has made the point dramatically by noting:

why, for example, do we find ourselves serenely contemplating a person's plan to climb a dangerous peak at the same time that we propose making it illegal for her to buy a can of Tab?

It seems clear that the saccharin controversy originated within the medical community—several times, in fact. The dispute has become highly politicized as a protective reaction by powerful vested interests which have successfully exploited the freedom of choice issue, and the ambiguity of the scientific evidence, to forestall federal regulation of saccharin.

Laetrile

We have written extensively on the Laetrile dispute (Markle and Petersen, 1980; Petersen and Markle, 1979a and b), one of the most politicized medical disputes in American history. Amygdalin, the chemical name for Laetrile, was first isolated in the 1830s and was apparently used in cancer therapy as early as 1843. The current controversy may be traced back to 1952 when Ernst Krebs, Jr. produced Laetrile from an extract of apricot kernals. Two years earlier Krebs and two colleagues had published a paper, "The Unitarian or Trophoblastic Thesis of Cancer," (Krebs, Krebs, and Beard, 1950) which provided a theoretical basis for Laetrile therapy.

The medical community responded to the Laetrile challenge with a series of laboratory studies on rodent tumor systems. Each claimed that Laetrile had no efficacy. But each, particularly a series of studies at Sloan-Kettering, was itself surrounded by charges of misrepresentation. In 1977 a Loyola biologist (Manner, 1977) claimed that Laetrile dramatically reduced tumors in mice. Though the study was scientifically deficient, it received front-page newspaper coverage.

The Laetrile controversy has been politicized by a broad coalition of groups devoted to Laetrile and other alternative cancer treatments, holistic and nontraditional medicine, health food and nutritional groups, and right-wing politics. The specific issue joining these divergent forces has been "freedom of choice." As we have noted in the saccharin dispute, this issue of the right of user-risk is a powerful one in a democratic society. Indeed, in direct contravention to the FDA, twenty-three states have legalized Laetrile. (Even so, no Laetrile is legally produced in the U.S.).

Several voluntary associations with widespread grassroots membership support the Laetrile movement. Three of the largest, The Committee for the Freedom of Choice in Cancer Therapy, The Cancer Control Society and The International Association for Cancer Victims and Friends, devote most of their agenda to Laetrile. These three organizations regularly publish magazines which publicize the Laetrile cause. In addition broader purpose organizations such as the National Health Federation actively support the movement.

In 1979 we wrote that Laetrile had become a "household word." A 1977 Harris Poll showed that three-quarters of all Americans had heard of Laetrile and two-thirds favored enactment of pro-Laetrile legislation in their own states. In the late 1970's the controversy was the subject of hundreds of news stories, including a Newsweek cover, and the subject of popular culture. Johnny Carson included Laetrile jokes in his monologue and cartoonist Gary Trudeau depicted the character Duke planning to make a fortune by buying an apricot farm and marketing the pits in Tijuana.

We have previously argued (Petersen and Markle, 1979a:149-151) that the Laetrile dispute began within, or at least at the edges of, the scientific community. Only when the use of Laetrile was prohibited, and only when Laetrile advocates were prosecuted, did a social movement form around the drug. Thus, the dispute expanded from the scientific to the lay community, and then back again in an iterative manner, to produce an intense social and scientific controversy.

DISCUSSION

Sociologists have previously paid little attention to cancer-related disputes. Much sociological literature on social problems and social movements is, however, relevant in understanding these disputes. In our examination of five cancer-related disputes, we find that conflicts are expanded and politicized as actors in the dispute seek to gain greater resources to improve their chances of victory. Given the role of the FDA in approving new drugs, it is frequently one of the original disputants in innovative conflicts. In revisionist conflicts the disputants may force the government into the controversy as part of an effort to politicize the dispute.

Other organizational actors have played key roles in the most politicized conflicts—Laetrile, ERT, and saccharin. At the core of the Laetrile movement are a set of voluntary associations devoted almost solely to the promotion of Laetrile. ERT, however, is one of a number of health-related feminist issues. While most feminist organizations have opposed the routine use of estrogen replacements, a few have given it central attention. For example, the Women's Hormone Information Service has given the ERT controversy considerable attention in its newsletter *Whistlestop*.

In contrast, economic organizations such as trade associations for the diet and soft drink industry were prominent actors in the saccharin dispute. Such vested interests seem to be especially important in revisionist controversies such as saccharin when the existence of a product for a period of time has permitted the development of strong financial interests.

The Vitamin C and FU disputes, on the other hand, show no important organizational involvement. Rather in both disputes the personal prestige of the challenger—Pauling and Moertel—is the major resource. In the case of Vitamin C, the larger orthomolecular and health food movements have also served as resources.

All of our disputes seem to begin over knowledge controversies. Knowledge claims may escalate into public disputes or they may stay dormant for a long period of time. Knowledge claims related to cancer etiology and therapy are frequently ambiguous. For example, the debate over dose-response curves for carcinogens has developed the "intensity of a jihad," according to Maugh (1978:37). There is little hard scientific evidence to support either the view that there are safety thresholds for carcinogens or the view that even low doses of carcinogens are harmful (for the difficulties of estimating cancer risks from radiation see Land, 1980).

Resource mobilization theory has ignored the role of knowledge claims as resources in social conflicts. Laboratory studies, clinical findings, epidemiological data, and expert opinion all are important resources (see Nelkin, 1975) which might be mobilized in social controversies. Our case studies offer evidence that such resources have been mobilized and played crucial roles in the cancer-related disputes.

For a controversy to expand into a public dispute, it must, in part, be recast as an issue of values. Whether value controversies arise naturally out of a dispute, or whether they are tactical devices of the disputants, is probably unimportant. What is important is that the value claim is consistent with prominent social values. Thus in our two most politicized cases, saccharin and Laetrile, appeals are made to "freedom of choice," an ideal consistent with the dominant American value of individualism. Our least politicized disputes, FU and Vitamin C, do not as yet have a strong value component. Finally, the intermediate politicization of ERT represents a successful value appeal to feminist interests.

Taken as a group of related controversies, the case studies demonstrate the utility of resource mobilization theory for the analysis of medical conflicts. The particular details of how resources have been mobilized varies from case to case. The expansion of disputes, however, is patterned. Those motivated to expand the scope of disputes can do so only if resources are available and successfully mobilized.

REFERENCES

American Druggist
    1971   Should Saccharin be Banned. (May 3):41.
Antunes, C., P. Stolley, R. Rosenheim, J. Davis, J. Tonascia, C. Brown, L. Burnett, A. Routledge, M. Pokempner, and R. Garcia
    1972   "Endometrial cancer and estrogen use." New England Journal of Medicine 300: 9-13.
Atkins, H., J.L. Hayward, D.J. Klingman, and A.B. Wayte
    1972   "Treatment of early breast cancer: a report after ten years of clinical trial." British Medical Journal 20:423-429.
Barkan, Steven E.
    1979   "Strategic, tactical and organizational dilemmas of the protest movement against nuclear power." Social Problems 27:19-37.
Broadcasting
    1977   "Build-up on both sides over possible ban for saccharin." (July) 11:14.
Byar, D.P.
    1972   "Survival of patients with incidentally found microscopic cancer of the prostate: results of a clinical trial of conservative treatment." Journal of Urology 108:909-913.
Cameron, Ewan
    1966   Hyaluronidase and Cancer. New York: Pergamon Press.
Cameron, Ewan, and Linus Pauling
    1978   "Supplemental ascorbate in the supportive treatment of cancer: re-evaluation of prolongation of survival times in terminal human cancer." Proceedings of the National Academy of Sciences 75: 4538-4542.

Cameron Ewan, and Linus Pauling
    1979a   "Ascorbate and cancer." Proceedings of the American Philosophical Society. 123:
             117-123.
Cameron, Ewan, and Linus Pauling
    1979b   Vitamin C and Cancer. Menlo Park: Linus Pauling Institute of Medicine.
Chemical Week
    1977   Saccharin Ban Modified. (April) 20:19.
Creagan, E.T., C.G. Moertel, J.R. O'Fallon, A.J. Schutt, M.J. O'Connell, J. Rubin, and S.
        Frytak
    1979   "Failure of high-dose vitamin C, (Ascorbic Acid) therapy to benefit patients with
            advanced cancer: a controlled trial." New England Journal of Medicine (September
            27).
Culliton, Barbara
    1977   "Cancer Society takes pro-saccharin stand." Science 196:276.
Enstrom, J. E., and D.F. Austin
    1977   "Interpreting cancer survival rates." Science 195:847-851.
Epstein, Samuel
    1978   The Politics of Cancer. San Francisco. Sierra.
Feinstein, A.R., and R.I. Horowitz
    1979   "A critique of the statistical evidence associating estrogens with endometrial can-
            cer." Cancer Research 38:4001-4005.
Fitzgerald, Joseph C.
    1979   "Ethical questions in chemotherapy of patients with gastro-intestinal cancer." New
            England Journal of Medicine 300:436.
Frazzano, Joseph
    1978   "The 1977-78 diet soft drink market." Beverage World.
Goodman, Louis S., and Alfred Gilman
    1975   The Pharmacological Basis of Therapeutics. New York: Macmillan.
Greenberg, Daniel
    1975a   "Progress in cancer research—don't say it isn't so." New England Journal of
             Medicine 292: 707-708.
Greenberg, Daniel
    1975b   "The critical look at cancer coverage." Columbia Journalism Review (January/
             February).
Greenberg, Daniel
    1977   "The Unhappy Lessons of Cancer Politics (November 1)." Washington Post.
Gusberg, S.B.
    1947   "Precursors of corpus carcinoma estrogens and adenomatous hyperplasia." Ameri-
            can Journal of Obstetrics and Gynecology 54: 905-926.
Havender, William R.
    1979   "Ruminations on a rat: saccharin and human risk." Regulation (March/April):
            19-24.
Hulka, Barbara S., C.J.R. Hogue, and B.G. Greenberg
    1978   "Methodological issues in epidemiological studies of endometrial cancer and exo-
            genous estrogen." American Journal of Epidemiology 107:267-276.
Ingis, D.A., and R.G. Farmer
    1975   "Adenocarcinoma of the bile ducts: relationships of anatomic location to clinical
            features." American Journal of Digestive Diseases 20: 253-261.
Kennedy, Donald
    1978   "What animal research says about cancer." Human Nature (May) 84-89.
Kolata, Gina Bari
    1976   "Estrogen drugs: do they increase the risk of cancer." Science 191: 838-841.

Krebs, Ernst, Jr., et al.
    1950   ''The Unitarian or Trophoblastic Thesis of Cancer.'' Medical Record 163:149-174.
Kriesberg, Louis
    1973   The Sociology of Social Conflicts. Englewood Cliffs, N.J.: Prentice-Hall.
Land, Charles E.
    1980   ''Estimating cancer risks from low doses of ionizing radiation.'' Science 209: (12
            September) 1197-1203.
Lepkowski, Wil
    1977   ''The saccharin debate: regulation and the public taste.'' The Hastings Center Report
            7: 5-7.
Levine, Carol
    1977   ''The first ban: how Teddy Roosevelt saved saccharin.'' The Hastings Center Report
            7: 6-7.
Li, Min C., and Stuart T. Ross
    1976   ''Chemoprophylaxis for patients with colorectal cancer.'' Journal of the American
            Medical Association 235: 2825-2828.
Manner, Harold W.
    1977   ''The remission of tumors with Laetrile.'' presented at the annual meeting of the
            National Health Federation. Chicago.
Markle, Gerald E., and James C. Petersen
    1980   ''Politics, science, and cancer: the laetrile phenomenon.'' AAAS Selected Sympo-
            sium Series. Boulder: Westview Press.
Markle, Gerald E., James C. Petersen, and Morton O. Wagenfeld
    1978   ''Notes from the cancer underground: participation in the laetrile movement.'' Social
            Science and Medicine 12:31-37.
Maugh, Thomas H.
    1978   ''Chemical Carcinogens: how dangerous are low doses?'' Science 202: (October 6)
            37-41.
Mazur, Allan
    1981   The Dynamics of Technical Controversies. Communication Press.
McCarthy, John D., and Mayer N. Zald
    1973   The Trend of Social Movements in America: Professionalism and Resource Mobili-
            zation. Morristown, N.J.: General Learning Press.
McCarthy, John D., and Mayer N. Zald
    1977   ''Resource mobilization and social movements: a partial theory.'' American Journal
            of Sociology 82:1212-1241.
Moertel, Charles G.
    1976   ''Fluorouracil as an adjuvant to colorectal cancer surgery: the breakthrough that
            never was.'' Journal of the American Medical Association 236: 1935-1936.
Moertel, Charles G.
    1978   ''Chemotherapy of gastrointestinal cancer.''·New England Journal of Medicine 299:
            1049-1052.
Moertel, Charles G., A.J. Schutt, R.G. Hahn, and R.J. Reitmeier
    1974   ''Effects of patient selection on results of Phase II chemotherapy trials in gastro-
            intestinal cancer.'' Cancer Chemotherapy Reports 58: 257-259.
Nelkin, Dorothy
    1975   ''The political impact of technical expertise.'' Social Studies of Science 5:35-54.
Oberschall, Anthony
    1973   Social Conflict and Social Movements. Englewood Cliffs, N.J.: Prentice-Hall.
Petersen, James C., and Gerald E. Markle
    1979a   ''Politics and science in the laetrile controversy.'' Social Studies of Science 9:139-
            166.

Petersen, James C., and Gerald E. Markle
 1979b "The laetrile controversy." In Dorothy Nelkin (ed.), Controversy. Politics of Technical Decisions. Beverly Hills: Sage Publications.
Pfeffer, R.I.
 1977 "Estrogen use in postmenopausal women." American Journal of Epedimology
  105:21-29.
Rettig, R.H.
 1977 Cancer Crusade. Princeton, N.J.: Princeton University Press.
Schattschneider, E.E.
 1960 The Semi-Sovereign People. New York: Holt, Rinehart and Winston.
Solomon, Joan
 1972 "Menopause: a right of passage." Ms (December) 16-18.
Strickland, S.P.
 1972 Politics, Science and Dread Disease. Cambridge,Mass.: Harvard University Press.
Studer, Kenneth, and Daryl Chubin
 1980 The Cancer Mission: Social Contexts of Biomedical Research. Beverly Hills, Ca.:
  Sage Publications.
Wilson, Robert A.
 1966 "Estrogen: a key to staying young." Look Magazine (January): 66-73.
Young, James Harvey
 1980 "Laetrile in historical perspectives." Pp 11-60 in G. Markle and J. Petersen (ed.),
  Politics, Science and Cancer: The Laetrile Phenomenon. Boulder, Co.: Westview
  Publishers.

THE MIAMI RIOTS OF 1980:
ANTECEDENT CONDITIONS, COMMUNITY RESPONSES AND PARTICIPANT CHARACTERISTICS

Robert A. Ladner, Barry J. Schwartz,

Sandra J. Roker, and Loretta S. Titterud

I. INTRODUCTION

The winter of 1968 marked the end of a half-decade of bloody and costly racial violence in the United States. During those five years, the violence had evolved from specific acts of terrorism in Birmingham and Selma to the epidemic of urban violence of the summer of 1967.

By 1968, the nation had begun a period of cautious optimism about the future of race relations. The racial disorders of the summer of 1968 were more sporadic and easily contained than the widespread riots of the previous year; the Kerner Commission had made recommendations to the Federal govern-

Research in Social Movements, Conflict and Change, Volume 4, pages 171-214
Copyright © 1981 by JAI Press Inc.
All rights of reproduction in any form reserved.
ISBN: 0-89232-234-9

ment and legislation was in progress under the Johnson administration. Elaborate plans were underway for the solution of the major racial problems of the 1900s: urban unemployment, substandard housing, poverty. Sociologists were sifting through data from Detroit and Watts, examining alternative theories regarding the epigenesis of urban unrest, and posing hypotheses about the personality of the rioter, relative deprivation and social disorganization.

And in Dade County, Florida, an area untouched by the urban violence of the decade, a public opinion poll was conducted in the black community by *The Miami Herald*. The major problems perceived by Miami blacks were "too many school dropouts," "parents don't control their children," and "dirty neighborhoods." Police brutality was mentioned as a serious problem by less than one black out of four. Yet there was tension: the massive Cuban immigration that had begun less than ten years earlier was creating competition for jobs and housing and resentment about government refugee benefits, and the overall levels of dissatisfaction expressed by Dade County blacks were actually higher than those expressed by Detroit blacks after the riots of 1967.

But there was no overt indication of strain. There was no rioting in Miami after Martin Luther King was murdered in April, and the racial disturbances that did take place elsewhere throughout the country were much less serious and more easily localized than the widespread riots of 1967. Even when three days of racial violence in Miami took three lives in Liberty City in August, it was easy to consider the disturbance an outgrowth of the presence of the Republican National Convention held at that time on Miami Beach.

Twelve years later, after an all-white jury in Tampa acquitted four white Dade County policemen in the beating death of Arthur McDuffie, a black man, three days of rioting in Miami shattered that calm. It was the first severe occurrence of collective racial violence that the nation had witnessed in more than a decade. Eighteen deaths and over $100 million in property damage made it the worst the nation had seen in the century.

The Miami rioting did more than disturb the belief that major urban disorders were a thing of the past, an outgrowth of 1960s activism that the country had outgrown. The riots pointed out that the social conditions that had given rise to the worst of the urban riots of the 1960s had not disappeared, and that community calm could not be taken as an indication of community complacency. In at least one American city, racial conflict capable of escalating into a full-scale riot had been growing steadily, even as it was being ignored: In how many other American cities were these same tensions brewing?

Less than two weeks after the curfews were lifted, research sociologists from the Behavioral Science Research Institute (BSRI), a private nonprofit social science research organization in Miami, conducted a series of face-to-face interviews with 450 residents of the riot area. This survey was substantially underwritten by *The Miami Herald*, and drew extensively on a body of data on both the attitudes of Miami blacks in 1968 and the attitudes of Detroit blacks immediately after the riots of 1967. As such, the survey was designed to allow fruitful comparisons in specific areas between post-riot attitudes in Detroit and in post-riot Miami, and between Miami black attitudes in the 1960's and post-riot attitudes in 1980.[1]

In this chapter, we will examine the Miami riots from several perspectives, presenting both historical data on the development of organizational and economic strains in the black community and contemporary data obtained from between the economic and social status and attitude structure of blacks in the BSRI survey. In doing so, we will illustrate some remarkable similarities Miami in 1980 and of blacks in other riot cities in the 1960s, and will show how a combination of rapid social change and economic competition from Cuban refugees laid the foundation for the riots.

II. THE RESEARCH CONTEXT

In the wake of the major urban riots of the 1960s, sociologists began to assemble the accumulating data on disorder and the characteristics of the people and situations that gave rise to them. Although early research efforts were directed toward identifying ideological and social characteristics of rioters themselves—the "rioter as deviant" school of thought (Caplan and Paige, 1968; Fogelson and Hill, 1968; Sears and McConahay, 1969)—it became evident that individualistic explanations did not account for the genesis of urban riots throughout the major northern cities. In effect, although the research indicated a social basis for the participation of certain kinds of people (predominantly unemployed, male and young) and for the timing and location of the riots (on weekends and at places where residents tended to congregate), none of these issues had anything to do with the question of why riots occurred in one city and not another. The mere presence of unemployed males on the street in naturally-occurring public areas did not mean that there would be another Watts or Detroit.

Accordingly, a second major set of theories was introduced into the literature. These theories were more concerned with the issue of discriminating riot cities from non-riot cities, rather than riot participants from non-participants, and ranged from predominantly structural (e.g., Spilerman, 1970; Jiobu, 1971) to those which were more oriented toward social process (e.g., Downes, 1968; McPhail, 1971). In general, these theories were used to characterize a particular city as (in Spilerman's terms) more or less "disorder-prone," and essentially drew upon four major schools of thought: disorganization, deprivation, frustrated expectation and political structure. These explanatory systems are of considerable relevance to an understanding of the Miami riots, and will be discussed in some detail here.

A. Social Disorganization

This approach accounted for urban violence on the basis of a lack of community integration, where community norms for behavior are weakened

constrained, and rioting and violence are predictable (Downes, 1968). Al-
and collective deviance replaces more formal ways of achieving goals. In cases
of rapid population change, for example, large increases in population or
radical differences in the racial composition of a neighborhood produce a
residential population that has not developed community ties and accepted
norms for social behavior. Under these circumstances, individual action is less
though there were indications that neighborhood characteristics were often
contributing factors, the relationship between structural indicators of disorganization and riot activity was never direct (Warren, 1970; Rossi and Berk,
1972; Spilerman, 1970). In Spilerman's analysis, for example, the magnitude
of the effect of social disorganization was reduced by half when the variance
associated with geographic region and percent nonwhite was entered into the
analysis. Downes (1968), in a review of earlier writings, suggested that much
of the variance associated with *disorganization explanations* could be ascribed
as easily to *deprivation explanations* (e.g., percent nonwhite, percent dilapi-
dated housing).

B. Economic Deprivation

The crux of deprivation models of riot activity is the concept of the disaffected underclass, either discontented because of their low status in absolute
terms (Lupsha, 1968; Downes, 1968; Geschwender and Singer, 1970), or
relative to another reference group (Gurr, 1968; Matza, 1966:622). Of the two
explanations, relative deprivation theories are generally seen as more powerful, linked to notions of intergroup competition, resentment, frustrated expectations and anger. Clearly, the "objective position" of blacks varies widely
from city to city and between neighborhoods within cities; an explanatory
system based solely on absolute conditions would have predicted rioting in
various cities at widely disparate points in time, rather than accounting for the
epidemic of violence in the mid-1960s.

With respect to black urban rioting, relative deprivation theories are not
complete until the reference group is specified: is the comparison with middle-
class whites, with bourgeois blacks, or with other immigrant groups (e.g.,
Cubans in Miami) who are seen to have prospered at the expense of black
economic progress? In addition, differences between the black population and
the reference group must be perceived and felt as frustrating by blacks themselves before the theory works: it is not enough that blacks are deprived relative
to a particular group. In order for discontent to be shared and to form the basis
for collective action, the group must be identified in the minds of the community (Williams, 1975: 147).

C. Frustrated Expectations

While relative deprivation theorists concentrate on a gap between the perceived progress of one group and the perceived progress of another, expecta-

tional theories refer to anticipated—and not realized—progress of a single group. In effect, the reference group that is the cause of the resentment is not an external reference group or other body, but the desired position of the discontented group itself, i.e., where it thinks it should be but isn't. When conditions are rapidly improving, or are supposed to rapidly improve, hopes for the future may outstrip reality, and anger and hostility produce a climate of discontent and riot (Berkowitz, 1968). In contrast to the relative deprivation theories, which postulate that the riot potential is greatest where the differences between underclass and reference group are greatest, riot theories based on frustrated expectations postulate just the opposite: riot potential is highest where the differences are smallest (Lupsha, 1968).

Again, however, the targets of the violence are not specified in the theory. Granted that there are frustrations in the inability of a group of people to close the perceived gap between where they are and where they feel they should be, this discontent—no matter how intense—is not alone sufficient to account for the incidence of rebellion. At what point, for example, does a group feel that further progress toward economic equity has been irrevocably blocked? Furthermore, what factors act to change a social perception that is highly individualistic in experience (i.e., the feeling that one is not where one should be in society) into riot activity which is largely collective (Feagin and Hahn, 1973; Rossi and Berk, 1972)? Although some process of geographic contagion may be seen as a means by which black rioting in one city can crystallize the frustarions of blacks in another city, the first riot still needs to be explained.

D. Political Structure

When the local political structure is seen as unresponsive to the needs of the governed, frustration with the system is more likely to take the form of collective revolt than conventional due process (Lieberson and Silverman, 1965). In effect, regardless of whether the "disorder-proneness" of the community is a function of social disorganization, absolute or relative deprivation or frustrated expectations, the unresponsiveness of the political system is seen as a necessary element in the genesis of a riot. In this formulation, urban civil disorders are not seen as unfocused acts of rage (characteristic of disorganization, deprivation and expectation theories), but have elements of political protest and become collective actions aimed at communicating a message and demanding change (Fogelson, 1971; Skolnick, 1969).

Although political structure theories are often quite argumentative and tend toward a subjective rather than objectively neutral explanations of riot behavior, they provide an important bridge between the existence of conditions which may be seen as precursors to a riot and the actual riot itself. In effect, the perception of the political system as being terminally unresponsive may well bring residents of a disorganized neighborhood to disruptive behavior, identify a target reference group and intensify feelings of relative deprivation, and convert individual feelings of frustration into collective action. It also accounts for the predominance of police/citizen conflict as the precipitating factor in urban riots: as the Kerner Commission report pointed out in 1968, the police are not only symbolic of the law but of the entire (arbitrary, repressive, unresponsive) political system as well (Kerner, 1968: 299).

III. DADE COUNTY: PRELUDE TO THE RIOT

Understanding the black riots in Miami demands more than a recitation of the litany of policy/community incidents that had taken place over the eighteen months previous. It is necessary to view Metropolitan Dade County and the City of Miami as a northern city in a southern setting, changing from a vacation and retirement area of less than one million residents in 1960 to a burgeoning urban community of over 1.8 million in 1980.[2] During those 20 years, Metropolitan Dade County had absorbed over 700,000 Cuban refugees, such that almost two out of every five persons in the County in 1980 were Spanish. In the 15 years from 1965 to 1980, Metropolitan Miami experienced the successive waves of urban decay, residential succession and migration, white flight and social service shortfalls that most American cities had taken 30 to 40 years to experience.

A. Dade County Demography

From its earliest days in 1896 when a few hundred residents were called upon to vote on incorporation and to choose a name for the city (interestingly, 162 of the 368 signators were black railroad workers, newly-enfranchised for the occasion, who later had their voting rights eliminated by the Florida legislature), the City of Miami and Dade County have grown primarily through extensive and steady in-migration. The large numbers of military brought into Miami during World War I, for example, was the beginning of a postwar boom that increased the population tenfold from its 1896 level of 3,000 residents to 30,000 in 1920. Although the depression resulted in a much slower population gain in the late 1920s and 1930s, Dade county had almost doubled in size by 1940.

Postwar migration dominated the decade of the 1940s, as the County population climbed to 495,000 in 1950; by 1960, Dade County had grown to 935,00 persons, an increase of almost 90% over the 1950s. The increases in population size were strongly influenced by migration of retired persons from the North, a pattern of persons leaving the East Coast and settling in Miami Beach, North Dade and other receptor areas in the County.

1. The Cuban Influx. The decade of the 1960s, however, brought about a significant change in the pattern of migration to Miami and to Metropolitan Dade County. After Fidel Castro's regime came to power in Cuba in 1959, more than 446,000 refugees entered the United States through Miami, almost five percent of the total population of Cuba. Many of these persons stayed in Dade County: the 1970 Census lists the Cuban population at 218,000 persons, fully 73 percent of Dade County's Latin population, and almost half of the entire Cuban population then in the United States.

The Cuban migration during the 1960s consisted of two waves of refugees, the first wave composed of relatively wealthy professionals who had the means to leave the country on their own when Batista was overthrown. Beginning in late 1965, the Freedom Flights allowed about a quarter of a million refugees to come to America (Clark, 1975). The airlift was accompanied by a massive relocation effort within the United States, as efforts were made to settle the refugees in major cities outside the Miami area. The exodus during these years tended to over-represent persons from the middle- and upper-middle classes, largely because these persons had the resources to endure from the time they announced their intention of leaving Cuba (and lost their jobs) and the time they actually left. Although relocation efforts were facilitated by this class difference, a sizeable proportion of the refugees remained in Dade County.

From 1970 to early 1980, there were essentially three Cuban migrant streams into Dade County. One group consisted of the last days of the Freedom Flights, which were ended in 1973; a second group consisted of boat-and-raft refugees, a steady trickle of desperate refugees with few resources, many of whom were farmers or fishermen in Cuba. The third group, by far the largest, consisted of persons who had been initially settled elsewhere in the United States, but who *returned to Miami when they had the opportunity*. This "returnee" trend began in the early 1970s and developed momentum rapidly: in 1972, an estimated 27 percent of the Dade County Cuban population were "returnees"; by 1978, a *Miami Herald* survey placed the figure at 40 percent (Levitan, 1980). In late 1980, a fourth stream of Cuban immigrants entered Dade County: the Mariel boatlift. During a period of less than 45 days, over 125,000 additional refugees entered Miami. In contrast to most of the earlier waves, these refugees were destitute and largely unskilled.

The Cuban influx from 1960 to 1975 had two principal effects on the demographic composition of Dade County. The primary effect was the "Latinization" of large areas of the County—predominantly in the City of Miami and Hialeah—within the span of about a decade. The second effect was indirect, in that this massive immigration was accompanied by a massive suburbanization, as thousands of non-Latin whites left the City of Miami and settled elsewhere in Dade County. Between 1965 and 1970 alone, over 103,000 non-Latin whites fled to the suburbs (Ladner, et al, 1976).

2. Effects on Black Neighborhoods. The rapid influx of Cuban refugees and returnees into the central Miami area did more than encourage white flight to the suburbs. Uban renewal of the black Overtown district in the downtown area was slated to begin in the 1960s, involving an extensive planned community revitalization program and slum clearance project timed to coincide with the construction of an interchange between the East-West Expressway and Interstate 95. This latter project involved multi-level aerial cloverleaves, requiring a large-scale land acquisition program by the State Highway Department. Between this construction and the projected urban renewal, about half of Overtown was razed by the early 1960s.

At that time, Overtown had been the cultural hub of the urban black population of Dade County, and had been a thriving religious, residential and commercial center. With the coming of urban renewal plans, a proportion of the residents took the initiative and moved several months before the land clearing began—sometime between 1958 and 1960. Residents with fewer resources waited until they were forced into relocation. Had it not been for the rapid influx of Cuban refugees into the transitional housing south of the Miami River, many of the Overtown residents could have relocated a relatively short distance into a downtown residential area immediately south of Overtown, a site now known as Little Havana. Church membership and business patronage would have continued and would have imparted both cultural and economic solidarity to the black community.

As it was, this migration was utterly blocked by the Cuban immigration. During the period from 1959 to 1965, almost one-third of the entire Cuban refugee population took up permanent residence in the City of Miami and settled in Little Havana. During that same period, virtually all of the Overtown evictions took place. Blocked by the Cuban influx to the south, Overtown blacks migrated north into Model Cities, Allapattah, Edison-Little River and other northern Dade County areas. Here, they not only competed for housing with existing residents and refugees, but they competed with other blacks migrating to Dade County from elsewhere in the South. Some Census tracts went from exclusively white in 1960 to exclusively black in 1970; in one Model Cities tract, 88 percent of the housing units changed from white ownership to black within two and a half years (Ladner, et al., 1980).

3. Demographic Change and Social Problems.   The processes of in-migration, urban renewal, relocation stress and "white flight" are certainly not unique to Miami. The typical historical pattern of urban migration and residential succession repeated in northeastern and midwestern cities involves a multi-stage process: after the turn of the century, European immigrants converged on older sections of cities because of low-cost housing and the availability of public transportation, and gradually dispersed to outlying suburban areas as they assimilated into the larger society. Residential invasion of the suburbs (and long-term residential succession) was accompanied by competition for land and housing resources, and often resulted in social disorganization. In the years following the Supreme Court desegregation decision, southern blacks joined the migration into the cities, following in the footsteps of the European immigrants with one notable exception: once they moved into the inner city, they did not leave.

In the case of Dade County, the critical factor was the timing. The great European immigration and residential succession processes of northern cities took place before 1920, by which time 15 million immigrants had entered this country. In Dade County, the "European immigration" took place in 1960, virtually on the heels of the Supreme Court decision, and instead of the black migration following in the footsteps of the "European immigrant migration," it had to compete with it.[3]

Furthermore, these convergences took place in a city with no real social problem experience. Before 1960, the predominant concern associated with population influx was that it was not extensive enough to satisfy the developers and entrepreneurs who gambled their fortunes on the City's growth. The major concern in the early 1960s was that there was a housing glut. The black community, if not wealthy, was at least employed.

Within ten years, the entire composition of Dade County had changed. Hundreds of thousands of Cuban refugees (and later, returnees) had moved into Little Havana. Overtown was half paved over, and the residents moved into the southern portion of Model Cities, still largely within the boundaries of the City of Miami. Competition for jobs and housing had replaced abundance. The whites had moved to the suburbs, and the Cubans who could afford to do so followed them.

B. Riot Neighborhood Economic and Social Problems

The data in this section illustrate economic and social changes in the black riot neighborhoods from 1960 to 1970. For each neighborhood, Census data are compared with black population totals, Hispanic population totals and Dade County totals. The neighborhoods themselves are outlined in Figure 1 with the exception of Opa-Locka, all of these neighborhoods are wholly or partially within the municipal boundaries of the City of Miami.

a. *Model Cities*. With a population of about 78,000 residents, Model Cities is the largest black enclave in Dade County, amounting to 37 percent of the entire black population. The area includes the Liberty City and Brownsville subdivisions, both of which were identified as black neighborhoods since the 1920s, as well as a western portion of unincorporated Dade and a southeastern portion within the City of Miami. The Model Cities area was racially mixed until about 1950: between one-third and one-half of the Liberty City and Brownsville areas were white, and the western and southeastern sections were almost exclusively white.

After the Supreme Court housing desegregation decision in 1954, the Model Cities area experienced a threefold growth in population by 1960, and the white population of Liberty City and Brownsville was dramatically reduced.

Figure 1. Census Tract Areas for Major Riot Sites during the Miami Riots of 1968. The Model Cities and Overtown Areas are the Most Involved; Opa-Locka and Coconut Grove Were Least Involved.

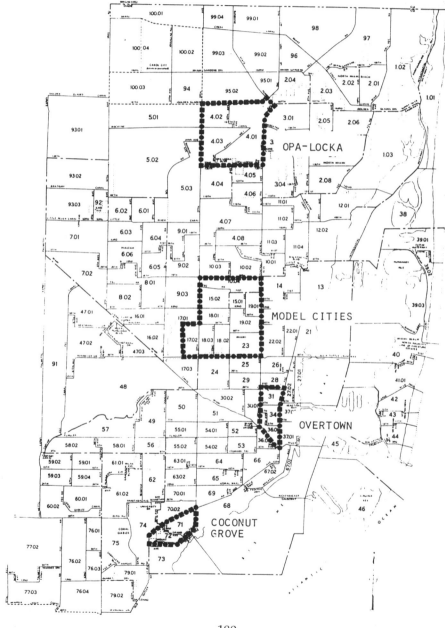

From 1960 to 1970, during the decade of the Overtown urban renewal, the net population increased by about 50 percent. The white population of Liberty City and Brownsville had been all but eliminated, and whites were rapidly moving out of the western and southeastern portion of Model Cities. In some cases—notably, the southeastern portion—Cuban refugees competed with black migrants for the available housing.

b. *Overtown*. Overtown is the second-oldest black neighborhood in Dade County, and was the "downtown district" to the black population since the turn of the century, when it was a residential and business area for blacks working on Henry Fagler's railroad or on farms along the Miami River. Even when Overtown residents began to migrate to the then rural Brownsville and Liberty City black neighborhoods in the 1940s, Overtown retained its role as the downtown business and religious center of the community.

By the 1950s and early 1960s, Overtown was overcrowded and run down. The low-rise concrete apartments that had been built in the 1940s were rapidly deteriorating, and residential segregation had severely limited the ability of the residents to spread out. By the end of the 1950s, the end of segregation and the land acquisitions planned for urban renewal encouraged many residents to leave the downtown area, and move to relatively open areas in Model Cities. The residents who stayed behind lacked the resources to move, and waited until they had to go.

The massive land acquisitions and demolition of the early 1960's forced many of the latter residents into a hasty, disorganized relocation. With the counter-pressures from the Cuban refugee influx, Model Cities again was the target for the displaced residents. The residents who remained faced rubble, vacant lots, concrete expressway overpasses and boarded-up shops.

c. *Opa-Locka*. The Opa-Locka area is outside the City of Miami, located in the northwest section of Dade County. In contrast to the poverty, dislocation and out-migration in Overtown and the migration and residential succession in Model Cities, the Opa-Locka black community is relatively small and very stable.

The town was built in the 1920s along an "Arabian Nights" theme, with pseudo-Moorish architecture and streets with names like "Scheherazade Boulevard" and "Ali-Baba Avenue." The name of the town itself has nothing to do with Arabic: it is a Tequesta/Seminole derivative meaning "big island covered with many trees in the swamp."

d. *Coconut Grove*. Coconut Grove is the oldest black neighborhood in Dade County, and shares many features with the Overtown community north of the Miami River. Like Overtown, Coconut Grove was settled by laborers, in this case Bahamian fishermen and ex-slaves from the Carolinas and Georgia, brought to the Grove to work the plantations and the Flagler railroad. Like Overtown, restrictive legislation constricted the growth of the Grove community, leading to overcrowding and economic marginality in the 1940s and early 1950s.

While migration to Model Cities created a massive attrition from Overtown in the 1950s and 1960s, no such migration occurred from Coconut Grove. In contrast to the high proportion of renter-occupied housing in Overtown, a larger proportion of Grove residents owned their own homes, and those who did migrate out of the Grove in the 1950s tended to move South to the agricultural Richmond Heights area. Urban renewal in the grove was not accompanied by wholesale property acquisition and expressway construction; rather, additional public housing was constructed and sidewalk and street repairs were made under Neighborhood Development Plan programs.

e. *Economic and social comparisons.* As may be expected from the migration patterns discussed above, the Model Cities and Overtown areas show the greatest economic problems (Table 1): note that although the Coconut Grove area was severely depressed at the time of the 1950 Census, conditions in the Grove had improved remarkably by 1970, and the economic condition of the area had begun to approximate the more stable Opa-Locka black community.[4] During that same period, the condition of blacks in the Model Cities and Overtown areas had actually deteriorated. Relative to other blacks, to the County as a whole and to the Hispanic population in specific, blacks in Model Cities and Overtown *suffered economic declines* from 1960 to 1970.

The social problem level indicators in Table 2 show a similar picture. In 1970, the proportion of black families with below-poverty incomes was twice as high for blacks as Hispanics, and was higher in the Model Cities and Overtown areas than for Opa-Locka and Coconut Grove. Likewise, the proportions of female-headed families with dependent children was higher for blacks than for Hispanics, and higher for Model Cities and overtown than for Opa-Locka and Coconut Grove.

Against the backdrop of demographic change, disruptive relocation and suburbanization in the 1960s, the economic and social conditions of blacks in Dade County had not improved. Not only did Dade County blacks show little improvement in income levels or economic stability during this decade, in many neighborhoods they actually fell further behind. Not only did they lose ground relative to the white population, which showed overall large gains during this decade, *they lost ground to the newly-arrived Cuban refugees.*

This relative shift is shown dramatically when the economic conditions and social problem levels of Dade's Hispanic and black populations are compared. For example:

- In 1960, the median family incomes of Hispanics (at that time, predominantly Puerto Ricans) and blacks were both well below the Dade medians, and were not significantly different from each other. By 1970, the Hispanic median income had increased by 142 percent, *twice as great an increase as among the blacks*, and was not significantly different from the Dade average. At the same time, black income relative to the Dade average had not changed: blacks were still substantially below average.

Table 1. Miami Black Economic Conditions

Neighborhood	Median Family Income: 1960		Median Family Income 1970		% Increase, 1960-1970	Male Unemployment 1960		Male Unemployment 1970	
	Amount	% Below Dade Median	Amount	% Below Dade Median		% Net	% Over Dade Mean	% Net	% Over Dade Mean
Model Cities	$3,460	77%	$5,687	77%	64%	6.6%	18%	4.7%	43%
Overtown	$3,181	85%	$4,846	86%	52%	10.9%	95%	7.8%	136%
Opa-Locka	$4,362	61%	$6,667	64%	53%	2.8%	-50%	3.3%	0%
Coconut Grove	$3,373	80%	$5,805	61%	72%	3.7%	-33%	4.4%	33%
All blacks in Dade	$3,367	79%	$5,093	74%	78%	7.1%	26%	4.2%	27%
All Latins in Dade	$3,777	71%	$8,091	57%	142%	8.0%	43%	3.2%	-4%
Dade Total	$5,348	50%	$9,245	50%	73%	5.6%	0%	3.3%	0%

Table 2. Miami Black Neighborhood Social Problem Indicators

Neighborhood	% Families in General	% Female-Headed Households with dependent children	Families with Incomes Below the Poverty Level*	% High School Dropouts**	% Overcrowded Housing***
			% Families Receiving Public Assistance		
Model Cities	30%	51%	24%	27%	31%
Overtown	34%	54%	31%	37%	33%
Opa-Locka	23%	37%	8%	14%	29%
Coconut Grove	29%	57%	25%	28%	33%
All blacks in Dade	28%	49%	27%	27%	33%
All Latins in Dade	14%	17%	29%	21%	33%
Dade Total	11%	27%	20%	16%	13%

*Calculated at $3,743 per annum for a nonfarm family of four (1970 Census).
**Calculated on the basis of persons 16 to 21 years of age who did not graduate (1970 Census).
***Calculated on the basis of household units with more than one person per room (1970 Census).

- In 1960, black and Hispanic unemployment levels were both well over the Dade average, and Hispanic unemployment levels were themselves even higher than those of blacks. By 1970, the overall unemployment levels had improved for all Dade citizens, but black unemployment levels were just as far above Dade averages as they were in 1960. By contrast, Hispanic unemployment levels were no longer different from the Dade averages.

IV. THE RIOT ITSELF: GRIEVANCE AND PARTICIPATION

The economic stagnation of the 1960s had carried over well into the 1970s. By the time of the riots, two recessions had worsened the economic condition of blacks in Dade County: the 1974 recession had severely hurt the construction industry, a major employer of blacks; and before Dade had fully recovered from the 1974 downturn, the recession of 1979 had begun to affect the Florida economy. Job competition with Hispanics was further exacerbated by the development of international retail, financial and tourist activity: at a time when the need for economic opportunity was at its peak, one prerequisite for participation was the ability to speak Spanish.

During the 18 months immediately prior to the riots, however, a set of police/community incidents created an atmosphere of disaffection and anger with the white establishment. In January, 1979, a 37-year-old Florida Highway Patrolman was accused of taking an 11-year-old black female into his car and sexually abusing her; an investigation by the State's Attorney supported the charge, but the officer was allowed to resign, was placed on probation and instructed to attend outpatient psychotherapy sessions. In February, 1979, narcotics officers of the Dade County Department of Public Safety conducted a forcible search, with a warrant, of the home of Nathaniel LaFleur, a black public school teacher. LaFleur resisted the search and was seriously injured; it was determined later that the address on the search warrant was not that of LaFleur's, and that the search was improperly conducted. The State's Attorney investigation resulted in no criminal indictments, although the officers were placed on disciplinary leave.

During the period when the LaFleur incident was receiving wide press coverage, the State's Attorney conducted an investigation of Dr. Johnny Jones, the Superintendent of the Dade County School system and a popular black leader, pursuant to his alleged use of several thousand dollars of school funds to purchase plumbing equipment for his vacation house. The day after the Grand Jury indicted Dr. Jones, the School Board met and dismissed him; after a lengthy—and publicly televised—trial, Dr. Jones was found guilty on April 30, 1980, and was awaiting sentencing when the riots broke out.[5]

In September, 1979, an off-duty Hialeah policeman working as a security guard shot and killed a 22-year-old black male, Randy Heath. The officer stated he had surprised Heath in a break-in; Heath's sister, a witness, stated that Heath had been shot when he stopped to urinate against a building. Later, the officer claimed his gun had gone off by accident, and the State's Attorney determined that the killing had been negligent, but not criminal.

On December 17, 1979, a 33-year-old black male, Arthur McDuffie, ran a red light on his motorcycle and was pursued by several units of the Miami Police Department and Dade County Department of Public Safety. He was apprehended after an extensive chase, and (according to the initial police report) had crashed his motorcycle and had been critically injured resisting arrest. McDuffie died of massive head injuries on December 21; shortly thereafter, the County Medical Examiner reported that his injuries were inconsistent with a motorcycle accident. Based on information supplied by one of the officers, an investigation into possible tampering with evidence (a police car was alleged to have backed over McDuffie's motorcycle and arrest reports were said to have been falsified) and manslaughter was conducted by the State's Attorney. Five Department of Public Safety officers were subsequently dismissed and faced criminal charges: four others were relieved of duty. Because of the publicity attending the incident, a change of venue was granted and the trial of the five officers began on March 31, 1980 in Tampa, Florida. Around the time the trial began, the occupation of the Peruvian Embassy in Havana by would-be refugees escalated into a massive uncontrolled boatlift of over 125,000 Cubans from the port of Mariel to Miami by way of Key West.

On Saturday afternoon, May 17, 1980, an all-white jury in Tampa acquitted the five accused policemen of all charges. The news was broadcast at 3:00 p.m. on that day, coincidently with the close of a community anti-crime rally in Africa Park in Model Cities. By 4:00 p.m., reports of random, scattered violence had been logged at the City of Miami Police Department, much of it in the Africa Park area. By 6:30, the rock and bottle throwing in Liberty City had escalated into violent assault, and a crowd was forming at the Dade County Justice Building in the Civic Center, near Overtown. By 9:00, disorders were reported throughout a 20-square-mile area, including Coconut Grove and Opa-Locka; the crowd at the Justice Building was out of control; widespread arson and looting was taking place; and ten persons had died. By 10:00, the National Guard had been called in and the riot area had increased to 40 square miles. The National Guard curfew was lifted nine days later, on Monday morning, May 26. Eighteen deaths and over $100 million in property damage were the consequence.

By far the worst of the rioting was in the Model Cities and Overtown areas. In Model Cities, the first reports of violence against individuals and arson against businesses came in around 6:00 p.m., when reports were logged in that several whites had been taken from stopped cars and had been severely beaten or killed. Verification of these incidents was hampered by confusion over the intersections where the incidents were supposed to have taken place; the verification was made easier when the bodies were recovered later in the evening. The Zayre's department store was looted; the Norton Tire Company was burned; the majority of specific acts of violence against individual persons and businesses took place in this area.

By contrast, the Overtown disturbances were more of the nature of mob action, as the crowd at the Justice Building vandalized the building and set fire to police cars. Sniping and scattered violence against individuals continued throughout the riot period, but the violence in Overtown did not have the ferocity of the violence in Model Cities. By midnight Saturday, the worst of the Overtown rioting was over.

In Coconut Grove and Opa-Locka, the violence and property damage were even more restrained, although it continued until Thursday morning. Although the police department and National Guard were able to contain the violence, it was never actually controlled, and the containment itself was limited to the downtown/Liberty City area after the second night of the riots.

A. The BSRI/Herald Survey

Even before the National Guard curfew was lifted, Behavioral Science Research Institute (BSRI) had begun negotiations with the *Miami Herald* to survey the attitudes and concerns of the residents of the riot areas, as a means of understanding the motivations of the riot participants and as a means of clarifying post-riot political issues. The major impetus for the *Herald's* interest in the research came from Philip Meyer, a Knight-Ridder news executive who had been responsible for a survey of the attitudes of Detroit blacks by the Urban League and *Detroit Free Press* (a Knight-Ridder newspaper) after the 1967 riots, as well as a *Herald* survey of black attitudes in Miami in 1968. The final form of the *Herald*/BSRI research project was that of a joint venture, with both the *Herald* and BSRI contributing to the costs of the research, providing the *Herald* (and, by separate contract with the *Herald*, the *Washington Post*) with rights of first publication of the findings and allowing BSRI unrestricted use of the data thereafter.

Survey development and pretesting within the black community were accomplished by the close of May: data collection fieldwork, using black casework staff from the James E. Scott Community Association (JESCA) as interviewers, took place from June 3 to June 11. By the close of that week, 450 respondents of the riot neighborhoods had been interviewed. During data cleaning and editing, data from six respondents were discarded as unusable.

The sampling design was intended to divide 450 respondents among the five major areas affected by the riot. Because of the dispersion of the population and the small size of the sample, respondents were selected according to a cluster-sample design, filling age-specific quotas within each cluster to minimize sampling bias.

The first stage of the sampling involved population estimation within riot areas. Based on the over-15 black population reported for these areas in the 1970 Census, Opa-Locka was allocated 12 percent of the cases, Model Cities was allocated 64 percent, Overtown was allocated 17 percent and Coconut Grove was allocated 7 percent. A second stage stratified the over-15 population into age categories, such that persons 15-24 accounted for 28 percent of the total, persons 15-44 accounted for 40 percent and persons 45 and over accounted for 31 percent. These parameters were adjusted to fit a 10-case cluster, resulting in sampling quotas that closely approximated the neighborhood size and age stratification of the population. Opa-Locka was allocated five clusters; Model Cities, twenty-nine; Overtown, eight and Coconut Grove, three.

Clusters were assigned to each riot area on the basis of Census tracts. Within each area, tracts were sampled with replacement until there was at least one designated tract for each sample cluster. Because there were more clusters than tracts, this resulted in an average of three clusters per tract. Street intersections were identified within each tract through Census maps, and the four contiguous blocks were considered the cluster area. Within this cluster area, interviewers were to survey ten area residents who were also U.S. citizens, such that three would be under 24, four would be between 25 and 44 years of age and three would be 45 or over.

Interviews were conducted in public places, homes, parks, restaurants and other naturally occurring places where residents congregate. The interviewers were not restricted to daylight hours, and conducted interviews into evening hours. All days of the week were included in the sample timing, including weekends.

Given a random sample of 450 cases, the maximum expected error under a 95 percent confidence interval would normally be 4.6 percent; however, because cluster samples are less efficient than simple random sampling, the maximum error estimates are closer to 5.6 percent.

B. Riot participation: Patterns of Activity

Based on the measures used in the survey, riot activity in Miami was broader in scope than the riot activity of the 1960s. In contrast to a level of participation of about 12 percent to 15 percent discussed in the Kerner Commission report, for example, 26 percent of the blacks interviewed in the riot areas indicated they had "been active" in the rioting. Although this figure must be treated with caution—it is not possible to determine whether more riot participants under-represent or over-represent their involvement—it is *significantly higher than the response obtained from Detroit blacks in 1967.* At that time, black response to the identical question indicated 12 percent net acknowledged participation in the disturbances (Urban League, 1968). The highest levels of reported involvement were in the Model Cities (28 percent and Overtown (41 percent) areas, sites of the major violent assaults and arson (Model Cities) and the crowd disturbances around the Metro Justice Building (Overtown). In Coconut Grove, 25 percent of the residents acknowledged participation; in Opa-Locka, 14 percent.

The specific content of the riot participation is shown in Table 3. Note that along with activities that can be used to suggest antisocial behavior (e.g., ''went out into the riot area''), there were other activities that clearly were counter-riot in intent:

- Sixty-one percent of the active participants and 32 percent of the non-actives reported *protecting their property from rioters*.
- Forty-three percent of the active participants and 24 percent of the nonactives reported *bringing children off the streets*.

Table 3.   Patterns of Riot Activity Among Participants and Non-Participants

Activity	Riot Participation	
	Active	Not Active
(Sample size)		
	(113)	
	(291)	
During the riots, did you:		
Protect property from rioters?	61%	32%
Observe the disturbance from own property?	48	38
Stay at home?	45	68
Bring children off the streets?	43	24
Go into disturbance area?	43	8
Help injured blacks?	22	4
Direct traffic around area?	18	3
Leave neighborhood entirely?	15	9
Call fire department?	12	4
Help injured whites?	9	2
Were you or any member of your family:		
Physically hurt?	6%	2%
Have property damaged?	4	3
Have business damaged?	5	2
Lose a job because of business or property damage?	18	7

In general, persons who were active participants were three times as likely to have been physically hurt themselves, twice as likely to have their businesses damaged, and almost three times as likely to have lost jobs because of the business or property damage.

The actual riot behaviors in Miami are strikingly similar to those reported in Detroit in 1967. Table 4 compares the reported activity level in the postriot survey conducted by the Urban League and the *Detroit Free Press* with the levels of activity reported after the Miami riots in the *Herald*/BSRI survey. The higher overall levels of activity in Miami are shown in the proportion of persons describing themselves as "not active": of the persons agreeing to answer questions about their riot involvement, 83 percent of the Detroit blacks and 72 percent of the Miami blacks described themselves in this way. This difference is statistically significant, as is the over-representation of Miami blacks indicating they were "slightly" involved. The proportions of "somewhat" and "very" involved respondents are not different from one riot population to the other.

Table 4.   Comparison of Riot Behavior: Detroit (1967) and Miami (1980)

Activity	Detroit 1967	Miami 1980
	(437)	(444)
A. *Activity Level*		
Not active	83%	72%
Slightl	9	19
Somewhat	4	5
Very	4	4
	100%	100%
B. *Specific actions*		
(% yes)		
Went out into riot area?	14%	17%
Observe the disturbance from own property?	38%	40%
Stay at home?	44%	58%
Protect own property from rioters?	33%	39%
Call fire department?	7%	6%
Leave neighborhood entirely?	7%	11%

In terms of the actual activity, the pattern of actions taken by persons acknowledging participation is similar for the Detroit and Miami groups. With the exception of "protecting own property" and "stay at home" proportions, which show a higher level of activity in Miami than in Detroit, there are *no significant differences between the two groups*.

In 1968 the Kerner Commission report described the typical rioter of the summer of 1967 as an unmarried male between the ages of 15 and 24, was not a high school graduate and was employed in a menial job. This profile effectively led to a stereotype of the black rioter as a streetcorner youth, and some researchers after the 1968 riots posed the "riff-raff" hypothesis, suggesting that black rioters were a deviant subgroup within the black community (cf. Caplan and Paige, 1968; Fogelson and Hill, 1968).

The data in Table 5 illustrate the difference between active participants and nonactive participants in the Miami riots. In contrast to the stereotype presented by the Kerner Commission summary and to some of the data collected after the Detroit riots, the differences between the active and nonactive participants do not suggest a street-corner culture of violence. Rather, they suggest that although there was one component of the active participant population that does fit the notion of street youth, there is a large—and involved—population of persons who are more broadly representative of the community at large.

Table 5.   Comparison of Salient Attributes of Riot Participants and Non-Participants

	Riot Participation	
	Active	Non-Active
(Sample size)	(113)	(291)
A. *Marital Status*		
Single	65%	41%
Married	22	29
Divorced/separated	12	21
Spouse deceased	1	9
	100%	100%
B. *Education*		
Less than high school	38%	44%
High school	39	37
Post-high school training	23	19
	100%	100%
C. *Criminal justice system involvement* (% yes)		
Had brush with law	42%	24%
Arrested for misdemeanor	32	17
Convicted of misdemeanor	21	6
Arrested for felony	12	4
Convicted of felony	9	4
D. *Occupation*		
White collar	21%	19%
Blue collar, skilled	27	27
Blue collar, unskilled	18	18
Unemployed	23	16
Disabled, housewife, student, retired	11	20
	100%	100%
E. *Method of learning about McDuffie verdict* (% yes)		
Watched on television	85%	93%
Heard on radio	94	79
Read in newspaper	77	74
Heard on street	90	77

- Educational levels are strikingly similar for the two groups, and show a higher proportion of less-than-high-school persons in the *nonactive* group. In this, the Miami data is quite similar to the data reported after the Detroit riots: in general, those who were active in the riots show *slightly more education* than those who did not participate.

- Persons who were active in the Miami riots were about *twice as likely to have been involved with the law*. Across the board, the rates for active participants are higher than for nonactives.

- Occupational status shows a *higher degree of underemployment or unemployment among the active participants,* relative to the non-actives. The difference is made up in the higher numbers of non-actives who are disabled, retired, students or housewives. In all other categories, the *occupational status of active participants was indistinguishable from that of the non-participants*. About 20 percent of both groups held white-collar jobs; an additional 27 percent held blue-collar skilled labor positions. These figures are in marked contrast to the Detroit numbers, which show a lower overall proportion of white-collar and blue-collar skilled positions among the active participants.

- Media consumption by both active and non-active participants is somewhat similar, although *non-participants were more likely to have learned about the McDuffie verdict on television* and were less likely to have heard about the verdict on the radio or on the street than active participants.

Table 6 illustrates the age difference between active and nonactive participants in the Miami riots, and compares them both with levels of participation and with the age distributions of active and nonactive participants in the Detroit riots. The younger Miami participants considered themselves to be more actively involved, and the older participants to be less actively involved. Note, however that *fully 20 percent of the active participants were over 35 years of age*, a significantly higher proportion than the 13 percent reported in Detroit in 1967.

The proportion of males and females engaged in active participation was not significantly different from the proportion of males and females in the non-active population. Among the active participants, the ratio was exactly 50-50; among the nonparticipants, the ratio was 45-65. These differences are not significant.

Table 6. Age Distributions of Participants and Non-Participants

	Miami Level of Activity, 1980				Miami, 1980		Detroit, 1967	
Age	Not Active	Slightly Active	Somewhat Active	Very Active	Not Active	Active	Not Active	Active
(Sample)	(263)	(73)	(17)	(22)	(263)	(112)	(287)	(44)
15-24	26%	37%	29%	82%	26%	45%	23%	61%
25-35	27	36	59	14	27	35	16	25
35-50	27	25	12	4	27	19	32	11
Over 50	20	3	0	0	20	1	29	2
	100%	100%	100%	100%	100%	100%	100%	99%

C. Attitude Similarities Between Active and Non-Active Participants

Table 7 compares the perceived neighborhood social problems of not participants and non-participants, and reveals a remarkable similarity between the perceptions of major community problems by active participants and the perceptions by nonactives.[6]

Table 7.   Comparison of Salient Attitudes of Riot Participants
and Non-Participants

	Riot Participation	
	Active	Not Active
(Sample size)	(113)	(291)
A. *Perception of major problems in the community* (% yes)		
Lack of jobs	93%	97%
Police brutality	88%	94%
Poor housing	87%	92%
Drug use	81%	93%
Poverty	86%	90%
Broken political promise	82%	87%
School dropouts	80%	85%
Anger with police	88%	84%
Dirty neighborhoods	77%	86%
Overcrowded living	78%	84%
Disappointment with white officials	78%	82%
Lack of strong black leaders	73%	81%
B. *Perceptions of the effects of riots on the community* (% true)		
Riots won't change anything.	36%	37%
It will be harder to get businesses in the riot neighborhoods.	66%	70%
Police will let up on us.	18%	24%
People will pay more attention to the needs of the black community.	68%	74%
The riots will make things better for the community.	45%	43%
Blacks who get ahead can only do it by fighting for their rights in the streets.	36%	26%

- In 10 out of 12 top-ranked major problems in the community, as ranked by the active and nonactive residents, there were *no significant differences in the levels of importance ascribed to each problem.*

- In five out of six major attitudes reflecting the way the riots would affect or not affect the community, there were *no significant differences between active and nonactive rioters.* In these areas, both active and nonactive participants expressed mixed feelings about the effects of the riots on their future: it would be harder to get businesses to locate in the neighborhoods, but the riots may change things and at least people will pay more attention to the community. Active participants supported fighting for rights in the streets more than nonparticipants; note that this attitude was measured after the riots, and may represent a *justification* of the activity level of the participant, rather than a predisposition toward street violence.

The data on the concerns of the black community in Miami in 1968 stand in stark contrast to the post-riot data from blacks in Detroit for that same year, and for Miami blacks in 1980 (Table 8). Post-riot Detroit blacks were most concerned about three issues: the police, their housing and jobs. The post-riot Miami black population was concerned with the same three major issues. While *lack of jobs* ranked first in post-riot Miami and fifth in post-riot Detroit, however, it ranked *thirteenth* in Miami in 1968. *Police brutality*, ranked first and second in post-riot Detroit and Miami, respectively, was ranked 20th in Miami in 1968.

These data would suggest that for blacks in Miami in 1968, the specific urban problems and frustrations that characterized black living conditions in northern cities were remote. There were real problems in the community, but the issues of police brutality and unemployment that were raised in Detroit during the same period—and were raised in Miami 12 years later—were distant.

Table 8.   Comparison of Complaint Levels
Miami (1967), Detroit (1968), and Miami (1980)

Complaint	Miami 1980		Miami 1968		Detroit 1967	
Lack of Jobs	95%	(1)	50%	(13)	45%	(5)
Police brutality	90%	(2)	23%	(20)	57%	(1)
Poor housing	89%	(3)	59%	(6)	54%	(3)
Broken political promises	84%	(6)	58%	(8)	44%	(7)
Too many school dropouts	83%	(7)	77%	(1)	39%	(8)
Anger with the police	83%	(7)	–		51%	(4)
Dirty neighborhoods	82%	(9)	67%	(3)	44%	(6)
Overcrowded living conditions	81%	(10)	59%	(7)	55%	(2)
Disappointment with white public officials	78%	(11)	32%	(11)	–	
Lack of strong black leaders	75%	(12)	57%	(9)	29%	(14)

The perceived seriousness of the existing black community problems in Miami in 1980 may be measured by the proportion of blacks rating a given problem as serious. In Detroit in 1967, for example, the *five most pressing problems* were mentioned by an average of 52 percent of the black respondents. In Miami in 1968, without a riot to trigger an awareness of community problems, the average response for the top five problems was 68 percent. In Miami in 1980, after the riots, the average perception level for the top five problems was 90 percent. In effect, the top problems were perceived by post-riot blacks in Miami in 1980 in a more consistent and more widespread manner than the problems seen by either Miami blacks in 1968 or Detroit blacks after the riot in 1967. Even more importantly, *the problem perception levels in Miami in 1968 were higher and more uniform than the problem perception levels in Detroit in the previous year.*

The relative ranking of problem areas across Miami black neighborhoods after the 1980 riots is remarkably consistent (Table 9). Lack of jobs, police brutality, poor housing, too much drug use, poverty and broken political promises are rated *as most serious by residents in every black neighborhood;* there are few cases where any other problem is rated more serious than one of these top six.

Table 9. Comparison of Complaint Levels
For Individual Black Neighborhoods
(% Indicating Serious Problems)

	Model Cities	Overtown	Opa-Locka	Coconut Grove
Lack of jobs	97%	92%	96%	97%
Police brutality	95	91	86	87
Poor housing	92	90	86	97
Too much drug use	92	82	92	90
Poverty	90	87	88	93
Broken political promises	86	85	84	90
School dropouts	88	82	78	80
Anger with police	87	79	88	77
Dirty neighborhoods	88	86	62	83
Overcrowded housing	86	80	62	97
Disappointment with white politicians	81	74	90	83
Lack of strong black leaders	78	70	72	100
Anger with politicians	79	69	79	66
Failure of parents to control children	75	68	76	83
Too much drinking	73	68	70	83
Anger with judges	71	62	80	71
Hatred of whites	65	73	68	50
Poor transportation	66	50	70	70
Not enough welfare	65	57	59	67
Disappointment with black politicians	63	52	63	66
Poor schools	59	49	57	43
Lack of recreational facilities	56	48	54	33
Anger with local businessmen	48	42	39	40

At the time of the 1980 riots, Miami blacks saw themselves as less well off than blacks in other cities and less likely to see improved attitudes. Table 10 shows a comparison of post-riot attitudes in Detroit and Miami, and the pessimism of the Miami black community is well evident.

Table 10.   Comparison of Black Attitudes:
Detroit (1967) and Miami (1980)

Attitude Area	Detroit 1967	Miami 1980
A. Registered to vote?		
% yes	72%	76%
B. Blacks can only get ahead by fighting for rights.		
% agree	67%	26%
C. Over the next five years, white attitudes toward black rights in this city will:		
- get better	57%	26%
- get worse	8	25
- stay same, don't know	35	49
D. Compared to blacks in other cities, blacks in this city have:		
D.1 more income	46%	5%
less income	8	53
same, don't know	46	42
D.2 better jobs	39%	5%
worse jobs	8	41
same, don't know	53	54
D.3 better educations	25%	8%
worse educations	10	34
same, don't know	65	58

- After the Detroit riots, 57 percent of the black population in that city expected white attitudes to improve, 8 percent expected them to deteriorate. In Miami after the 1980 riots, by contrast, 26 percent expected white attitudes to improve and 25 percent expected them to deteriorate.
- In the areas of income, jobs and education, blacks in Miami after the 1980 riots saw themselves as *substantially worse off than blacks in other cities*. The difference between the perceptions of Miami blacks and the post-riot perceptions of blacks in Detroit are consistent and remarkable: most Detroit blacks either have no opinion about their relative status or consider themselves better off, while most Miami blacks have no opinion or consider themselves worse off.

V . FROM SECOND PLACE TO THIRD: BLACK RESENTMENT TOWARD CUBANS

To blacks in Dade County, the decade of the 1970s may have seemed like one long bad dream. The modest economic gains of the 1960s were turning to ashes in the recession of 1974. Welfare programs and government aid were being re-deployed to meet the problems of the Cuban refugee population, and competition for jobs at all ends of the scale were stepping up. In 1968, when blacks were interviewed by the *Miami Herald*, two attitude questions were included as a means of measuring black feeling toward Cubans: blacks were asked whether they were bothered by Cuban success, and by Governmental aid to Cubans. Both were answered in the affirmative (Table 11).

Ten years later, a *Herald* survey of Cuban community relations posed several questions to both the black and non-Latin white communities: 28 percent of the black respondents considered that Cubans had better jobs than other people in Dade County (vs. 18 percent among the whites), and 56 percent agreed that Cubans "want to gain control" in Dade County (vs. 46 percent for whites). More remarkable were the apparent differences in the perceived importance of bilingualism: 77 percent of the blacks felt that stores should have both English- and Spanish-speaking help (vs. 47 percent for whites), and 43 percent felt every public school student in Dade should be required to become proficient in Spanish (vs. 15 percent for whites).

By the time of the Mariel boatlift in 1980, black attitudes toward the erstwhile Cuban refugees had hardened. Although a *Herald* survey of community reactions to the new refugees showed no significant difference in the attitudes of whites and blacks toward the newcomers, the expressed attitudes of blacks toward the existing Cuban population was much more strongly negative than the attitudes of whites. The survey was published in May, 1980, six days before the outbreak of the rioting.

After the rioting, the BSRI survey showed black attitudes toward all Cubans to be equally pessimistic, regardless of when they came to Miami.

One measure of the perceived economic competition of Cubans was a question regarding who the black respondents considered their biggest competitors for jobs. Table 12 illustrates the responses to this item, along with breakdowns of the other attitude statements regarding black/Cuban relationships. Across the board, Cubans are seen as being the biggest competitors for jobs, outranking other blacks and whites. There are no significant differences between the pattern of response of active and nonactive rioters.

The sole significant relationship between black respondent characteristics and the perception of economic rivalry is shown in Table 13. Although Cubans remain the predominant economic rivals across all types of occupational level and status, there are important variations: black respondents with white-collar

Table 11. Development of Black Attitudes Toward Cubans, 1968-1980

Attitude Statement	% in Agreement	
	Blacks	*Whites*
1968 Miami Herald Survey	(n=530)	
It bothers me to see Cubans succeeding more than Americans who were born here.	76%	n.a.
The government does more to help Cubans than Blacks.	60%	n.a.
1978 Miami Herald Survey	(n= 75)	(n=125)
Cubans have better jobs than other people in Dade County.	28%	18%
Cubans want to gain control of government and business in Dade County.	56%	46%
Every store in Dade Country should have Spanish- and English-speaking people to help customers.	77%	47%
Every student in the public school system should be required to become proficient in Spanish.	43%	15%
1980 Miami Herald Survey (May 11, 1980)	(n=200)	(n=243)
Cubans who came here since 1960 have been bad for Dade County.	45%	29%
The new refugees will be bad for Dade County.	57%	68%
Reasons why more people are concerned about the arrival of more Cuban refugees:		
There are not enough jobs	88%	86%
There is not enough housing	88%	90%
It would make it more difficult for people who don't speak Spanish . . .	84%	79%
1980 BSRI/Herald Survey (June 11, 1980)	(n=404)	
Cubans who came here over the past 10 to 15 years have hurt black economic chances.	87%	n.a.
The new wave of Cuban refugees will hurt black economic chances.	91%	n.a.
Too many employers hire only people who can speak Spanish.	82%	n.a.

Table 12. Levels of Perceived Economic Competition
Between Cubans and Blacks

	Riot Participation		Neighborhood			
	Active	Not Active	Model Cities	Overtown	Opa-Locka	Coconut Grove
(Sample size)	(113)	(291)	(259)	(75)	(47)	(27)
A. If you were looking for a job today, who are biggest competitors?						
Miami Blacks	4%	4%	3%	4%	0%	7%
Haitians	7	1	3	11	0	0
Cubans	57	59	61	51	49	85
Whites	31	34	30	29	51	7
Other	1	2	3	5	0	0
B. Too many employers hire only people who can speak Spanish.						
True	80%	83%	84%	80%	79%	85%
False	20	17	16	20	21	15
C. Cubans who came here over the past 10 to 15 years have hurt black economic chances.						
True	84%	88%	92%	77%	80%	91%
False	16	12	7	23	20	9
D. The new wave of Cuban refugees will hurt black economic chances.						
True	89%	92%	89%	78%	100%	92%
False	11	8	11	22	0	8

jobs are more likely than other blacks to see Cubans as job competitors, and blacks with transient, unskilled jobs are more likely to see other blacks as their competitors.

Table 13.   Relationship Between Occupational Status
and Perceived Economic Rivalry

Competing Ethnic Group	*Reported occupational status of adult respondents*				
	White Collar	*Blue Collar, Skilled*	*Blue Collar, Unskilled*	*Occasional, Unskilled*	*Unemployed*
(sample)	(82)	(114)	(48)	(20)	(69)
Miami blacks	1%	3%	4%	20%	3%
Haitians	6	2	2	5	4
Cubans	72	55	58	50	61
Whites	18	38	35	20	30
Others	2	3	0	5	1
	99%	101%	99%	100%	99%

VI. PRINCIPAL ELEMENTS OF BLACK COMMUNITY CONCERNS

As a means of organizing the welter of riot participation data, attitudes and respondent characteristics measured in the survey, a large number of variables was subjected to principal components factor analysis, with iterations. In this analysis, the main diagonal of the correlation matrix is altered by substituting squared multiple correlations between each variable and all other variables in the matrix; this provides a set of inferred factors. The first unrotated factor solution was evaluated according to the guideline suggested by Guertin and Bailey (1970), such that factors associated with 5 percent or more of the common variance are considered important. Variables with less than a .20 maximum initial (unrotated) loading were deleted from the analysis. Over the course of sequential factorings, changes in the composition of the variable resulted in alterations in the total number of factors: the unrotated matrix stabilized at six factors and 70 variables, and the final set of factors was rotated to achieve the best orthogonal solution to the factor matrix. The SPSS PA2 factor analysis program was used throughout (Kim, 1975).

The orthogonal solution was chosen in order to yield factors which would be as *statistically independent* of each other as possible. These forced ''zero correlation'' relationships among factors tend to isolate riot participation indicators into one factor, thus presumably making it clear as to what is most highly correlated with riot participation and what is statistically unrelated. The orthogonal solution statistically simulates the psychological independence of the factors, such that the factors can be considered independent, free-standing aspects of the psychology of the neighborhood residents: as the factor scores indicate, major citizen concerns with social service delivery, criminal justice system abuses, anger with the system and riot attitudes and behavior are *all independent issues*. The fact that overt riot behavior is independent of other salient attitudes provides support for the attitude similarities shown between participants and non-participants. By the same token, it indicates the pervasiveness of those concerns and angers, and shows the breadth of the ideological support for the causes and concerns that are seen as underlying the riots.

Table 14 through Table 19 illustrate the variables in each factor and their loadings on all factors.

Table 14.   Factor 1: Perceived Police Brutality (29.5%)

	FACTOR SCORES					
	I	*II*	*III*	*IV*	*V*	*VI*
Policemen lack respect or use insulting language.						
– Happens to people in your neighborhood?	.583	.030	.124	.073	.067	.039
– Happened to anyone you know?	.740	−.037	−.004	−.019	.009	.059
– Happened to you?	.761	−.008	−.113	.008	.070	.005
Policemen roust, frisk or search people without good reason.						
– Happens to people in your neighborhood?	.589	.048	.110	.005	.088	−.039
– Happened to anyone you know?	.754	−.012	.017	.029	−.002	.021
– Happened to you?	.850	.004	−.078	.009	−.006	−.030
Policemen stop or search cars or homes for no good reason.						
– Happens to people in your neighborhood?	.530	.094	.095	.009	.002	−.021
– Happened to anyone you know?	.740	.028	−.072	−.093	−.063	−.041
– Happened to you?	.761	−.021	−.057	−.083	−.072	−.030
Policemen use unnecessary force in making arrests.						
– Happens to people in your neighborhood?	.582	−.009	.046	−.053	−.012	−.052
– Happened to anyone you know?	.762	.026	−.009	−.050	−.057	−.055
– Happened to you.	.694	.032	−.052	−.074	−.034	−.033

Factor 1: Perceived Police Brutality

The first factor to emerge from the rotated solution contained a set of items related to police abuse, i.e., lack of respect, stop-and-frisk, unreasonable search and unnecessary force. For each action, the respondents were asked to indicate whether it happens to people in their neighborhood, happened to someone they knew, or happened to them personally, and (if it happened to them) whether they reported it. These were not the only measures of dissatisfaction with police activity, however: other measures included attitude statements regarding the seriousness of "police brutality" and statements regarding the degree of justice for blacks expected from white juries.

Note that all coefficients in this factor are positive; this indicates an internal consistency among the responses, such that persons who report one kind of police abuse tend to report experiencing them all, and vice-versa.

Several items are of interest in this factor. First, the loadings are limited to experienced police abuse, and did not include attitudes regarding police brutality, biased court systems or the respondent's own response to abuses directed toward him or her. Secondly, although the primacy of this factor is indicative of the importance of the issue to the respondents, it is *independent of other social problem variables* and of any indication of riot behavior or activity level by the respondent. In effect, the factor appears to represent a generalized anger toward police for maltreatment, unrelated to other issues in the respondent's mind.

B. Factor 2: Social Problems

The second factor contains two elements: a listing of perceived problem levels (see Table 9) for a set of identified social problems, and a statement regarding black leadership in Dade County. The factor indicates widespread agreement that these problem areas go together and are either all very important or not important; furthermore, respondents who think these problems are important also believe that there are not enough strong black leaders in Dade County and vice-versa.

Again, no mention is made in this factor of any riot activity by the participant. In effect, the perception of high social problem levels and lack of black leadership is just as independent of riot participation as is perceived police abuse (Table 14).

Unlike Factor 1, there is some factor overlap for certain variables between this factor and Factor 4: concerns with "broken political promises," "police brutality," "anger with local businessmen" and "disappointment with black officials" show up both in this "social problems" grouping and in Factor 4 ("roots of anger"). Attitudes regarding "strong black leaders" appear both in this factor and in Factor 5 ("biased judiciary").

Table 15.   Factor 2: Social Problems (25.7%)

		FACTOR SCORES				
	I	II	III	IV	V	VI
Perceived Problems*						
− Poor housing	.087	.444	−.068	.090	.086	−.057
− School dropouts	.111	.554	.039	−.045	.020	.009
− Broken political promises	−.068	.284	.012	.254	.020	−.015
− Police brutality	.120	.302	.012	.222	−.036	−.037
− Poor schools	.056	.575	−.037	.070	.168	.007
− Lack of strong black leaders	−.025	.324	.005	.089	.006	.005
− Anger with local businessmen	.062	.421	.038	.379	.146	−.014
− Parents can't control children	−.013	.370	−.179	.147	−.005	−.163
− Disappointment with black officials	.012	.343	−.001	.403	.004	.094
− Lack recreational facilities	.964	.508	.048	.123	.144	−.028
− Poor transportation	.028	.609	.083	.153	.042	.011
− Dirty neighborhoods	.032	.687	−.015	−.031	−.116	.040
− Overcrowded living conditions	−.070	.588	−.070	.061	−.119	−.003
− Too much drinking	−.046	.427	−.192	.112	−.089	.123
− Too much drug use	−.058	.275	−.210	.110	−.121	.111
− Not enough welfare	−.053	.525	.168	−.011	.001	.202
Attidtudes						
− There aren't enough strong black leaders in Dade County.	.008	−.271	.019	−.044	.221	.059

*Reverse coded. High scores indicate low perceived level of importance.

C. Factor 3: Riot Involvement

Factor 3 includes an ordinal measure of degree of participation (see Table 4, above), specific riot activities and consequences (see Table 3), and the measures of active reporting of police abuse mentioned in Factor 1. Note that several of the riot activity indicators in Table 3 had *dropped out of the analysis* by the time these factors were generated.

Within the factor, the negative coefficients for riot activities and the positive coefficients for the responses to police brutality indicate only that the two sub-clusters are negatively correlated: persons who were active in the rioting did not report acts of police abuse when they happened, and vice-versa. As in the case of Factor 2, some variables overlap from one factor to another. "Calling police and fire department" appear in Factor 6 ("economic position"); "protected property" and "lost job" appear in Factor 4 ("roots of anger"); and "lost job" and "reported frisking" appear in Factor 5 ("biased judiciary").

Table 16.   Factor 3: Riot Involvement (16.7%)

| | *FACTOR SCORES* | | | | | |
	I	II	III	IV	V	VI
Riot activities						
— Overall riot participation	−.034	.085	−.556	−.011	−.105	−.045
— Called Police Department	.017	−.082	−.276	.134	.031	.246
— Called Fire Department	.030	−.146	−.314	.180	.029	.279
— Helped injured blacks	.053	.008	−.467	.100	.061	.152
— Protected property from rioters	.009	−.034	−.400	.256	.076	.028
— Went out into riot area	−.061	.136	−.479	−.040	.072	.035
— Lost job because of riots	.025	−.087	−.236	.223	−.238	.113
Response to police brutality						
Reported incidents of insults	−.008	−.033	.589	.072	.053	.145
— Reported incidents of unreasonable frisking	−.003	−.051	.556	.050	.222	.057
— Reported incidents of unreasonable search	.003	.022	.456	.049	.015	.021
— Reported incidents of unreasonable force	−.004	.026	.590	.071	.101	.012

D. Factor 4: Roots of Anger

While the problems outlined in Factor 2 were general and related to social problems in the Miami black community, the issues and problems raised in Factor 4 clearly reflect the displacement of frustration and anger on both the black and white leadership structure. There are two major themes in Factor 4: a generalized *anger and disappointment* with officials, and *economic frustration*, including poverty, perceptions that blacks in other cities have better jobs than blacks in Miami, and frustration with the perceived effect of Cuban refugees on black economic chances. Persons who are angry and disappointed believe that blacks have it better elsewhere, that white leaders don't represent their interests, and that Cubans have hurt them. "Having a business damaged in the riots" is negatively related to this frustration: blacks with businesses damaged in the riot are not as angry or disaffected as blacks who did not have businesses damaged.

In a manner similar to the overlap reported for Factor 2 and Factor 3, there is some overlap here: "blacks in Miami have worse jobs" appears in Factor 6 ("economic position"); and "business damaged" and "white leaders" appear in Factor 5 ("biased judiciary").

Table 17. Factor 4: Roots of Anger (10.5%)

	FACTOR SCORES					
	I	II	III	IV	V	VI
Perceived problems						
– Poverty*	−.032	.124	−.064	.324	−.210	−.136
– Broken political promises*	−.068	.284	.012	.254	.020	−.015
– Hatred of whites*	−.037	.213	.023	.337	−.009	.001
– Anger with police*	−.036	.212	.132	.537	.049	−.017
– Anger with judges*	−.085	.207	.107	.561	.080	−.140
– Anger with politicians*	−.039	.261	.064	.555	.006	−.105
– Anger with local businessmen*	.062	.421	.038	.379	.146	−.014
– Disappointment with white officials*	−.017	.198	.080	.479	.118	−.058
– Disappointment with black officials*	.012	.343	−.001	.403	.004	.094
– Blacks in Miami have worse jobs than blacks in other cities	−.042	−.042	−.183	−.277	−.104	.279
– Ertswhile Cubans hurt black economic chances	.000	.029	.077	−.266	.138	−.100
– Recent Cubans hurt black economic chances	.016	.007	.140	−.322	.090	−.170
Riot activities						
– Had business damaged in riots	−.010	−.011	−.122	.305	−.231	.224
Attitudes						
– White leaders don't represent respondent's interests	.067	−.102	.012	−.268	.389	.097

*Reverse coded. High scores indicate low perceived level of importance.

E. Factor 5: Biased Judiciary and Riots as Protest

The attitude statements in Factor 5 represent an activist orientation toward the white political system. On one hand, the respondents believe that blacks cannot get a fair trial, white juries do not deliver justice to black defendants, whites can do anything to blacks and get away with it, there aren't enough strong black leaders (cf. Factor 2), and white leaders don't represent black interests. On the other hand, voting is the only way to have a say, riots draw attention to black needs and make things better for the community, blacks gain more than they lose by rioting, and white attitudes toward black rights will improve. In effect, blacks who are pessimistic about their position in the white political system are optimistic about the benefits of both riots and voting as instruments of social change.

Table 18.   Factor 5: Biased Judiciary and Riots as Protest (9.4%)

	FACTOR SCORES					
	I	*II*	*III*	*IV*	*V*	*VI*
Attitudes						
– White attitudes toward black rights will deteriorate.	–.001	.019	–.188	.217	–.323	–.006
– Voting is only way to have say.	.001	.071	.267	–.027	.419	.125
– Blacks can't get fair trials in Dade.	.003	–.089	.051	–.156	.424	.088
– Blacks get no justice from all-white juries.	–.015	–.001	.087	–.194	.428	–.031
– Whites can do anything to blacks and get away with it.	–.004	–.093	.022	–.130	.461	.185
– Riots will make people pay attention to black needs.	.013	–.002	.066	.133	.399	–.125
– Riots will make things better for the community.	–.016	.041	–.071	.084	.426	–.118
– Blacks lose more by rioting.	.037	–.100	.171	–.009	–.461	.085
– White leaders don't represent respondent's interests.	.067	–.102	.012	–.268	.389	.097

F. Factor 6: Economic Position

This factor combines interval-level measurements of where blacks see themselves on an imaginary 10-rung ladder with perceptions of the relative status of blacks in Miami and in other cities and perceptions of the effects of Haitian refugees on black economic chances. The more optimistic blacks are about where they were five years ago, at present and five years hence, the more pessimistic they are regarding their position relative to blacks in other cities, the less they think Haitian refugees have hurt black economic chances, the more likely they were to have called the fire department during the rioting and the more likely they were to be employed. These findings are consistent with a relative deprivation explanation, in that the better off the black respondents think they are, the more they see themselves as less well off than blacks in other cities. Conversely, economically marginal blacks see themselves as no worse off than blacks in other cities, and see Haitian refugees as potential competitors.

Table 19. Factor 6: Economic Position and Relative Deprivation (8.3%)

| | | | FACTOR SCORES | | | |
	I	II	III	IV	V	VI
Attitudes						
– Perceived economic position five years ago	–.073	.081	–.079	.119	–.179	.430
– Perceived economic position at present	–.071	.153	.083	.110	–.136	.543
– Perceived economic position in five years	–.089	.058	–.005	.132	.052	.406
– Blacks in Miami have lower incomes than blacks in other cities	.004	–.169	–.183	–.144	–.001	.324
– Blacks in Miami have worse jobs than blacks in other cities	.042	.042	–.183	–.277	–.104	.279
– Blacks in Miami have less education than blacks in other cities	.005	–.114	–.169	–.164	–.103	.299
– Ertswhile Hatian refugees hurt black economic chances	081	–.267	–.035	–.021	–.051	–.402
– Recent Haitian refugees hurt black economic chances	.101	–.243	–.036	–.021	–.115	–.267
Riot activities						
– Called Fire Department	.030	–.146	–.314	.180	.029	.279
Respondent characteristics						
– Respondent is unemployed	.034	–.010	–.065	.127	–.015	–.274

G. Factor Structure Summary

Although the individual factor components are complex, the aggregate set of factors presents a picture of the post-riot attitude configuration of Miami blacks. Because the orthogonal rotation produces factors which are independent of each other, it is possible to identify six major elements in the thinking of Miami blacks:

- A perception that police act abusively toward blacks.
- A concern about the social conditions of blacks in Dade County, and a linkage of that concern with a feeling that black leadership is insufficient.
- A willingness to engage in antisocial behavior rather than to seek redress for police abuse through conventional channels.

- Pervasive anger directed toward the courts, businesses, black and white politicians, whites in general and Cubans as economic competitors in particular.
- A feeling that the white criminal justice and political structure is biased against blacks, coupled with a willingness to resort to both conventional and unconventional means to draw attention to (and reduce) these biases.
- A feeling among blacks who see themselves as relatively well off that blacks in other cities are better off than blacks in Miami.

These issues are entirely independent of each other, such that those blacks who feel they have experienced police abuse are not necessarily concerned about social problem levels and black leadership, nor may they be assumed to have participated in the riot. This is an important point: experiences with police abuse (Factor 1) are unrelated to cynicism about bias in the white judicial system and the perception that riot behavior is a productive means of protest (Factor 5); similarly, concerns about social problem levels in the community (Factor 2) are unrelated to economic status and feelings of relative deprivation (Factor 6); likewise, anger at authority figures and Cubans (Factor 4) is unrelated to riot participation (Factor 3).

VII. DISCUSSION AND SUMMARY

In an earlier section, we outlined a set of theories that had become accepted as the "conventional wisdom" of sociologists seeking to explain the urban race riots of the 1960s. Some theorists had suggested that there were special characteristics of rioters that made them different from nonrioters; others, that there were elements of social disorganization that gave rise to riot behavior, or that the rioters were economically deprived, either in terms of some objective standard or in terms of reference groups they saw as competitors. Still other theorists posed accounts that were based on frustrated expectations, or dissatisfaction with existing political and municipal systems of the cities in which the riots took place.

If there is any prevailing characteristic of the literature on riot incidence, it is the existence of overlapping issues from one explanatory system to another. Social disorganization overlaps with absolute deprivation; relative deprivation overlaps with frustrated expectations; frustrated expectations overlap with political unresponsiveness and with the intrapersonal explanations of those who sought to differentiate rioter from nonrioter on the basis of values, personality or social condition; in turn, the latter systems overlap with theories of social disorganization.

In Robin Williams' analysis of the literature on civil disorders, these perspectives were ordered into a semiformal system, predicated on the development of "collectively shared discontent" among the rioting population (Williams, 1975). In effect, Williams argued, there are several interlocking components to the genesis of urban civil disorder: the production of shared discontent (which cannot be generated solely by deprivation), the acceptance of that discontent as an accepted ideology, the raising and subsequent blocking of hopes for change within channels of legitimate authority, and a set of ecological conditions which allow collective action.

In Miami in 1980, all of these elements were present. On one level, the genesis of the riot is itself easily linked to the sequence of police/citizen conflicts in 1979 and early 1980, a sequence that satisfies the requirements of both the production and legitimation of shared discontent, the raising of hopes when the McDuffie assailants were indicted and the dashing of hopes when they were acquitted, and the coincidence of the verdict announcement taking place on a Saturday afternoon when a public rally was breaking up in the largest black neighborhood in Miami.

To take this approach would be to ignore the development of a much larger set of issues in Dade County, issues that reflect much more extensively on the conditions that gave rise to a 1960s race riot in 1980. Although there are aspects of Miami's recent cultural and social history that could be considered exceptional—most notably, the Cuban migration—there is an isomorphic relationship between the expressed concerns of the Miami blacks at the time of the 1980 riots and the concerns of Detroit blacks at the same point in 1967. In point of fact, the similarity is much more extensive: in the Kerner Commission report, the first-tier concerns and second-tier concerns of blacks in riot cities are identical to the top-ranked concerns of blacks in Miami in 1980. In effect, Miami in 1980 was like most northern cities of the 1960s: crowded, conflicted, with an apparently-unresponsive political bureaucracy and an economic deprivation that intensified the conflict between rival ethnic groups.

We have seen how the Model Cities and Overtown areas went through enormous social upheaval within a relatively short period of time. During the 1960s, Overtown lost population drastically as urban renewal forced migration; those who remain under such circumstances are almost invariably the most marginal. During the same period, the population of Model Cities burgeoned, with entire Census tracts turning color in a matter of a few years and migrants from Overtown competing both with blacks from outside Dade County and with Cubans from outside the United States. By itself, the changes in these two neighborhoods would constitute a field day for social disorganization theorists.

At the same period of time, black economic progress was stymied, again especially in these neighborhoods, as circumstance constricted opportunity and competition came from an unexpected quarter. Again during the 1960s, waves of Cuban refugees competed for housing, for low-scale jobs and for welfare dollars as the Cuban Refugee Assistance Program provided stipends for resettlement. Not only was the gross population influx disruptive by itself, the peculiar characteristics of a Spanish-speaking group with strong middle-class orientations and Caucasian racial heritage made it worse. In effect, an additional middle class had wedged its way between black achievement and black aspirations; the developing Spanish subcultural economy did nothing to enrich the blacks, and made it all the harder to find work. White standards of living became even more inaccessable: Cubans became the reference group for feelings of relative deprivation.

During the 1970s, the conditions of the 1960s did not improve. The recession of 1974 cut deeply into black employment; the returnee refugee stream continued to swell the Spanish-speaking middle class; and the economic advantage of trade with South America simultaneously opened up untapped economic options even as it further closed off avenues of participation for blacks. Blacks saw themselves booted down from second-place status to third; it must not have been a pleasant sensation.

The problems of Miami in the 1970s were not unique to that city, however, as the National Advisory Commission on Criminal Justice Standards and Goals reported in 1976:

> In many ways, the state of the great cities is more desperate than it was during the most serious riots of the 1960s. An unstable economic situation has forced substantial curtailment of public services in many cities and caused a general deterioration in the quality of life for the poorer classes. Crimes of violence, damaging to both criminal and victim, continue at an unacceptably high level. Unemployment has risen markedly, and job opportunities for the disadvantaged have dwindled. These facts may well have contributed to the present quiescence. But this is a false calm, and we must see in the current social situation an accumulation of trouble for the future (*NACCJSG*, 1976: 2).

In effect, the promises and expectations of the Great Society of the 1960s were rapidly being mortgaged in the 1970s. The reality of social conditions was falling well short of expectations.

Against this tapestry, social service shortfalls and police behavior in the latter part of the 1970s may be easily perceived by the community in Dade County as evidence of political unresponsiveness. Requests for welfare assistance were denied as categorical relief programs—many aimed at refugees, both Haitian and Cuban—drew against limited Federal resources. Latins were elected to municipal and County government; blacks were not.

Without other influences, the conditions outlined here would have been enough to bring Dade County to a crisis point. Add an additional set of circumstances—eighteen months of strained police/community relations, which the most dispassionate observer would have to acknowledge reflected poorly upon the police—and the County would be at the flash point. With the addition of the Mariel boatlift and the promise of an instant replay of the Cuban migration problems of the 1960s, the collective strain would be intolerable.

But there also had to be a sense of agreement on the ideological basis for the strain. The McDuffie verdict provided it. Blacks in Dade County didn't riot when Johnny Jones was put on trial and found guilty; they didn't riot when Arthur McDuffie died; they rioted when five policemen, accused by one of their own of bludgeoning McDuffie to death and faking the reports to make it look like an accident, were found not guilty of all charges in Tampa.

It is hardly surprising that the level of riot participation was higher in Dade County in 1980 than it was for any urban riot of the 1960s. It is not surprising that no substantial ideological differences are found between participants and nonparticipants, from heavily-involved riot neighborhoods to lightly-involved neighborhoods. There is every evidence that extensive consensus existed regarding the justifiability of the riot, both among participants and nonparticipants. In particular, the factor analysis shows quite clearly that the disaffection with the criminal justice system, the anger and resentment against power structure figures and Cuban economic competitors, the understanding of the social problems and impotence of black leadership were all *independent of riot participation*, as were ideological positions on the effectiveness of riots as a form of political expression. Both active participants and nonparticipants were disaffected with the white establishment's response to black needs, and were prepared to consider the riots as having made an important contribution to progress. Some of the participants and nonparticipants, by the same token, felt that social problem levels were not as high, did not experience this disaffection and felt that the riots may have done more harm than good. Even if the Dade County riots had a broad ideological base, they did not arise out of a revolutionary consensus.

For that reason, looting Zayre's department store, setting fire to the Norton Tire Company and crippling Andy Vasquez were not well thought out expressions of political protest. Quite the contrary. But then, the black rioters in Dade County had had little sophistication in collective social protest. Dade County had turned into a northern city too fast for that to happen. Even as there was widespread disillusionment with black leadership, there was hardly consensus regarding exactly who those should be and what they should represent. The black residents of Dade County, although clearly angry and overtly bitter, had yet to develop the consensus necessary to make the riots an act of negotiation, to transcend the heat of the moment and forge active political alliances.

There is a moral to this experience. For over a decade, American cities had not experienced serious racial disturbances. There was a disarming calm to race relations in the 1970s, a calm born of the belief that the riots of the 1960s were outgrowths of ideologies and experiences peculiar to that age, and that the problems that had given rise to the riots had been solved with a federal alphabet soup of programs. But these programs require support, support which is not always there when the economy is coping with inflation, and massive population mobility and demographic changes tax the ability of existing agencies to respond to even the most minimal human service demands.

The Miami riots demonstrate that the underlying causes of the social problems of the 1960s have not been addressed, that although there may be cosmetic revision of the outward appearance of the problems the basic problems have not been solved. In addition, it may be that one more decade of dependence on the federal government has intensified the frustration of population groups that have learned to expect aid; that the large-scale internal migration from the Northeast to Sunbelt states is placing additional strain on the ability of southern cities to manage their population growth; that the growth of the Spanish-speaking minority population—expected to surpass the black population in size by the mid-1980s—will provide a basis for inter-ethnic conflict.

The Miami riots cannot be dismissed as an accident of fate, an outgrowth of a freakish Cuban migration and an unfortunate set of police actions. When Dade County changed from a vacation and retirement mecca to a congested urban environment, it set the stage for the worst urban riot of the century. And there are many other cities that are developing like Miami.

NOTES

1.   The Detriot survey was cited extensively in the Kerner Commission report, and was used in several post-riot analyses (e.g. Warren, 1969). Indicators of riot activity, social problem levels, police abuse, involvement with the criminal justice system and attitudes toward the white political system were identical in the Miami 1980 survey to insure comparability of the data, even where Detroit study operationalizations were considered questionable (e.g., riot participation was scaled from "very active" to "slightly active").

2.   Throughout this report, "Miami" and "Dade County" are used largely interchangeably. Where it is necessary to refer to the central incorporated area, rather than to the metropolitan area as a whole, "City of Miami" is used as the appropriate designation.

3.   The Cuban immigration to Dade County was very "European" in style. Not only were there language differences that helped the Cubans maintain cohesion and which separated them from the blacks, there were also racial differences. Although blacks made up about 25 percent of the population of Cuba at the time of the 1958 Census, less than 4 percent of the refugees before 1980 were black (Portes, 1969).

4.   A more comprehensive tract-by-tract analysis of black neighborhood social problem levels, migration, housing stability and economics was produced for the United States Commission on Civil Rights (Ladner, et al., 1980). Copies of this report are available at cost from the Behavioral Science Research Institute.

5.   During the worst of the rioting, Dr. Jones asked to be allowed to speak on local television; all but one television station refused. In his address, he pleaded with the rioters to "give the criminal justice system a working chance," indicating that although he had been found guilty, he was seeking redress through the appeals process. Despite his conviction, Dr. Jones' stature as a leader in the black community was undiminished: 64 percent of the blacks surveyed considered him an effective leader, the second-highest rating given to any black person in Dade County.

6. Attitude data has sometimes been criticized because of the chronological sequence in which it is gathered, i.e., after the fact of the riots. We are not considering these attitudes to be characteristic of the black residents of Miami before the disorders, but of their concerns after the riots, and will be using them only as points of comparison with other surveys of the Miami black population or with the post-riot Detroit black population of 1967.

REFERENCES

Berkowitz, William
    1974   "Socioeconomic indicator changes in ghetto riot tracts." Urban Affairs Quarterly 10: 69-94.
Caplan, Nathan, and Jeffrey Paige
    1968   "A study of ghetto rioters." Scientific American 219: 15-21.
Clark, Juan
    1975   The Exodus from Revolutionary Cuba: A Sociological Analysis. Unpublished Doctoral Dissertation, University of Florida, Gainesville.
Downes, Brian
    1968   "The social characteristics of riot cities: a comparative study." Social Science Quarterly 49: 504-520.
Feagin, Joe, and Harlan Hahn
    1973   Ghetto Riots: The Politics of Violence in American Cities. New York: Macmillan.
Fogelson, Robert
    1971   Violence as protest. Garden City, N.Y.: Doubleday.
Fogelson, Robert, and Robert Hill
    1968   "Who riots? A study of participation in the 1967 riots." Supplemental Studies for the National Advisory Commission on Civil Disorders, Washington, D.C.: U.S. Government Printing Office.
Geschwender, James, and Benjamin Singer
    1970   "Deprivation and the Detroit riot." Social Problems 17: 457-463.
Guertin, William and John Bailey
    1970   Introduction to Modern Factor Analysis. Ann Arbor: Edwards Brothers.
Gurr, Ted
    1968   "Urban disorder: perspective from the comparative study of civil strife." American Behavioral Scientist 2: 50-55.
Jiobu, Robert
    1971   "City characteristics, differential stratification and the occurrence of interracial violence." Social Science Quarterly 52: 508-520.
Kim, Jae-On
    1975   "Factor analysis." Pp. 468-514 in Norman Nie, et al., Statistical Package for the Social Sciences (2 ed.). New York: McGraw-Hill.
Ladner, Robert et al.
    1976   Social problems and resources in the City of Miami. City of Miami Comprehensive Neighborhood Development Plan, Technical Appendix II.
Ladner, Robert, Loretta Titterud, Barry Schwartz and Sandra Roker
    1980   The Miami Race Riots of 1980: Historical Antecedents and Riot Participation. Report to the United States Commission on Civil Rights. Miami: Behavioral Science Research Institute.
Levitan, Aida
    1980   Hispanics in Dade County: Their Characteristics and Needs. Dade County (Florida) County Manager's Office, Office of Latin Affairs.

Lieberson, Stanley, and Arthur R. Silverman
   1965   The precipitants and underlying conditions of race riots.'' American Sociological
            Review 30: 887-898.
Lupsha, Peter
   1968   ''On theories of urban violences.'' Paper presented at the 1968 meeting of the
            American Political Science Association, Washington.
Matza, David
   1966   ''Poverty and disrepute.'' Pp. 619-669 in Contemporary Social Problems. New York:
            Harcourt, Brace and World.
McPhail, Clark
   1971   ''Civil disorder participation: a critical examination of recent research.'' American
            Sociological Review 36: 1058-1073.
National Advisory Commission on Civil Disorders
   1968   Report of the National Advisory Commission (''Kerner Commission'') on Civil
            Disorders. New York: Bantam Books.
National Advisory Commission on Criminal Justice Standards and Goals (NACCJSG)
   1976   Report of the Task Force on Disorders and Terrorism. United States Department of
            Justice, Law Enforcement Assistance Administration.
Portes, Alejandro
   1969   ''Dilemmas of a golden exile: integration of Cuban refugee families in Milwaukee.''
            American Sociological Review 34: 505-518.
Rossi, Peter and R. Berk
   1972   ''Local political leadership and popular discontent in the ghetto.'' Pp. 292-308 in
            James Short and Marvin Wolfgang (eds.), Collective Violence. Chicago: Aldine -
            Atherton.
Sears, David and John McConahay
   1969   ''Participation in the Los Angeles Riot.'' Social Problems 17: 3-19.
Skolnick, Jerome
   1969   The Politics of Protest. New York: Simon and Schuster.
Spilerman, Seymour
   1970   ''The causes of racial disturbances: tests of an explanation.'' American Sociological
            Review 35: 627-649.
U.S. Bureau of the Census
   1963   1960 Census of Population and Housing, Miami, Florida Standard Metropolitan
            Statistical Area. Washington, D.C.: U.S. Government Printing Office.
   1973   1970 Census of Population and Housing, Miami, Florida Standard Metropolitan
            Statistical Area. Washington, D.C.: U.S. Government Printing Office.
Urban League of Detroit
   1968   A Survey of Attitudes of Detroit Negroes After the Riot of 1967. Detroit: Urban
            League.
Warren, Donald
   1969   ''Neighborhood structure and riot behavior in Detroit: some exploratory findings.''
            Social Problems 16: 464-484.
Williams, Robin
   1975   ''Race and ethnic relations.'' Pp. 125-164 in Alex Inkeles, James Coleman and Neil
            Smelser (eds.), Annual Review of Sociology (Volume I). Palo Alto, Cal.: Annual
            Reviews.

WELSH NATIONALISM IN CONTEXT

Charles Ragin and Ted Davies

INTRODUCTION: NATIONALISM

In one way or another a developmental conceptualization of societal change is embodied in most macrosociological perspectives (Nisbet, 1969). This conceptualization is often based on a pre-modern/modern dichotomy which contrasts a predominance of primordial sentiments (Geertz, 1963) in pre-modern settings with a predominance of rational interests (Weber, 1947) in modern settings. Nationalism cuts across this dichotomy. On one hand, nationalism is similar to the primordial sentiments predominant in pre-modern settings because it is an affective bond linking the individual to a collectivity. (Because of this affective character, nationalism is often considered sinister or reactionary.) On the other hand, however, nationalism is a truly modern social force. This seemingly primitive instinct arrived in Europe with the French Revolution and has yet to depart (Smith, 1971). The intensification of nationalist sentiment in Third World countries and the resurgence of subnationalisms in Western countries since World War II testify to the continued modernity of nationalism. (See Said and Simmons, 1976.)

Research in Social Movements, Conflict and Change, Volume 4, pages 215-233
Copyright © 1981 by JAI Press Inc.
All rights of reproduction in any form reserved.
ISBN: 0-89232-234-9

How can this affective sentiment flourish in an increasingly rational world? A recent attempt to account for this contradiction is found in Gellner's (1969) theory of reactive ethnic nationalism. In a nutshell, he argues that nationalism results from the uneven spread of modernizing forces, particularly industrialization, over the surface of the earth and from the disparities this unevenness creates between culturally distinct groups. Hechter (1975) has modified Gellner's arguments and applied his own version of the theory to ethnic resurgence in advanced societies. Specifically, Hechter attempts to account for the emergence of Celtic nationalisms in Britain. Hechter calls his perspective the ''theory of reactive ethnic cleavages.'' Below we contrast the arguments of Gellner and Hechter with the developmental arguments of mainstream political sociology, particularly those of Lipset and Rokkan (1967). We then assess the relevance of these theories to the Welsh case. We examine Wales because it closely approximates the conditions specified by the reactive theories (see below and Cohen, 1976) and because both perspectives have been applied to the Welsh case. Our assessment involves historical analyses of Welsh ethnicity and political expressions of Welsh ethnicity and quantitative analyses of third party voting in Wales and England.[1]

THE DEVELOPMENTAL PERSPECTIVE

The developmental argument converges with classical Marxism and nineteenth century liberalism in predicting the decline of both ethnicity and nationalism. The liberal view assumes that both of these sentiments are primitive, antithetical to modern reason; the classical Marxist view argues that ethnic and national affinities will become superfluous as capitalism is transcended by socialism.[2] (See Gellner [1969] and Nisbet [1953] on the convergence of liberalism and classical Marxism; see also Nielsen [1980].) Developmentalists, by contrast, argue that modernizing forces, particularly industrialization and urbanization (Lipset, 1959; Alford, 1963; Cox, 1970), lay the foundation for the rise in the modern setting of rational, functional ''interests'' (Weber, 1947, pp. 122-3) and that, as a result, ethnic and other cultural affinities become secondary or forgotten altogether.

The developmental perspective has been applied to the analysis of political cleavages in advanced societies by Lipset and Rokkan in *Party Systems and Voter Alignments* (see also Lipset, 1959; Alford, 1963; Allardt and Littunen, 1964; Cox, 1970). Briefly, they argue that in the development of a modern polity, political cleavages that are based on geography or culture are superseded by functional cleavages that reflect the economic interests of groups of political actors. This growing predominance of functional cleavages in European polities, according to Lipset and Rokkan, was brought on by the Industrial Revolution and was manifested in the more or less uniform establishment of mass, working class political parties in Western European countries. Their interpretation of the European experience is based on the view that cultural cleavages reflect value communities and that diverse economic interests cut across value communities. In the developmental framework, therefore, ethnic mobilization in the modern setting is unlikely because industrialization disrupts value communities by (1) magnifying the importance of economic interests and (2) eroding the particularism inherent in the constitution of value communities.

Implicit in this developmental interpretation of intranational political cleavages is a general diffusionist model of social change (Cox, 1970; Hechter, 1975). Before functional cleavages can become predominant on a national scale, it is necessary for the modernizing forces embodied in the process of industrialization to engulf the different value communities contained within the boundaries of an emerging nation-state. To the extent that value communities are attached to specific territories, this means that industrialization, and economic modernization in general, must connect the different geographic areas and draw then into a common economic life (Hannan, 1979). The subsequent assimilation of "peripheral" areas with "core" areas (Hechter, 1975) should progress as a function of the intensity of inter-regional interactions. Thus, peripheral cultural traditionalisms which, in this perspective, may serve as a basis for ethnic nationalism will survive only if there is a failure to incorporate peripheral areas into the national economy.

GELLNER'S THEORY OF REACTIVE ETHNIC NATIONALISM

Gellner's (1969) theory is a sociological theory of ethnic nationalism, for he treats ethnic nationalism as a cultural phenomenon. In his perspective the question of ethnic nationalism is a question of cultural affinity and the conditions that increase the importance of cultural affinity.

According to Gellner, these conditions are associated primarily with the eneven spread of development, particularly industrialization, over the surface of the earth. The uneven spread of development creates more advanced and less advanced groups attached to geographic areas. Often, more and less advanced areas are created within the territorial boundaries of large multi-cultural political entities (e.g., empires), and sharp cultural differences may coincide with developmental differences. If cultural and developmental differences do coincide, as is often the case, the two will tend to re-inforce one another, especially in the allocation of scarce roles, rewards and resources. Gellner (1969, p.168) argues: " ... when ... new entrants in the industrial world aren't markedly distinguishable from the older, they cannot hardly be excluded ... This is where culture, pigmentation, etc., become important: they provide means for exclusion for the benefit of the privileged, and a means of identification, etc., for the underprivileged." For this reason, nationalism should not be seen as a great collective awakening, but rather as a product of the exclusionary practices that accompany the uneven spread of industrialization.

HECHTER'S THEORY OF REACTIVE ETHNIC CLEAVAGES

Hechter's (1975) modifications of Gellner's theory are substantial, even though the two agree in spirit. Hechter's divergence from Gellner mostly reflects his attempt to apply the reactive theory to the Celtic nationalisms in Britain, examples of ethnic national resurgence in a modern setting.

The most important theoretical modification Hechter introduces is his de-emphasis of the temporal association of ethnic national mobilization with the arrival of the culturally distinct in an industrial setting. In Gellner's framework, there are only two possibilities: cultural assimilation or ethnic mobilization; in Hecter's, the spread of industrialization creates a cultural division of labor which provides a persistent, latent basis for ethnic nationalism. This latent basis, according to Hechter, may coalesce into an avowedly ethnic nationalist movement when the appropriate political and economic conditions obtain (see below).

Two other modifications follow from this temporal dissociation of ethnic nationalism and industrialization: (1) In Hechter's scheme the cultural markers which provide a basis for economic exclusion may be very subtle (e.g., accent). Gellner argues that if cultural distinctions are not sharp, the culturally subordinate will simply forgo their distinctive cultural practices in favor of assimilation. (2) Hechter asserts that even a partial coincidence of economic and cultural subordination will provide a latent basis for ethnic nationalism; Gellner emphasizes absolute or near-absolute exclusion, not relative exclusion.

THEORETICAL REFORMULATION

Both of the perspectives discussed above, developmental and reactive, are primarily theories of ethnic political mobilization; they are not theories of nationalism. The developmental perspective speaks only of the waning importance, given industrialization, of political cleavages based on cultural or "status" (Weber, 1946) distinctions, while the reactive ethnicity perspective points simply to the disruptive potential of a persistent coincidence of class and ethnicity.[3] Thus, the developmental perspective seems to deny the possibility of ethnic nationalism in its de-emphasis of the political relevance of ethnic affinity, while the reactive ethnicity perspective must assume, after showing a structural basis for continued ethnic affinity, that the jump from ethnic-class consciousness to ethnic nationalism is more or less automatic. It is not. There are many world-wide examples of ethnic class consciousness leading to ethnic mobilization without ethnic nationalism.[4]

It is difficult to address nationalism sociologically, for national identitites are both historically and politically defined and shaped. They are politically defined in the sense that the way in which a nation-state is constituted shapes the nature of the national sentiments which join a subject population to a national collectivity. For the national government of a particular country disfranchise ethnic minorities, for example, surely would alter the meaning of national identity in that country for both the dominant and subordinant populations. National identities are historically defined in the sense that they refer to the collective histories that result from the intersection of large-scale historical events. To claim a national identity is to claim a collective history and a collective fate. Large scale events continue to create new national identities (e.g., in the Third World) and to reshape old ones. For these reasons national identities must be seen as fluid; changes in national identities are induced by large scale events (often exogenetic in origin) and by ontogentic political actions and events (see Weber, 1946).[5]

Variations in the nature and intensity of existing nationalisms have a profound effect on the viability of subnationalisms such as ethnic nationalism. Subnational identities, like national identities, are historically and politically shaped. Indeed, to define a national identity is to define potential subnationalisms, for the national identity defines what is and what is not national. Virtually all nation-states confront historically induced ethnic and cultural heterogeneity (i.e., variant collective histories). To the extent that these heterogeneous collective identities are at odds with each other, subnational identities are likely to coalesce and to persist.

Lipset and Rokkan fail to address national identities historically; their approach to nation-building, in their own words (1967, p. 26), is "distinctly developmental." They (1967, p. 14) argue that the resolution of conflicts associated with the "National Revolution" (involving, among others, "the conflict between the central nation-building culture and the increasing resistance of the ethnically, linguistically, or religiously distinct subject populations of the provinces and the peripheries") precedes and lays the foundation for the resolution of conflicts engendered by the Industrial Revolution (e.g., the conflict between workers and owners). The reasoning behind this argument is straightforward: Economic conflicts that are cross-territorial can become of decisive political significance only in territorially integrated political entities. Once territorial integration is achieved, functional cleavages should predominate over all other cleavages.

While it is true that working class political mobilization was the rule in the polities of Western Europe and that this mobilization seemed to place Western polities on apparently convergent paths, this mobilization did not erase subnational identities. Viewed historically rather than developmentally, subnational resurgence is always a latent possibility given the existence of variant collective histories and a conducive national political or international context.

By equating territorial integration, which can be an accomplished fact, with nation-building, which is much more fluid, Lipset and Rokkan exclude the possibility of subnational resurgence. In fact, however, territorial integration is most often achieved in the face of persistent subnational identities. Perhaps a more reasonable developmental argument would be one that affirms both the primacy of functional cleavages and the probable persistence of culturally-based cleavages. In this revised developmental perspective, a subnational resurgence is possible whenever functional cleavages subside in a modern polity. However, it is also true in this revised perspective that a resurgence in the importance of functional cleavages would again reduce the salience of culturally based cleavages.

PRIOR EMPIRICAL RESEARCH ON THE WELSH CASE

The developmental perspective has been applied to the Welsh case by Cox (1970). Briefly, he argues that the industrialization of South Wales led to the rise of class politics in that area and its subsequent integration into the British polity via the Labour Party. Citing Alford, he states, "Increasing class militancy in South Wales at the end of the nineteenth century has been traced to English influences and militant centralized unionism . . . These are examples of the diffusion of class polarization on a macro-scale." (Cox, 1970, p. 159). By contrast, Cox argues, Welsh cultural traditionalism survived in the agrarian North of Wales and provided a basis for continued Liberal Party support. The traditionalism of the North thus accounts for its lack of integration with the British polity.

Cox conducted his study of Welsh and British politics prior to the resurgence of support for Welsh nationalism in the late 1960s. Given his emphasis on the predominance of functional cleavages in industrial Wales, however, it is likely that he would argue that support for Welsh nationalism could be strong only in the more traditional, less industrial areas of Wales where, historically, the Liberal Party has been successful. Further, noting the great magnitude of the differences between North and South Wales, he would probably discount the possibility that a national party of Wales could unite the Welsh in opposition to the British national government.

Hechter (1975) argues that the industrialization of South Wales led to the creation of an ethnically Welsh industrial working class dominated by English or anglicized middle and upper classes. This industrial cultural division of labor according to Hechter resulted from a pattern of "internal colonial" industrial development which carried with it the exclusionary practises described by Gellner. A cultural division of labor was also the rule in agrarian North Wales and in pre-industrial Wales as a whole. This agrarian cultural division of labor consisted of a Welsh-speaking, Nonconformist tenantry dominated by an English-speaking, Anglican landlord class. (See also Cox, 1970.)

Hechter argues that the cultural division of labor in industrial Wales created and maintained a latent basis for ethnic political mobilization. This latent basis for ethnic mobilization, in turn, according to Hechter, has been manifested in persistent Welsh anti-Conservatism and, more recently, in support for the Plaid Cymru (the Welsh nationalist party) following the disillusionment of Celtic voters with the Labour Party.[6] According to Hechter, the failure of the Labour Party to stymie the relative economic decline of Wales has resulted in the defection of Welsh workers from the Labour Party. In his perspective, Welsh nationalism is anomalous in the context of the British political system, for English voters do not have a subnational outlet comparable to that provided by the Plaid Cymru for Welsh voters.

As we show below, however, the historical record of industrialization and ethnicity in Wales does not conform very neatly to the picture provided by Hechter.

INDUSTRIALIZATION AND ETHNICITY IN WALES

The act of 1536 which formally joined Wales to England claimed to confirm a political unity that had always existed. Indeed, the border between Wales and England has never been distinct; Monmouth was treated as a county of England as late as the early 1900s (Morgan, 1970). With formal union came an abolition of distinctive Welsh political and legal institutions, and from Tudor times it became official governmental policy to eradicate the language and culture of the Welsh (Evans, 1973).

Most of the historical evidence indicates that the assimilation of the Welsh began very early. G. Williams (1971) points out that there have been large communities of English speakers in South Wales for centuries. It is believed that most of the Welsh were bilingual in Welsh and English or Welsh monoglot in 1800 (G. Williams, 1971); however, census takers did not undertake the enumeration of Welsh speakers until 1891. This census showed that the proportion of Welsh monoglots was only about .250; the proportion of Welsh-English bilinguals, about .30. By 1911, the proportion of Welsh monoglots had declined to .085; the proportion of Welsh-English bilinguals, to .265.

This remarkable decline in Welsh-speaking was the result of two complementary processes. One was the imposition of the English language in state financed schools following the Education Act of 1870. Evans (1973, pp. 38-9) comments, "The Welsh language was . . . excluded from them [the schools] not only as a medium of instruction but as a subject on the timetable, and even as a means of communication between the pupils themselves." The influx of thousands of English workers into South Wales between 1870 and 1900 furthered the decline of the Welsh language. "This solid body of English monoglots . . . hastened the anglicisation of the Welsh children with whom they played . . ." (Evans, 1973, p. 39). Eventually, an earlier pattern of immigrant English-speakers learning Welsh was reversed, and Welsh speakers were forced to give up their native tongue in what gradually had become English-speaking communities.

The nineteenth century was one of linguistic assimilation for the Welsh; it was also one of industrialization. Coal and the metallurgical industries were the first to develop, and they remained the most important industries until recently. An initial, modest industrial expansion in the last two decades of the eighteenth century laid the foundation for an explosion of industrial activity after 1840. "A local traffic to nearby coastal areas was transformed on a world-wide scale, with a massive expansion of output and the development of great ports such as Cardiff and Barry to link the growth of Wales to international demands." (Morgan, 1970, p. 10). "Between 1815 and 1914 the population of Wales rose four-fold, more so in Glamorgan and Monmouthshire [in South Wales] which together contained by 1914 over 60 percent of the entire population of Wales." (Philip, 1975, p. 3).

Partial, if not almost complete, assimilation resulted from this intensive industrialization of South Wales. A contemporary observer remarked that industrial Wales had become "American Wales" while rural Wales remained "Welsh Wales" (Morgan, 1970, p. 10). Indeed, the available quantitative evidence shows that Welsh-speaking survived only in the least industrialized areas; the cross-sectional correlations between the percentage of Welsh-speakers and the percentage of adult males employed in agricultural occupations for the thirteen counties of Wales are all over .60 (decennial census data, 1891 through 1971).[7]

Despite clear longitudinal and cross-sectional evidence of industrialization-linked assimilation, there is also evidence that a cultural division of labor of the sort described by Gellner and Hechter accompanied industrial development. D. Williams (1950, p. 246) argues, for example:

> The ironmasters, many of whom had their origins in English middle class Dissent, became allied through marriage, and association with the gentry, and adopted their Anglicanism. Seldom did the Welsh workmen attain to high administrative posts. 'In the works,' says a government investigator in 1847, 'the Welsh workman never finds his way into the office. He never becomes either clerk or agent. He may become an overseer or contractor, but this does not take him out of the labouring and put him into the administering class.'

Scholars do not agree on the extent of these conditions, however. Morgan (1970, p. 11) asserts that:

> Many of the later industrialists, particularly the coal owners and their managers . . . were Welsh in speech and Nonconformist by religion, preserving an intimate, personal relationship with their employees, with whom they could combine against the anglicized squires who ruled Welsh society.

Neither account, of course, gives a full picture. In all likelihood a cultural division of labor did develop to some degree in the more anglicized areas of South Wales, particularly those areas closer to England or the coast. The more western and northern portions of the South Wales industrial belt remained more Welsh in the sense that the upper strata were less anglicized and less Anglican. Yet, these areas probably appeared anglicized to immigrants from the North of Wales, for Welsh cultural traditionalisms were much weaker even in these seemingly more Welsh industrial areas.

To argue that Welsh culture and ethnic identity were preserved in industrial Wales by a cultural division of labor, therefore, distorts the reality presented by a comparison of the industrial South with the agrarian North. In other words, while it is quite true that industrial Wales was distinctive relative to England, it was also distinctive relative to North Wales. It is probably more appropriate to treat industrial Wales not as a bastion of Welsh ethnic identity, but as a synthesis of rural Wales and the peripheral industrial areas of England. This interpretation would account, for example, for the fact that while many of the social tendencies of Wales as a whole, such as Nonconformity and Liberalism, were *amplifications* of English peripheral social patterns, these amplifications were muted by industrialism in South Wales. The overall pattern of industrialization and ethnicity in Wales, therefore, lends some support to the developmental view and only slight support to Hechter's reactive view.[8]

Even though an agrarian cultural division of labor was the rule in preindustrial Wales as a whole, over time this agrarian cultural division of labor was dismantled throughout Wales. In the South it was dismantled by industrialization. In the North, ownership of farms gradually passed into the hands of the tenants. Indeed, most Welsh farmers today "own their own freeholds" (Madgwick et al., 1973, p. 125). This change in ownership is due to the fact that farming is much less profitable than it was in the past and that the importance of the agricultural sector has diminished markedly.

THE WELSH IN BRITISH POLITICS

Despite significant but incomplete assimilation, there have been stirrings of Welsh nationalism for over a century (Morgan, 1970). Throughout most of this period, agitation for a more independent Wales has occurred within the context of Welsh (and British) Liberalism. The first such movement was the Cymru Fydd, or Young Wales movement, founded in 1886. Most of its early members were South Wales Liberals, often middle class and Nonconformist. While literary and cultural interests predominated initially, the movement began to press for recognition of the unique social and economic problems of Wales by the Liberal Party before Parliament. The movement rapidly gained support in all areas of Wales; eventually it came to be dominated by the more radically and culturally Welsh North Wales Liberal Association.

The Cymru Fydd collapsed after only a few, intense years of activity. The proximate causes for its collapse were mostly political. North Wales Liberals favored greater independence from the national Liberal Party and, ultimately, from the British nation. South Wales Liberals, however, doubted the feasibility of severing economic ties with England and favored Liberal agitation for special treatment of Wales by Parliament (Morgan, 1970). Ultimately, however, these political differences sprang from a growing divergence of the more anglicized, industrial South and the more Welsh-traditional, agrarian North (Morgan, 1970).

Liberals representing Welsh parliamentary constituencies continued to voice the interests of Wales even after the collapse of the Cymru Fydd. Most often, these interests were educational and religious, but there were also serious efforts for a "home-rule all round" plan (provoked primarily by Irish nationalism) that included provisions for home-rule for Wales. Today the Liberals are the major proponents of a federal system for Britain, a plan that would allow Wales a good deal of autonomy.

The modern Welsh nationalist party, the Plaid Cymru or Party of Wales, was founded in 1925, long after the demise of the Cymru Fydd. The Plaid Cymru hoped to avoid the mistakes of the Cymru Fydd and disavowed formal association with the Liberal Party. Though sound in principle, this strategy cost them popular recognition; it was not until after World War II that they gained even scattered electoral support, and it was 1970 before they won the approval of even ten percent of Welsh voters. The Plaid Cymru's appeal always has been, at least in part, a cultural appeal; the three goals originally established by the party in 1925 all concerned the Welsh language. More recently, however, the party has argued the merits of economic independence from England before the Welsh electorate and in 1970 formulated a national economic plan for Wales.

Both the Plaid Cymru and the Liberal Party fared well in Wales during the 1960s and early 1970s. The Plaid Cymru's percentage of the poll climbed from about five percent in 1959 and 1964 to over ten percent in 1970 and 1974. The Liberals' share climbed from about six percent to about fifteen percent over the same period. While to some it appeared as though the Plaid Cymru would eclipse the Liberal Party in Wales (their respective shares of the 1970 poll were almost identical), the Liberals outdistanced the Plaid Cymru by more than five percentage points in 1974.

HYPOTHESES

Does the resurgence of support in Wales for the Plaid Cymru and the Liberal Party indicate that Wales is on a political path which diverges sharply from that of the British nation? The revised developmental perspective presented above argues that, examined within the context of British polity-wide patterns, Welsh patterns are probably not distinctive for two reasons.

1.   The dissaffection in Wales with the two class based parties, Labour and Conservative, is more properly seen as part of a British polity-wide dissaffection. This dissaffection, further, indicates a polity-wide decline in the salience of class cleavages. Relevant to this argument is the fact that third party (i.e., Liberal) support in England increased from

about nine percent in 1959 and 1964 to 13.6 percent in 1970 (282 seats contested) and to 24.2 percent in 1974 (February, 452 seats contested). Thus, the increase in Plaid Cymru and Liberal support in Wales is not unique; it reflects an increase in support for the Liberal Party in England. Thus, dissaffection in Britain with the two class based parties, according to this reasoning, has taken on a nationalist tone in Wales, but the origins and magnitude of dissaffection are probably the same throughout the British polity.

2.   Also relevant to the developmental argument is the fact that Welsh cutural traditionalisms have persisted in the more remote (i.e., less industrialized) areas of Wales. These cultural traditionalism, no doubt, continue to provide a social basis for Welsh political distinctiveness (Cox, 1970). If third party support is greater in Wales than in England, it may be greater only because of the culturally based political malintegration of these more traditional areas of Wales.

Proponents of the reactive theories, however, argue that support for third parties in Wales is a product of the disillusionment of Welsh workers with the Labour Party. Ethnic national mobilization in this perspective did not simply fill the political void left by the partial submergence of class cleavages. Ethnic-class conscious Welsh voters forsook the Labour Party for what appeared to be more viable alternatives, the Plaid Cymru and the Liberal Party. These parties, unlike the Labour and Conservative Parties, attempt to represent Welsh people as a nation, not as members of one of two social classes. Welsh voting patterns should differ markedly from English patterns since no such subnational alternative exists for English voters.[9] In Wales third party voting is a positive act, indicating support for the subnational alternative; in England, however, third party voting indicates only a dissaffection with the two class-based parties.

An adherent to the reactive theories might also point out that most of the population of Wales is industrial, even more industrial than that of England. If the developmental argument is correct, then one would expect *less* third party support in Wales, not more, since class should remain more salient in industrial areas. Thus, raw percentages showing support for third parties in Wales and England must deflate Welsh distinctiveness, for they do not control for industrialization. Once these controls have been introduced, the true political distinctiveness of Wales should be magnified.

These competing interpretations of Wales in British politics inform the empirical test we present below utilizing historical census and election data on Welsh and English counties. Basically, the two arguments run as follows: The developmental perspective does not completely deny Welsh political distinctiveness; net of the effect of Welsh cultural persistence, however, this perspective predicts that differences in support for third parties in England and Wales should disappear. The reactive ethnicity perspective, however, sees differences in support for third parties as an indication of a persistent basis for ethnic nationalism. Controlling for industrialization, these differences should be magnified, while controlling for indicators of tradtional Welsh culture should not reduce the political distinctiveness of Wales as indicated by level of support for third parties.

DATA AND MEASURES

The measures used in this study are based on data from the *County Reports* of the *Census of England and Wales* for the years 1921, 1931, 1951, 1961, and 1971, from *Parliamentary Election Results* (1918 to 1945 and 1950 to 1970) compiled by F.W.S. Craig and from the *Annual Reports* of the Registrar of Births, Deaths and Marriages. The 1974 election results were taken from Butler and Kavanaugh (1975). The constituency election results were aggregated into counties to conform to the census data. To match the census data to the election data we interpolated and extrapolated the decennial census data to conform to election dates. We analyze the results of the elections of 1924, 1929, 1931, 1935, 1945, 1950, 1955, 1959, 1964, 1966, 1970, and 1974. The election of 1924 was selected as the starting point because: (1) It predates the founding of the Plaid Cymru by one year; (2) it follows the political turmoil of the 1918 to 1923 period during which the Liberal Party was divided and the Labour Party made great headway (Kinnear, 1968); and (3) it follows the extension of the franchise in 1918 which gave the vote to all adult males (before this date many Welsh and English workingmen were not allowed to vote).

These data were used to construct our dependent variable and two independent variables.

The dependent variable is third party support defined as the proportion of the electorate voting for the Liberal Party in English counties and as the proportion of the electorate voting for either the Liberal Party or the Plaid Cymru in Welsh counties. By contrasting Liberal and Plaid Cymru support in Wales with Liberal Party support in England, we are able to examine the support of the Welsh for parties sympathetic to Welsh interests within the context of third party voting in the British polity considered as a single system.

The independent variables we constructed with the census data are a measure of industrialization and a measure of the persistence of traditional Welsh culture.

Our measure of industrialization is based on urbanization and occupational data; it is simply the sum of two proportions: the proportion of a county's population living in cities of over 20,000 in population and the proportion of a county's male labor force employed in manufacturing occupations. Thus, counties that are completely urban and contain a large proportion of manufacturing workers score almost 2 on this measure while rural, agricultural counties score around 0.

Our measure of the persistence of traditional Welsh culture is simply the proportion of the population able to speak Welsh. As noted above, this more than any other measure of Welsh cultural persistence shows the erosion of traditional cultural patterns by industrialization. The proportion of Welsh-speakers has declined over time as Welsh speakers have become more concentrated in the least industrial counties. Other measure of Welsh cultural distinctiveness do not indicate as directly the waning persistence of Welsh traditional culture. Note that the scores of Welsh counties on this measure range from a low of around 0 to a high of around .5. Thus, some of the counties of Wales are indistinguishable from the counties of England on this measure.

The third independent variable is a dichotomously coded variable indicating the counties of Wales. The thirteen counties of Wales are coded 1 on this measure and the forty counties of England are coded 0. Regression coefficients attached to this measure in our analysis of third party support indicate the magnitude of all England-Wales differences in third party support. If, for example, a positive, significant coefficient is attached to this measure, then we conclude that the other independent variables in the equation do *not* account for the differences between Wales and England in their respective scores on the dependent variable, third party support. In regression analyses below the Welsh counties binary variable serves as an index of the differences in third party support between Wales and England for hypothesis testing purposes. We turn now to a discussion of this method.

MODELLING WELSH DIVERGENCE WITH REGRESSION TECHNIQUES

As noted above it is important to examine differences between English and Welsh counties in third party support to see if these differences are statistically significant net of other possible explanatory factors. The developmental perspective, for example, argues that net of the effect that the waning persistence of traditional Welsh culture has on third party support in Wales there should be no statistically significant differences between third party support in Wales and England. The reactive ethnicity perspective, however, sees Welsh political distinctiveness as a phenomenon induced primarily by an industrial cultural division of labor. Thus, according to this perspective, differences in third party support should not be reduced once controls for Welsh traditonal culture have been included in the statistical analyses, while the introduction of controls for industrialization should magnify differences in third party support.

To test these arguments we analyze with regression techniques the aggregate census and election data described above. We first regress third party support on the binary variable indicating the counties of Wales. This analysis shows the magnitude of the differences between England and Wales without controlling for any of the variables thought to reduce or to magnify these differences. It is a simple difference of means test. In the second step of the analysis we include our measure of industrialization in the equation. This tests the argument based on the reactive ethnicity perspective that Welsh political deviance is especially anomalous given Wales' high level of industrialization. In the third step of the analysis we include our measure of the persistence of Welsh traditional culture, Welsh-speaking, to test the argument of the developmental perspective that the political distinctiveness of Wales is the result of the persistence, in some of the less industrialized areas, of traditional Welsh culture.

RESULTS

We report the results of our statistical analysis in Table 1. We examine third party support in twelve elections from 1924 to 1974. In each of the statistical analyses we weight the county data by population. For purposes of significance testing, however, we set the number of degrees of freedom at 53, in line with the actual number of observations.

Three equations were computed on the data for each election. The first regresses third party support on the binary indicator of the counties of Wales; the second, on this binary variable and the measure of industrialization; the third, on the binary variable, industrialization and the proportion of Welsh speakers, as follows:

(a) $T = a + b_1 C + e,$
(b) $T = a + b_1 C + b_2 I + e,$
(c) $T = a + b_1 C + b_2 I + b_3 W + e;$

where:

T = third party support,
a = regression constant,
b_1, b_2, b_3 = unstandardized regression coefficients,
e = error term,
C = binary variable indicating counties of Wales,
I = industrialization (proportion urban plus proportion in manufacturing occupations), and
W = proportion of Welsh speakers.

Table 1 shows the results of these analyses. The following patterns are observable in the results: (1) In nine of the twelve elections, third party support is greater in Wales than in England. The equations denoted by (a) show that these differences range from .063 to .183. The temporal patterning of these differences is somewhat contradictory. In the four elections since 1959 only one (1970) shows a statistically significant difference between Wales and England in third party support. This difference in support, however, is the largest difference reported in Table 1. (2) The inclusion of industrialization, in equations denoted by (b), has little effect on these differences; the effect at all

Table 1.   Stepwise Regression of Support for Third Parties on
Welsh Binary Variable, Industrialization and Welsh Speakers*

Dependent Variable		Independent Variable			
Proportion of Vote for Third Parties	Constant	Welsh Binary Variable	Industrialization	% Welsh Speakers	R^2
1924(a)	.172	.128			.138
(b)	.349	.120	−.149		.439
(c)	.320	(−.089)	−.124	.566	.583
1929(a)	.237	.096			.143
(b)	.425	.085	−.156		.776
(c)	.418	(.038)	−.151	.129	.791
1931(a)	.076	.136			.165
(b)	.216	.128	−.116		.367
(c)	.206	(.036)	−.108	(.280)	.392
1935(a)	.064	.125			.187
(b)	.201	.117	−.113		.442
(c)	.191	(.030)	−.105	.278	.474
1945(a)	.094	.064			.057
(b)	.264	.046	−.142		.482
(c)	.245	(−.059)	−.126	.379	.563
1950(a)	.094	.063			.091
(b)	.223	.046	−.107		.484
(c)	.220	−.067	−.088	.429	.662
1955(a)	.025	.087			.138
(b)	.130	.073	−.087		.337
(c)	.095	−.084	−.058	.626	.648
1959(a)	.062	.082			.101
(b)	.207	.059	−.119		.399
(c)	.180	(−.055)	−.097	.473	.550
1964(a)	.122	(.034)			.015
(b)	.309	(.003)	−.152		.400
(c)	.287	−.081	−.134	.380	.477
1966(a)	.088	(.048)			.031
(b)	.265	(.019)	−.143		.376
(c)	.243	(−.058)	−.126	.376	.449
1970(a)	.075	.184			.395
(b)	.233	.168	−.131		.601
(c)	.207	.091	−.110	.400	.673
1974(a)	.213	(.052)			.037
(b)	.431	(.030)	−.181		.493
(c)	.421	(.000)	−.173	.154	.506

*Unstandardized regression coefficients are reported; nonsignificant coefficients, p greater than .10, are reported in parentheses. The county data are weighted by population; the degrees of freedom has been set at the true number of observations, 53.

twelve points in time is to *reduce* very slightly the size of the coefficient attached to the binary indicator of the counties of Wales. (Note that at each point in time the effect of industrialization on third party support is negative. This supports the developmental argument that support for the two class based parties is greatest in the most industrialized areas.)[10] (3) The inclusion of proportion of Welsh speakers in the regression equations either reduces the coefficient associated with the binary indicator of Welsh counties to nonsignificance (elections of 1924, 1929, 1931, 1935, 1945, 1959, 1966, 1974) or changes its sign to *negative* and significant (elections of 1950, 1955, 1964). The reduction to nonsignificance indicates that Welsh political distinctiveness is due to the persistence of traditional Welsh culture. The change to significant, negative coefficients indicates that relative to their level of industrialization and their cultural traditionalism, Welsh counties on the whole are *less* supportive of third parties than English counties. (4) The one election which does show a statistically significant, positive difference in step (c) is that of 1970. This election supposedly was the nationlist breakthrough in Wales, for it followed a period of agitation by the Plaid Cymru and modest electoral success at by-elections. However, the results of 1974 election show this success to be only temporary, for third party support in Britain as a whole caught up with third party support in Wales in the election of 1974.

DISCUSSION

The findings presented above do not support the reactive ethnicity perspective. They support instead the revised developmental view that Welsh political distinctiveness must be viewed within the context of factors which increased the support for third parties throughout the British polity.

According to some scholars the British polity-wide factors that have contributed to the rise of third parties are related to the very success of the class appeal. Developmentalists and others (e.g., neo-Marxists such as Habermas, 1968) have argued that there has been a decline in the salience of class in advanced democratic countries following the political incorporation of the working class and the provision of economic and social security via the welfare state. (See also Giddens, 1974; Mann, 1973; Dahrendorf, 1959.) The findings of this study support the argument that these are polity-wide events and should be examined in that context. We recommend, therefore that research be directed toward questions that address the fate of class cleavages in whole polities, not toward questions that deal only with the political behavior of peripheral groups.

The decline in the salience of class, noted prior to the resurgence of the Celtic nationalisms by Alford and Butler and Stokes, may be only temporary. In the British general election of 1979 the nationalists in both Scotland and Wales fared poorly. In part, their poor showing can be traced to the stance taken by the Conservative Party during the election. Specifically, the Conservatives were more actively anti-labor and anti-socialist than they had been in the recent past; this increased the class relevancy of the general election and decreased support for third parties throughout Britain. By presenting itself to Celtic voters as much more of a class party, the Conservative Party increased its attractiveness to some third party supporters and drove others back to the Labour Party. The Welsh nationalists lost the few seats in Parliament they had won in the general election of 1974, and their share of the total vote declined. The Liberal Party suffered serious setbacks in all areas of Britain.

This turn of events suggests that the best way for the Conservative Party to combat the appeal of the Celtic nationalists is to maintain its class rhetoric, even if this results in a greater loss of Celtic Britain to the Labour Party. In any event, the results presented in Table 1 showing the equivalence of Welsh political distinctiveness and Welsh cultural traditionalism suggest that as long as the appeal of the Welsh nationalists is predominantly cultural, support for the nationalists will not be strong outside of the more traditional, less industrial areas of Wales.

NOTES

1. We compare the support for two third parties in Wales (Liberal and Plaid Cymru) with the support for a single third party in England (Liberal). This comparison is the organizing principle of the statistical analyses we present, for it is our contention that ethnic national sentiment in Wales must be examined within the context of third party voting in Britain as a whole. For a somewhat different approach, see Ragin (1979).

2. The national question has been debated extensively by Marxist writers, mostly in recognition of the difficulties of the classical Marxist position. Austro-Marxists such as Otto Bauer and Karl Renner favored limited cultural autonomy and argued that this autonomy could be achieved without political autonomy. Other Marxists, such as Lenin and Stalin, however, discounted the feasibility of this and other such schemes.

3. This disruptive potential is well known among developmentalists. Many of Lipset and Rokkan's arguments are based on an identical logic; see Ragin (1976).

4. The case of Blacks in the U.S. immediately comes to mind. Perhaps a crucial consideration here is the degree to which the culturally distinct population resides in a single definable territory such that the greater the territorial concentration, the greater the likelihood that ethnic political mobilization will take on a nationalist character (see Ragin, 1980).

5. Weber long ago pointed out the fluid nature of national identities and the problem this presents for nation-building. It is unfortunate that his discussion of the nation is largely ignored.

6. Ragin (1977) has shown that cultural factors associated with Celtic ethnicity do not enhance Labour's support in Celtic Britain. This casts considerable doubt on Hechter's ethnic-working-class interpretation of Celtic anti-Conservatism, for he argues that the Labour Party has served as an outlet for the expression of Celtic peripheral sectionalism.

7. A similar pattern obtains when a second indicator of Welsh cultural traditionalism, the percentage of Nonconformist marriages, is substituted for the percentage of Welsh-speakers. The cross-sectional correlations between these two indicators of Welsh cultural traditionalism are around .90.

8. Hechter acknowledges the consistency of the data on Welsh-speaking with the developmental argument and emphasizes instead the persistence of Nonconformity. The cross-sectional

correlations between these two indicators are very strong and positive, however, showing an inherent link between these two as indicators of the persistence of traditional Welsh culture in the less industrialized areas.

9. The party in England which claims to represent the whole nation is, of course, the Conservative Party. This claim is valid, for, historically, the Conservative Party has been the national party of England. It is thus impossible for English voters to escape class politics. To vote for the Conservative Party is to vote for a party which is both a class party and a national party.

10. Statistical analyses, not shown here, reveal that the negative effect of industrialization on third party support is *greater* in Wales than in England.

REFERENCES

Alford, Robert
1963   Party and Society. Chicago: Rand McNally.
Allardt, Erik and Yrjo Littunen
1964   Cleavages, Ideologies and Party Systems. Helsenki: Academic Bookstore.
Butler, David and Dennis Kavanaugh
1975   The British General Election of February 1974. New York: Macmillan.
Butler, David and Donald Stokes
1969   Political Change in Britain. New York: St. Martin's.
Cohen, Ira
1976   ''On Hechter's interpretation of Weber.'' American Journal of Sociology 81: 1160-2.
Cox, Kevin
1970   ''Geography, social contexts, and voting behavior in Wales, 1861-1951.'' Pp. 117-
          59 in Erik Allardt and Stein Rokkan (eds.), Mass Politics. New York: Free Press.
Dahrendorf, Ralf
1959   Class and Class Conflict in Industrial Society. Stanford: Stanford University Press.
Evans, Gwynfor
1973   Wales Can Win. Llandybie, Wales: Christopher Davies.
Geertz, Clifford
1963   Old Societies and New States. New York: Free Press.
Gellner, Ernest
1969   Thought and Change. Chicago: University of Chicago Press.
Giddens, Anthony
1974   The Class Structure of the Advanced Societies. London: Hutchinson University
          Library.
Habermas, Jurgen
1968   Towards a Rational Society. Boston: Beacon.
Hannan, Michael
1979   ''The dynamics of ethnic boundaries in modern states.'' Pp. 253-75 in Michael
          Hannan and John Meyers (eds.), National Development and the World System:
          Educational, Economic and Political Change, 1950-1970. Chicago: University of
          Chicago Press.
Hechter, Michael
1975   Internal Colonialism: The Celtic Fringe in British National Development, 1536-
          1966. London: Routledge and Kegan Paul.
Kinnear, Michael
1968   The British Voter, New York: Cornell University Press.
Lipset, Seymour
1959   Political Man: The Social Basis of Politics. New York: Doubleday.

Lipset, Seymour and Stein Rokkan
1967   Party Systems and Voter Alignments. New York: Free Press.
Madgwick, Peter et al.
1973   The Politics of Rural Wales. London: Hutchinson.
Mann, Michael
1973   Consciousness and Action Among the Western Working Class. London: Macmillan.
Morgan, Kenneth O.
1970   Wales in British Politics, 1868-1922. Cardiff: University of Wales Press.
Nielsen, Francois
1978   ''The Flemish movement in Belgium after world war II: a dynamic analysis.''
        American Sociological Review 45: 76-94.
Nisbet, Robert
1953   The Quest for Community. New York: Oxford University Press.
1969   Social Change and History. New York: Oxford University Press.
Philip, Alan
1975   The Welsh Question: Nationalism in Welsh Politics, 1945-1970. Cardiff: University
        of Wales Press.
Ragin, Charles
1976   ''Review of Michael Hechter's 'internal colonialism: the Celtic fringe in British
        national development.' '' Social Forces 55: 553-4.
1977   ''Class, status and 'reactive ethnic cleavages:' the social bases of political regional-
        ism.'' American Sociological Review 42: 438-50.
1979   ''Ethnic political mobilization: the Welsh case.'' American Sociological Review 44:
        619-35.
1980   ''Celtic nationalism in Britain: political and structural bases.'' Pp. 249-65 in Terence
        Hopkins and Immanuel Wallerstein (eds.), Processes of the World-System. Beverly
        Hills, CA: Sage.
Said, Abdul and Louis Simmons
1976   Ethnicity in an International Context. New Brunswick, NJ: Transaction Press.
Smith, Anthony
1971   Theories of Nationalism. New York: Harper and Row.
Weber, Max
1946   From Max Weber: Essays in Sociology. New York: Oxford University Press.
1947   The Theory of Social and Economic Organization. New York: Oxford University
        Press.
Williams, David
1950   A History of Modern Wales. London: J. Murray.
Williams, Glanmor
1971   ''Language, literacy and nationality in Wales.'' History 56: 1-16.

SOCIAL MOBILITY AND MODERN ART:
ABSTRACT EXPRESSIONISM AND ITS
GENERATIVE AUDIENCE

Judith Huggins Balfe

To discuss the experience of art as a process is to say nothing new: it always involves interaction between past or newly-created works of art and previous or present audiences. But any sound analysis of that process must go more deeply than is usually the case into the ways in which the perception and understanding of art by any audience is socially constructed by its previous exposure to other artworks and their aesthetic traditions. These traditions interact with socio-historical events in complex ways, depending (among other things) upon the homogeneity, duration, and power of the tradition itself, the life-experience of the audience generation which perpetuates or changes it, and its synchrony with various other artworld and social institutions.

Research in Social Movements, Conflict and Change, Volume 4, pages 235-251
Copyright © 1981 by JAI Press Inc.
All rights of reproduction in any form reserved.
ISBN: 0-89232-234-9

We have often analyzed revolutionary or counter-revolutionary changes in other areas of culture in this fashion, but we have seldom done so with the arts (Willett, 1978), since these remain around to deny by their similarly framed artifactuality the changes they once exemplified. This makes even more complex the already difficult analysis of artistic innovation, because if one can rightly state that art creates its audience, one must also say that the audience creates the work of art according to its own needs for change or stability. This is through the necessary "re-creation" of the work by members of the audience as they individually experience it, of course. Less obviously, it is also created through the begetting of self-recruited artists, distributors, and critics by that wider audience.

These four key artworld roles and their inter-relationships are thus subsumed under one master role-interaction, that of audience confronting the art; the art is product and producer, in a continual and ever-changing feedback loop. Specific audiences are recruited by and for particular art forms, and even the artworld specialists always remain members of the audience for their own work and for works and activity produced by other artists (Adler, 1979; Becker, 1974; Bensman & Lilienfeld, 1968; Kadushin, 1976). These may apprehend such other works differently than does the wider lay-audience because of their supposedly greater expertise (Child, 1969), but there is a great range in the expertise possessed by both artworld and lay audiences (Stebbins, 1979). The latter is composed of amateur artists, connoisseurs, collectors, and the like, as well as by the strictly nonpracticing onlookers and nonlookers. All are involved to different degrees in maintaining or changing particular audience traditions, and thus affect the soon-to-be-traditionalized artworks which confront them in turn.

The "master audience" for any art is thus affected by many variables. These determine the possibility of synchronies and the probability of multiple dissynchronies in the art-audience interaction: different audience members may occupy the same space and time, but they arrive and leave on different timetables and in different directions, at different speeds. Among the possible dissynchronies is the semi-inevitable "generation gap", but there are other such "gaps" as well, equally conditioned by specific historical events and particularly acute in periods of rapid social change and/or mobility. In all such instances, artists may separate themselves from the traditions of their "audience of origin" and adhere in turn to different "audiences of affiliation" in adulthood. Thus produced is the self-conscious denial of one's own "bourgeois" class origins, in adherence to an avant-garde anti-bourgeois ethic (Poggioli, 1968); the reverse may also occur.

Even without a quasi-political shift, contemporaneous generations obviously differ between as well as within themselves in standard SES terms involving relative degrees of mobility, power, wealth, education and homogeneity. These affect the age of their first exposure to different artworks, as well as the intensity and duration of that exposure (e.g., one trip to a museum or opera in college vs. listening to Milton Cross each Saturday afternoon or living across the street from the "people's mural" since childhood); the context of that exposure and the situational definitions imposed thereby (e.g., the arts as something to dress up for and be very polite about on rare occasions, as a mark of social status, vs. the arts as what everybody plays around with for fun); the degree of activity or passivity of involvement according to the art in question (e.g., very early activity is necessary if one is to become an artist in ballet or in instrumental performance, but not to such a degree in literature or theater). All of the audience variables interact with the specifics of the art form and its own traditions and innovativeness of style. Together, they affect the recruitment of new artists, and thus the creation of new works of greater or lesser difference from earlier ones.

As an example of the mix of generational and SES differences, those born in the United States before World War II tended to have a different reaction to the Vietnam War, or to late 60s popular music, than did their children, the "under 30, Spock generation". This was not just on account of the parents' less permissive up-bringing during the Depression. More importantly, the kind of social mobility experienced by that older generation differed as well. Many of them became full-fledged members of higher SES groups by emigrating out of the marginal restrictiveness of "lower" ethnic or class locations, via their own efforts and the G.I. Bill. They saw the world and hence the arts differently than did their "second generation" children who were born to the luxuries of split-level suburbia (Bensman & Vidich, 1971; Toffler, 1964). If acceptance of the art forms produced by any younger generation depends in part upon the degree to which they fit already established artistic traditions and institutions, this was a particularly difficult problem for the "immigrant" cohort which was upwardly mobile during the 40s: existing cultural institutions were less prepared for their entrance, and were therfore more hostile, than was the case a generation later in the 60s era of Pop art when "art as innovation" was the prevailing ethic to a far greater degree.

Differences in social mobility between generational cohorts, as in this instance, are enormously important even today when there is a vast expansion of the general multi-generational audience for all of the arts. The media which have made mass culture possible have also done much to make "high" culture accessible to a much wider public, thus expanding the recruitment base for future "high" culture artists as well. So too the printed book expanded the numbers of writers of and the audience for literature and visual images (Ivins, 1967, 1973; Mukerji, 1979). Rather than regarding the concomitant "Mid-cult" with horror (MacDonald, 1957)—what, after all, is the novel but an archtypally middle-class art form (Watt, 1957)—we should note that artists who create or perform "elite arts" are very seldom recruited from the elite audiences that ostensibly monopolize their patronage. This is virtually as true today as it was during periods of true aristocratic art patronage, e.g., by the Medici, or Louis XIV. By itself this fact undercuts any easy correlation of art, artists, and *Zeitgeist* based upon different "fantasy dispositions" in different historical and class locations (Kavolis, 1968). It suggests that there may be more change going on, even in periods of apparent stability, than might otherwise be realized from cultural evidence alone. Today, as in the past, without some vast (if undefined and often ignored) mid/mass cultural audience for presumably elite arts, the pool of potential self-electing artists would be much reduced.

Now, of course, boundaries between elite and mid/mass culture are highly porous indeed, with influences and artists moving in both directions. So as Gieseking and Horowitz frequented New York jazz clubs to hear Art Tatum in the late 30s, Dizzie Gillespie and other street-trained jazz musicians were studying the harmonics of Stravinsky and Bartok (WBGO Guide, 1980). Similar shifts in social status and the production of works of high aesthetic quality occurred in medieval Paris, Renaissance Florence, or Elizabethan England just as in 20th C. Berlin or New York. The difference is that in the former cases, artists and artisans were recruited from an often illiterate peasantry (e.g., Giotto), rather than from the literate middle classes. In either case, however, nonelite groups were included in the intended audience for the public arts which decorated churches, palaces, and museums, or were performed in other public settings; even restricted artists' guilds of past or present variety wanted a wider public than themselves or their elite patrons, if only to broaden the recruitment base.

The generational and historical dynamics discussed surely affect the lay audience, the artworld, and therefore the changing or "changeless" art more than is often recognized. They do much to determine not only the variety and the nature of the culture produced by different co-existing generations, but also the particular characteristics of the audience of producers and patrons, consumers and nonconsumers, and the degree to which any of these is prepared to understand art that is very different in origin or style from that of their own manufacture (Gaertner, 1955). Stylistic traditions for audiences and artists may be dormant or latent for years until the times are ripe for their re-emergence and rediscovery; indeed, because those traditions are encapsulated in the artworks themselves, they can exist independently of an unappreciative response by any particular audience and thus survive for a future and warmer public. (So post-Renaissance Mannerism was "discovered" as an independent style in the 1930s, after centuries of denigration).

This reminds us that the social relations of the role incumbents of the artworld and the surrounding social structure may determine less than we think about the endless and changing parade of the muses, because the arts themselves are actors, and not merely symbols, in the interaction. The human roles themselves are played in front of the artworks, and help to determine the inherent value and the price of the innumerable objects which are competing for audience consideration as art (Dickie, 1974; Kubler, 1962). However, it is the artworks which determine the aesthetic attitudes which the role players use to apprehend and evaluate those objects (Bensman & Lilienfeld, 1968; Duvignaud, 1972). But while created work and responsive audience may reflect each other over time, this is more commonly understood years later, when analysts have begun to see the forest despite the trees. When aggregated audiences have simultaneously available many art and audience traditions in different stages of development, it is difficult indeed to know just what is to be understood as "a product of its time." Who is more representative of the experience of modernity, Norman Rockwell or Jackson Pollock (Balfe, 1979b)?

It is for all of these reasons that it is necessary to go beyond the two most common approaches to the history or sociology of art, if we are to understand how it changes and/or use it to illustrate social movements. The usual approaches tend to see the arts as cultural symbols, primarily dependent upon the social structure. Otherwise, they explore descriptively the ways in which such culture is produced (Berger, 1972; Bourdieu, 1968, 1973; Hauser, 1951; Kavolis, 1968; Peterson, 1976, 1979; Sorokin, 1937). But either approach makes it difficult to get at the interaction between the arts and the audiences, the symbols and the social structure: to the degree either deals with specific artworks at all, these are all too often seen as an expression of the *Zeitgeist* or as a cultural product of the social structure, which then, in circular fashion, is defined from the evidence of the art expressed and produced. I have already shown the difficulty of such an easy assessment. Both approaches derive from the understandable tendency for sociologists to concentrate on the organizational structure of the current artworld (DiMaggio & Hirsch, 1976; Ennis, 1979; Graña, 1964a, among many others). Not surprisingly, such relations are usually structured in ways similar to the structures of the wider society, especially in their economic aspects, and thus the wider society is viewed as the independent variable. Given the replication of structural features, macro-level theory can be applied as readily as it is to other areas of social statics or dynamics (Karbusicky, 1968; Parsons, 1973). Other sociological methods and perspectives (e.g., sociology of occupations, small-group analysis) are equally germane. I have no quarrel with any of these approaches; indeed, the data they provide are necessary if the audience-art interaction is to be analyzed as I would suggest. They simply do not go far enough if we are to establish any causal arrows in the otherwise recognized interaction, or understand why so many seemingly contradictory styles can coexist in one era and not in another.

One problem is that we cannot merely ask the artworld audience what arts it likes, and why, and then go on from there: however they understand it, professional and lay artworld members alike usually find it difficult to articulate the private meanings which they may find in any work of art, created by themselves or by others. Most sociologists of art have tried to circumvent this problem by determining the social characteristics of those playing the four artworld roles, which would allow us to plot degrees of social similarities and differences within and between them. These data are hard enough to obtain for the artists, critics, and producers; they are virtually impossible to get for the audience, even when granted full cooperation from the art institutions which often commission such studies (Chicago Arts & Culture Survey, 1977; Metropolitan Museum Visitors Survey, 1975; Research in the Arts, 1977; DiMaggio, Useem, & Brown, 1978). In the age of mechanical reproduction and recording, let alone the mass media, the real and potential audience for any art is wide and diffuse indeed, and it is seldom examined for the full range of the arts it likes and dislikes at the same time. The usual justification for such audience studies as do exist (of past as well as contemporary audiences) is to determine the sources of patronage, either to link it with particular styles (Henning, 1970; Haskell, 1976; Hauser, 1951; Kavolis, 1968), or to attract it for the ongoing political and financial support of current institutions and programs (Netzer, 1978; Zolberg, 1980).

Such studies are both valid and necessary, but we cannot stop there if we are to understand the changing art-audience relation. Only if we use as well an egg theory of chickens, and view the audience as the means by which a work of art produces another work of art (perhaps one or many generations later), can we understand the relation of particular aesthetic streams (Ennis, 1979) to the society that produces or merely tolerates them, and to the synchronic or dissynchronic changes that occur in both over time (Kubler, 1962). After all, what in this flux remains fixed enough to serve as basis of such an investigation? The answer is an old one: *"vita brevis, ars longis"*. So by starting with the stream of art objects, we can then get at specific and varied instances of their interaction with the artworld itself, and their inter-relation with the wider society.

In sum: traditions established and maintained by existing works of past and present art, and in the minds' eyes of past and present audiences, contribute to the social constriction and construction of perception and appreciation in future audiences—and artists. What is true of language (Whorf, 1971) is true of paintings and music as well (Child, 1969). Innovation in the arts is a function of the perceptual and evaluative boundaries established by existing works; current and future definitions and uses of the arts depend upon what they have been, upon the rigidity or elasticity of previous definitions, upon the nature and number of rival definitions, and upon the social locations of all of these.

As a specific illustration of the foregoing approach to the study of innovation in the arts as an index of social movement, let us look at the social origins of Abstract Expressionism. The story we are usually told (Chipp, 1968; Geldzahler, 1970; Hobbs & Levin, 1978; Sandler, 1970) is that certain gifted and creative Americans came together in New York in the late 30s, learned much there from European artists exiled from Nazi Germany and elsewhere, and with native American exuberance and genius, suddenly exploded with "action painting" (Greenberg, 1973)—otherwise called Abstract Expressionism and often simply "the New York School." Peggy Guggenheim gave Jackson Pollock his first showing in her new gallery in New York in 1942, although he was not a

Surrealist like most of the other artists in her "stable." It would not have seemed an auspicious beginning. Yet a mere five years later, so great was the power of his style, so gifted were his fellow practitioners, and so evidently wide-spread was its audience appeal (in certain regions at least) that the Chicago Art Institute's nationally-prestigious annual exhibition of contemporary American painting was limited only to works in this style and in its close cousin, Abstract Surrealism. No entries were even permitted of works done in previously dominant American traditions of romantic realism or cubistic semi-abstraction. How did such an abstract and emotional style triumph so quickly, when for 40 years American modernists had met with near-total incomprehension? And why was the warmth of reception for the New York School demonstrably greater and earlier in the Midwest than in the East, including the Museum of Modern Art, in the city of its "birth"? What was its symbolic meaning, what social changes did it express?

Ignored by most critics and art historians who describe this period is precisely the matter of the audience, both the one of 1945-50 and the one out of which the painters themselves were self-recruited. Also ignored are differences between the audience which provided these recruits and/or applauded their innovative efforts, and other contemporaneous audiences which did not. Yet there can be a sociological accounting for such differences of taste, and for this particular instance of "culture lag" within the stream of "ideal culture" itself, once the audience question is settled.

New York School artists (and also their sympathetic critics, patrons, and historians) seldom saw the movement as maintaining a stylistic tradition. (Gorky is one possible exception, as he worked through a variety of modern styles to evolve his own.) Rather, they were often highly conscious of breaking both European and American traditions, even those of the avant-garde itself (Poggioli, 1968; Wolfe, 1975). Surrealism's ideology of freeing the unconscious was clearly influential, but stylistically it had much less impact upon the expressionistic style of the young Americans. Indeed, they had seen little Surrealism prior to arriving in New York as aspiring artists, although they had been in the audience for other styles of 20th C. European art. In the presentday "museum without walls" (Malraux, 1953), this may seem an unwarranted assumption, but there is considerable evidence for it. It is really only since World War II that Malraux's image could have come to mind and find widespread acceptance, because it is only since then that enormously expanded numbers of art books have been published, with good color illustrations and color slides widely available as well. Before the war, when future members of the New York School artworld were finding their respective paths to self-identification as painters, critics, or patrons, anyone's exposure to art was far more a matter of face-to-face or face-to-original-painting interaction than is the case today. Even if many originals were unavailable, or if the would-be artists were seldom taken to a museum or art gallery by their parents (Rosenberg & Fliegl, 1965), they were taught by someone who had seen certain originals, framed as art in particularly limited social situations. The artistic sensibility of such teachers was far less a product of slides and photographs than is the case today.

In order to learn what those originals were, as well as their social definitions, we must start with the artists as young members of a geographically and socially restricted audience. (The tourist strata of the 20s did not produce many painters, and young people seldom traveled far from home on culture tours during the Depression.) Almost all of the American-born artists who became widely recognized as members of the New York School actually came as adults to New York from elsewhere, generally from the Mid- or Far West, and from towns and small cities (Cummings, 1971; Geldzahler, 1970). If they did come from the East (let alone from New York City), they were Jewish, and from relatively stable second-generation ''gemeinschaftlich'' ghettoes. Many European émigrés were in New York at the time, working in a variety of artistic styles, but those who became influential or prominent in this movement as mentors, followers, dealers, or patrons were Jewish and/or from Northern or Eastern Europe: they were not out of the Parisian artworld (Chipp, 1968).

The elective affinity of American and European-born artists was not simply due to ethnic traditions, and the fact that so many Midwesterners had German ancestry. The main artistic traditions of the influential European artists were in each case expressionistic, given to depicting emotions rather than to the intellectual exploration of formal relationships. However, artists from those same socio-geographic areas had produced in the 20s an antithetical and highly geometric style at the Bauhaus. Among these artists, Albers and Mondrian were in New York during the formative years of Abstract Expressionism, and Moholy-Nagy was in Chicago. Yet the Bauhaus diagrammatic style, close to the Cubism which had attracted the first generation of American modern painters and (largely) Eastern collectors, failed to recruit many American artists to perpetuate it until 15 years or so after Abstract Expressionism had swept the field. Being German was not enough—especially not during World War II!

The dealers, critics, and most early patrons of the New York School shared with the artists similar social origins, whether native or foreign-born. They too emigrated to the New York art ''center'' from what it regarded as ''the provinces,'' or they were otherwise members of socially ''marginal'' groups, such as Jews. Common experience as immigrants aside, more important was the fact that all shared audience traditions of exposure to expressionistic work and to certain aesthetic attitudes which accompany it, however geographically distant may have been their places of birth. This is clearly true of the European and American-born Jews. But it is also true of the native American Midwesterners who became so prominent in the New York School (even those without German ancestry), as it was not true of their non-Jewish contemporaries who were raised in the Eastern locale which gave its name to the movement.

How do we know this? We can take museums as crucial institutions in the establishment of public tolerance for particular art styles, since even if privately funded, they must maintain wide public credibility in order to exist. And prior to World War II, regardless of the size and supposed sophistication of the supporting city, Midwestern museums exhibited a far greater proportion of European and American modern and particularly abstract art than did Eastern museums (Balfe, 1979a). From 1913 on, when America was first exposed to a massive exhibition of European artistic modernism with the Armory Show, museum exhibitions in Chicago, Detroit, St. Louis, Cleveland, and especially Buffalo were much more avant-garde than were those in New York and other Eastern cities. Not only did the ''provincial'' musuems exhibit such work, they actively collected it, with local assistance. This pattern continued despite the disregard of New York institutions for such modernism, and despite (rather than because of) the aggressive promulgation of avant-garde art by the Museum of Modern Art, founded in 1929.

This is demonstrable because the styles collected and exhibited varied by region. The Midwest gave far more prominence to German and other expressionistic artists than did the East, which virtually ignored them in favor of more structured and intellectual (primarily French) styles. When Eastern museums finally did start to catch up to the 20th century innovations in art, it was these latter styles which were displayed. Again, this is without regard to ethnic or national origin, as the East promoted Bauhaus and International Style geometrics of German origin just as the Midwest ignored them, as noted above. Obviously, what was available to be experienced as art differed in different parts of the country; however wide and diffuse the arts audiences were, they had geographic and therefore cultural limitations.

Of perhaps even greater influence than face-to-painting exposure to different styles were different regional definitions of what art was for. Midwestern museums geared their education programs around a John Deweyan ideal of art as experience (Dewey, 1934; Graña, 1964b), as means of emotional expression seen as beneficial for everyone regardless of age, class, or cultural level. This mirrors general Midwestern populism, of course, and is exemplified in both form and content in the paintings of John Steuart Curry and Thomas Hart Benton, neither of whom were regionally scorned as ''uncouth'' as were members of the New York City-based ''Ash Can School''. In contrast, Eastern museums were far more historical, intellectual, and elitist in their approach to art education, more steeped in and thus restricted by the Old Masters and European aristocratic taste.

The different philosophies of the uses of art, and of the appropriate aesthetic attitude, were taught in art schools as well as in museums, and not just to would-be artists, but to would-be art teachers. (Included in the latter category were the lecturers who fanned out from Chicago, giving chatauquas all over the Mid-West during the 20s and 30s.) The Art Institute in Chicago contained the largest art school in the world; in the 20s, it alone trained a fifth of all the art teachers in the United States, many of whom went on to teach in the region of their training. And it taught the Deweyan view altogether, to all classes and ethnic groups.

Thus even the undifferentiated audiences which did not elect to join the more structured artworlds of the Mid-West or East found different prevailing social and aesthetic traditions "in the air". This should come as no surprise in the visual arts, since similar regional schools have long been recognized in literature (e.g., the writings of Dreiser, Norris, Sinclair, Rolvaag, Cather, or Sandburg are distinctly Midwestern, rough, realistic, and unpolished compared to their Eastern counterparts). In architecture, the Chicago School of Louis Sullivan and Frank Lloyd Wright emphasized the unique and individual creativity of the architect, the authetic expressivity of materials of all kinds, the warmth of handcrafted work, and human scale and living patterns. In contrast, pre-30s Neo-Classicism of Eastern architectural styles had more in common with the International Style of Bauhaus elitism and aesthetic purity, to which it succumbed when the latter (and its proponents) arrived here in the early 30s (Gowans, 1964). The same regional difference is evident in contemporary and popular forms of music: 1930s Chicago Style jazz was improvisational, elaborating an underlying theme in different ways as the spirit moved the individual players at the moment of performance. New York popular music of the period was different: "big band" and structured, it required musicians to read and play the notes as written. And it can hardly be forgotten that American sociology itself acquired its particular and distinctive empirical characteristics in Chicago, before taking a different and more intellectual and theoretical turn in the East.

In every instance, the Midwestern style is not to be regarded (as many Easterners surely saw it) as inferior, crude, or provincial variants of Eastern (or dominant) culture. Indeed, in many instances noted above, the Midwest was distinctly more modern, advanced and concerned with broad humanistic values as well. Both ordinary life and rapid movement and change were acceptable in content and in style, but idealized universal forms were not. In the arts especially, innovation and emotional expression for everyone were taken for granted as the underlying reason for creating art at all, thoroughly undercutting any class-conscious "anti-bourgeois" or "anti-establishment" posture as a necessary ingredient in avant-garde work.

Lungs accustomed to breathing freely, Midwest fashion, did not readily adjust to the air encountered upon migration to New York, even though that city had the reputation of welcoming artistic innovation. Even given the legendary tolerance of Greenwich Village, New York liberalism extended far more to some styles than to others. Rather than accepting the Eastern taste and becoming more polished and "sophisticated" as had earlier immigrant artists who arrived in New York as solitary individuals, these artists reacted with vigorous counter-definitions instead. In sufficient numbers to constitute a critical mass, and otherwise sure of themselves, they embraced their "marginalism" with entrepreneurial zeal, and used it against both the elegantly stuffy "establishment" and philistine middle class society whether advanced or traditional in taste.

This situation cannot be understood just according to the European model of "épater le bourgeoisie" (Poggioli, 1968). The marginality that contributes to innovation was here clearly not determined by class differences, and, indeed, these artists may have succeeded in establishing themselves so quickly because of that fact (Rogers and Shoemaker, 1971). But if not a matter of such status hierarchies (even though the Easterners may have viewed it as such), what were the characteristics of the situation? Here were different regional and generational cultural traditions interacting, along with different dominant social structures as well. Long prevailing in the East more than in the Midwest, and far more in its native WASP art patron elites than in its ethnic or immigrant populations (Cuddihy, 1974) was a rationalized, Protestant-ethic self-control, underlying even robber-baron conspicuous consumption. This discipline helped in the early Eastern establishment of enlarged bureaucratic and technological institutions in cultural, economic, and political spheres. The late 40s and 50s, the era of the New York School, were precisely the years during which such "universalized rationality" became fully established throughout American society, without regard to geography, education, or class level. Military and academic institutions produced first the G.I., and then, through the G.I. Bill, the Man in the Gray Flannel Suit, caught in the "iron cage" of the corporation and the split-level trap.

While few of the prominent New York School artists themselves served in the military in World War II, let alone joined the ranks of corporate executive trainees, their own migration to New York City in the late 30s seemed in many respects traumatically similar to that experienced by those a decade younger. The discipline which was required for survival in modern "Easternized" institutions seemed to come more naturally to those who had been raised to its prevailing ethic of "don't scare the horses". Among other media, this was taught through the arts: "read and play the notes as written"; "good form does not show" (Arnheim, 1966); "great art teaches restraint" (Gombrich, 1954). But that demand was met with anxiety, rage, and hostility by those of whatever generation who were more subject to the strains of upward *or* horizontal mobility into that discipline, and whose view of themselves as artists or audience had been predicated upon different definitions of art and what its audience was entitled to experience from it.

Thus it is only by including in our discussion issues of ethnic, regional, and generational traditions of "audience of origin" and their possible variance with "audiences of affiliation" that we can understand not only the creation, but also the immediate and widespread acceptance of the New York School in the Midwest—and the lag of some years before its acceptance by the Eastern "establishment". (Indeed, in many such quarters, it has yet to become accepted.) The art audience which may never have left Detroit or Buffalo nevertheless similarly encountered as alien the institutions of mass society which reached out and engulfed them. While those who had grown up with the impulse control which those insititutions required found meaning in the geometric constructions of Mondrian or Albers, the Abstract Expressionists Pollock, Gorky, Motherwell, or de Kooning "put form on intuitions" (Langer, 1953) which these Easterners did not possess, and so could not comprehend in visual form. Indeed, final acceptance of the New York School by WASP purists at the Museum of Modern Art was largely determined by the influx into the New York art audience of overwhelming numbers of intellectuals, dealers, collectors, art historians and critics (especially Harold Rosenberg and Clement Greenberg) with the same social roots as the "immigrant" artists who had created this style. Thus the "established" artworld audience expanded to include (and even be dominated by) many who had previously been excluded, and the style speaking most directly to their experience of geographic, cultural, and social mobility from one particular location to another also became dominant, as the New York School. While the "center" may have expanded to dominate the "margins" economically, culturally something closer to the reverse happened if this evidence is to be taken seriously.

The perspective used so far, examining the audience as producer of both innovative artists and artworks, affords a sociological explanation of the eclipse of Abstract Expressionism and the emergence of the recently dominant styles of geometric minimalism and of Pop, and hyper-realism. It permits us to recognize that a different generation is now dominant in the established artworld (and affluent enough, if not altogether dominant elsewhere, to affect the economics of the art market). Involved are artists, critics, distributors, and both appreciative and speculative audience. The recent styles are socially and geographically widespread in terms of recruitment of artists, and in exhibition and location of creation (although still the Eastern art establishments give more prominence to geometric work than have the Midwestern ones). But differing from their parents, this new audience generation of artists and patrons matured with the realization that open self-expression was not the answer to emotional survival in the adult world, despite the views of Spock on which many were raised. Rather, they found that a cool distancing, a noninvolvement of self, was the better route to getting along in the even-more advanced and universalized modernity into which they had been born. Pollock met such institutions as a mature adult; those younger than he grew up through them and found that free-flowing emotion did not help in a setting that seemed both highly rationalized and irrational at the same time. Thus their view of art, and of life, became one of self-effacement, masking, ironic detachment, mannerism—and these are characteristics of both geometric minimalism and Pop or hyper-realism (Lucie-Smith, 1976). The one style enhances a sense of intellectual order, the other of every-day objective reality, both of which seemed to need such enhancement and reinforcement in the early 60s. To be sure, both styles are as much a reaction against the world, and the art, of the "father's generation" as had been that of the New York School in its day. At the same time, they are characterized as well by the positivistic science and technology created by those "fathers," for which this generation had also been audience in the post-war television era in which they matured (Davis, 1977).

Television had helped to broad that audience's exposure to vastly different arts and dissynchronic styles, of course, and it also taught that reproductions could be equal in aesthetic importance to originals. A further lesson was that the manner in which the artist played his role was often as important as the art which was produced. Neither view was held by the earlier generation, who are still insisting (to the end: Harold Rosenberg died, "unconverted," in 1979) on the primacy of individual-to-painting interaction, and of the emotional power of unique symbols which alone are to be understood as "art."

There is insufficient space here to discuss the details of this, comparable to our examination of Abstract Expressionism, and to explain the complexities of the audience which has produced "post-modernism" in art as well as else-where. Still, even this brief treatment indicates the usefulness of this audience-centered approach in explaining the emergence and decline of particular styles in ways that study of their immediate moment of creation cannot do, as it affords evidence of how the works of art work back on the audience to perpetuate themselves in different or less congenial contexts. Synchronies and dissynchronies in the creation and acceptance of different styles (as cultural indicators of other forms of social movements) become more comprehensible when generational factors are included, along with regional or ethnic audience traditions. Using this approach, it would be worthwhile looking at the Beat Generation of writers and their mixed reception in different quarters, or the sudden and enormous expansion of dance companies in the last decade (a matter not totally determined by vastly increased federal funding), or the apparent evolution of rock music into a "higher" art form in recent years, or the latest revival of Victoriana. It could be profitably used in sociohistorical studies as well, helping to explain both change and continuity in the production of art in the present and the appreciation of the arts of the past.

Such an art-historical emphasis need not be the primary focus of such studies, of course: works of art, like other cultural artifacts, are social and, thus, sociological. They can be used to illustrate sociological theories of the processes of modernization, or social change or conflict in general, by paying careful attention to their own traditions and socializing impacts upon audi-ences (and, thus, upon artists). Because the arts are always created by a tiny minority, it is too easy to assume *either* that they are elitist and nonrepresentative of major social forces *or*, on the contrary, that they are uniquely expressive of these forces because of the greater sensitivity and awareness of those who produce them. As demonstrated by this close examination of one such instance, neither of these conclusions is warranted. Avante-garde or innovative art no more successfully predicts the future than does rétardataire or traditional work; the same is true of the kinds of sociological prediction to which we are all too prone, as we try to make comprehensible the staggering complexity of our social world. Awareness of the perils of reductionism in the one sphere might save us from the greater errors inevitable in its practice in the other.

REFERENCES

Adler, J.
1979   Artist in Offices. New Brunswick: Transaction.
Albrecht, M.
1970   ''Art as an institution.'' Pp. 3-26 in M. Albrecht, J. Barnett, and M. Griff (eds.), The Sociology of Art and Literature. New York: Praeger.
Arnheim, R.
1966   Toward a Psychology of Art. Berkeley: University of California Press.
Balfe, J.
1979a   ''The institutionalization of modern image: modern art in American museums 1913-1963.'' Unpublished Ph.D. dissertation. Rutgers New Brunswick University.
Becker, H.
1974   ''Art as collective action.'' American Sociological Review 39(6):767-776.
Bensman, J., and I. Gerver
1958   ''Art and mass society.'' Social Problems 6: 4-10.
Bensman J., and R. Lilienfeld
1968   ''A phenomenological model of the artistic and critical attitudes.'' Philosophy and Phenomenological Research 38(3): 353-367.
Bensman, J., and A. Vidich
1971   The New American Society. Chicago, Il.: Quadrangle.
Berger, J.
1972   Ways of Seeing. New York: Viking Press.
Bourdieu, P.
1968   ''Outline of a sociological theory of art perception.'' International Social Science Journal 20(4): 589-612.
Bourdieu, P.
1973   ''Cultural reproduction and social reproduction.'' Pp. 71-99 in R. Brown (ed.), Knowledge, Education, and Cultural Change. London: Travistock.
Child, I.
1969   ''Esthetics.'' Pp. 853-916 in G. Linzey and E. Aronson (eds.), Handbook of Social Psychology, 2nd edition. Reading: Addison-Wesley.
Chipp, H.
1968   Theories of Modern Art. Berkeley, Ca.: University of California Press.
Cuddihy, J.
1974   The Ordeal of Civility. New York: Dell.
Cummings, P.
1971   Dictionary of Contemporary American Artists. London: St. James Press.

Davis, D.
   1977   Artculture: Essays on the Post-Modern. New York: Harper and Row.
Dewey, J.
   1958   Art as Experience. New York: Capricorn Press.
Dickie, G.
   1974   Art and the Aesthetic: An Institutional Analysis. Ithaca, N.Y.: Cornell University
            Press.
DiMaggio, P., and P. Hirsch
   1976   ''Production organizations in the arts.'' American Behavioral Scientist. 19(6): 735-
            752.
DiMaggio, P., M. Useem, and P. Brown
   1978   Audience Studies of the Performing Arts and Museums. Washington: National En-
            dowment for the Arts.
Duvignaud, J.
   1972   The Sociology of Art. New York: Harper and Row.
Ennis, P.
   1979   Expressive Symbol Systems: Theory, Morphology, and Process Methods. Middle-
            town: Wesleyan University.
Gaertner, J.
   1955   ''Art as the function of an audience.'' Daedalus 86(1): 80-93.
Geldzahler, H.
   1970   New York Painting and Sculpture: 1940-1970. New York: Metropolitan Museum.
Gombrick, E.
   1954   ''Visual metaphors of value in art.'' Pp. 255-281 in L. Byron, et al. (eds.), Symbols
            and Values: an Initial Study. New York: Harpers.
Goodman, N.
   1968   Languages of Art. New York: Bobbs-Merrill.
Gowans, A.
   1964   Images of American Living. New York: Harper and Row.
Graña, C.
   1964a   Bohemian v. Bourgeois. New York: Basic Books.
Grāna, C.
   1964b   ''John Dewey's social art and the sociology of art.'' Pp. 175-190 in R. Wilson (ed.),
            The Arts in Society. Englewood-Cliff, N.J.: Prentice-Hall.
Greenberg, C.
   1973   Art and Culture. Boston: Beacon Press.
Haskell F.
   1976   Rediscoveries in Art. Ithaca: Cornell University Press.
Hauser, A.
   1951   The Social History of Art. New York: Vintage Books.
Henning, E.
   1970   ''Patronage and style in the arts.'' Pp. 353-362 in M. Albrecht, J. Barnett, and M.
            Griff (eds.), The Sociology of Art and Literature. New York: Praeger.
Hirsch, P.
   1969   The Structure of the Popular Music Industry. Ann Arbor: Institute for Social Re-
            search.
Hobbs, R., and G. Levin
   1978   Abstract Expressionism: The Formative Years. New York: Whitney Museum.
Ivins, W.
   1967   How Prints Look. Boston: Beacon Press.
Ivins, W.
   1973   On the Rationalization of Sight. New York: Plenum.

Kadushin, C.
1976   ''Networks and circles in the production of culture.'' American Behavioral Scientist
        19(6): 769-784.
Karbusicky, V.
1968   ''The interaction between 'reality-work of art society'.'' International Social Science
        Journal 24:4, 642-655.
Kavolis, V.
1968   Artistic Expression: A Sociological Analysis. Ithaca: Cornell University Press.
Kubler, G.
1962   The Shape of Time. New Haven: Yale University Press.
Kuhn, T.
1970   The Structure of Scientific Revolutions. 2nd ed. Chicago: University of Chicago
        Press.
Langer. S.
1953   Feeling and Form. New York: Scribner's.
Loesser, A.
1954   Men, Women, and Pianos. New York: Simon and Schuster.
Lucie-Smith, E.
1976   Late-Modern: The Visual Arts Since 1945. 2nd ed., New York: Praeger.
MacDonald, D.
1957   ''A theory of mass culture.'' Pp. 59-73 in B. Rosenberg, and D. White (eds.), Mass
        Culture. New York: Free Press.
McMullen, R.
1972   Art, Affluence, and Alienation. New York: Praeger.
Malraux, A.
1953   The Voices of Silence: Museum Without Walls. Garden City: Doubleday.
Martorella, R.
1977   ''The relationship between box office and repertoire.'' Sociological Quarterly 18:
        354-366.
Meyer, L.
1967   Music, the Arts, and Ideas. Chicago: University of Chicago Press.
Mueller, J.
1951   The American Symphony Orchestra. Bloomington: University of Indiana Press.
Murkerji, C.
1979   ''Mass culture and the modern world system.'' Theory and Society 8: 245-268.
Netzer, D.
1979   The Subsidized Muse. New York: Cambridge University Press.
Parsons, T.
1973   ''Culture and social system revisited.'' Pp. 33-46 in L. Schneider and C. Bonjean
        (eds.), Culture in the Social Sciences. New York: Cambridge University Press.
Peterson, R.
1976   ''The production of culture: a prolegomena.'' American Behavioral Scientist 19(6):
        669-684.
Peterson, R.
1979   ''Revitalizing the Culture Concept.'' Annual Review of Sociology 5: 137-166.
Poggioli, R.
1968   The Theory of the Avant-Garde. Cambridge: Belknap Press.
Research in the Arts: Proceedings of a Conference on Social Policy, Related Studies of the
        National Endowment for the Arts.
1977   Baltimore: Walters Art Gallery.
Rogers, E., and F. Shoemaker
1971   Communication of Innovations. 2nd ed., New York: Free Press.

Rosenberg, B., and N. Fliegl
    1965   The Vanguard Artist. Chicago: Quadrangle.
Sandler, I.
    1970   The Triumph of American Painting. New York: Harper and Row.
Sorokin, P.
    1937   Social and Cultural Dynamics. Vol. I, New York: American Book.
Stebbins, R.
    1979   Amateurs. Beverly Hills: Sage Publications.
A Study of Out-of-Town Visitors to the Metropolitan Museum
    1975   New York: Yankelovich, Skelly and White, Inc. for the Metropolitan Museum of Art.
Survey of Arts and Cultural Activities in Chicago
    1977   Chicago: Chicago Council on Fine Arts.
Toffler, A.
    1964   The Culture Consumers. New York: Random House.
Watt, I.
    1970   ''Private experience and the novel.'' Pp. 105-120 in M. Albrecht, J. Barnett, and M.
              Griff (eds.), The Sociology of Art and Literature. New York: Praeger.
WBGO Program Guide
    1980   Newark: Public Radio 88 FM, October.
Whorf, B.
    1971   Language, Thought, and Reality. Cambridge: M.I.T. Press.
Willett, J.
    1978   Art and Politics in the Weimar Period. New York: Pantheon.
Wolfe, T.
    1975   The Painted Word. New York: Farrar, Straus, and Giroux.
Zolberg, V.
    1980   ''Displayed Art and Performed Music.'' Sociological Quarterly 21: 219-231.

SUBORDINATED TECHNOLOGICAL DEVELOPMENT:

THE CASE OF MEXICO

James D. Cockcroft

This work is a preliminary attempt to elaborate—through examination of the Mexican case—the role played in capital accumulation by technology sales from the more-industrialized countries to the less-industrialized developing countries (so-called LDCs). The argument is that technology sales not only serve the purposes of capital accumulation for the seller but also contribute to the subordinated capitalist development of the buyer. Both the Mexican and the non-Mexican bourgeoisies, directly or indirectly, manage to accumulate capital as a result of these technology "transfers," at the expense of the working class which activates the technology. Yet the non-Mexican bourgeoisies accumulate far more capital and at faster rates in this area. Consequently, in spite of economic growth in Mexico, there develops an historical pattern of relative decapitalization of Mexico, manifested in the outflow of remitted profits, payments on technology, debt amortization, etc. The work is

Research in Social Movements, Conflict and Change, Volume 4, pages 253-282
Copyright © 1981 by JAI Press Inc.
All rights of reproduction in any form reserved.
ISBN: 0-89232-234-9

divided into three parts: theoretical formulations; technology, capital accumulation, and the cult of technocracy; and the case of Mexico.

I. THEORETICAL FORMULATIONS

The centralization tendency of capital is what underlies the present monopoly stage of capitalism: the merger of banking with industrial capital. This fusion is called "finance capital." Lenin (1972) summarized imperialism as "the domination of finance capital," characterized by the export of capital and "the formation of international capitalist monopolies which share the world among themselves."

Over sixty years since Lenin's study of imperialism, one finds this part of his theory still useful—although there is less "world" for the imperialists to share, given the rise of socialist revolutions and anti-imperialist wars of national liberation. One now observes continued centralization of capital; the internationalization of capital and select production "sectors" (*e.g.*, automotive); and monopolization of the means of production and of international markets or segments thereof (without ever eliminating competition).

I shall employ the concept "imperialism" in Lenin's sense, keeping in mind that imperialism is not itself a mode of production (MOP) but rather is a stage of development of the capitalist MOP. This understanding of the analytical concept "imperialism" proves more precise and scientifically applicable to the case of Mexico than broader conceptualizations based on notions of territorial imperatives, human greed, or nationalist acts of expansion disguised as ones of self-defense.[1]

Concomitant with the emergence of imperialism is a sharpening of the fundamental contradiction of the capitalist MOP: the contradiction between the progressive socialization of production and the private appropriation which fuels it, that is, the contradiction between labor and capital, proletariats and bourgeoisies. Through its own inner laws of motion, capitalism lays the basis for its own expansion and yet its own demise. It socializes labor throughout society, thereby, "disciplining, uniting, and organizing" the very class strategically placed to challenge or overthrow it (Marx, 1933, Vol. I, Ch. 23). In its inexorable drive to accumulate more surplus value, capitalism destroys land and workers. Yet capitalism depends on land and workers to continue the process of capital accumulation. An ever more acute tension builds between the social productive forces (socialized labor based on the division of labor and cooperation), on the one hand, and the capitalist relations of production, on the other. The international rivalries and wars generated by capitalism in its imperialist stage only heighten the tensions inherent in the capitalist MOP and have been seen to speed the replacement of capitalist MOPs with socialist ones (or at least transitional ones) in those areas where anti-imperialist liberation struggles triumph. While the character of these transitional MOPs varies, their birth in the fires of world war and national and international class struggles, and their subsequent impact on such struggles, are widely recognized.

Sociologists and economists of whatever theoretical persuasion have almost universally come to recognize the great importance of transnational corporations (TNCs) in the modern world (Barnet & Muller, 1975; Baird & McCaughan, 1979; Bernal Sahagún, 1976; Braungart & Braungart, 1980; Fajnzylber and Martínez Tarrago, 1976; Gilpin, 1975; Hernández, 1973; Kreye, 1974; Levinson, 1971; Newfarmer & Mueller, 1975; Palloix, 1973; dos Santos, 1973; U.N., 1973; Vernon, 1977). TNCs are corporations which have their base in one country but draw much of their income, raw materials, and operating capital from several other countries, through ownership of foreign subsidiaries, joint ventures with foreign governments or investors, and a host of other means. [2]

The compelling force behind the rise of TNCs is the need for coporations to grow and maintain their profitability, as well as to gain control over as much of the world's resources and capital as possible. TNCs are the logical outgrowth of monopoly capital which has outgrown nations.

As capital and production transcend national boundaries, becoming "transnational," labor also becomes more mobile, crossing national boundaries, *but at a slower rate* than does capital. For monopoly capital based in the most industrialized countries, this constitutes the basic cause of its obtaining overseas a higher rate of surplus value and access to a growing reserve army of labor. Distribution and exchange relations flow through the same dynamic of a capitalist MOP gone international in its imperialist stage. All the familiar statistics about "unequal exchange" are, in terms of the source of all value in labor's production, the empirical and *historical* reflection of *surplus-value circulation*. This international circulation of surplus value is part of the realization of production, *i.e.*, the actualization of products through their exchange and consumption. It is an important part of the process of contemporary accumulation of capital on an extended scale.

It is commonly recognized that historically LDCs have sold commodities to more industrialized countries relatively cheaply and "in exchange" bought commodities dear—"unequal exchange"—often raw materials or primary products for finished manufactured goods. But this unequal exchange is in the realm of prices, which in turn reflect costs, profits, and the fetishism of commodities in its ultimate form: money. Such fetishism conceals what in fact are relations between people. Unequal exchange is a social and historical phenomenon based on power relations which historically have colonized, dominated, and impacted on the evolution of the social formations of LDCs. In the imperialist stage of capitalism, these power relations have tended to strengthen and deepen economically.

Writing on these factors of power and history which lurk behind the contemporary fetishism of commodities in the context of unequal exchange, Harry Magdoff (1978, p. 163) points out:

"Whatever equality of exchange one may assume exists between the products of the metropolises and the periphery, one thing is obvious: it contains within it an inequality in wages that conceals a long and bitter history of force and oppression. The costs that enter into prices are determined not only by the costs of living labor but also by the exertion of the past, dead labor—the way labor was used to create harbors, canals, railroads, machinery. . . . needed to extract and export the resources of the periphery. . . . from whichever angle we approach the cost-price relations, we find that prices and costs are themselves the products of the social system and the current as well as the congealed past power relations of that system.

In the capitalist MOP, surplus value—*i.e.*, surplus labor, or the value of the total product of social labor beyond the equivalent of the socially necessary labor time requisite for the maintenance of the workers and their families— when circulated into markets, assumes prices. This surplus-value circulation, when occurring internationally, is unequal for LDCs not only for historical reasons. Modern forms of monopoly provide additional power advantages for TNCs. Such phenomena as the following deepen unequal exchange and its corresponding benefits for the TNCs' accumulation of capital: TNCs' export of capital or intermediate goods at exhorbitant prices (made possible by monopoly or oligopoly); direct and indirect investment in LDCs, where TNC exploitation of low-wage labor permits exaggerated rates of surplus value; pressures applied on LDCs by international credit institutions dominated by monopoly capital—*e.g.*, the International Monetary Fund (IMF), World Bank, etc.; monopoly capital's direct or indirect domination of the market into which an LDC's petty-commodity producers (*e.g.*, poor peasants) channel their surplus product; a TNC's conversion of the materialized human labor congealed in products imported from an LDC—often from a TNC subsidiary— back into products for sale or export; and many others.

Thus, international pricing mechanisms produce unequal exchange. Both are based on the exploitation of labor over many decades of uneven power relations within and between social formations. Historically, the creation and distribution of surplus labor occurs on an international level, with national differences in wage levels relating in part to the power advantages accruing to imperialist nations over time. Theoretically, Amin (1979, p. 89) points this out when he asserts:

National differences in the price of labor power are not to be explained by differences in average national levels of development, but rather by the [international] fragmentation of the working class. . . . The price of labor power in the imperialist centers is not independent of the price of labor power in the dominated periphery, because the 'average price' of the totality of labor power must correspond to their value, which is in relation to the development of productive forces on a world scale. The [higher] price of labor power at the center is indissolubly bound up with the imperialist international character of the system of capitalist exploitation.

TNCs epitomize the twentieth-century fusion of banking capital with industrial capital, that is, the domination of finance capital. The reproductive cycle of social capital assumes three material forms—money capital, productive capital, and commodity capital—each of which is activated by three corresponding types of capital: banking capital, industrial capital, and commercial capital (all of which are fused, to one degree or another, in finance capital). Finance capital articulates itself in the process of production of commodities (industrial capital), the circulation of commodities (commercial capital), and the credit system that supports circulation (bank capital). The internationalization of the production process, fueled by these capitals, is *itself* the expression of finance capital's domination. Finance capital, a fusion of distinct forms of social capital, guides and expresses the internationalization process of production, distribution, and exchange. Technology sales are an important part of this process.

TNCs initiate and develop a set of international relations of production, which serve to reorganize the basis of exploitation and the conditions of employment and unemployment. However, completion of this process of internationalization of the relations of production is barred by countervailing forces, themselves generated by contradictions inherent to the capitalist MOP in its imperialist stage. These countervailing forces include anti-imperialist wars of liberation, inter-imperialist rivalry, uneven devolopment patterns within each capitalist nation, etc., all of which are but *forms*, or *partial expressions*, of the fundamental and underlying contradiction which fuels the expansion of the capitalist MOP, its internal decay, and its external threats: the contradiction betwen labor and capital.

II. TECHNOLOGY, CAPITAL ACCUMULATION, AND THE CULT OF TECHNOCRACY

Key to the understanding of technology's role in capital accumulation is the centralization tendency of capital, and here again the monopoly character of modern captialism shows up. According to a study by the U.N. Conference on Trade & Development (UNCTAD, 1971, pp. 24-25):

> Fifty percent of all patents which were obtained by companies and whose corresponding research was financed by the Federal Government of the U.S. between 1946 and 1962 belong to twenty firms . . . market control and monopolistic concentration is reinforced through the system of crosslicensing between companies, which in turn reduces a worldwide oligopolistic structure into a, regionally, monopolistic one.

A recent trend in the export of capital is the commercialization of technology ("technology transfers"). Most TNCs are now interested in exporting investment capital, technology, and capital goods rather than merely exporting manufactured products as they had done, in large part, earlier in this century (manufactured products, in turn, are often exported to regional common markets after being produced abroad). So important is this process that the UNCTAD study (1971, p. 4) views TNCs as carving up among themselves foreign markets for technology: "arrangements of patent cross-licensing among transnational corporations, cartel agreements, tacit segmentation of markets . . . (etc.) often constitute common behavior rather than the exception." Although U.S. technological advantages have dwindled in recent years, in the 1960s the U.S. still accounted for more than two-thirds of all receipts based on patents and licenses accruing to the six capitalist nations most active in patent activity (*The Financial Times*, Feb. 3, 1969). R & D figures also show the U.S. far ahead in technology-development investments (although quantity does not entail quality, as any American consumer can verify). In brief, TNC activity in technolgy is as elsewhere: monopoly or oligopoly, with U.S. advantages quantitatively measureable but qualitatively insecure.

The UNCTAD study (1971, p. 15) shows how important technology has become in the export of capital from the imperialist nations to Latin America:

> For the whole of Latin America it has been estimated that during the period 1960-65 about $1,870 million were spent annually for the importation of machinery and equipment. These imports amounted to 31% of the total import bill of the area. They also constituted about 45% of the total amount spent by Latin America on capital goods during the same period.

A consulting firm for TNCs, Business International Corporation (1970, pp. 21, 29) suggests that:

> a new era of international investments has dawned, in which the predominant characteristic is the exploitation of technology . . . If licensed technology and management contracts can afford sufficient income and control without equity ownership, all the better in terms of economic nationalism.

Not surprisingly, U.S. Secretary of State Henry Kissinger made technology a key agenda item at the 1976 meetings of the Organization of American States in Chile.

TNCs use their monopolies on technology to accumulate capital in less obvious ways, through various tricks of internal bookkeeping known as "transfer pricing." TNCs can readily underprice or overprice (price-fix) because trading is done between related parties, sometimes using a fictitious third party "dummy office" as intermediary. Over half of Latin American trade comes under potential transfer pricing (Barnet & Muller, 1975). The Mexican pharmaceutical industry, controlled by foreigners, has been reported as making up to $400 million a year through transfer pricing (*El Día*, Aug. 20, 1974). Transfer pricing decapitalizes LDCs through overpricing technology imports and underpricing exports (making local profits look smaller and thereby reducing taxes owed). In other words, transfer pricing on both technology and its products is a mechanism of accumulating capital for TNCs.[3]

The importance of technology sales in capital accumulation is suggested by the enthusiasm that Cold-War-oriented captialists show in negotiating investment packages with the Soviet Union and Eastern Europe. These technology sales should not be viewed in isolation from the larger whole of which they are a part, including capitalism's need for international stability ("detente").

But other questions are involved, besides super-power rivalry. Classically, when dealing with weaker countries, TNCs use technology sales to help "denationalize" strategic economic sectors, mainly through the capitalization of technological inputs. Whether through joint-venture deals or pure licensing agreements, a TNC can stipulate that part or all of the technology furnished may be paid through "equity participation" (together with a lump-sum payment or a running royalty usually calculated as a percentage of net sales, or one of these). Later renegotiations of technological agreements may include the demand for equity participation. Or the terms of payment for technology may imply an increase of the debt/equity ratio that can lead to some sort of equity "sale" or "transfer" to the supplier of the technology.

This raises a number of questions for further research, questions which can be addressed only in a preliminary fashion here. What are the relationships between the international commercialization of technology and direct foreign investment? What are *all* the implications (including cultural ones) of the fact that technology agreements between TNCs and other parties increasingly involve the sale or licensing of "know-how"? To what degree is transfer pricing on "technology transfers" supplementing direct industrial production in the accumulation-of-capital process, and what are the limits to that? To what extent is it possible under the capitalist MOP to advance technologies to such a point that human labor becomes relatively superfluous in the production process itself?

This last question confuses overall development of machine production, which rests on objectified labor and permits expanded production of use-values and chains of employment, with *automation*, which in its fullest application tends toward an absolute displacement of human labor. The capitalist MOP which generates automation also generates countervailing forces, such as the tendency for the rate of profit to fall as a result of increased investment in machinery relative to living labor (the only source of surplus value).

Cognizant of the source of capitalist production in the sale of living labor power to the capitalist, Marx (1973), far from positing the elimination of living labor under the capitalist MOP, observed toward the end of one of the longest passages he ever wrote on this question: "The most developed machinery thus forces the worker to work longer than the savage does, or than he himself did with the simplest, crudest tools" (even though in the long run it may reduce the relative demand for labor). This derives from the drive of capitalists to accumulate, not from automation or machine technology as such. Technology, in fact, has the potential to release humankind from long workdays and alienated labor *once* the relations of production have been brought into line with the forces of production under socialism, or collectivized ownership of the means of production by those who make and work them—an alignment yet to occur in any of the more industrialized countries.

Far from heralding a new lease on life for capitalism, automation and increased investments in constant capital relative to variable capital (labor power) contribute to the ultimate decline of the capitalist MOP in a twofold manner. First, they lay the conditions for capitalism's dissolution *via* the socialization of the means of production and the ever greater contradiction between that socialization and the appropriation of its products by a few. Second, they tend to reduce the rate of profit, as well as the relative rate of investment in the source of surplus value, *i.e.*, in living labor, use and reproduction of which are essential to capitalism's existence and survival. Thus, ideological discourse about capitalism's triumph through technological miracle-making, post-industrial social utopias, an age of abundance, and "post-capitalist" forms of production (by which is usually meant production based on the latest technology) serves to mystify a much larger and more explosive contradiction within the capitalist MOP, the effects of which are currently being struggled around in a multitude of ways.

Capitalism tends to reproduce itself wherever it asserts its dominance as an MOP, and this reproduction, however uneven in practice, occurs also in the superstructural areas of science and culture. Anyone who has experienced the spread of the English language and U.S. cultural norms abroad, along with the export of Coca Cola, Donald Duck, and U.S. technology, can readily appreciate the validity of the concept "cultural imperialism." Much of the success of imperialism's historic expansion and survival derives from its maximization and maintenance of advantages in technology and its intellectual sources: science and education.

In 1970, R & D funding in the U.S., over half of it paid for by taxpayers' monies even though most of its products remain within TNC hands, approached $40 billion a year, or an amount far greater than most countries' gross national product and 2 and one-half times more than that spent on R & D by all the West European nations combined (Sergeyev & Strugatshya, 1971; UNCTAD, 1971). Insofar as LDCs engage in R & D, their research and norms are oriented toward those of the more-industrialized countries, and in practice their scientists tend to sevice foreigners more than their fellow citizens. Research for meeting the needs of the local masses is practically nonexistent. The tendency in LDCs is to draw up "comparative-cost tables" and on that basis decide that it is more economical and conducive to development to import foreign "known-how" and entire productive installations than it is to invest in developing one's own science and technology.

Given the fact that TNCs link science and technology in export "packages," cultural questions for a LDC become inseparable from questions of production and technology. A country usually cannot import a piece of machinery without importing the whole package, including "know-how."[4]

In most LDCs the results have already become obvious. Foreign standards of production, consumption, and education generate a materialistic, consumption-oriented bourgeoisie and middle strata which increasingly imitate the life styles of affluent families in the more-industrialized countries. This is more than a question of the influence of mass media or cultural "fads." It is rooted in the altering shape and relationships of the combined forms of production in the LDCs themselves. Not only the local bourgeoisies but also many people from the petite bourgeoisie and parts of the working class—merchants, shop-keepers, service workers, and aspiring intellectuals, scientists, and bureaucrats —are locked into a productive process dominated by TNCs and their technol-ogy, and a distribution, exchange, and educational process which accom-panies that. These social classes and groups, then, increasingly come to define the continued presence of such technology and its *models* of value, economic development, and education as being within their *own* class interests.

Their life style, rooted partly in the technology that allows it to exist, is reinforced by a form of ideological, or cultural, imitation characterized by the *cult of technocracy*, which exaggerates the importance of "expertise" and deference to technocratic solutions at every level of social and political organ-ization. Zuck and Cockcroft (1973) introduced the concept "cult of technoc-racy" because it is a cult. It is a cult because the majority of humankind have come to accept its dynamics of expertise, specialization, unique skills, and unquestionable authority on a level of both "commonsense" and respect, admiration, or worship. This cult serves to discourage creativity, imagination, and self-reliance among the masses. Technocracy itself is deferred to.

I say "technocracy," rather than bourgeoisie, because I am speaking here of a technocracy composed of a cross-section of classes and personnel which in effect behaves as a technologically shaped and informed group which carries out tasks from positions of power and authority in government, economic production, and education. The cult of technocracy is an ideological and cultural phenomenon because so many people accept, believe in, and live by the cult of technocracy, however severe the frustration or alienation which accompanies it.

The cult of technocracy is a crucial ideological creator and perpetuator of economic dependence in LDCs because it so elevates and mystifies technology as to make independent experimentation next-to-impossible. Workers and peasants are excluded from control over technology and made to feel "unpre-pared" to tackle technological questions, even at the workshop level of broken parts, repairs, etc. Furthermore, the cult of technocracy and the technocrats who participate in and benefit from it, can help lay a potential power base of upper and middle-level officials and bureaucrats upon which the forces of counter-revolution can build and rely—especially in situations where the normal supply of consumer goods or replacement parts is suddenly reduced or cut of. A good example is Chile under Allende (1970-1973), with the corre-sponding disastrous results that most Chileans have suffered since the imposi-tion of military dictatorship.[5]

Although historically rooted in capitalism, the cult of technocracy affects LDCs attempting socialist solutions to social production as well. For example, the Chinese, by their own accounts, confronted problems of relying too heavily on the expertise of Soviet technicians in the 1950s. A decade later, during the Great Proletarian Cultural Revolution, one of the major ideological directions of the revolutionary process was the struggle against dependence on China's *own* ''experts,'' with a renewed emphasis on ''self-reliance.'' The technocrats were told to ''go to the people, in order to learn from the people.'' Presently (1980), the Chinese leadership is still struggling with the problem in what appears to many as a complete reversal of earlier positions. The Chinese experience testifies to the gravity and depth of problems associated with the cult of technocracy in LDCs attempting socialist-oriented industrialization.

This raises questions for further exploration and research. What is the role of an indigenous science and technology capability in breaking the bonds of dependence? Is the quest for such capability, as *normally* conceived, in fact doomed to be counter-productive? *Normally*, this quest is conceived in terms of ''closing the gap'' between a LDC and a more-industrialized country. This ''closing-the-gap'' mentality, itself not unrelated to the cult of technocracy, tends to impose upon the developing country a set of already-existing standards of technological development, ''models'' and ''strategies'' for economic development, and all the baggage of related cultural attitudes and educational biases. Should not developing countries think rather in terms of alternative models, strategies, and approaches to science and technology, developing less constrained approaches to knowledge, education, scientific development, and technological advance? How can the developing of such alternatives, which presumably would also maximize the participation of the masses and their creative potential, occur without succumbing to the concomitant danger of turning one's back on much of the ''know-how'' already available on the world scene?

III. THE CASE OF MEXICO

Prior to World War II, Mexican economic development had been conditioned by an international economy through which Mexico imported manufactured goods in exchange for primary exports. Structural changes made under President Lázaro Cárdenas (1934-1940) provided a basis for increased industrialization. So did the contingencies of World War II, when Mexico's principal trading partner, the United States, was unable to export to Mexico its usual quantity of manufactured goods. To finance its war production, the U.S. purchased huge amounts of Mexican silver. Thus, internal and external conditions permitted Mexico to embark upon an import-substitution program of industrialization, which was undertaken over the next three decades.

Mexico's capitalist state, consolidated by the social and political reforms of the Cárdenas period, helped stimulate and guide this program in various ways, including tax incentives for private industry, state investments in economic infrastructure (transport facilities, energy, construction, education, etc.), and maintenance of a disciplined labor force receiving, for the most part, low wages and no social -welfare guarantees. The unbalanced class structure and uneven income distribution in Mexico (still today more unequal than in India or Puerto Rico), combined with the existing demand structure and the character of Mexico's bourgeoisie and state, contributed to Mexico's concentrating on light industry and durable and nondurable consumer goods mainly for the upper-income brackets of the population.

Mexico's industrialization program failed to emphasize local production of industrial equipment and producers' goods, that is, Department I of the total product (production of the means of production). Table 1 shows the distribution of manufacturing activity by 1960—and the slow changes beginning to appear by the 1970s in new efforts to confront the lack of Department I development. Producers' goods increasingly had to be imported from abroad just to keep the import-substitution process going. By 1968, capital goods represented 50 percent of Mexican imports; raw materials for industrial production accounted for another 32 percent. Mexico had become the sixth largest buyer of U.S. goods in the world. Import-substitution turned out to be import-intensive (*The Economist Intelligence Unit*, 1970, p. 19; Reynolds, 1970, p. 252; Villarreal, 1975).

Table 1. Manufacturing Percentage Structure, Mexico
(At constant 1960 prices)

	1960	1970	1974
Nondurable consumer goods	61.1	50.3	47.0
Intermediate goods	27.6	31.7	33.5
Durable consumer & capital goods	9.1	15.7	17.5
Other industries	2.2	2.3	2.0
Total	100.0	100.0	100.0

Source: Banco de México, annual reports.

Moreover, by permitting relatively free remittance of profits abroad and special tax breaks, the state encouraged foreign investment. The U.S. advanced large credits for Mexican industry during World War II, after which U.S. corporations entered with their own largescale investments, buying out many of Mexico's nascent industries. Direct foreign investment in Mexican more than doubled between 1940 and 1960; it nearly tripled between 1960 and 1970 (Table 2). Of the 1974 foreign investment, 76 percent was in manufacturing, 14 percent in commerce, 6 percent in mining and metallurgical industry, 1 percent in agriculture, and 3 percent in other areas. U.S. investors accounted for almost 80 percent of all foreign investment.

Table 2.   Direct Foreign Investment in Mexico, 1940-1974
(Millions U.S. dollars, Total; percentages, sectors)

Year	Total	Agri-culture	Mining & Metallurgi-cal industry	Manufac-turing	Elect-ricity	Com-merce	Trans-portation	Other
1940	418	1	28	7	30	3	31	0.3
1945	583	1	28	15	23	7	25	1
1950	566	1	20	26	24	12	13	3.1
1955	919	2	19	34	20	13	6	5.2
1960	1,080	2	16	56	1	nd	nd	5
1965	1.744	1	8	69	1	16	0.5	5.5
1970	2.822	1	6	74	0.2	15	0.3	3.5
1974	4,275	1	6	76	0.07	14	0.02	3

Source: Prepared by Sergio Ramos G., in Baird % McCaughan (1979); Banco de México, annual reports.
nd - no data

As Table 3 reveals for the decade 1960-1970, foreign investors took out more than twice what they put in, a trend which has continued relatively unabated to the present. For example, in the two-year period 1975-1976, a time when Mexican private capital was "fleeing" the country because of the populist rhetoric of President Luis Echeverría and the start of a recession in 1974, new direct foreign investment amounted to a whopping $693 million (ca., twice the 1969-1970 amount), while the flow of dividends, interests, and other payments to foreign investors added up to $1,480.6 million, more than double what came in (Banco de México, annual report, 1976).

Table 3.   Foreign Investment in Mexico, 1960-1970
(thousands U.S. dollars)

Year	New direct foreign investments	Total net foreign income on investments*	Reinvested profits
1960	62,466	141,566	10,570
1961	81,826	148,067	25,178
1962	74,871	159,344	36,190
1963	76,090	182,907	34,363
1964	83,075	242,202	56,339
1965	110,058	234,928	73,493
1966	111,112	277,434	73,700
1967	105,389	321,444	105,328
1968	11,116	367,728	112,216
1969	166,332	435,477	139,593
1970	183,932	473,552	154,175
TOTAL	1,166,267	2,984,649	821,145

Source: Nacional Financiera (1970) & Banco de México (n.d.), Cuadro 5.
*Profits remitted abroad & profits reinvested, interest, royalties, and other payments.

This "suction-pump" effect of foreign investment in taking surplus value out of Mexico (capital accumulation for foreigners)—combined with Mexico's increased foreign credits, unfavorable terms of trade, and periodic flight of capital—has generated a process of growing Mexican indebtedness and relative decapitalization. Interest and amortization payments on foreign debt alone typically absorb half of Mexico's export earnings (Table 4).

Chronic balance-of-trade deficits (last column of Table 4) relate to technology sales accompanying the industrialization process, as Mexico keeps importing the machinery and materials needed to maintain an expanded manufacturing industry aimed primarily at sustaining the consumer appetites of the bourgeoisie (Tables 1 and 5). To pay for these technological imports, Mexico has gone increasingly into debt (Table 5). At the same time, the presence of foreign technology has helped pave the way for increased foreign investment, sharply rising foreign profits, and an intensification of the "suction-pump" effect (Tables 3 and 6). A vicious circle of trade imbalance and debt has thus become institutionalized, greatly benefitting U.S. capital accumulation (and to a lesser degree that of other imperialist powers).

Table 4.   Mexico's Debt Payments & Foreign Trade
(Millions U.S. dollars), 1965-1975

Year	Payments of interest & amortizations	Imports	Exports	Exports as % of imports
1965	522	1,560	1,114	71
1966	539	1,605	1,163	72
1967	551	1,748	1,104	63
1968	673	1,960	1,181	60
1969	631	2,078	1,385	67
1975	1,657	6,580	2,859	44

Source: Nacional Financiera (1970); Banco nacional de Mexico (1977).

Table 5.   Production Goods Imported and Foreign Debt of Public Sector,
Mexico, 1965-1975
(Millions U.S. dollars)

Year	Capital goods	Raw Materials	Total production goods	Year	Foreign debt
1965	700	500	1,200	1966	2,343
1968	900	700	1,600	1970	4,262
1971	1,000	800	1,800	1973	7,070
1975	2,400	3,000	5,300	1977	25,000

Source: Banco de México, annual reports: Banco de México, Indicadores Económicos, May, 1973, Sept., 1974, June, 1976, cited in *El Día*, Sept. 5, 1976.

Table 6.   Profits from Direct Foreign Investments Plus
Interest Payments on Foreign Debt, Mexico, 1974-1977
(Millions U.S. dollars)

Year	Foreign profits plus interest
1974	1,222
1975	1,549
1976	1,839
1977	3,544

Source: Banco de México, annual reports.

Mexico has experienced economic growth. Table 7 shows the Gross Domestic Product (GDP) increasing at a rate of 7.3 percent in the 1960s and 5.5 percent from 1970 to 1976. As a factor in this growth, manufacturing industries have increased their share of the GDP from 19 percent in 1960 to 24 percent in 1976 (Table 8), a time when foreign investments were moving from 56 percent to 76 percent in manufacturing (Table 2). The share of manufactures in total exports has moved up from 11 percent in 1960 to 22.5 percent in 1968 to between 35 percent and 43 percent in 1978/1979 (Banco de México, annual reports). Inflation has accompanied growth, reaching 30 percent in 1980.

Table 7.   Average Annual Rates of Growth of Gross Domestic Product (GDP)
and Inflation at Constant Prices (%), Mexico

Years	GDP	GDP Per cap.	Government final consumption expenditure	Private final consumption expenditure	Gross fixed capital formation	Inflation
1960-1970	7.3	3.8	8.8	6.7	10.2	3.3
1970-1976	5.5	1.9	12.9	4.9	7.2	12.7

Source: U.N. Annual Statistical Yearbook, 1977.

Table 8.   Gross Domestic Product (GDP) by Kind of Economic Activity,
Mexico (GDP, 1,000 million pesos; kind of economic activity, %)

Year	GDP	Agriculture	INDUSTRIAL ACTIVITY: Total	INDUSTRIAL ACTIVITY: Manufacturing industries	Construction	Wholesale & retail trade	Transport & communication	Other*
1960	150.5	16	25	19	4	34	3	18
1963	196.0	16	26	19	4	32	3	20
1970	418.7	11	29	23	5	32	3	20
1975	1000.9	10	29	24	6	31	3	20
1976	1220.8	9	30	24	6	31	3	21

Source: U.N. Annual Statistical Yearbook, 1977
   *insurance, real estate, social services, public administration, and defense

Many of these manufactured exports have been sugar and tinned and pre-pared fruits, heavily influenced by foreign capital, or products generated by the U.S. *maquiladora* (assembly) plants in Mexico's free-trade border area with the United States. Nearly a third of the value of U.S. components sent abroad for assembly in 1972 was concentrated in Mexico where, as Table 9 shows, wages paid Mexicans in typical *maquiladora* plants are from 1/4 to 1/6 of those paid corresponding U.S. workers (Chapoy Bonifaz, 1975, p. 226). Also, labor productivity in Mexico in sub-contracted assembly operations is usually higher than in the U.S. (Van der Spek, 1976).

Table 9.   Comparison of Average Hourly Wage in Mexico and U.S.,
by Type of Activity, 1969

Type of activity	Average hourly wage (U.S. dollars)		Realtion of U.S. wage to Mexican wage
	Mexico*	U.S.	
Electronic products for domestic use	0.53	2.31	4.4
Office-machine parts	0.48	2.97	6.2
Semiconductors	0.61	2.56	4.2
Garments	0.53	2.29	4.3
Toys, dolls, models	0.65	2.59	4.0
Scientific instruments	0.85	3.01	3.6

Source: Villalbos Calderón, 1973, p. 14
   *includes compensatory supplements

What has happened is that U.S. investors are not merely sending obsolete machinery at high prices to Mexico to be assembled there with cheap labor, as in the boom days of Mexico's wasteful, expensive, and irrational development of its automotive industry (Fenster, 1969). They are now emphasizing modern technology as well and investments in assembly plants and original production plants inside Mexico, using reinvested profits or Mexican capital and cheap, highly productive labor to produce and sell finished goods for the Mexican market, pocketing exhorbitant profits, or tying into the flow of trade of "Mexican" manufactured goods back to the U.S. or to other Latin American countries through the Latin American Latin American Association for Inte-grated Trade and, prior to its demise, the Central American Common Market.

Between 1965 and 1970, Mexican private or public capital financed 71 percent of all foreign direct investment (Banco de México, n.d., Cuadro 24). Using largely Mexican sources of capital for their increasing takeover of key sectors of the economy, U.S.-based TNCs by 1970 had come to obtain the following percentages of control: automotive, 57 percent; petroleum products and coke, 49 percent; paper and cellulose, 33 percent; rubber, 76 percent; mining and metallurgy, 53.6 percent; copper and aluminum, 72.2 percent;

tobacco, 100 percent; industrial chemicals, 50 percent; food & beverages, 46.8 percent; chemicals and pharmaceuticals, 86.4 percent; electrical machinery, 50 percent; non-electrical machinery, 52 percent; transportation equipment, 64 percent; computers and office equipment, 88 percent; commerce, 53.4 percent; construction materials, 38.9 percent (Ceceña, 1970; Fajnzylber & Martínez Tarrago, 1976).

Foreign capital also dominated the cement, synthetic fibers, and communications industries, and had influence in such sectors as textiles, iron & steel, agriculture, etc. U.S. firms dominate TV-programming, tourist hotels, and related services. Many firms are 100 percent foreign-owned, e.g., General Motors, Ford, Chrysler, Volkswagen, General Electric, Kodak, Sears, and Anderson-Clayton.

It is mainly U.S. monopoly capital which accounts for foreign investment in Mexico. Of the top 500 U.S. manufacturing companies ranked by sales, 277 or 55 percent had Mexican manufacturing operations in 1977. Of the top 100 U.S. companies, 71 percent had Mexican manufacturing investments (Baird and McCaughan, 1979, p. 190).

Most significantly, TNCs locate in those sectors of industrial production having the highest levels of capital concentration. According to Fajnzylber and Martínez Tarrago (1976), almost two-thirds of TNC investments, compared to less than one-third of Mexican investments, are in sectors with more than 50 percent concentration (i.e., four largest firms in a sector accounting for over half the sector's total production). These monoploy sectors of the economy also tend to be the most dynamizing ones, responsible for Mexico's relatively consistent rates of economic growth since World War II.

Mexico's economy is characterized by historic trends toward concentration and centralization of capital in the hands of the Mexican bourgeoisie and foreign captialists (mainly U.S.). According to a study completed in 1970 by economist José Luis Ceceña, of 2,040 companies with the largest incomes, foreign capital controls 36 percent of the income of the largest 400 and strongly participates in another 18 percent, while Mexican private capital controls 21 percent and the state 25 percent. Foreign capital is concentrated in the most dynamizing areas, particularly the capital goods and basic intermediate goods industries, where transfer pricing on technology sales further augments foreign capital accumulation.

Mexican private capital, most of it in light industry, tourism, and consumer goods, is highly centralized. According to a study published by economist Alonso Aguilar (1967), about 6 percent of non-foreign manufacturing firms account for 94 percent of those firms' fixed capital, 90 percent of their value of production, and 70 percent of their employed personnel. Of non-foreign commercial firms, 1.8 percent absorb 73 percent of such firms' captial and 63.9 percent of their income. By 1965, some 77 percent of all industrial capital in Mexico was controlled by 1.5 percent of industrial corporations.

Such centralization of capital has led to largescale accumulation of capital for not only TNCs but also private Mexican capital. Between 1972 and 1977, for example, the social capital of the largest fifty private enterprises in Mexico increased 130 perecent from $200 million to $456 million (*Business Trends*, 1972, 1977).

The cooperation of the state in keeping wages down and labor disciplined has greatly benefitted capital accumulation for private monopoly capital. Only 25 percent of Mexico's wage workers are unionized, and only 30 percent of the economically active population are incorporated in the social security system (*Estrategia*, No. 25, Jan.-Feb., 1979, pp. 44-45). Since 1938, most unionized industrial workers have been corporatively organized from the top down, with the official labor organization being one of the three "sectors" of the official "revolutionary" political party in Mexico's one-party system. In the 1970s and 1980s a strong independent workers' movement from below developed, fighting corrupt labor bureaucracy and demanding democratic reforms; it was strongly repressed by the state, and partially coopted.[6] According to the official labor organization Congreso del Trabajo, wages account for 24.4 percent of national income, the state 11.1 percent, and private capital 63.2 percent (*Ceteme*, Nov. 11, 1978). The proportion of salaries, wages, and benefits to the value of industrial production declined from 15.4 percent to 13.3 percent in 1978 (Secretaría de Programacíon y Presupuesto, 1978, p. 14).

Fanjnzylber and Martínez Tarrago (1976) have emphasized the inappropriateness of technology imported by Mexico, both in terms of costs and of labor utilization. They conclude that "fewer and fewer productive jobs have been created per unit of capital invested" and that capital has been increasingly remunerated "at the expense of workers' incomes."

Because of dependence on foreign capital and technology, because of largescale state participation, and because of domination by domestic and foreign monopoly capital, Mexico's economy may be described as dependent state monopoly capitalism. U.S. capital does not control the economy in its entirety, but it wields sufficient influence to make a critical difference—and therein lies Mexico's structural economic dependence.

Part of U.S. capital's influence has derived from the immense advantages enjoyed by U.S. capitalists over their Mexican counterparts in technology and capital reserves. Aguilar's study (1967) indicates that Mexican industrial output increased five times between 1940 and 1965, while imports of foreign (mainly U.S.) industrial or capital goods and replacement parts increased 12.5 times. This not only added directly to capital accumulation for U.S. corporations but also provided them critical leverage for increasing their investments in related areas of the economy. U.S. companies "tied" their sales of technology to further sales and expansion possibilities, using a panoply of means, including patents, licences, know-how agreements, etc.

By 1965, Mexico was an industrializing LDC with a high degree of centralization of capital in technology-intensive industry. According to Ricardo Cinta

Table 10.   Centralization of Industrial Capital According to
Value of Gross Fixed Capital, Mexico, 1970

Size by gross fixed capital	Number of firms		Total gross production		Gross value added	
	Absolute	%	1000s of pesos*		1000s of pesos	
Small industry (up to 3,000,000 pesos)	115,295	96.9	44,471,339	21.5	17,906,665	22.6
Medium industry (from 3,000,001 to 20,000,000 pesos)	2,712	2,3	53,392,653	25.8	20,366,698	25.8
Heavy industry (From 200,000,001 pesos and up)	968	0.8	108,756,145	52.7	40,780,731	51.6
Total	118,975	100	206,620,137	100	79,054,094	100

Source: Industrial Census, 1970
*1 peso = $.08 (U.S.)

Table 11.   Distribution of Industries by Size, Employed Personnel,
and Wages, Mexico, 1970

Size (see Table 10)	Number of firms		Employed personnel		Wages		Average annual wage per worker
	Absolute	%	Absolute	%	Absolute (1000s of pesos*)	%	
Small industry	115,295	96.9	713,368	45.9	7,928,242	25.0	11,113
Medium industry	2,712	2.3	471,837	23.9	8,530,894	26.9	22,942
Large industry	968	0.8	469,969	30.2	15,240,470	48.1	32,438
Total	118,975	100	1,555,174	100	31,699,606	100	20,383

Source: Industrial Census, 1970
*1 pesos = $.08 (U.S.)

(1972), some 938 firms, a mere 0.82 percent of all industrial firms, accounted for two-thirds of total production while providing employment for only one-third of the employed industrial labor force. Of the 938 firms, 27 percent were foreign-owned. Of the top 116 of these firms, which accounted for over half the production of the 938, some 53 percent were foreign-owned. In other words, foreign ownership tends to concentrate at the productive heights of the economy. Development of local monopoly has been accompanied and stimulated by foreign monopoly in Mexico's industrialization process.

Tables 10 and 11 reveal the centralization of capital according to the Industrial Census of 1970. Some 78.5 percent of total production is accounted for by 3.1 percent of industrial firms (*i.e.*, big and medium industry). Labor's productivity is greater there, as are wages. Big industry employs 30 percent of the industrial labor force, with an average of 485 workers per firm; medium industry employs 24 percent with an average of 137 persons per firm; small industry employs 46 percent with an average of six persons per firm (Osorio Urbina, 1975). The tables show that centralization of capital is accompanied by concentration of workers in technology-intensive industry which produces great surplus value, on the one hand, and a dispersal of workers in numerous small industries which produce far less surplus value, on the other.

Table 12.   Mexico's Economically Active Population by Sector, 1940-1975 (percentage)

Year	1940	1950	1960	1965	1970	1975
Total workforce (in thousands)	5,858	8,272	11,274	12,240	13,181	16,597
Agriculture*	65	58	54	46	39	40
Industry (all)	15	15	19	20	22	24
Mining/petroleum	2	1	1	1	1	1
Manufacturing	11	12	14	15	17	18
Construction	2	3	4	4	4	5
Electricity	0.4	0.3	0.4	0.4	0.4	0.4
Services (all)	19	26	27	32	38	35
Trade	8	8	10	9	9	10
Trans./commun.	3	3	3	3	3	3
Others	9	11	13	17	20	nd
Unspecified	–	4	0.7	3	6	–

Source: 1940-1950, General Population Census;
1960-1970, Nacional Financiera (1974);
1975, *Primer Informe de Gobierno*, Anex I-1977.
*includes livestock raising, forestry and fishing
nd - no data

Table 12 shows the stimulating effects of capital centralization in Mexico's industrialization in terms of the shifts in the economically active population out of agriculture and into industry and services between 1940 and 1975. Yet comparison of Table 12 with Table 8 shows that 40 percent of the workforce remained in agriculture in 1975, even though agriculture accounted for only 10 percent of the GDP. In other words, modern industry is not absorbing workers rapidly enough to uplift the rural poor or their migrant kinfolk who constitute the majority of Mexico's unemployed and underemployed (estimated at 50% in 1979 presidential addresses).

Technology sales as a method of capital accumulation derive from the tendency of capital to expand more rapidly in Department I (means of production) than in Department II (articles of consumption). This tendency has led to the more-industrialized countries' advances in Department I production, their periodic crises of over-production in that Department, and their increased export of capital, a defining characteristic of imperialism. For a LDC, even one with the relative headstart that Mexico enjoys compared to most other LDCs, the effort to "close the gap" or to develop its own nationally controlled Department I of production is doomed to failure so long as it follows a capitalist road of development through importation of capital goods from the more-industrialized countries' Department I of production. Such a procedure only increases the power advantages of the imperialists while putting a LDC like Mexico in an increasingly subservient position *vis-à-vis* imperialism, in terms of both capital accumulation and foreign debt.

In 1970, Mexico was importing 75 percent of its Department I goods (*i.e.*, machinery and auxiliary raw materials). In addition, as Perzabal (1979, p. 128) has shown, the enterprises in Mexico producing capital goods were dominated by foreign capital, which received 70 percent of the income from Mexico's Department I production (the other 20 percent went to state enterprises and 10 percent to private Mexican firms).

Technology sales help both to generate increased foreign domination of Mexico's economy and to evade "nationalist" laws ostensibly aimed at regulating foreign investment. As the manager of one U.S. affiliate in Mexico has stated: "the use of payments for technology is the easiest legal way to transfer profits out of the country" (Newfarmer & Mueller, 1975, p. 17).

In other words, by disguising profits as *costs*, TNCs increase their capital accumulation in two ways. First, they conceal profits by not declaring them and thereby do not have to pay taxes on them. Second, by raising their declared "costs," they reduce what remaining profits they do declare and pay taxes on. These disguised parts of imperialist capital accumulation never appear in the statistics on foreign profits, which nonetheless show a sharp upward curve in Mexico in the middle 1970s (Table 6). So-called "technology transfers" remit to the United States almost *twice* as much money as officially declared profits (Fajnzylber & Martínez Tarrago, 1976; Sepulveda & Chumacero, 1973).

Tables 3, 5 and 6 provide an illuminating insight into the multiplying character of foreign capital accumulation accompanied by ever-increasing technology sales. In one year (1977), declared foreign capital accumulation ($3,544 million) exceeded all the declared foreign capital accumulation of a recent decade, 1960-1970 ($2,984 million). As Table 5 reveals, some of this jump derived, in a way more exaggerated than normal, from the Echeverría government's deliberate emphasis on technology imports as a supposed step toward establishing a more independent and productive Department I for future Mexican capitalist development.

Yet it is precisely this effort by the Echeverría government, planned in the early 1970s and strongly implemented in the middle 1970s, which confirms the futility of a capitalist solution to the problem of developing a viable national Department I of production in the context of modern imperialism. From 1970 to 1976, some 80 percent of Mexican imports were capital goods. Of all

Mexico's capital goods developed during the same period, 80 percent were imported (Banco de México, *Indicadores Económicos*, June, 1976).

The figures in Table 5 for Production Goods Imported underestimate the actual costs, since they represent only the value of specific goods imported and omit a significant quantity of related costs. Even so, the six-fold increase in Mexico's foreign debt between 1970 and 1977 corresponds rather closely to the quadrupling of capital goods imports between 1970 and 1976. Mexico's huge trade imbalance and foreign debt flowed logically from its development strategy (and that of imperialism, as will become clear) of the 1970s: massive importation of foreign technology, "know-how" contracts, etc., and related loans to finance them. By 1975, payments of interest and amortizations on Mexico's foreign debt equalled 80 percent of the value of Mexican exports. These interest payments had tripled since a decade earlier (*Review of the Economic Situation of Mexico*, Feb., 1977, p. 47).

Based on the arguments presented in the preceding section, I suggested in 1973 to some of President Echeverría's top advisors during an international congress on science and technology in Mexico City that their technology development plans coincided, consciously or not, with those of U.S. imperialism. I pointed out that the TNCs, reeling from the waste of resources in the Vietnam War and the detrimental economic and social impact of the defeat suffered by imperialism there, were committed to a new export drive euphemistically called "technology transfers" (*i.e.*, sales) as one means to solve the cash-liquidity crisis, since many technology sales are paid for promptly through cash transfers achieved *via* international credit institutions. Because of increased costs at home, the TNCs were also committed to a strategy of selling more industrial installations abroad, particularly to the expanding home markets of the more-industrialized LDCs like Mexico. Such technology commercialization was becoming the fastest growing means of capital accumulation for U.S.-based TNCs.

Technology commercialization, I added, was crucial for the survival and growth of TNCs precisely because imperialism found itself on the defensive: the Vietnam setback; the dollar no longer hegemonic on international money markets; the terms of trade stiffened by OPEC and similar LDC cartels; depression or crisis at home, accompanied by world-wide capitalist "stagflation" (high unemployment with inflation); intensified inter-imperialist rivalry; and the rise of revolutionary governments and liberation movements in key LDCs throughout the world. U.S. monopoly capital would react not only by tightening up on the social-welfare programs and wage levels of U.S. workers but also by seeking to displace its crisis abroad and to increase its rate of capital accumulation there.

Thus, Mexico would become one of the first test cases for imperialism's strategy to displace its own crisis onto the backs of the working classes of LDCs while finding abroad new, quick sources of capital through the commercialization of technology. President Echeverría's advisors responded that the 1972 "Law on Registration of Technology Transfers," implemented through

CONACYT (National Council on Science and Technology), would meet the challenge. This was utopian, since these advisers conceded there existed no adequate ways of disciplining TNCs short of opening their accounting books, which itself would take a revolution. Three years later, CONACYT acknowledged the failure of the 1972 law and the previous thirty years' development strategy in general. The savings derived from the registering of technology sales were insignificant; the registering occurred irregularly and only after the conclusion of negotiated contracts (*El Día*, Nov. 22, 1976).

And so, Mexico's crisis of the 1970s unfolded in all its horror, climaxing with the 1976 devaluation of the peso by almost 100 percent, massive unemployment, inflation rates of from 20 percent to 50 percent a year, and the utopian attempt to "recover" through delivering much of the nation's oil wealth to imperialism. This delivery is, though meeting much resistance from nationalist workers and intellectuals, already beginning to occur through yet more technology contracts, relaxing of the law regulating foreign investment in petrochemicals, and construction of a 750-mile natural gas pipeline from Chiapas to Texas. This "gasoducto," if completed, will make an appropriate symbol of imperialism's "suction-pumping" out much of Mexico's surplus value.

Yet Mexico has committed itself more strongly than ever to its old strategy of capital goods imports. According to a national plan for 1979-1982 (Nafinsa-Unido, 1977), Mexico would not only eliminate dependence on capital goods imports—it would also begin to export capital goods. Imports of production goods increased to 43 percent in 1978 (*Latin America Economic Report*, March 23, 1979). To encourage more production of Department I goods, Secretary of National Properties and Industrial Growth (Sepafin) José Andrés de Oteyza was reported in 1978 as having devised new incentives for TNCs like the following: elimination of all *ad valorem* import duties on raw materials and components and 75 percent of *ad valorem* on machinery; cuts of 75 percent on sales taxes; cuts of 15-20 percent on income taxes; and increase of depreciation allowances (*Business Latin America*, April 12, 1978).

The demand for capital goods is projected to rise in the 1980s at an intense rate. Machinery imports alone for 1980 were projected at 45,000 million pesos or over $2,000 million (Perzabal, 1979, p. 129). In spite of increased oil production for export and for subsidizing foreign and local capital in its industrial development, Mexico continues to run a trade deficit. According to *Latin America Weekly Report* (Jan. 25, 1980), the nonoil deficit in trade for 1980 was running at a staggering annual rate of $10,000 million.

A 1959 "Regulation of the Petroleum Law" act had opened the doors to various U.S. concerns in secondary petrochemicals, including unrestricted areas of investment like pharmaceuticals, paints, and synthetic fibers, all U.S.-controlled today. The secretary-general of the petrochemical workers' union has been reported as saying 80 percent of the petrochemical industry is "in the power of the transnationals," including 40 percent hidden by *"prestanombres"* (Mexicans lending their names to foreign capitalists). In the same report, TNC researcher Bernal Sahagún added that TNCs control more than 90 percent of the industry's machinery; 80 percent of its transport and chemical-pharmaceutical production; 70 percent of its production of chemicals; and 60 percent of its electrical machinery (*Unomásuno*, Jan. 15, 1978).

Before the recent oil discoveries, U.S. companies already had invested over $600 million in Mexican chemical operations. The private sector has slated 69 new investment projects in petrochemicals. The state-owned oil company PEMEX plans to float petro-bonds both in the international money markets and internally. National energy concerns are already heavily mortgaged to foreign creditors. PEMEX's debt in 1975 was $2,560 million, while that of the CFE (government electric company) was over $3,000 million, or 67 percent of the value of the company. The majority of new investments by PEMEX traditionally have been financed by foreign loans (*Siempre*, Sept. 3, 1975, pp. 26-27). Thus, private capital has strong leverage to dominate, if not control, the "national" energy industry: ownership does not necessarily mean control.

Related to TNC's capital accumulation *via* technology sales is the penetration of Mexican agriculture by foreign agribusiness, more through technical supplies (machinery, fertilizer, seeds, etc.) and marketing than actual land ownership. Mexico's agrarian crisis by 1980 was a matter of public record: over 50 percent of the rural population landless; high import bills not only for technology but also for such traditional food staples as maize, beans, sugar, etc. (production being geared for local and foreign agribusiness's exports of cotton, tomatoes, meat, etc.); and a policy pushed by international lending agencies like the World Bank to tie small subsistence producers to more technology sales and the national and international market in a process where nonsalaried agricultural producers have all their surplus product appropriated by capitalists (Bennholdt-Thomsen, 1980; Lorenzen, 1980; Payer, 1979; Rama and Vigorito, 1980).

Since imperialism also dominates the World Bank, IMF, and similar lending institutions, and since it is both paid and unpaid (subsistence) Mexican labor which ends up producing the economic surplus used to pay much of Mexico's debt, capital accumulation for foreign monopoly capital occurs in this sphere of circulation and not just production. The role played by the LDC debt-structure in capitalist accumulation is not just interest payments or the opening up of new investment opportunities. It is the actual control that accrues to imperialism in the shaping of critical national decisions of an LDC. This was illustrated with Mexico's 1976-1977 devaluation of the peso and acceptance of stringent IMF terms for continued "credit-worthiness." The IMF imposed on the incoming López Portillo government restrictive guidelines on the federal budget, Mexico's trade policies, and the wage structure, all steps favoring monopoly capital in its efforts to squeeze more surplus value out of labor's production.

Mexico's own credit and banking system in turn increasingly is penetrated and dominated by foreign capital. The industrial development bank Nacional

Financiera (Nafinsa), a ''mixed'' body with the state holding majority shares, increased its resources five-fold between 1975 and 1978 (to $10,000 million). A fourth of this went to service its *own* foreign debt for the preceding year. Some 72 percent of Nafinsa's resources in 1978 came from abroad, as its foreign debt reached $6,800 million, almost half of which was owed the World Bank (Aguilar, 1979). The world's largest private financial institutions (Chase Manhattan Bank, Bank of Tokyo, etc.) have often extended credits to Nafinsa. The state's top financial officials are often drawn from the Board of Directors of Nafinsa. Most of Nafinsa's loans (72 percent) have gone to industry in recent years, especially heavy industry, while 21 percent have gohe to economic infrastructure, *e.g.*, irrigation works (Brandenburg, 1964; Aguilar, 1979). In planning increased investments in the petrochemical industry, Nafinsa in its 1978 annual report said it would use ''the criteria of tripartite association, that is, public sector, foreign firms providing technology, and private national investors.''

The Bank of Mexico, like Nafinsa a ''mixed'' body with a slim government majority, has more resources than Nafinsa and is the equivalent of Mexico's ''central bank.'' It works closely with the IMF and follows IMF's conservative, pro-monopoly approach to banking. A third major state banking institution is the Banco Nacional de Comercio Exterior (Báncomex), which receives 85 percent of its resources from foreign bankers (mainly U.S.). It works in close association with the agro-export sector of the economy and the gigantic agrarian state bank Banco Nacional de Crédito Rural, which in turn owed foreign creditors $1,100 million in 1977 (Aguilar, 1979).

In brief, the state banking sector is well integrated with national and foreign monopoly capital. Through its rapidly increasing capitalization and its diversification into the ''mixed'' banking sector and state and ''mixed'' industrial investment, it had come to account for almost half of all credit resources in Mexico by 1980. As Aguilar (1979) observes:

> The recent expansion of large private mining, iron-and-steel, metallurgical, and petrochemical firms, many of them foreign, would have been impossible without state investment and the backing of government banks. . . . state banks also are an important factor in that they maintain a low-wage policy and high rates of exploitation of workers.

Also important are the private banks Banco Nacional de México and Banco de Comercio, which in the early 1970s controlled almost half of all Mexico's banking resources. At that time, seven private banking *groups* controlled an estimated 85 percent of all capital in Mexico. This powerful financial bourgeoisie retains close links to other banks, insurance companies, investment houses (*financieras*), industries, and TNCs (Barkin, 1975; Niblo, 1975).

If these private banks encounter problems, as they did during the capital-flight and devaluation crisis of 1976, those banks with state participation (*e.g.*, Bank of Mexico), on whose boards the leading private bankers often sit, step in with huge credits. This saves the private banks, but who saves the state banks? In 1976, some 90 percent of the emergency credits procured by state banks were in foreign currency (Banco de México, annual report, 1976). The monopolistic character of Mexican banking, closely tied to giant foreign banks, is thus a near-perfect expression in the sphere of circulation of capital of how surplus value is transferred from workers and peasants to bankers and industrialists, national and foreign, in a dependent state monopoly-capitalist social formation.

IV. CONCLUSION

In terms of value (materialized human labor) and its reproduction on an extended scale (capital accumulation), Mexico finds itself borrowing heavily to maintain or stimulate its capital accumulation. The observed result has been its combining a subordinated industrialization with relative decapitalization and a further integration of the state, local monopoly capital, and TNCs. This in turn has had a transforming impact on Mexico's class structure, with peasant and labor protests rising and deepening in the 1970s and 1980s, as I discuss elsewhere (Cockcroft, 1979 and 1982), precisely in areas most influenced by monopoly capital.

Mexico's experience suggests that development of Department I productive capacity, if dependent on the "good will" of TNCs, will only accelerate the accumulation of capital at the centers of world capitalism and further tie Mexico to imperialism and its lending institutions (IMF, etc.). A successful strategy would have to put considerably more emphasis on developing education—from literacy campaigns to R & D institutes—in order to assure a long-term capacity for indigenous technology growth. In 1973, Mexico's R & D expenditure was only about $100 million, two-thirds of it financed by the government (U.N. Annual Statistical Yearbook, 1977). To succeed, such a strategy would have to break through the integrated blocs of power established in the triumvirate of state/private capital/foreign capital, nationalize the commanding heights of the economy (and probably the plateaus also), and, through national planning, bring into ever greater convergence the nation's own resource uses, community needs, economic demands, and production in a socialist economy.

Without implementation of such a strategy, it is likely that the state's occasional anti-imperialist foreign-policy proclamations will continue to be an exercise in futility unless accompanied by an anti-imperialist practice and a class (social) revolution. The populist-style "nationalism" of recent bourgeois governments in Mexico has actually served to mask the continued and deepening provision of proletarian and peasant labor power at low costs to foreign capital and its associated partners within the Mexican bourgeoisie and the state bureaucratic sector. The resultant intensification of class struggle in

Mexico has provided a new opportunity for forging a socialist alternative, suggested in part by the state's own frenetic efforts to carry through a tokenistic "political reform" in an effort to deflect or absorb the opposition.[6]

ACKNOWLEDGMENT

A half-year sabbatical granted by Rutgers University, 1980, helped make this work possible.

Abbreviations Used in This Work

LDC: less-industrialized developing country

MOP: mode of production

TNC: transnational corporation

IMF: International Monetary Fund

Nafinsa: Nacional Financiera

R & D: research and development

NOTES

1. Recent writings on imperialism (Amin, 1974; Cohen, 1973; Diamond, 1979; Emmanuel, 1972; Insurgent Sociologist, 1977; Magdoff, 1978; Sweezy, 1974) recognize the usefulness of the original formulations of authors like Lenin or Hobson, yet indicate a need to expand or refine them further. This is necessary in part to take into account phenomena historically new in their importance (like the one examined here), as well as to account for forms of imperialism practiced by self-declared "socialist" nations which in fact also have forms of monopoly and finance capital (*e.g.*, the Soviet Union). On centralization of capital, wherein "the larger capitals beat the smaller," see Marx (1933), vol. I, p. 686.

2. I employ the term "transnational" rather than "multinational," because it is a less ideological and more accurate concept, combining the control aspects implicit in "national" with the global aspects of "trans." For elaboration, see Cockcroft (1975).

3. For a case study of the Mexican pharmaceutical industry, see Gereffi (1977). For further specifics on patents, technology pricing, industry takeovers, etc., consult: Bazin & Anderson (1977); Goulet (1977); Katz (1972); Lipton (1971); Science for the People (1973); Sergeyev & Strugatshya (1971); Stanzick & Godoy (1972); U.N. (1974); UNCTAD (1978); & Vaitsos (1973). On the Mexico case, in addition to other works cited in the text, consult: Aguilera (1975); María y Campos (1974); Wences Reza (1977); and Vuskovic (1979).

4. The "package" is priced cheaper as a whole than it would be if its component parts were sold separately. According to UNCTAD (1971, pp. 2-3): "Technology in the process of its commercialization is usually embodied in intermediate products, machinery and equipment, skills, whole systems of production (like turnkey plants), even systems of distribution or marketing (like cryogenic technology in ships that transport liquid gas), etc. Thus, know-how represents a part integrated in a larger whole . . . This market integration of various inputs creates noncompetitive conditions for each one of them since they are sold in a package form."

5. Rutgers Chile Research Group found that 24 of the top 30 U.S.-based TNCs controlled two-fifths of Chile's largest 100 corporations and held additional advantages through monopolistic control over markets and technology. It also found the same 24 TNCs the one ultimately guiding U.S. foreign policy and behind the coup against Allende. *Cf.*, Cockcroft (1972, 1975); Johnson (1973); and Petras and Morley (1975).

6. I examine the new rank-and-file labor militancy, as well as the relationship of the informal alliance of the state, foreign capital, and private Mexican capital to the heating up of the class struggle in the 1970s and 1980s, in my forthcoming book on modern Mexico (Cockcroft, 1982).

REFERENCES

Aguilar, Alonso
  1979   "La burguesia no solo manda, gobierna." Esstrategia 28(July-August): 2-32.
Aguilar, Alonso and Fernando Carmona
  1967   Mexico: riqueza y miseria. Mexico: Editorial Nuestro Tiempo.
Aguilera, Manuel
  1975   La desnacionalizacion de la economia mexicana. Mexico: Fondo de Cultura Economica.
Amin, Samir
  1974   Accumulation on a World Scale: A Critique of the Theory of Underdevelopment. 2 Vols. New York: Monthly Review Press.
  1979   "Reply to Weeks and Dore." Latin American Perspectives 21(Spring): 88-90.
Baird, Peter and Ed McCaughan
  1979   Beyond the Border: Mexico and U.S. Today. New York: North American Congress on Latin America (NACLA).
Banco de Mexico
  n.d.   Estadisticas basicas de la inversion extranjera en Mexico. Mexico.
Barkin, David
  1975   "Mexico's albatross: the U.S. economy." Latin American Perspectives II, 2 (Summer): 64-80.
Barnet, Richard J. and Ronald E. Muller
  1975   Global Reach: The Power of the Multinational Corporations. New York: Simon & Schuster.
Bazin, Maurice and Sam Anderson
  1977   Ciencia e Independencia. 2 Vols. Lisbon: Livros Horizonte.
Bennholdt-Thomsen, Veronika
  1980   "Investition in die Armen. Zur Entwicklungsstrategie der Weltbank." Lateinamerika, Analysen und Berichte, No. 4 (Berlin).
Bernal Sahagun, Victor
  1976   The Impact of Multinational Corporations on Employment and Income: The Case of Mexico. Geneva: International Labor Office.
Brandenburg, Frank R.
  1964   The Making of Modern Mexico. Englewood Cliffs, NJ: Prentice-Hall.
Braungart, Richard G. and Margaret M. Braungart
  1980   "Multinational corporate expansion and nation-state development: a global perspective." Pp. 169-86 in Louis Kriesberg (ed.), Research in Social Movements, Conflicts and Change, Vol. 3. Greenwich, CT: JAI Press Inc.
Business International Corporation
  1970   Nationalism in Latin America. September.
Cecena, Jose Luis
  1970   Mexico en la orbita imperial. Mexico: Ediciones "El Caballito."
Chapoy Bonifaz, Alma
  1975   Empresas multinacionales. Mexico: Ediciones "El Caballito."
Cinta, Ricardo
  1972   "Burguesia nacional y desarrollo." Pp. 165-99 in El perfil de Mexico en 1980, Vol. III. Mexico: Siglo XXI.

Cockcroft, James D.
1972   "Las companias multinacionales y el gobierno de Allende." In Siempre (September 13) and, revised, Johnson (1973): 3-24 (with Henry Frundt & Dale L. Johnson).
1975   "Impact of transnational corporations on Chile's social structure." Summation 5 (1 & 2): 7-32; revised in Cuadernos Politicos 10 (Oct.-Dec., 1976): 64-82.
1979   El imperialismo, la lucha de clases y el estado en Mexico. Mexico: Editorial Nuestro Tiempo.
1982   Modern Mexico: Capital Accumulation, Class Formation, and the State. New York: Monthly Review Press.
Cohen, Benjamin
1973   The Question of Imperialism. New York: Basic Books.
Diamond, Larry
1979   "Power-dependence relations in the world system." Pp. 233-58 in Louis Kriesberg (ed.), Research in Social Movements, Conflicts and Change, Vol. 2. Greenwich, CT: JAI Press Inc.
Emmanuel, Arghiri
1972   Unequal Exchange: A study of Imperialism of Trade. Includes Bettleheim's critique. New York: Monthly Review Press.
Fajnzylber, Fernando and Trinidad Martininez Tarrago
1976   Las empresas transnacionales: expansion a nivel mundial y proyeccion en la industria mexicana. Mexico: Fondo de Cultura Economica.
Fenster, Leo
1969   "Mexican auto swindle." The Nation June 2:693-97.
Gereffi, Gary
1977   "Drug firms and dependency in Mexico: the case of the steroid hormone industry." Yale University and Harvard University Center for International Affairs.
Gilpin, Robert
1975   U.S. Power and the Multinational Corporation: The Political Economy of Foreign Direct Investment. New York: Basic Books.
Goulet, Denis
1977   The Uncertain Promise: Value Conflicts in Technology Transfer. New York: IDOC/ North America, Inc.
Hernandez, Salvador
1973   Un ensayo sobre el imperialismo norteamericano en Mexico. Mexico: Cuadernos del Centro de Estudios Politicos, No. 1, UNAM.
Insurgent Sociologist
1977   Imperialism and the State. Vol. 7, No. 2 (Spring).
Johnson, Dale L. (ed.)
1973   The Chilean Road to Socialism. New York: Anchor.
Katz, Jorge
1972   "Patentes, corporaciones multinacionales y tecnologia." Desarrollo Economico, April-June (Buenos Aires).
Kreye, Otto (ed.)
1974   Multinationale Konzerne. Munich: Reihe Hanser.
Lenin, V.I.
1972   Imperialism, the Highest State of Capitalism. New York: International Publishers.
Levinson, Charles
1971   Capital, Inflation, and the Multinationals. New York: Macmillan.
Lipton, Michael
1971   "The international diffusion of technology." In Dudley Seers and Leonard Jay (eds.), Development in a Divided World. Baltimore: Pelican.

Lorenze, Hannes
1980   "Investment in the poor: a World Bank project in Mexico." Mimeo. Zurich (Gartenhofstrasse 27): Rome Declaration Group.
Magdoff, Harry
1978   Imperialism: From the Colonial Age to the Present. New York: Monthly Review Press.
Maria y Campos, Mauricio de
1974   "La politica mexicana de transferencia de tecnologia: una evaluacion preliminar." Comercio Exterior May: 463-77.
Marx, Karl
1933   Capital. Chicago: Charles Kerr & Co.
1973   Grundrisse. Trans. Martin Nicolaus. New York: Vintage.
Nacional Financiera
1970   La economia mexicana en cifras 1970. Mexico: Nacional Financiera.
1974   La economia mexicana en cifras 1974. Mexico: Nacional Financiera.
Nafinsa-Unido
1977   "A strategy to develop capital goods in Mexico." Mexico: Nacional Financiera.
Newfarmer, Richard S. and W.F. Mueller
1975   Multinational Corporations in Brazil and Mexico: Structural Sources of Economic and Noneconomic Power. Washington, DC: Report to the Subcommittee on Multinational Corporations of the Committee on Foreign Relations, U.S. Senate (August).
Niblo, Stephen R.
1975   "Progress and the standard of living in contemporary Mexico." Latin American Perspectives II, 2 (Summer): 109-24.
Osorio Urbina, Jaime
1975   "Superexplotacion y clase obrera: el caso mexicano." Cuadernos Politicos 6 (Oct.-Dec.): 5-23.
Palloix, Christain
1973   Les firmes mutinationales et la proces d'internationalization. Paris: Maspero.
Payer, Cheryl
1979   "The World Bank and the small farmers." Journal of Peace Research XVI (4): 293-312.
Perzabal, Carlos
1979   Acumulacion capitalista dependiente y subordinada: el caso de Mexico (1940-1978). Mexico: Siglo XXI.
Petras, James and Morris Morley
1975   The United States and Chile: Imperialism and the Overthrow of the Allende Government. New York: Monthly Review Press.
Rama, Ruth and Raul Vigorito
1980   Transnacionales en America Latina: el complejo de frutas y legumbres en Mexico. Mexico: Editorial Nueva Imagen.
Reynolds, Clark W.
1970   The Mexican Economy: Twentieth Century Structure and Growth. New Haven, CT: Yale University Press.
Santos, Theotonia dos
1973   Imperialismo y empreses multinacionales. Buenos Aires: Galerna.
Science for the People
1973   Science & Technology in Latin America. June.
Secretaria de Programacion y Presupuesto
1978   Boletin mensual de informacion economica. Vol. II, No. 9.
Sepulveda, Bernardo and Antonio Chumacero

1973   La inversion extranjera en Mexico. Mexico: Fondo de Cultura Economica.
Sergeyev, Y.U.A. and N. Yu Strugatshya
1971   ''Scientific and technical development, the monopolies and the patent system.''
          Reprinted from Russian Research Journal SSHA: Ekonomik, Politika, Ideologiya, in
          Idea 15:2 (Summer).
Stanzick, Karl-Heinz and Horacio H. Godoy (eds.)
1972   Inversiones extranjeras y transferencia de tecnologia en America Latina. Santiago,
          Chile: Ed. Universitaria.
Sweezy, Paul
1974   ''Some problems in the theory of capital accumulation.'' Monthly Review May:
          38-55.
U.N.
1973   Multinational Corporations in World Development. New York: ST/ECA/190, Sales
          No. E.73.II.A.11.
1974   The Acquisition of Technology from Multinational Corporations by Developing
          Countries. New York: ST/ESA/12, Sales No. E.74.II.A.7.
UNCTAD
1971   Transfer of Technology. New York: U.N. Conference on Trade and Development
          Secretariat, Junta del Acuerdo de Cartagena. TD/107 (December 29).
1978   Transfer of Technology: Its Implications for Development and Environment. New
          York: UNCTAD, TD/B/C.6/22.
Van der Spek, Peter G.
1976   ''Mexico's booming border zone: a magnet for labor-intensive American plants.''
          Journal of Interamerican Economic Affairs 29 (Summer-Spring).
Vaitsos, Constantino V.
1973   Comercializacion de tecnologia en el pacto andino. Lima: Instituto de Estudios
          Peruanos.
Vernon, Raymond
1977   Storm over the Multinationals: The Real Issues. Cambridge: Harvard University
          Press.
Villalobos Calderon, Liborio
1973   ''La industria maquiladora extranjera en Mexico: mal necesario de una sociedad
          subdesarrollado.'' Relaciones Internacionales (UNAM, April-June).
Villarreal, Rene
1975   ''Del proyecto de creciminento y sustitucion de importaciones al de desarrollo y
          sustitucion de exportaciones.'' Comerico Exterior 25, 3 (March): 315-23.
Vuskovic, Pedro
1979   ''America Latina ante nuevos terminos de la division internacional del trabajo.''
          Economia de America Latina March: 15-28.
Wences Reza, Rosalio
1977   ''Ciencia y tecnologia: bosquejo historico y el caso de Mexico.'' Problemas del
          Desarrollo February-April: 51-64.
Zuck, Daniel G. (with assistance of James D. Cockcroft and Rutgers-Livingston TNC Research
Group)
1973   ''Technology, dependence, patents, and transnational corporations, with special
          emphasis on Chile.'' Science for the People (July), Siempre (June 27).

TRANSNATIONAL NETWORKS AND RELATED THIRD CULTURES:

A COMPARISON OF TWO SOUTHEAST ASIAN SCIENTIFIC COMMUNITIES

John Useem, Ruth Hill Useem, Abu Hassan Othman, and Florence E. McCarthy

This study[1] mediates between several research traditions on the interdependencies among human societies and endeavors to introduce a fresh perspective on one segment of these relationships.

One powerful tradition has focused on the processes of development around the world. In this tradition, discussions about the interrelationships between the more and less developed countries have assumed science and technology to be crucial both for the development of the less developed societies and for creating a viable future for mankind in an increasingly interdependent world. Recent examinations of the place of science and technology in both inter- and

Research in Social Movements, Conflict and Change, Volume 4, pages 283-316
Copyright © 1981 by JAI Press Inc.
All rights of reproduction in any form reserved.
ISBN: 0-89232-234-9

intra-societal relationships have become critical of earlier assumptions and have searched for more sophisticated concepts and methods for understanding what has become an inherently complicated set of relationships.

In the aftermath of three decades of experience of the more developed countries assisting in the building of academic and scientific communities in the less developed countries, there is substantial consensus that despite many accomplishments, the fundamental goals have yet to be significantly fulfilled. The critics come from a wider range of societies than earlier and increasingly include both scholars and policymakers in third world countries. The literature stemming from the 1979 UN Conference on Science and Technology for Development is representative of this three-decades-old tradition.

A second and recent influential research tradition has as its central organizing concept the growth of world systems and their consequences for societies which become core or peripheral to these systems. Still another conceptual scheme has centered on the development of underdevelopment and the significant characteristics of dependency among the more vulnerable countries of the third world.

Paradigms are not confirmed or disproved—they offer empirically-oriented researchers of cross-cultural relations fresh questions to pursue in order to deepen our knowledge and understanding of what is actually occurring around the world.

While there have been significant contributions at the macro level to our thinking concerning international cooperation and conflict in the organization of science and technology on a worldwide scale, we discern one largely neglected yet crucial domain in most discussions, namely, recognition that world systems, policies, and programs are carried by individual human beings whose lives, scientific careers and professional roles are embedded in particular historical, economic, technological and political settings. Where these concerns have surfaced, we have been hampered both by a weak knowledge base about the particularities and an inadequate conceptual framework for making meaningful summaries.

To pursue the micro-level study of the linkages of working scientists in developing countries with their counterparts in the world system of science, we trace the specificities of their transnational networks and delineate the norms of the third cultures which pattern their interaction. Third cultures are created, carried and changed by persons who are relating segments of one society with segments of one or more other societies. Although affected by macro-level changes in the relationships between societies and by redefinitions of the position of the segment within a society, still each third culture has a history of its own which can be traced. These third cultures, in turn, impact on other segments of societies through the roles which carriers play. Viewed sociologically, the aggregate of third cultures constitutes a social structure which functions as a linkage system between the scientific communities of developing societies and the centers of world science. Through these corridors of personalized and professional networks flow the ideas, skills, knowledge, technology and visions of modern science. In function, they are the contemporary equivalent of what the anthropologist Kroeber (1960) termed the Oikoumene, the Old World civilization which linked the widely dispersed and distinctive social and cultural units from Gibraltar to Japan (Useem, et al., 1963; Useem and Useem, 1967; Useem, 1971; Kumar, 1979).

Although developing countries share some commonalities, each also has a unique history which impinges on the nature of the linkages which its scientists have to the world system of science. We chose to look at the scientific communities of two countries, the Philippines and Malaysia, to explore the commonalities and uniquenesses.

COUNTRY SETTINGS OF THE SCIENTISTS

Among the world's 125 countries with a million or more population, the Philippines, with a population of 44 million, ranks seventeenth in size. Malaysia, with 13 million, ranks forty-ninth. Ecologically, the former is an extended archipelago and the latter a peninsular society with some off islands. Both lie in the region which has come to be known as Southeast Asia. The seven countries (Indonesia, Malaysia, the Philippines, Thailand, Singapore, Vietnam and Cambodia) which comprise this region have a total population of approximately 296 million.

Both countries are classified by the World Bank (1979) as "middle income developing countries," being two of the 55 countries with a per capita GNP between $310 and $3190 which rank above the 37 "low income countries" with less than $300 per capita GNP. The Philippines' per capita GNP of $450 gives it a rank of 11 among the middle income countries; Malaysia, being more affluent with its per capita GNP of $750, ranks 31.

Since independence from the United States in 1947 for the Philippines and from Great Britain in 1957 for Malaysia, the two nations have been among the many third world societies which have a small but growing modern-educated middle class. Collectively, the members are influential in the central institutions of a modernizing society and have roles in relating segments of their own society to the rest of the world. Most of the middle class members are highly educated, having graduated from institutions in their own countries which, for the most part, have been developed only in the last thirty years. A considerable proportion of those in professions, in senior policy-making and administrative positions and in influential roles in colleges and universities have secured education in the West.

One segment of this modernizing middle class in developing third world countries is composed of academic research scientists, the subject of our report. We shall concentrate on the interconnections of the scientists with the world system of science and deal with only those aspects of the domestic scene as are related to this emphasis.

ACADEMIC SETTINGS

Before being established as nation-states, the Philippines were incorporated for more than three centuries into the Spanish and, subsequently, the American colonial third cultural systems of education and science; Malaysia for over a century was part of the British colonial world with its own distinctive set of practices (Furnival, 1948; Jamais, 1962; Van Hise, 1957; Wong and Hean, 1972; Wong and Hong, 1975; Carson, 1978). There were several important differences in the colonial traditions of the two countries which have significance for post-independence development of the scientific community.

The Spanish introduced higher education into the Philippines largely under the aegis of its Catholic missionary orders which also developed feeder elementary and secondary educational institutions for both boys and girls. To this system was added, in the American period beginning in the early twentieth century, an emphasis upon mass public education and the development of a public university which combined the philosophies of education of American state universities and "land grant" colleges. However, efforts of church-related organizations, both Catholic and Protestant, and other private groups to provide education at all levels were not discouraged. Foreign educators and scientists were present who had ties into the American and to some extent European centers of science, but there was an early emphasis upon developing "native" scientists who shared these transcultural ties.

The British, in what is now divided into Malaysia and Singapore, were more concerned with developing a small indigenous "elite" rather than a mass educated populace. They maintained control over institutions of higher education, dominated the faculties, discouraged the efforts of both foreign and local groups to establish institutions of higher education, and included only an occasional "native" in the academic scientific comunity.

The institutions of higher education in Southeast Asia, like most of the third world, have passed through a period of high growth rates since the end of colonialism and the start of development (Hoong, et. al. 1973; Huq, 1975; Presidential Commission, 1970; Silcock, 1964, 1979; Tapingkae, 1974). The Philippines now have 23 public and 556 private universities and colleges with about 13,000 faculty members who are classified as scientists. Malaysia has five public universities with about 1000 scientists on their faculties.

Reflecting the differing colonial traditions in educational emphases are the statistics for literacy rates of those above 15 and the numbers enrolled in tertiary education expressed as a percentage of the population, 20-24. The Philippines has a literacy rate of 87 compared to Malaysia's 60, and a higher education enrollment rate of 20 compared to Malaysia's 3 (World Bank, 1979).

STUDY DESIGN

In order to get an understanding of the academic scientists of non-Western developing societies, our field work consisted of three types of information gathering: 1) assembling widely scattered and often unpublished data on academic institutions, exchange of students, scientific publications and library holdings, faculty compositions, etc.; 2) ethnographic in nature—interviewing key informants and senior figures important in the growth of the scientific communities.

The third was data collected from a sample of academic research scientists in the two countries. From each scientist we secured a biodata form, including publications, and a self-administered questionnaire. In addition, each individual was interviewed in depth for two to five hours.

DEFINITION OF THE POPULATION OF ACADEMIC RESEARCH SCIENTISTS

Who is defined as a scientist varies significantly according to the purposes of particular gathering units and the methods used for collecting information about a population of scientists (Harbison and Myers, 1964; UNESCO, 1968; Moravcsik, 1975; Merton, 1973; Barber, 1962; Basalla, 1968; Crane, 1972; Hagstrom, 1965; Spiegel-Rösing and Price, 1977). We defined the population in which we are interested as academic research scientists: those having a primary attachment to an institution of higher education and having been actively, although not exclusively, engaged in research in the physical, life, and social sciences.

As can be seen in Table 1, the different traditions in higher education of the two countries result in quite different proportions of those classified as academic scientists who fall in the population of our definition of research scientists—less than ten percent of Philippine and over half of the Malaysian academic scientists. In the Philippines, the research scientists are attached to a very few of the close to 600 institutions of higher education which are primarily engaged in teaching. Malaysia has but five higher educational institutions.

Table 1. Percentage of Philippine and Malaysian Academic Scientists in the Physical, Engineering, Life and Social Sciences Engaged in Research.

Scientific Fields	Philippines[a]		Malaysia[b]	
	Academic Scientists No.	Percent Researchers %	Academic Scientists No.	Percent Researchers %
Physical Sciences	2,909	7	119	52
Engineering Sciences	1,454	2	246	24
Life Sciences	4,668	14	302	73
Social Sciences	4,193	5	195	56
Total	13,224	8	862	52

[a]*Source:* Adapted from Table A-2 of the *Survey of Scientific and Technological Manpower in the Philippines, Educational Institutions and Non-Profit Organization*, Volume II, *Statistical Tables*, National Science Development Broad Project, University of the Philippines Statistical Center.

[b]These figures are for only four of the five universities in Malaysia. Missing is a provincially-located university which was not included in the study. Excluded are foreigners.

In both countries the life sciences are the leading fields and the most active in research. Almost two-thirds of the Philippine and one-half of the Malaysian productive scientists are in the life sciences, even though they constitute slightly over a third of the total number of scientists in both countries. In contrast to the West, the physical sciences lag both in terms of their numbers and the proportion engaged in research. In the Philippines they comprise 22 percent of all academic scientists and 18 percent of those active in research. In Malaysia they are but 14 percent of the academic scientists and 14 percent of the academic researchers. The engineering scientists form 11 percent of the Philippine academic scientists and three percent of its research population. The Malaysian proportion in academic engineering sciences is higher (28 percent) than the Philippines owing to a recent upgrading of the Institute of Technology to university status, but as yet the proportion of all scientists engaged in engineering research (13 percent) is lower than their percentage of the academic population. The social sciences in the Philippines make up 32 percent of academic scientists and 18 percent of the researchers and in Malaysia, 23 percent of the academic scholars and 25 percent of the researchers.

Except for occasional visiting foreign professors and a few foreign members of religious orders, the Philippine community had been "nationalized" by the time we did our interviewing. In Malaysia, there are still numbers of expatriates in regular academic positions, but they were excluded from the population from which the sample was drawn.

THE SAMPLES

In both the Philippines and Malaysia, we drew a disproportionate, stratified, cluster sample of scientists who had authored at least one research publication according to the variables of institutional affiliation, scientific field, gender, and age of scientist. We estimate that our Philippine sample of 160 is about 14 percent of the 1150 research scientists; the Malaysian sample of 80 is 18 percent of the published academic scientists.

In both countries there is a great gap in the proportion of published scientists at the primate universities and the percentage at other institutions of higher education. We undersampled the former and took almost all from the latter. The Philippine sample came from 17 public and private universities and the Malaysian from the four universities in Greater Kuala Lumpur (excluded was one provincial university).

Nearly all of the conventional disciplines and a few of the most advanced specialties within disciplines are represented in these two Southeast Asian countries, but there is not a critical mass of scholars in any one with the exception of research on rice in the Philippines. Hence, we did not try to study specific disciplines or subdisciplines, as these are defined at the world centers, but rather sampled scientists in clusters of related disciplines which are here termed "scientific fields." The largest cluster, the life sciences, we divided into three scientific fields—general life sciences, medically-related life sciences, and agriculturally-related life sciences. In order to have sufficient numbers in the six scientific fields, we oversampled engineering and social scientists in the Philippines and the weaker agriculturally-related sciences in Malaysia.

Philippine women (Filipinas) have long had a well-established place in all levels of higher education and science. Thirty-nine percent of academic scientists are women, in contrast to the 10 percent which constitutes the percentage in most societies for which we have records. Malaysian women began to enter the science fields only in the 1960s and are 12 percent of the published research scientists. We slightly undersampled Filipinas and oversampled Malaysian women.

We tried to get sufficient number from all generations of scientists in order to look at the changes in the scientific community over time. This meant oversampling older scientists in Malaysia because they were so few.

The additional variables of nature of present research being applied or basic, what higher degrees they held, and where they obtained them were secured from biodata sheets.

The overall distribution of the two samples by the seven variables can be seen in Table 2.

CHARACTERISTICS OF THE SCIENTIFIC COMMUNITIES

The characteristics of the scientific communities of these two developing societies can be described in terms of the seven variables whose meanings were developed in the course of the field work and in the analysis of the biodata forms and depth interviews: 1) institutional setting; 2) scientific fields; 3) basic and applied research; 4) education; 5) generations; 6) ethnicity; and 7) gender.

Institutional Affiliation. In both countries, the first affiliation of scientists with an institution of higher education normally is enduring for their academic careers. This contrasts sharply with the reported interuniversity mobility in the career histories of American scientists. Scholars who leave their original institution of affiliation before retirement (65 in the Philippines, 55 in Malaysia) join an international organization, enter into the private sector or the national government, or, in the case of Filipinos, migrate to another country. As a result, most scientists are less aware of the research being done by their counterparts in other academic institutions in the country than they are of research going on in foreign universities, research sponsored by international organizations and to some extent the national government. Scholarly societies and professional organizations are relatively weak.

Table 2.   Characteristics of the Philippine and Malaysian Scientific Community Samples of Academic Research Scientists, in Percentages[a]

Variables	Philippines %	Malaysia %
1. *Institutional Affiliation*		
Primate Universities	59	64
Other Universities	41	36
2. *Scientific Fields*		
Physical	16	15
Engineering	9	16
Life—General	16	18
Life—Agricultural	19	16
Life—Medical	15	16
Social Science	25	19
3. *Nature of Present Research*		
Basic	42	41
Applied	52	59
No Present Research	6	0
4. *Education*		
Highest Degree Earned		
Bachelor	2	1
M.D./M.B.B.S.	6	15
Master[b]	31	25
Doctorate[c]	61	59
Foreign Education		
Yes	91	94
No	9	6
5. *Generations—Philippines*		
Received Bach/M.D. between		
1922-1946	11	
1947-1951	16	
1952-1956	32	
1957-1961	24	
1962-1968	17	
Generations—Malaysians		
Received Bach/M.B.B.S. between		
1945-1956		10
1957-1961		18
1962-1968		59
1969-1975		14
6. *Ethnicity (Malaysia Only)*		
Malay		34
Chinese		45
Indian		21
7. *Gender*		
Male	68	81
Female	32	19
	(N=160)	(N=80)

[a]Sum of percentages within each variable equals 100.
[b]9 Filipinos also have M.D.s
[c]3 Filipinos also have M.D.s, 1 Malaysian also has M.B.B.S.

Scientific Fields. The acculturation of the European-American conceptions of higher education and scientific disciplines to the social situation and cultural environment of Southeast Asia is a continuing and many-sided process. As new scientific thrusts within various disciplines come to the fore at the world centers of science, they are introduced into Southeast Asian universities and adapted to the local scene in several ways. The new returnees with foreign education bring their recently acquired specializations into their research which must come to terms with the local environment and, because most researchers also teach, they introduce new approaches into their courses of instruction. Most try to assemble local data and to complement and test their foreign-derived generalizations. Some of the newer emphases from the world centers enter university curricula and research through the widely-used foreign literature, professional journals, and textbooks.

Seldom are there institutionally-imposed constraints on academic scholars to stay within fixed disciplinary boundaries in their research. Indeed, because of their being affixed to a particular institution, the incentives of a succession of new internationally (and occasionally domestic) sponsored and funded research opportunities encourage researchers to shift the emphasis of their work. Some even change disciplines.

Basic and Applied Research. There is little consensus in the literature as to what is basic and what is applied research. One meaning of basic stems from the world's disciplinary groups in the primate institutions of a national society. In less-developed countries, basic research problems may derive from questions arising from application of foreign knowledge. This usage of basic may or may not fit into the epicenters' definition of basic research. In the colonial period, the process of defining was lodged in the combinations of colonial governors, foreign educational administrators, and expatriate scientists. Since the establishment of independent states with their own educational and scientific communities, the persons who define what is basic or applied are nationals.

To get at the meaning of these terms for our samples, we simply asked them to define their main research work as primarily basic or applied. We then asked them to characterize their current and main research. Those who designated their main research as basic described it as being "in great part" theoretical, experimental, taxonomic, or methodological. The self-classified applied researchers characterized their current research as "in great part" policy-oriented, technological, teaching-related, or highly useful to a segment of their own or other societies.

The proportions of the two samples who define their main research work as primarily basic or applied are similar. Forty-four percent of the Filipinos and 41 percent of the Malaysians classify their research as basic. There are some differences, however, from this overall proportion in the various clusters of disciplines. About 60 percent of the sample of published physical scientists in both countries refer to their main research thrust as primarily basic. A major reason is that the multinational and foreign corporations which dominate the industrial sector do their ''applied'' research in their home countries and do not support to any appreciable degree the indigenous scientific communities.

Of all life scientists grouped together, the proportion in basic research is higher in the Philippines (52%) than in Malaysia (35%). The discrepancy is especially large in the bio-medical researchers, with 48 percent of the Filipinos and 23 percent of the Malaysians in this disciplinary cluster seeing themselves as being involved in basic research. In the social sciences, the opposite prevails. Twenty-nine percent of the Philippine and 47 percent of the Malaysian social scientists regard their main current work as largely basic.

It should be emphasized that this variable applies only to their main research. Almost all have work roles in universities that include teaching, committee work and administration. Inasmuch as they are in developing countries which have a scarcity of the very highly educated, they are called upon to perform consulting work outside the universities. Two-thirds of the basic, four-fifths of the applied Filipinos and 60 percent of both basic and applied Malaysian scientists function in the capacity of consultants outside the university.

Education. Over ninety percent of both the Philippine and Malaysian sample scientists have had foreign education. The patterning of that foreign education differs somewhat in the two countries. In the Philippines, the scientists typically secure their undergraduate education in one of the local universities, are employed upon graduation as an instructor or research assistant in the same institution, and only then go abroad for advanced graduate work or post-graduate specialization while on leave from the employing institution. Faculty members play a decisive role in sponsoring their students as new entrants into a particular field (usually in a specialization in which the faculty member feels weak), gaining their commitment to a scholarly future, and helping them secure opportunities for study abroad. A similar sequencing prevails for slightly less than half of the Malaysian sample. The other half secure their undergraduate as well as their graduate education in foreign countries.

Reflecting the linkages established in the colonial period and continuing in the post-colonial era, study abroad is heavily weighted in the direction of the ex-colonial power. Ninety percent of the 124 Filipinos who were granted their highest degree in a foreign university received it in the United States. Fifty-six percent of the 70 Malaysians who earned their top degree in a foreign country studied at U.K. universities; an additional 30 percent received their higher education in Commonwealth countries (Australia, Canada, New Zealand, and India); only 13 percent received their highest degrees from the United States— a recent phenomenon largely related to the field of agriculture.

Generations.   We have classified the scientists into generations according to
the period in which they received their first academic degree (Bachelor, M.D.,
M.B.B.S.) and took their initial steps into the academic scientific community.
The concept of generation, as we use it, refers to a group of scholars who enter
into their professional field at a particular point in time with reference to the
historical development of their own societies, the relationship of their own
society to other societies, and the changing character of world systems of
science. There are five distinguishable generations in the Philippine sample
and four in the Malaysian.

The Philippines, due to American colonial policy, developed more indigenous scientists during its colonial period than did Malaysia under the British.
Malaysia still has a large number of foreign faculty, whereas most foreigners in
the Philippines have been replaced and the few remaining have had to keep a
low profile during the period of high nationalistic fervor in the 1970s.

The pre-independence generation (pre-1947) in the Philippines was formed
during the peak years of colonialism and was concentrated largely in the life
sciences. It was relatively small in number during those years and has diminished even more in size in recent years through death, retirement, and movement into leadership positions in national, regional and international organizations, particularly the agricultural scientists.

A second and somewhat larger generation emerged in the reconstruction
years following World War II (they received their first academic degree
between 1947-1951). Although women were early in the sciences, this generation has a higher proportion of women than the other generations due to the
war-related deaths of men. The third generation was formed in the 1952-1956
period of increasingly self-conscious building of science-related systems to
meet the widely recognized need for expanding higher education and national
development programs.

The fourth (1957-1961) and fifth (1962-1968) generations entered science
during a period of growing domestic turbulence and intensifying Philippine
nationalism. Many did their graduate work in American universities in the late
'60s and early '70s when there was radicalization of campus life.

The generations in Malaysia follow a somewhat similar, but delayed-in-
time, development. Independence did not come to Malaysia until 1957, and
the pre-independence period was characterized by extremely limited participation of Malaysians in the one existing colonial university. As a result, the
pre-independence generation is very small. The transitional years following
independence, when the second generation of scientists were completing their
undergraduate education, saw some quickening in the process of developing
undergraduates who later went on for higher education as Malaysia began to
recognize the value of science and of having their own scientists available.
Malaysia's third generation (1962-1968) grew quickly in response to the
opening of new opportunities for higher and professional education abroad as

well as the establishing of new academic institutions and support systems for science at home. The youngest generation (1969-1975), many of whom returned from a foreign education only a short time before being interviewed, has yet to fashion their own professional lives in ways distinctive from the prior generations.

One indication of the recency of entrance of Malaysians into the scientific world, in contrast to the longer tradition of Filipinos being part of academic science, is the age of the scientists. Thirty-four percent of the Philippine and 75 percent of the Malaysian scientific community samples were less than forty years old at the time they were interviewed.

A brief comparison of the history of the life and agricultural sciences in the Philippines and Malaysia serves to illuminate some aspects of these scientific-field generational patterns. Due to the emphases of its colonial third culture, the Philippines had an earlier and more numerous founding generation in the life sciences than did Malaysia, which did not have a strong native generation in the life and agricultural sciences until after independence in 1957. The general life sciences in the Philippines continue to have an influential and active leadership among the "second" generation. Some have retired from their academic positions, but many are still engaged in research and take an active interest in promoting the careers of their former students among the newer generations. They are highly supportive of these newer generations' vigorous efforts to create a national sector in which their knowledge and skills will contribute to national development. However, because of fundamental changes in theoretical conceptualizations, the senior generations, though they have been deeply committed to research, have not left a powerful scholarly legacy of findings that continue to be cited in the present work of the newer generation of scholars in the life sciences.

Ambivalent feelings permeate inter-generational interaction in the life sciences. The newer generations regard the work of the "old-timers" as pioneering but outmoded studies. However, they respect the achievements of a generation which earned a strong international reputation in their time for their contributions. Some of the senior surviving generations admire the advanced character of the work carried out by the newcomers who have brought back to the Philippines complex technological skills and fresh approaches. However, some are uneasy about the intensification of nationalism among the younger generation as to what it implies for Philippine science in relationship to world science. The academic agricultural sciences regularly lose their senior generations to government, to regional, and to international organizations. Hence, there is no gerontocracy in the agricultural sciences, and the recently educated can move up quickly.

Thrusts in world science which have become central to established disciplines or disappeared from the core countries as important research problems make for generational divisions in some disciplines. In others, such as the bio-medical sciences, it is common for senior scholars to return to foreign research centers for post-doctoral training in new fields of research. The younger scholars do not feel their "elders" are outmoded.

Thus the stratification between generations reflects values which mix international and domestic status systems in the scientific community.

Ethnicity.   Ethnicity in Southeast Asian societies is unevenly interwoven into the patterning of the modern-educated middle classes, secondary and higher education institutions, the newer organizations in the public and private sectors, and in the cultural definitions of personal identities (Arles, 1971; Esman, 1972; Hirschman, 1975; Purcell, 1967; Sandhu, 1969; Takei, Bock and Saunders, 1973; Banks, 1976; Amyot, 1973; Gowing and McAmis, 1969; Majul, 1973; Wernstedt and Spencer, 1967).

The lineaments of ethnicity are more openly evidenced in Malaysian historical development and present development policies with respect to the academic and scientific communities than they are in the Philippines. Malaysian urban Chinese of both genders have long had access to quality secondary-school instruction and facilities in the sciences and mathematics. This has encouraged them to pursue university education and to subsequently enter into a variety of professional occupations. They number 36 percent of the total population of Malaysia and 45 percent of our sample of the scientific population. The Malays, who total 53 percent of Malaysia and 34 percent of our sample, are largely newcomers to the world of science. Their interest in higher education, and especially in the sciences, was not vigorously activated until the 1960s. Previously, only a few amongst the Malay elite and almost none from the rural areas where most Malays reside had the experience of attending secondary-level schools with adequate libraries, laboratories, and instructional staffs in the sciences. Talented Malays often were directed into civil service rather than into scientific careers. The Indians, though a minority of nine percent in Malaysia, have customarily attached great status and value to education. They comprise 21 percent of our sampling of the scientific community. These demographic trends have precipitated a disproportionately large Chinese and Indian group of scientists in the senior generations. Since independence, the stress in public policy is to expand the opportunities for Malays in educational institutions and in higher-status occupations, including the academic world. This has made for a high concentration of Malay scientists in the newer universities and among the younger generations.

The history of Philippine ethnicity is more difficult to summarize for the society as a whole and for its scientific populations. The social and political-legal definition of a Chinese identity has proved at times negotiable and continues to change. The largest but still small (7 percent of the population) cultural minority are the Muslims in the southern island of Mindinao. The Muslims early resisted becoming involved in the educational systems of the colonial powers. And tensions have long existed and still persist between the Muslims and the dominant Christian population. One new and state-sponsored university in the south contains the few Muslims in the academic community and most of them are in the younger generation.

The regional-linguistic divisions within the majority Christian population form the basis of everyday identity among scientists. There are variations in the proportions of the various linguistic groups going on for post-collegiate education, but these linguistic groupings are not consistently dividing. There is a high rate of endogamy among the highly educated, with marriages across ethno-linguistic lines common.

Although each ethno-cultural group has its own language, and although both countries have moved toward establishing a national language, the medium of teaching the sciences in English, and all scientists read and speak English. This makes them especially open to continuing cultural contact with those parts of the world in which science is carried on primarily in that language.

Gender. On most of the measures used, there were few consistent differences between Philippine men and women scientists in their involvement in research, patterns of participation, publications, or attitudes within the Philippines. Because of women's relatively recent entrance into the academic scene in Malaysia, there are some differences between the sexes, particularly in their acceptance into administrative roles. For both academic communities, however, there is more equal participation within the country than in the world of international science, where men are advantaged.

LINKAGES BETWEEN NATIONAL AND WORLD SCIENCE SYSTEMS

We shall confine this account to four aspects of the interrelations between the academic research scientists of the Philippines and Malaysia, and the world systems of science. We take them up under four dimensions: 1) Cognitive maps of the world's leading centers of science; 2) Sources of recognition, places of publication, and international citations; 3) Patternings of transnational networks; and 4) Values as to where the scientists want to make their contribution.

Cognitive Maps of the World's Leading Centers of Science. One starting point in a search for the matrices of trans-societal networking is to examine the responses of our Philippine and Malaysian sample academic scientists to the broad question: ''Where are the leading centers in your field of specialization?'' No one had difficulty in identifying particular countries and regions of the world in which were located the leading research centers and outstanding scholars in their own specialization, discipline, or field.

There were considerable differences in how well informed each person was and the sources of their personal knowledge. The most fully informed usually offered detailed accounts of the current work under way in specific laboratories and institutions; knew either a well-established research center was currently at the forefront, stagnant, or slipping; and could assess the value for their field of the studies being done by individual scholars. Such knowledge and appraisals were based on past experience as graduate and post-doctoral students, visits to foreign centers at various times in their career histories, recurrent participation in international conferences, regular reading of the main journals and the sending for reprints of articles to which they had no direct access, occasional visits to their group by foreign scholars in the same specialization, and the exchange of news in correspondence with foreign colleagues. The less aware were commonly well informed about the places where they had studied, but about other places they would say, ''I know something important is going on there, but I don't know any more about it.''

Table 3 summarizes their responses by the countries or regions in which were located their designated ''leading centers.'' Overall, American and British scientific communities and institutions are perceived as being foremost in the present world of science in nearly half (44 percent) of the Philippine and three-fourths (70 percent) of the Malaysian responses. Slightly more than one-third of the leading centers cited by both the Filipinos (34 percent) and Malaysians (36 percent) lie in the United States. Another third of the Malaysian-mentioned centers, but only ten percent of those cited by Filipinos, were located in Great Britain. Eleven percent of the leading centers cited by the Filipinos, and 18 percent by the Malaysians, were located in Commonwealth countries. These patterns, to considerable extent, reflect the opportunities for funded advanced training, research, and international conference attendance. The differentials between the two countries in their ties into the first world in part reflect continuation of networks originally established in the colonial period.

In each of the six scientific fields, Philippine scientists exhibit a more global outlook than the Malaysians who, beyond the U.S. and U.K., reveal a cognitive map of the most important centers of world science that is confined primarily to Western Europe and the Commonwealth countries (Australia, New Zealand, Canada, India) and, to some extent, Southeast Asia. Other places referred to by Philippine scientists as having important centers in their field and which were not mentioned by any Malaysian scientists were: Japan, Taiwan, Korea, Pakistan, Iran, Israel, Brazil, Mexico, South Africa, and Rhodesia.

Western European countries are seen as containing outstanding science centers by some scientists in all six scientific fields. Neither Russian nor mainland Chinese science has been directly accessible to most Philippine and Malaysian scholars. Research strengths of the U.S.S.R. comprised only three percent of the Philippine and one percent of the Malaysian responses. Apart from a bit of speculation, no one listed any center in the People's Republic of China.

Table 3.   Percentage Distribution of the Responses by Scientific Fields of the Philippine and Malaysian Scientific Community Samples to the Question, "Where Are the Leading Centers in Your Field (Specialization)?"

| | Physical | | Engineering | | Life-Gen. | | Life-Agri. | | Life-Med. | | Soc. Sci. | | Total | |
	Phil %	Mlys %	Phil %	Mlys %	Phil %	Mlys %	Phil %	Mlys %	Phil %	Mlys %	Phil %	Mlys %	Phil %	Mlys %
USA	34	29	44	31	34	33	23	43	37	35	44	46	34	36
UK	10	34	4	53	8	46	11	13	12	35	11	23	10	34
Aust/NZ	2	6	4	6	9	3	8	17	2	15	4	8	5	9
Canada	2	9	0	3	0	6	4	7	0	6	0	0	1	5
Europe	20	17	13	6	11	6	8	3	22	3	25	8	16	8
USSR	12	3	9	3	2	0	0	0	2	0	1	0	3	1
Japan	14	—	4	—	19	—	14	—	10	—	4	—	12	—
India	5	0	0	0	6	6	7	10	5	6	3	8	5	5
S E Asia	2	3	22	0	9	0	12	7	10	0	7	8	9	3
Asia	0	—	0	—	1	—	8	—	0	—	0	—	2	—
Other	0	—	0	—	1	—	5	—	1	—	1	—	2	—
Total	100	100	100	100	100	100	100	100	100	100	100	100	100	100
N =	59	35	23	36	65	33	91	30	60	34	73	39	371	207

298

Japan and the cooperating Southeast Asian countries are two special places in the mapping of world science for these two Southeast Asian academic research scientists. Japan is the major Asian country in higher education and research which is extensively tied into the international scientific community. It is also a major economic power with large and growing investments in both the Philippines and Malaysia. Nevertheless, there are ambivalent reactions in both countries to Japan's academic and scientific communities. These stem from historical experiences of Japanese wartime occupation, language barriers, and divergent culturally prescibed attitudes and behaviors. In Philippine scientific circles, especially in the general life and agricultural sciences, the Japanese research establishment is well regarded and its science centers are more often positively appraised than even those in the U.K. Whereas 12 percent of the Philippine responses were to centers in Japan, none of the Malaysians mentioned Japan.

The newest reference group is Southeast Asia as a region. During recent years, some of the older higher-educational and research organizations and a few new regional research and training centers have assumed responsibility for providing regional leadership in particular scientific and technological fields. The Philippines were early in sponsoring a regional network and institutionally participating in collaborative research and educational exchange programs. Among our Philippine sample, nine percent of the world's leading centers in their fields are seen as located in the region—more specifically, the Philippines and Thailand. Malaysia has more recently begun to use regional networks in higher education and science. The Malaysian sample's responses include but three percent of all the prominent centers as being in Southeast Asia.

The life sciences in both countries have greater depth and better established research traditions than have the physical, engineering and social sciences. Scientists among the latter three groupings see the foremost centers of science primarily as outstanding universities for advanced training. The life scientists exhibit a more sophisticated awareness of research centers and the specializations of particular universities, and include places in countries with whom they would exchange knowledge as well as send outstanding students to pursue advanced degrees. This is especially true of the agricultural sciences in the Philippines, which are quite well established.[2]

Thus, despite seventy years of close ties between Philippine and American academic institutions in the agricultural sciences, exceptionally large-scale cooperative research and training programs between Philippine universities and American land-grant colleges in the development-oriented years, and the use of agricultural research and extension consultants from America in some crucial national undertakings, less than a fourth of their listing of the world's leading agricultural science centers is located in the U.S. In contrast, for

Malaysia, with limited American involvement in the agricultural sciences and the agricultural sector of the national society, almost half (43 percent) of the centers named by the Malaysian agricultural scientists are in the U.S. The agricultural research and development fields in Malaysia are relatively new, and they are looking to the U.S. for specialized training in the various aspects of the agricultural sciences for the building of their "second generation" of academic agricultural scientists, rather than for exchanging knowledge.

Sources of Recognition.   For scholars located at the cores of the global scientific community, there is little self-consciousness about whether it is more important to gain recognition from their national colleagues or from their foreign colleagues. Scientists at world centers, for whom publishing in their "national" journals assures world-wide distribution of their research, seldom debate whether it is more important to publish in a local or foreign journal. Scientists in the peripheries give much more thought as to who are their significant others and where to publish their research results. The choices to be made often involve a subtle blending of the local maturity of their professional field, the availability of quality national publication outlets, their generation, and the degree of nationalistic commitment.

Recognition Inside Versus Outside the Country.   As can be seen in Table 4, under three percent of the Philippine and none of the Malaysian scientists feel that the process of choosing between the alternative sources of recognition has been an unimportant question for them, and only 20 percent of the Filipinos and 15 percent of the Malaysians resolve the issue in their own minds by deciding that recognition for their own achievements inside and outside their country are equally desirable. Of the 112 Filipinos who limited their choice to either inside or outside, upwards of two-thirds (63 percent) opted for inside recognition, while for the 69 Malaysians who restricted their options to one or the other, two thirds decided that outside recognition is more important.[3]

Philippine research scientists in three fields—physical, general life, and medical life sciences—are closely divided between wanting inside/outside recognition. Among engineering, agricultural-life and social sciences, preference is given to gaining recognition within the domestic scientific community. Malaysians in every scientific field give higher priority to outside over inside recognition.

As can be derived from Table 5, intergenerational comparisons serve in part to add historical perspective to the two samples' "definition of the situation." While the pre-independence (1922-1946) Philippine first generation of scientists strongly stress the relative importance of recognition within the country (67 percent), this emphasis is sharply reversed in the following or second generation, among whom only 38 percent view home-country recognition as being more important, and one-third think recognition is desirable in both

Table 4. Percentage Distribution of Scientific Fields of Philippine and Malaysian Scientific Community Samples by Where They Think It Is More Important to Gain Recognition for Their Research— Inside or Outside Their Country.

	Where Important to Gain Recognition				
Scientific Field	Inside Country	Outside Country	Both Desirable	Not Important	Total
Physical					
Philippines	35	42	15	8	N=26
Malaysia	25	58	17	0	N=12
Engineering					
Philippines	62	15	23	0	N=13
Malaysia	39	46	15	0	N=13
Life—General					
Philippines	44	39	17	0	N=23
Malaysia	21	57	21	0	N=14
Life—Agriculture					
Philippines	59	7	34	0	N=29
Malaysia	31	61	8	0	N=13
Life—Medical					
Philippines	41	46	9	4	N=22
Malaysia	23	62	15	0	N=13
Social Science					
Philippines	56	22	19	3	N=32
Malaysia	33	53	13	0	N=15
Total					
Philippines	49	28	20	3	N=145
Malaysia	29	56	15	0	N= 80

places. From then on, through the third, fourth and fifth generations (the decades of the 1950s and 1960s), the proportion who are nation-oriented steadily mounts with each successive generation and reaches 61 percent in the fifth generation who identify their personal and professional reputation with preferring recognition for their research work in the Philippines.

In Malaysia, unlike the Philippines, from the first pre-independence generation to the fourth and youngest, there is a steady increase in the proportion of each generation who look to outside countries as the important source of recognition. The percentage who do so climbs from 38 percent with the first to 73 percent in the fourth generation.

Scientists who classify their current main research as primarily applied are pulled in the direction of thinking it is important to gain recognition inside the country. In the Philippines, 60 percent of primarily applied scientists think recognition inside the country important, whereas only 38 percent of those whose present main research is basic opt for inside recognition. In Malaysia, 36 percent of the applied and only 18 percent of those in basic research desire in-country recognition.

Place of Publication.[4]   Appearing in a journal which has an international reputation in one's specialized field has many meanings. It assures scientists of reaching significant others doing similar work in the leading centers of research for their field. To publish in an outstanding foreign journal often signifies to the Philippine and Malaysian scientists a testing and validation of the quality of their work by more universalistic scientific norms than is true of publications in their own national journals. This seems especially important to those scholars who, being "one of a kind" in their country, have few peers to react meaningfully to the substantive content of their work. Some save what they feel are their "best" studies for publication in the main international journals of their field. A number in the forefront of the general, agricultural, and medical life sciences and a few in the social sciences called our special attention to their foreign-published articles which enlarged, refined, or altered generalizations which heretofore had been derived from data about plants, animals, and humans specific to the part of the world where the leading science centers are located. Philippine and Malaysian scientists typically observe that

Table 5.   Percentage Distribution of Generations of Philippine and Malaysian Scientific Community Samples by Where They Think It Is More Important to Gain Recognition for Their Research— Inside or Outside Their Country.

Filipinos Received First Degree (Bach, M.D.) Between:	*Where Important to Gain Recognition*				
	Inside Country	*Outside Country*	*Both Desirable*	*Not Important*	*Total*
1922-1946	67	13	13	7	N=15
1947-1951	38	24	33	5	N=21
1952-1956	45	37	14	4	N=49
1957-1961	46	32	22	0	N=37
1962-1968	61	17	22	0	N=23
Total	49	28	20	3	N=145
Malaysians Received First Degree (Bach, M.B.B.S.) Between:					
1945-1956	38	38	25	0	N=8
1957-1961	29	42	29	0	N=14
1962-1968	32	60	8	0	N=47
1969-1975	9	73	18	0	N=11
Total	29	56	15	0	N=80

they receive more requests for reprints and letters about the detailed contents of their published studies from colleagues in foreign countries than they do from associates in their own country. Furthermore, it is considered a violation of norms to take the initiative in sending out reprints to scientists who are not close associates, friends, or relatives.

Aside from gaining recognition from other scientists for the substantive content of their research, there are also differential rewards for foreign versus domestic publications in terms of advancement within their own universities. Although there is no ''publish or perish'' tradition in either country, there are rewards for publication. Malaysian institutions in their appraisal for advancement of scholars allocate a larger amount of recognition to foreign over domestic publications. The Philippine reward system varies somewhat on this score, with some institutions clearly assigning more weight to foreign over domestic publication and others giving equal weight to both, but in no case is greater weight given to local over Western publications.

Part of this difference in recognition of publication outlet is a reflection of the colonial and post-colonial patterns in the two countries in the storing of knowledge. All scientific fields in the Philippines have at least one domestic-published journal, some going back to the early 1900s.[5] Philippine scientific journals have been numerous, with many more starting than continuing to publish regularly. Current editors of many of the leading journals in different fields claim there is a constant need for more quality research articles than are normally available.

A survey of the domestic and foreign periodicals located in the libraries of the four Malaysian universities found that 99 percent of all journals and scientific bulletins are imported from abroad. Only 36 (less than one percent) of all scientific journals are Malaysian in origin, and many are recent in inception. Although every scientific field has at least one journal, 14 are in the social sciences, 10 in the agricultural, and 6 in the engineering sciences. The remaining six are scattered in the physical, medical and general life sciences.

The interaction of these factors of wanting recognition for their research from core members of the global scientific community, securing wide distribution of their research results, gaining rewards within their own university,

Table 6. Distribution of Philippine and Malaysian Samples by Place of Publication of Articles in Scientific Journals

Place of Publication	Philippines %	Malaysia %
Own Country *Only*	40	19
Both Own Country and Foreign	54	59
Foreign *Only*	6	22
Total	100	100
	(N = 153)	(N = 80)

availability of domestic outlets, and where they secured their foreign education results in different publication patterns in the two countries.

As is summarized in Table 6, twice as many Filipinos (40 percent) publish
solely in their own country as do Malaysians (19 percent). And proportionately
three times as many Malaysians publish in a foreign journal *only* as do
Filipinos (23 percent to 6 percent). Over half of the sample scientists published
in both local and foreign publications.

Table 7 gives the countries in which the scientists have published. Again the
ties to the former colonial power are evident in that the highest proportion of
the scientists publishing outside their country publish in journals of their
former governors. Worthy of note, however, is that the American journals
have a greater attraction for Malaysians than do British and Commonwealth
journals for Filipinos.

There is a fairly similar incidence in both countries in the distribution of
publishing outside the country for most fields. The life and medical sciences
exhibit the highest proportion of foreign-published scholars in both countries.
A cluster of fields next to them are the physical, engineering and agricultural
sciences. However, there is a large difference between Philippine and Malaysian social sciences: twice as many Malaysians (73 percent) as Filipinos (36
percent) in the social sciences are foreign published. We attribute this difference, in part, to the availability of comparatively strong Philippine journals in
many social-science disciplines and the depth of the concern in some of the
Philippine social-science circles for the development of an authentic Philip-
pine-based scholarly tradition of thought and writing.

As might be predicted, there is a fairly close correspondence between each
scientific community's perceptions of the leading centers of world science and
the foreign countries in which they have published. The two leading centers of

Table 7. Percentage of Philippine and Malaysian Sample Scientists Who
Published at Least One Article in Various Countries and Regions

Place of Publication	Philippine Scientists %*	Malaysian Scientists %*
Own country	93	78
U.S.A.	50	30
U.K.	6	44
Europe	8	28
Canada	1	8
Asia (except SE Asia)	3	11
Southeast Asia (except own country)	3	28
Australia/N.Z.	0	25
Number of Scientists	(N=153)	(N=80)

*Does not add to 100 percent because percentage is of scientists, not their publications. Most had multiple
publications.

world science for Filipinos, the U.S. and Europe, are also the location of the journals in which they most often publish. For Malaysia, the U.K. and U.S. are considered the two leading centers in that order, but a slightly higher proportion publish in the U.S. than consider it the locus of the leading centers in science. For the Philippine sample, Japan is a special case. Well-regarded by many as a major center of creativity (third in rank order), its journals, because of language inaccessibility problems, are not easily open to Filipinos.

International Citations.   The question can be raised as to whether or not the scientists are correct in assuming that foreign publication is more likely than domestic publication to bring notice of their work in the international scientific community. To answer this question, we checked the *Science Citation Index* to see if their published articles were referred to by others.

We found that nearly four out of every ten in both the Philippine and Malaysian scientific communities had one or more citations to their publications (39 percent in both countries). For articles published in a scientific journal in their own country, 20 percent of the Filipinos and 13 percent of the Malaysians had at least one citation of their locally published articles, even though no Philippine or Malaysian publication was abstracted in the *Science Citation Index* during the period we checked. Fifty-four percent of the Philippine scientists received at least one citation to articles published in the U.S.A. The comparable percentage for Malaysians is 71 percent. If the scientists published in the U.K., 80 percent of the Filipinos and 46 percent of Malaysians were cited at least once.

The medical and general life scientists are the most often cited among both Philippine and Malaysian groups and for their local as well as their foreign publications. About half of the medical researchers in the two countries were cited for articles which appeared in their home-country journals and two-thirds of them for their foreign publications. Among the general life scientists, 30 percent of the Filipinos and a somewhat smaller percent of the Malaysians were cited for their locally published studies; for their foreign publications, 44 percent of the Filipinos and 64 percent of the Malaysians received citations.

To summarize for all fields: when a Filipino or Malaysian publishes in a Western journal (the North Atlantic-community countries plus Australia and New Zealand), the likelihood is one in two of being cited; if in an Asian scientific journal, about one in eight; if in a Philippine publication, one in five; and if in a Malaysian journal, one in six.

Patternings of Networks and Their Cultures.   A close study of the social structures and related cultures which are generated out of the personal interaction between scientists in less-developed countries and their counterparts in other countries with influential science centers can reveal important aspects of a scientific community in the third world. We shall cover in this section the incidence of participation in differing types of cross-national networks and the norms which characterize their professional ties with foreign-based colleagues.

A useful distinction can be made between the commonplace process of encountering foreigners and the more differentiated process of participating in a reciprocating set of relationships with foreign scholars. Every segment of the academic and scientific communities and every person in our Philippine and Malaysian samples have had direct contacts with foreign scientists. Besides foreign scholars in their midst[6], nine out of ten of both of our samples have studied in a foreign university, primarily in the first world. Participating in international conferences consistently is reported as very significant for maintaining ties with foreign colleagues. Forty-four percent of the Filipinos and 66 percent of the Malaysians attended conferences in foreign countries in the three years before being interviewed.[7] In addition to conferences, one-fourth of both samples of scientists are called upon to do consulting work with Southeast-regional and international agencies and organizations.

We shall focus on the outcomes of these encounters as they are evidenced in several modal types of interpersonal ties which exist between Filipinos or Malaysians and their consociates in other countries. We classified our scientists into those who have no active networks and those who have "extensive," "intensive," or "slim" transnational networks. Perhaps the nature of the networks can best be understood by presenting a brief profile of each type.

Extensive Transnational Networks.   Scientists with extensive third-cultural networks are persons who have commanding knowledge of their field and are considered to be the leading representatives within the Philippines or Malaysia of the worldwide scientific community. Their daily conversations touch upon the latest problems and issues of interest in their specialty and, to some degree, in science and technology in general. They are nationally and often internationally recognized scientists, have established reputations in their specialization but also understanding of the problems in adjacent fields. They attend foreign-held international conferences, teach as exchange scholars or serve as guest speakers at a series of institutions abroad. Typically they are members and fellows of foreign scientific societies and have given papers both locally and abroad. Their continuous communication with foreign colleagues is the primary source of information for keeping up to date. They often exchange reprints and preprints with their "significant others" abroad in the same specialty. Scientists with extensive international ties know what is being worked on in their field and who is working on these projects.

Within their own countries, they can be described as influentials or brokers —those persons who are likely to influence the direction of scientific research by controlling appointments, promotions, and the distribution of special subsidies and awards; they can secure admission for their best students in foreign universities, and are instrumental in establishing arrangements between their home university and a foreign foundation, agency, or institution. They are "insiders" among highly mobile people who know or know about each other before meeting, and hence are aware of the norms of moving swiftly into "shop talk."

Those with extensive networks interact with many others, but only in narrowly defined segments of the total person. The personal dimension is not so much ignored as respected and used for making realistic judgments concerning the "business" at hand.

Intensive Transnational Networks. Intensive networks are both professional and highly personalized. They occur with one or a few scientists in foreign countries, and encompass more of the totality of the individuals involved. They are multi-bonded relationships, often involve parts of the "private selves," and often include family members. Many have a long history of being together in various places and times—as fellow graduate students, as first teacher-student and subsequently colleagues in a study, as collaborators in a major research project, and as intimate friends who meet together while attending international conferences.

Slim Transnational Networks. Slim networks between our sample scientists and foreign counterparts refer to more tenuous and often more protean relationships than is true of the extensive or intensive networks. Some are nascent ties of young scientists with former teachers and fellow graduate students which have not yet had time or opportunity to develop. Some are those being developed at mid-career as individuals enter new fields of research or administrative roles, or have more opportunities to attend international conferences. Others are fading extensive or intensive networks as the participants shift away from research interests which were previously shared, or as changes in the allocation of funding have contracted opportunities to carry out research or directly interact with foreign colleagues. Other slim relationships might be classified as latent, and could be renewed should priorities of support change once more or political differences between the nations of their citizenship take a different turn.

No Networks. The scientists with no interpersonal, third-cultural networks include: some who have the potential of establishing personalized ties abroad and hope to do in the future, but have not done so up to now because of their newness to their academic and professional roles; others who have entered into full-time administrative roles soon after their return from their foreign education, or still others who after starting research become increasingly engaged in teaching, administrative roles, or extra-scholarly pursuits in private and public life and have curtailed their research and active communication with scientists in foreign countries; a few who for ideological-nationalistic reasons prefer to minimize further contacts with foreign scientists, institutions, and foundations; and some whose foreign counterparts have retired, died, or moved into other research emphases.

When we look at the process of networking from the standpoint of the content of the behavior and norms which are exhibited, we observe that around each of our selected variables (e.g., scientific fields, generations, gender, institutions), there are mini-traditions, brokerage functions, both reciprocated and asymmetrical exchanges, and intricate linkages to other networks—all of which can be identified as representing third cultures generated along the networks among scientists of two or more societies. Like all cultures, these particular third cultures and their networks have both symbolic meaning and practical utility. Participants in them manifest a sense of sharing and a feeling of being identified with a collectivity which transcends their immediate environs.

Because of the small scale of most fields in these two Southeast Asian countries, their marginality to the primary centers of global science, and the weaknesses of the local support systems, the scientists depend on their networks for getting critical readings of research papers in preparation for publication; securing articles, apparatus, materials, specimens, and animals which otherwise may be long delayed in transit or costly to obtain.

Having such networks facilitates the scientist's work being taken seriously. In the words of one distinguished Philippine biochemist, "If you are from a small and uninfluential country and you are not personally known in the international scientific community, then when you write, they tend to simply ignore and belittle your findings." Networks are activated for placement of one's students in foreign graduate schools and for arranging one's own post-doctoral appointments and invitations to conferences.

Benefits do not flow all one way, of course. Foreign, primarily Western scientists (particularly in the various life and social sciences) gain access to data and specimens from the region. In their visits to the country, they are provided with knowledgeable and supportive hosts. Many of these networks have served as sources for developing collaborative research between Filipinos or Malaysians and foreign scholars.

The international networking of basic and applied researchers in the Philippines and Malaysia reflects the growth of regional and world science systems. The basic scientists in Southeast Asia have been part of world science for generations. Their country-based studies in such fields as botany, geology, zoology, meteorology, and anthropology were integrated into world knowledge through the published literature, papers given at international conferences, and exchange of scholars. The applied fields have become internationalized with the evolving of applied research problems whose paradigms put together the common interests of scholars in both developing and developed countries. There are also Southeast Asian regional systems which are integrated into world systems concerned with development of the less-developed countries.

If there is any continuity in the particularized networks, it is because the cultural norms are continuously renewed and reworked, and the relationships activated on both sides. They are not inherited from others, but constantly created, negotiated, expanded, contracted by individuals within the setting of larger world movements, political realignments, and socio-economic changes.

Although our sample scientists differ in the nature of their networks, those who had them were eager to recall their origins and subsequent historical development, to describe the character of the interpersonal relations among the participants, and to review the specific ways in which the networks had influenced and facilitated their professional careers.

Based on the descriptions which each member of our sample gave us about the scope and content of their interaction with foreigners located abroad, we concluded that approximately six out of ten Filipinos and eight out of ten Malaysians in our samples participate in trans-societal networks. As can be noted in Table 8, this overall discrepancy between the two samples in the proportion having networks is largely accounted for by the Malaysians with slim networks, 51 percent as compared with 28 percent for Filipinos. And most of the discrepancy is due to recent entrants. The Philippine youngest generation came into the scientific community during the late 1960s and early 1970s, a period of heightened nationalism and its concomitant anti-foreignism. The Malaysian youngest generation did not enter their professional careers in such an atmosphere. Hence, 82 percent of the Malaysian youngest generation are hanging on to their slim ties and hoping to enlarge them, whereas 60 percent of the Philippine youngest generation reject foreign ties. This is further confirmed by looking at the proportion of those in the Philippines who have no networks. Sixty percent of those Filipinos without networks clearly opt for recognition inside the country in contrast to 16 percent of those without networks wanting outside recognition. Among Malaysians without transna-

Table 8.   Distribution of Philippine and Malaysian Sample Scientists by Type of International Network

Type of Network	Filipinos %	Malaysians %
Extensive	22	24
Intensive	12	9
Slim	28	51
None	38	16
Total	100	100
	(N=160)	(N=80)

tional linkages, 39 percent want within-country recognition and 39 percent want outside recognition.

The variable which seems to make the greatest impact on type of transnational network is that of scientific field. The general life sciences in both countries have the highest proportion of their numbers with extensive networks (Philippines, 42 percent; Malaysia, 43 percent). We are of the opinion that this reflects both the strength of the life sciences in these two developing countries and the global nature of life sciences, whose centers of research are both more geographically dispersed and interdependent than is true of the physical and engineering sciences, whose cores are less dependent on peripheries for comparison testing of scientific propositions. The engineering sciences are still weak in both countries, and fewer of their numbers have extensive networks compared to other clusters of scientific disciplines. In contrast to the life scientists who can reciprocate with foreigners, physical and engineering scientists have less to offer in exchange. It may also be that Western scientists in some of the physical and engineering sciences are not as ready to have their paradigms tested.

The incidence of intensive networks does not fluctuate as widely as the extensive networks among the fields. Most intensive network creators feel that their relationships with foreigners helped them to remain "scientifically alive." This evaluation is especially common for the "one of a kind" in an area of research interest. Some of those with intensive relationships are crucial links in a chain of "one of a kinds" around the world; others are singletons in the Southeast Asian area but their research interests do have large epicenters in the Western world.

Scientific Contribution to Whom.   As was mentioned earlier in distinguishing between basic and applied research, one of the dominant themes in the current literature about the expected contribution of scientists in the less-developed countries centers on their collective responsibilities and priorities in the development of their societies. Many, including national policymakers, foreign consultants, foundation representatives, and "science statesmen," assert that scientists in developing countries should work primarily on practical and applied scientific research problems that will be directly useful to and have immediate application to the needs of different sectors of the country. Others have argued that any independent society moving toward "self-sufficiency" in science and education needs to build a solid group of basic-oriented scientists along with applied scientists in order to avoid the neo-colonialism which is engendered by over-dependency on foreign scientists and their leading centers for the conduct of basic research.

It is not, therefore, very surprising to learn that so many of the present occupants of the status of scientist in the Philippines and Malaysia commonly confront multiple and sometimes highly discrepant claims on their time and energy. In addition, many scientists experience major disjunctures in planning and carrying out research due to sudden shifts in national and international research priorities among those who formulate and fund their work. Domestic and international conflicts and major political changes also impinge on scientists —advantaging some and disadvantaging others. There are enormous variations among fields in their involvement in development planning and in having effective access to different sectors of a society. And, as we have already reported, the published scientists are in the world system of science which has its own priorities according to the prevailing thrusts in each field or for each generation within a field.

The Philippine and Malaysian scientists are perforce caught up in the process of having to make value-laden choices as to how they envision their own professional roles and what they would like to accomplish in their research careers in the creating and contributing of knowledge.

Herein we analyze but one critical part of this intricate issue. We asked each of the sample scientists to rank order from "closest to my interests" to "furthest from my interests"whom they would like their knowledge to benefit. We purposely delimited alternatives so they were aligned with current arguments on the "proper" functions of scientists in a less-developed country within the wider context of the transnational community. The statements they were asked to rank order are: I want to build knowledge which will benefit a SPECIFIC GROUP (specify); I want to build knowledge which will benefit my COUNTRY AS A WHOLE; I want to build knowledge which will benefit SOUTHEAST ASIAN PEOPLES: I want to build knowledge which will benefit MANKIND AS A WHOLE; I want to SEARCH FOR TRUTH in my field, no matter who is benefitted.

Overall the two country samples do not differ greatly in the proportions who select the various categories as one of their first two choices. Several modal groupings of responses can be distinguished.

Benefit own country. Two-thirds of both the Filipinos and Malaysians rank "benefit their own country" either first or second in their scale of values. Foremost in being country-centered are the social sciences, with 90 percent of the Filipinos and 87 percent of the Malaysian social scientists ranking their own country as first or second in their scale of values. These goals are consonant with their publishing and consulting activities. Of all scientific fields, the social scientists have the largest proportion in both countries who publish inside their country and the lowest proportion who publish only in foreign journals. In the Philippines, over 80 percent of the social scientists consult with domestic agencies and groups. Malaysian groups do not as overwhelmingly call upon their social scientists but they do involve them more than the average.

Search for Truth no Matter Who is Benefitted. A second modality forms around the "search for truth no matter who is benefitted," with half of both samples making this value their first or second choice. The physical sciences and the social sciences differ the most on this value, with the former scaling high and the latter low. The medical scientists in the Philippines and engineering scientists in Malaysia are special cases owing to their historical development and continuing traditions. The medical and public-health schools of the primate Philippine university were originally designed to meet international standards in research and professional education, and this concern remains foremost in their scale of institutional values. The research group in engineering sciences at the primate Malaysian university also has strong emphasis upon maintaining international standards. Among the Philippine medical researchers, 84 percent list the "search for truth no matter who is benefitted" and 68 percent list "making a contribution to knowledge of benefit to mankind" as their top priorities, whereas Malaysian medical scientists are much lower. On the other hand, of Malaysian engineering researchers, 62 percent rank "truth no matter who is benefitted" and 85 percent choose contributing to mankind's benefit as their uppermost priorities.

If their value choices are related to the type of international network which the scientists maintain, of particular interest is the overwhelming proportion of those with intensive networks who are interested in the "search for truth no matter who is benefitted"—75 percent of Philippine and 86 percent of Malaysian intensive networkers. Many of those with intensive networks are following scientific problems which are not part of the central thrusts of their own political economy.

Benefit Mankind as a Whole. The building of knowledge which would "benefit mankind as a whole" evokes a first- or second-order interest among two-fifths of both the Philippine and Malaysian scientific community. Fewer social scientists in both countries, but particularly in Malaysia, value this option than do other scientists.

Southeast Asia. Southeast Asia has somewhat greater priority for Filipinos than Malaysians due to the former's greater involvement in exerting leadership in regional groupings, particularly in the social sciences.

Specific Groups. Specific groups mentioned by the sample range from malaria sufferers to the industrial sector, and occasionally include ethnic groups (e.g., the Muslims in the Philippines).

Historically speaking, there is a protean dimension to the distribution of values in the scientific communities of developing countries which is illuminated by inter-generational comparison. In the case of the Philippines, 79 percent of the pre-independence generation puts contributing knowledge to their own country at the highest level while all the other values attracted few responses. The next two generations following independence show a decline in country-centered interest and a shift to most of the other values. Then with the upsurge of nationalism and the growing preoccupation of the whole country with the increasingly visible national crisis, the newest generation again emphasizes making their contribution to their country. Eighty percent in the youngest generation rank at the top of their values making a contribution of knowledge to the Philippines.

The Malaysian experience discloses its own inter-generational changes. There has not been so much a change in the commitment to their own country as a small but steady increase in being concerned about specific groups within the country—the rural poor and the Malay ethnic group.

Altogether, these generational shifts in the primacy of values suggest that a culturally sensitive interpretation of a developing country's scientific community requires us to think about how working scholars personally respond to both intra-societal and trans-societal conditions in their times.

Finally, in this study of values, we return to the issue of basic versus applied, a subject permeated with ambiguities throughout the general literature on this topic, and yet one which has become a major theme in educational and science policies for developing countries. Using our operational definition of the distinction, we find that there is both a country-specific and a field-specific pattern in our study of the two scientific communities.

A comparison of the Filipinos and Malaysians shows the following. When we look at the Philippine scientific community as a whole, only 47 percent are in basic and 53 percent are in applied research at the time of our study. But if we take the Philippine scientists whose greatest preference is to make knowledge contributions in their own country, 39 percent are in basic and 61 percent are in applied. The colonial Philippine-American scientific third culture from its outset emphasized the importance of doing research which might prove directly useful to the country, and preserves this tradition in the continuing allocation of 90 percent of the National Science Development Board's funds for applied research. The Malaysian-British third-cultural heritage and its present themes move in a different direction. A contribution to basic knowledge by Malaysian scientists is envisioned as a contribution of benefit to their country. Accordingly, we find the opposite trend in the distribution of values among Malaysian scientists. Whereas only 41 percent of the overall sample is in basic research, 48 percent of those who value highly making a contribution to their own country are basic researchers.

CONCLUSION

It has become almost commonplace in the current literature to refer to the growing complexities of our interdependent world. Less common in our summaries of the world-wide situation are empirical studies within and between societies to search out the variables connected with these complex sets of social structures and cultures. If we are to proceed beyond broad macro-level interpretations, we must take our paradigms into actual environs to examine their closeness of fit and power of explanation—only then can we inform policy makers, change agents, leaders of revolutionary movements, or simply ourselves as scholars.

This particular small-scale, two-country comparative study of the commonalities and differences among academic-based research scientists in one part of the third world as to their networks, third cultures, and work situations constitutes an attempt to create fresh questions and concepts to guide further research in the study of cross-cultural relations in our times.

NOTES

1.   This report is part of a larger study sponsored by the Hazen Foundation. In the Philippines it was carried out in cooperation with the Philippine National Science Development Board and the Institute of Philippine Culture of Ateneo de Manila University. The Rockefeller Foundation assisted in the final phase of the field study. The Institute for International Studies in Education and the Center for International Studies and Programs of Michigan State University were supportive throughout the study. The Malaysian portion of the investigation was sponsored by the National University of Malaysia (Universiti Kebangsaan Malaysia).

2.   In 1973-74, the Philippine Council for Agricultural Research (PCAR) made the most complete survey of the research staffs in the adjacent fields of agriculture, fisheries and forestry for the 35 universities and colleges (government and private) and 13 other units which are partially involved in agricultural research. They found 918 persons who spend on the average of 28 percent of their time in agricultural research; 190 have Ph.D.s and 350 have Masters.

3.   An intensive reappraisal of the collective identity of Filipinos, the character of the established central institutions of the society, and the relations of Filipinos and Philippine social structures to the roles of foreigners in the country, permeated the intellectual world and the academic communities in the latter years of the 1960s and early years of the 1970s. It became a period in which numerous new bibliographies were prepared to rediscover past studies, including graduate theses, done by Filipinos on the Philippines. American scholars serving as technocrats, consultants, representatives of foundations, administrators of academic units, faculty members and the leaders of research projects often learned of the need for a low profile or found themselves circumscribed in what they could accomplish. Malaysians are just beginning to debate the issues.

4.   There is an influential medium of unpublished papers which circulate knowledge within both countries. The exchanges take place between the scientists and technocrats, leaders in particular sectors, and advanced and former students. Because we are concerned with cross-national linkages, they are not included in this account.

5.   The oldest and most widely respected journals include the *Philippine Journal of Science* (established 1906); *The Philippine Agriculturist* (1911) and *Acta Medica Philippina* (1939). In recent years the life scientists have started a quality journal, *Kalikasan*, and several of the agricultural and social scientists have expanded the number and improved the quality of their journals. In addition, most of the major universities have one or more professional journals which are broad rather than specialized in coverage.

We examined the footnote references of 17 of the leading Philippine scientific journals in all six scientific fields and found that 30 percent of all the citations were to other Philippine-published studies. We further examined the domestic and foreign subscriptions and exchange lists of 22 scientific journals. For this representative group of journals the average circulation is 252 copies in the country and 203 copies which go abroad to 121 different countries. Comparable Malaysian figures are not available.

6.   They are present as long-term expatriate professors, visiting professors for an academic year, visitors for a few days on study tours, longer term field researchers, representatives of foreign foundations and international agencies, students (enrolled mainly in Philippine schools of

veterinary medicine, human medicine and agriculture), and volunteers who serve as temporary instructors or in technical assistance roles.

7.   In contrast to the Philippines, which at the time of our interviews did not limit the number of times a scientist could accept invitations to attend foreign conferences, Malaysia tried to distribute the opportunities as widely as possible. Hence a higher proportion of the Malaysians than Filipinos attended foreign-held conferences, but the Filipinos who attended averaged more conferences (3.04) than did the Malaysians (1.72) in a three year period.

REFERENCES

Amyot, J.
    1973   The Manila Chinese. Quezon City: Institute of Philippine Culture, Ateneo de Manila University.
Arles, J.P.
    1971   ''Ethnic and socio-economic patterns in Malaysia.'' International Labour Review 104 (December): 527-554.
Banks, D.J.
    1976   Changing Identities in Modern Southeast Asia. The Hague: Mouton Publishers.
Barber, Bernard
    1962   Science and the Social Order. New York: Collier Books.
Basalla, George
    1968   The Rise of Modern Science: Internal or External Factors? Lexington, Massachusetts: D.C. Heath and Company.
Carson, A.L.
    1978   The Story of Philippine Education. Quezon City, Philippines: New Day Publishers.
Crane, Diana
    1972   Invisible Colleges: Diffusion of Knowledge in Scientific Communities. Chicago: University of Chicago Press.
Esman, Milton Jacob
    1972   Administration and Development in Malaysia: Institution Building and Reform in a Plural Society. Ithaca: Cornell University Press.
Furnival, J.S.
    1948   Colonial Policy and Practice. London: Cambridge University Press.
Gowing, P.G. and R.D. McAmis, Editors
    1969   The Muslim Filipinos. Manila: Solidaridad Publishing House.
Hagstrom, Warren O.
    1965   The Scientific Community. New York: Basic Books, Inc.
Harbison, Frederick, and Charles A. Myers
    1964   Education, Manpower and Economic Growth. New York: McGraw-Hill.
Hirschman, Charles
    1975   Ethnic and Social Stratification in Peninsular Malaysia. Washington: American Sociological Association Rose Monograph Series.
Hoong, Yip Yat *et al* (eds.)
    1973   Development Planning in Southeast Asia. Singapore: Regional Institute of Higher Education and Development.
Huq, Muhammad Shamsul
    1975   Education, Manpower, and Development in South and Southeast Asia. New York: Praeger Publishers, Inc.
Jamias, Juan F., Editor
    1973   The University of the Philippines and National Development Report on the 1972 U.P. Faculty Conference. Quezon City, Philippines: University of the Philippines, Diliman.
Kroeber, A.L.
    1960   The Nature of Culture. Chicago: University of Chicago Press.

Kumar, Krishna, Editor
   1979   Bonds Without Bondage: Explorations in Transcultural Interactions. Honolulu: University Press of Hawaii.
Majul, C.A.
   1973   Muslims in the Philippines. Quezon City: University of Philippines Press.
Merton, Robert K.
   1973   The Sociology of Science. Chicago: University of Chicago Press.
Moravcsik, Michael J.
   1975   Science Development. Bloomington: Indiana University PASITAM.
Pauker, G.J., F.H. Golay, and C.H. Enloe
   1977   Diversity and Development in Southeast Asia. New York: McGraw-Hill Book Co.
Presidential Commission to Survey Philippine Education
   1970   A Report on Higher Education in the Philippines. Mimeo.
Purcell, Victor
   1967   The Chinese in Malaya. Kuala Lumpur: Oxford University Press.
Sandhu, K.S.
   1969   Indians in Malaya: Some Aspects of Their Immigration and Settlement (1786-1967). Cambridge: Cambridge University Press.
Silcock, T.H.
   1964   Southeast Asian University: A Comparative Account of Some Development Problems. Durham, North Carolina: Duke University Press.
Spiegel-Rösing, Ina and Derek de Solla Price (eds.)
   1977   Science, Technology and Society. Beverly Hills: Sage Publications.
Takei, Y., J.C. Bock and B. Saunders
   1973   Educational Sponsorship by Ethnicity. Athens: Ohio University Center for International Studies.
Tapingkae, Amnuay
   1974   The Growth of Southeast Asian Universities. Singapore: Regional Institute of Higher Education and Development.
Useem, John
   1971   ''The study of cultures,'' Sociological Focus Vol. 4, No. 4.
Useem, John, John Donoghue, and Ruth Hill Useem
   1963   ''Men in the middle of the third culture: the roles of American and non-western people in cross-cultural administration,'' Human Organization 22:169-179.
Useem, John, and Ruth Hill Useem
   1967   ''The interfaces of a binational third culture: a study of the American community in India,'' The Journal of Social Issues 23:130-143.
Van Hise, Joseph B.
   1957   American Contributions to Philippine Science and Technology, 1898-1916. Doctoral Dissertation. Madison: University of Wisconsin.
Wernstedt, F.L., and J.E. Spencer
   1967   The Philippine Island World. Berkeley: University of California Press.
Wong, Francis H.K., and Gwee Yee Hean
   1972   Perspectives: The Development of Education in Malaysia and Singapore. Kuala Lumpur: Heinemann Educational Books (Asia) Ltd.
Wong, Francis H.K., and Ee Yiang Hong
   1975   Education in Malaysia. Kuala Lumpur: Heinemann Educational Books (Asia) Ltd.
World Bank
   1979   World Development Indicators. Washington D.C.: World Bank.

SOCIAL MOVEMENTS AND SOCIAL CHANGE:
PERSPECTIVES OF LINEARITY AND FLUIDITY

Joseph R. Gusfield

Kenneth Burke once said that every way of seeing is also a way of not seeing. The terms which we construct to provide an orderly understanding of the world arise as well from the problems and concerns of the observers and from the categories for making sense of events that are available to them as they do from the external phenomena themselves. The theories, paradigms, concepts and assumptions of sociological fields are often, however, couched in a language of Aristotelian science: the explanation of actions and processes whose factual nature bounds and compels the systems of understanding. A beginning to the study of social movements must then be inititated by a definition of what they are and what are their characteristics.

A more Platonist view of the scientific endeavor suggests a Schutzian world of multiple realities in which our language and our perspectives sensitize us to this or that piece of the universe of our interests. A beginning to the study of

Research in Social Movements, Conflict and Change, Volume 4, pages 317-339
Copyright © 1981 by JAI Press Inc.
ISBN: 0-89232-234-9

social movements in this vein avoids definition entirely and attempts to convey why it is that the observer wishes to study this phenomena and what experiences lead him or her to do so in this way. The Aristotelian realist feels safest when furthest from self; when the observer has been exiled from the observed. The Platonist is uncomfortable in such a posture and looks to place the self back in again.

This is a Platonist's paper and a way of seeing the study of social movements from a Platonic perspective. Again Burke, so much the grand Platonist of contemporary social analysis, has put it well:

> I do not see why the universe should accommodate itself to a man-made medium of communication. . . . Perhaps because we have come to think of ourselves as *listening* to the universe, as waiting to see what it will prove to us, we have psychotically made the corresponding readjustment of assuming that the universe itself will abide by our rules of discussion and give us its revelations in a cogent manner. Our notion of causality as a succession of pushes from behind is thus a disguised way of insisting that experience abide by the conventions of a good argument. (Burke, 1965. p. 99.)

All this murky philosophizing is a way of introducing a paper about the relation of social movements to social change and about how different frameworks for studying movements have different implications for this topic and this point in history. In describing and analyzing two perspectives—the linear and the fluid—I will argue that the latter has not been sufficiently used in sociology and that its adoption will help in studying some phenomena of change better than the former. Not that one perspective is better than the other but that one does some things that the other does not and vice versa. Having done this I will exemplify some of these issues by a brief examination of three movements.

SOCIAL MOVEMENTS AS COLLECTIVE ACTION

An effort to characterize a field or sub-discipline must necessarily gloss over many differences, distinctions and qualifications. In pointing toward certain commonalities in the study of social movements as a field I am undoubtedly doing injustice to significant nuances. Nevertheless I do so as a means of highlighting the similarities of many otherwise diverse sociologists.

Characteristically the field of ''social movements'' has been seen as a phase of collective behavior. The rationale behind this has stemmed from two considerations, both explicit in the classic and seminal paper by Herbert Blumer (Blumer, 1939). The first is that movements are viewed as attempts to change existing social relationships, process or institutions. Consequently they are differentiated from the normal, the status quo, the conventional in belief and action. Collective behavior served as a term of differentiation, dividing such behavior from ''social organization'' which attended to conventional, normalized thought and action.

Secondly, social movements could be conceptualized as a facet of collective behavior because they represented the action of collectivities—aggregates assuming shared goals and interests and acting in the name of group concerns. The ever-present natural history of social movements—from collective protest to social movement organizations to struggle for success to institutionalization is another form of this paradigm.

Even critics of these formulations have shared much of its imagery. Although McCarthy and Zald are highly critical of the "hearts and minds" approach to social movements, nevertheless they study collectivities in the form of social movement organizations and account for the development of movements by attention to how resources are mobilized toward conscious attempts to bring about change. (McCarthy and Zald, 1973).

Tilly is quite wisely sensitive to some differences in what is being studied by diverse frameworks. He distinguishes "collective action" from "social movements" suggesting that the latter attempts to study populations, beliefs, and actions. He defines a social movement as "a group of people identified by their attachment to some particular set of beliefs" (Tilly, 1978, p. 9.) It is clear from his text that is is not any set of beliefs, however, but those directed toward change. "Collective action" studies particular groups and events, such as violence, strikes, protests, etc. Such "collective behavior" has often been the concern of past students of social movements.

The field to which all of these point is, however, one characterized by the two models or frameworks or concepts discussed above:

1. Action is directed in a conscious effort to produce change in the society.
2. The unit of observation is an association organized to achieve change.

THE LINEAR IMAGE OF SOCIAL MOVEMENTS AND ITS IMPLICATIONS

This orientation toward phenomena involves the user in an image I term "linear" because it directs attention to a discrete association of people whose activity is perceived as using means to gain an end. The Labor Movement can be used as an anology, model or metaphor. The Movement can be studied through the development of a conception of labor goals, a series of actions in strikes and political mobilization to the achievement of goals or their frustration. The focus of attention on empirical events is on how they advance or deter the achievement of goals consciously stated in organizational programs.

For a variety of reasons not all implicit in the logic of its formulation, the linear image has had several characteristics which carry significant implications for the study of social change. These follow below:

1. *A preoccupation with the beginnings of movements*: A great deal of the social movements literature is intent on understanding how it is that move-

ments have occurred.[1] Because discontent, dissidence or attempted change appear as deviations from a norm of social conformity and convention, movements and their partisans seem to be unusual and hence problematic; something whose occurrence needs explanation. In the theoretical framework of much of sociology, especially in its functional formulations, the absence of conflict occasions less notice than its appearance. (Smelser, 1963; also the criticism of Smelser in Currie and Skolnick, 1970.)

Once movements are "seen" as directed against some *status quo* the alienation of partisans from "society" becomes a problem. Focus on origins, however, minimizes the attention to consequences. The current concern for mobilization is again another mode of studying how organization has developed but not what are the outcomes of movements.

2. *Focus on organizations and associations*. Much of what the literature of sociological studies of movements contains is the study of specific organizations of a population. What is studied is the HareKrishnas, the Woman's Christian Temperance Union, the Congress for Racial Equality, or the Students for a Democratic Society. "Social movements" as Zald and Ash put it, "manifest themselves, in part, through a wide range of organizations." (Zald and Ash, 1966, p. 327). The SMO (social movement organization) has become almost synonomous with the Movement.

In part this is also a function of defining movements as associations of people, as collectivities. In part, it is also a means of studying an otherwise elusive phenomena. Field work and other standard sociological methods and techniques make such discrete definition almost an essential.

3. *Focus on dissidence, protest, rebellion, deviance*: For a variety of reasons, well beyond the scope of this paper, sociologists have been preoccupied with political actions that attempt fundamental reforms and with collective behavior that appears to break with conventional procedures. The events of the 1960s have furthered this and produced a rash of interest in the genesis and development of violence and protest. Gamson's important work on *The Strategy of Social Protests* is one illustration. Charles Tilly's studies of protest actions is another. (Tilly, 1978, C. Tilly, L. Tilly and R. Tilly, 1975; Shorter and Tilly, 1974.)

An implication of this is found in the heightened concern for change directed toward the State. What I have referred to elsewhere as the "overpoliticalization" of sociology has haunted social movements. (Gustfield, 1980). Some would even define the field as the study of dissidence. (Denisoff, 1974.) It has also led to a focus on the value and consequence of specific strategies used by movement organizations or incipient movements. (Gamson, 1975.)

4. *Concern for change as success or failure of movements seen in their own terms*. Using an imagery of movements to deliberately achieve change, the movement becomes its own source for defining what happened. Whether success or failure was realized is found in the program or goal of the movement

as stated by its proponents and opponents. Thus, Gamson, in a careful discussion of operationalizing the concept of success, uses acceptance by the group's antagonists of the movement organization as legitimate leaders of a legitimate set of interests. In considering the realization of new advantages as a facet of success Gamson writes: "Did the potential beneficiaries of the challenging group receive what *the group sought* for them?" (Gamson, 1975, p. 34. Italics mine. JG) The impact of the movement on social structure or culture is then restricted to programmatic goals.

5. *The public area as the focus of movement actions*. The imagery of many social movement studies is that of a Romantic ideal of an "underdog" challenging a powerful authority. (Gamson uses the term "challenging group.") Victory is wrested from an unwilling foe; defeat comes at the hands of repressing elites. The emphasis of the studies are on the public arena. Legislation, institutional change, policy ended or begun; these are both the measures of success or failure and the points of attention.

A great deal of human life occurs at the day-to-day level of interactions, only dimly affected by public policies. (Gusfield, 1980; 1981.) A movement such as the Anti-Viet Nam movement may be oriented to change in public policy but a movement such as the Woman's Movement or the Gay Rights movement is, to a large extent, found not only among partisans and anti-partisans but in the myriad events of everyday life in which sexual and gender relationships are constructed and evaluated. The same is true even for linear movements. The Prohibition movement can be studied in its achievement of the 18th. Amendment and its enforcement. It can also be studied in the drinking behavior during that period and in the legacy it left, or did not leave, on America drinking habits. (Gusfield, 1968; Aaron and Musto, 1980.) Attention to political goals overstates the public as an arena of behavior and assumes a greater capacity for centralized social control than is warranted.

A MARX FOR THE MANAGERS; A MICHELS FOR THE MISBEGOTTEN

Whether explicit or implicit, the study of social movements seems pervaded by a practical, political concern about the movements studied. It is not only that political interests emerge in choices of what to study. (Elsewhere I have argued that Liberalism and its vicissitudes has been a major focus of sociological study of movements during the past four decades. Gusfield, 1978.) The image of the movement as directed toward change has made us emphasize the linearity of movements. The form of study appears addressed to those who want to know how to start or how to stop movements from occuring; to those who want to know how to succeed or how to frustrate purposive actions. The "power elite" can read Marx to learn to avoid revolution. ("A Marx for the Managers" is a paper by Gerth and Mills, 1942.) The "radical Left" can study Michels to prevent the "iron law of oligarchy" from deflecting organizations away from their movement goals. Piven and Cloward have done this in their advice to poor people that protest action is more effective than organized movements. (Piven and Cloward, 1979, Ch. 1.)

The point I am making is that the linear model and its emphasis on the deliberate pursuit of change by an association of partisans is one way of seeing social movements. Other ways are possible and their implications may be useful in other ways and for other interests.

THE FLUID CONCEPT OF SOCIAL MOVEMENT

Another model or image of "social movement" has persisted alongside the linear one, although its usage has not been extensive among sociologists. The vocabulary of social movements has included not only the discrete association but also vaguer, more diffuse phenomena such as Abolitionism, Humanitarianism, Feminism and "the egalitarian impulse." Such terms are more often the province of historians than sociologists. For example, in discussing the change in treatment of deviance in America, David Rothman analyzes the rise of the penitentiary as a manifestation of a changed orientation toward institutionalizing criminal offenders. He writes that "In the 1820s New York and Pennsylvania began a movement that *spread* through the Northwest and then over the next decade to many mid-western states." In the next paragraph he refers to the actions of state legislatures in creating prisons as "all this activity." (Rothman, 1971, pp. 79-80. Ital. mine, JG.) These are vague terms and the movement is discovered not in the actions of this or that organization in this or that event but in the quickening of actions, the change in meanings, and the understanding that something new is happening in a wide variety of places and arenas. The movement is seen as a change in the meanings of objects and events rather than the occurrence of associations.

Sociologists have often recognized the large ambits within which particular organized movements occur. Blumer, in his classic paper, distinguished between general and specific movements and referred to "cultural drafts" such as the labor movement or the women's movement which constitute the background for general movements. Drifts are "gradual and pervasive changes in the values of people, particularly along the lines of the conceptions which people have of themselves, and of their rights and privileges." (Blumer, 1939, p. 256.) Smelser, in a much different formulation, uses the distinction between norm-oriented and value-oriented movements to encompass a similar recognition of levels and scope of movements. (Smelser, 1962, Ch. 9, 10.) Recently the French structuralists, notably Michel Foucault, have focussed attention on the cognitive frameworks and the pervasive impact of changing cognitive structures on social and cultural transformations. (Foucault, 1973, 1975.)

Such perspectives operate with a more fluid and diffuse image of "movement" than the linear model encompasses. They blur the line between trend and movement, but they shift attention away from the association and its member-participants to the longer-run and less public areas in which meanings are undergoing transformation. They recognize the less directed aspects of social and cultural change. As Banks has been aware:

> Smelser's historical sequence, like that of sociologists who favor a natural history approach to the study of social movements, implies that the undirected phase *always* precedes the directed in time, or rather, that the directed phase *emerges* out of a previously inchoate groping toward the collective consciousness of similarities and differences and then in its turn accumulates around it a wider body of partisans." (Banks, 1972, p. 13.)

A more fluid perspective toward the meaning of movement emphasizes the quickening of change and the social sharing of new meanings in a variety of areas and places. It is less confined to the boundaries of organizations and more alive to the larger contexts of change at the same time as it is open to awareness of how the movement has consequences and impacts among nonpartisans and nonmembers as well as participants and devotees. Rather than success or failure of a movement, it is more likely to lead to questions about consequences: What happened?

To continue the liquid metaphor in the imagery of fluidity, we can liken the study of specific and organized movements to a ripple in the water rather than a shot in the dark. The perspective of fluidity emphasizes the cultural side of movements—the transformations of meaning—and the interactive side of consequences—the less public aspects of life. Politically, the focus shifts away from the short-run search for goals and goal realization and toward the less political parts of human life in long-run perspective. Society rather than the State becomes the area of analysis.

In a somewhat different usage Piven and Cloward also criticize conventional sociological studies of social movements for failure to recognize the significance of collective violence and protest actions in achieving poor people's interests. The focus on organized and directed activity toward articulated goals denies political meaning to much protest:

> The stress on conscious intentions in these usages reflects a confusion in the literature between the mass movement on the one hand, and the formalized organizations which tend to emerge on the crest of the movement on the other hand—two intertwined but distinct phenomena. (Piven and Cloward, 1977, p. 5.)

In exploring this distinction between a linear and a fluid conception of movements I want to stress two considerations: The utility of the fluid conception for 1.) understanding both social and cultural change and 2.) for analyzing contemporary movements in particular.

THE CONSEQUENCES OF MOVEMENTS

If we utilize a more fluid, expansive conception of movements, two implications become significant for the study of social change. First, we are led to examine any specific social movement organization in terms of consequences in a wide variety of areas and over a long run.

Given a more fluid image success or failure and consequences can no longer be gauged in terms intrinsic to the social movement organization. Recent evaluation of the movements of the 1960s have been filled with concerns for realization of movement goals. (Perrow, 1979; Oberschall, 1978; Snyder and Kelley, 1979.) But they have also indicated a number of ways in which other things occur. Thus Snyder and Kelly make the point that the outcomes of collective violence may vary as between impact on the group's concerns and on the total system. (The implications of racial violence on "white flight" for example.) Joel Handler has shown that achievement of legislation or favorable legal decision by no means implies that the behavior under concern has changed. Much depends on the precise character of the situations covered. Where bureaucratic discretion must be used in applying law to specific cases, there is less homogeneity between law and action than where a general rule can be enunciated and limited discretion is necessary. A law prohibiting construction of a building is far easier to apply than one declaring voting rights. (Handler, 1979.) A movement may be waning just when its aims are most supported. Hofstadter pointed out that the Anti-Trust movement had lost much of its public support at the point when anti-trust actions were at their height. (Hofstadter, 1965, ch. 6.) The institution of a structure—the Anti-Trust division of the Department of Justice—made for an autonomous operation, independent of beliefs.

One of the significant consequences of movements and movement organizations is the development of a cadre of movement personnel. Precisely as the movement is a more general concept than the SMO, so too people who participate in one movement or SMO are capable of being carriers to and for others. One of the outcomes of the 1960s was exactly that. Thus the present Anti-Nuclear movement draws on persons active in earlier movements. In the recent Anti-Nuclear movement in New England leading roles were played by residents of rural communes organized in the 1960s.[2] A similar cross-fertilization was commented upon at length by several historians of the 19th century. A number of leading figures in pre-Civil War movements had origins personally or through earlier generations in a district of Western New York State. Even a generation later in Nebraska there could be seen the working out of the movements that stirred "the burned-over district" of upstate New York. (Cross, 1950; Tyler, 1962.)

Recognition of such carry-overs and carry-ons between movements has great implications both for assessing the consequences for change of both

social movement organizations and movements seen as cultural transformations. Not only values but also cognitive structures are at work. The importance of such cultural implications exist at two levels. At the public level it
shifts the nature of public issues. At the private, everyday level it provides a
context of new meanings and actions dependent on them.

One of the residues of movements and SMOs is the existence of a vocabulary
and an opening of ideas and actions which in the past was either unknown or
unthinkable. Compare how the homosexual can be discussed in the contemporary generation with discussion in an earlier one. What was unthinkable in one
period has become thinkable and possible. Perrow, writing about his study of
the 1960s, observes:

> In every issue we considered, the contrast between the early 1950s and the late 1960s in
> our data source is extraordinary. . . . No one on the project team has failed to be astounded
> by the climate of the 1950s and the sharp contrast with the late 1960s. (Perrow, 1979.)

Significant also is the way in which major paradigms or structures of public
discourse and discussion are generated and retained. In a number of cases, the
specific movements of the past twenty years in America can be seen as
manifestations or instances of a larger egalitarian impulse at work. Such
unstated and yet crucial aspects of social and cultural change are significant
aspects of the context within which movements are operative. The struggle
over Gay rights, Women's rights and even the rights of handicapped operate
differently in the context of presumptions about equality in the 1980s than in
the 1950s. Even name changes carry such redefinitions and assume acceptance: Negro–Black; Homosexual–Gay; Feminist–Women's Liberationist.

As some writer's have seen, a longer-run approach to understanding how
general movements are formed and developed is necessary in studying social
and cultural change. E.P. Thompson studied the development of the English
working class as a movement over a long period of time. Carl Taylor studied
the specific movements of American farmers over more than a century and
substituted for specific studies of particular movements an entity called "the
Farmer's Movement." (E.P. Thompson, 1963; Taylor, 1953.) It is a matter
crying for study that movements remain dormant and remerge with their
rhetoric shining and seemingly unused. This occurs especially with ethnic
nationalism. (W.I. Thompson, 1967; Hechter, 1975.)[3] That old target of
American farmer's "Wall Street" disappears and reappears from time to time
in American politics. And what happened to the Women's Movement between
1920 and the late 1960s? (Green and Melnick, 1953.)

The second level of interest in the cultural changes of specific movements is
at the private or every-day level. Here it is necessary to introduce another
consideration: the reflexive character of movements.

THE REFLEXIVITY OF SOCIAL MOVEMENTS

A second implication of fluidity is that social movements, like other phenomena, are also objects of attention and perception. They are matters of interest and evaluation for those who consider themselves members and partisans. They are also objects for the perception and imagination of others. It is this aspect of movements which I refer to as reflexive. The effects of movements on change arises not only from their direct impact on institutions and on members but on those who perceive that a change is taking place; who reflect on the fact of the movement's occurrence.

The movement, specific or general, exists as well in the recognition of many that some matter of interest has now become an object of possible change; something is happening. There is a model implicit in the very sense of "movement;" the "normal" is undergoing movement and change. What was thought to be "taken for granted" has now become an issue. Relations between teachers and students become "problematic." Conceptions of "proper" relations between sexes are being challenged. Race relations are undergoing a new "charter." The existence and perception of a movement signifies that change is now possible.

This perception of a movement is part of the monitoring of "society" in which observers, spectators and audiences participate. It brings to them a view of the "generalized other" in the form of matters that are now in the realm of conflict and challenge. What was unthinkable is seen as now thinkable. What was taken for granted as an item of consensus can no longer be so taken. An example of this is the way in which co-habitation and marijuana use have moved from the realm of publicly-acknowledged deviation to the kingdom of public acceptance.

From this standpoint of fluidity, movements "exist" at the level of the private and the situated, as well as in the linear view of organized and public activities. The perception that a transformation may be happening in the larger society provides a background for the interactive and the micro-level in which people other than members or partisans participate. The Civil-Rights movement has meant more than the achievement of this or that legal or political right. It contributes to ambiguity where once there was norm in black-white interactions; to preferred and demanded equity where there was once dominance and subordination. The Woman's Movement happens where the housewife finds a new label for discontents; secretaries decide not to serve coffee and husbands are warier about using past habits of dominance.

The awareness of the movement is thus itself a crucial and significant phenomenon. It is part of the ways in which movements intersect social change; providing the appearance of new meaning in the spectrum of normalization and dissidence. From this perspective I might even say that a social movement occurs when people are conscious that a movement is occurring. It is a two-step conception of the role of movements in social change. The awareness of change is itself a second step in the production of change.

CONTEMPORARY MOVEMENTS AND THE MASS MEDIA

The recognition that a movement is occurring is a form of social sharing. Even in a mass form of society, where the members of the audience are not interacting, they are capable of understanding or perceiving that there are others who share their feeling or opinion. They are aware that there are others who make up a demand for transformation. A temperance official I once interviewed supported her stout defense of an old Prohibitionist stance by saying that she wanted it known that there were still some old-fashioned people who stood for Prohibition.

The kind of fluid concept of movement that I am espousing shifts our attention away from the origin of movements in the classical natural history model. It leads us to a concern for how awareness of a movement is constructed. Here McCarthy and Zald have been helpful in their recognition that the movement may emerge without a widespread constituency of partisans. (McCarthy and Zald, 1973.) So, too, Spinrad's analysis of the Sen. Joseph McCarthy movement demonstrates how a few and specific acts of complaint to agencies were treated as a movement and the emerging snowball impact of such treatment. (Spinrad, 1970.)

The fluid conception of movements is especially important in understanding the contemporary society and the ways in which change occurs as a consequence of movements. I will discuss two aspects of this; the role of the mass media in the construction of movements and the occurrence of movements of self-transformation and interpersonal relations.

The media of mass communications play a part that is both highly significant and unique to contemporary societies. (Gusfield, 1979.) it is not that television, movies, newspapers and journals persuade us to this or that set of opinions, this or that candidate. Rather it arises from the monitoring function of media of communications. They tell us what is happening and, alternately, do not tell us what is happening. In the telling they put together individual acts into general patterns; turn particular acts into movements. A good example of this is the hippie movement. Here no organization existed to provide a program; no highly dramatic events occurred to provide demonstrative confirmation of a direction toward change. It takes a generalization of specific events, a form of naming, to produce awareness, even among participants, that a movement is in process. How the movement becomes noticed and depicted bears not only on the general audience but even on the members and conscious partisans of specific movements. (Gitlin, 1980.)

The almost constant preoccupation of the media with movements brings home to the audience the existence of shared attitudes toward social transformation. Student protest, the Woman's movement, the anti-nuclear movement, the holistic medicine movement, the child abuse movement are examples of how the communication of shared directions in change is made part of the general monitoring system of the spectator. The disposition of commercial and competing forms of communication to dramatize events and movements enhances the awareness of living in a changing environment. The media do more than reflect ''society.'' They refract it and construct it. To that extent, the media may play a significant gate-keeping role.

This is especially important when movements are less organized and more fluid than linear. The very fluidity of such movements may elude their recognition. Perceiving their fluidity enhances them and generalizes them into something with a name and direction. The Woman's Movement seen as something of which the E.R.A. and equal pay are only parts strengthens the perception of a broader transformation in process that has implications at the micro level as well as at the macro. Putting together a variety of specific responses to changes in abortion, homosexuality and sexual openness in the form of ''the moral majority'' provides the spectators with a wider sense of sharing in a more general movement.

CONTEMPORARY MOVEMENTS: SELF-TRANSFORMATION AND INTERPERSONAL IMPROVEMENT

My second point about the contemporaneity of fluid movements heightens the importance of the constructing which mass media (and mass education) do in generating social and cultural change. The kinds of movements which assume importance in this period in American history are more fluid in character, less encompassed by organization and programmatic direction than is true of those movements caught in the net of linear images.

A turn away from public life as a major arena of action is a theme in recent and significant writings. Lionel Trilling, Richard Sennett and Ralph Turner have all commented on the disposition to blur the distinction between the public and the private and to expend private concerns into public attentions. For Trilling this was inherent in the movement away from the acceptance of public roles as valued and sincere and in the growing glorification of continuity between the private self and the public person in the concept of authenticity. (Trilling, 1972.) For Sennett it is found in a privatizing trend which sees public life as less significant. (Sennett, 1978.) For Turner it is manifest in the preoccupation of contemporary movements with problems of alienation and self-identity. (Turner, 1969, 1976.)

The linear perspective toward social movements fit much of the nineteenth and early twentieth century social structure. Specific attempts to remedy social ills were thought of in political and economic terms for which concepts of class and status stratification and political goals encapsulated much of the character of such movements. Tilly's and Gamson's formulations are thus appropriate.

They are less so when the movements that occupy attention are more fluid and less public. In a movement like the Woman's Movement or the human potential movement or the new fundamentalists the imagery is even more misleading.

Two changes in American life appear to me to enhance the utility of a fluid conception of movements. One is a tendency toward the break-up of homogeneous classes and status groups and their superimposition on other social categories. The Protestant-Catholic, worker-middle class splits of the past are less salient in American life today. "Social groups" are salient, not only in the older linear fashion in which organization could speak for a social base, but also as emerging and receding clusters of people formed around a specific area of concern. Cultural distinctions, such as "liberal" or "moral majority" or "youthful" may correlate with sociological categories of age or education but they fail to depict communities of people who share a communal life. The mass basis of such movements as Abortion or human potential rests more on common styles of life than on position in the division of labor or residential commonalities.[4]

The other change is a product of the absorption of leisure as a facet of central life interests. As problems of the division of labor have assumed less salience, issues connected with life style, with consumption, have achieved greater prominence. Living, as well as livelihood, becomes an object of attention.

What seems to be increasingly the case is that public arenas become the depositories of private worries. Here again the media of mass communication play a large role in making such areas of life as sex, parenthood, love and ambition into areas where private feelings are seen as socially shared. The self has become not only an object of transformation but an object whose change can be pursued in concert with others.

In short, the generalizing and normalizing processes by which movements influence change is more and more a process which should not be ignored. Movements are not only linear and directed; they are also fluid and undirected. They build up generalized contexts of cognitive and moral structure in both public and private; transcending and situated actions; at micro and macro levels. As W. I. Thompson put it, " . . . history is also the process by which public events become private imaginations." (W. I. Thompson, 1967, p. 235.)

PROBLEMS IN SOCIAL MOVEMENTS AND SOCIAL CHANGE

I bring this paper to a close with an examination of three movements. In each of these the relation between a specific and a more general movement is considered. Each represents a somewhat different problem in analyzing linear and fluid conceptions in the relation between social movements and social change.

1. The Social Security Act. The Problem of Protest and Change.

The passage of the Social Security Act of 1935 is seen by many historians of American life as a watershed in the development of a welfare state: from a reliance on voluntary, private activities to assure welfare to a commitment from public, governmental sources. (Lubove, 1968, Ch. 1; Schlesinger, 1959, p. 315.) In the light of the general discussion of protest and organized dissent in producing major change, the development of social security cries out for analysis.

Some historians and political scientists give a great deal of weight to the Townsend Movement and see its programs and agitation for pensions of $200 a month as crucial to the emergence and "successful" passage of the Act. (Holtzman, 1963; Sanders, 1973.) For these observers the social movement organization created a protest movement for which the Act was a response. Piven and Cloward, however, use the Townsend Movement as an example of how organization blunts the effectiveness of opposition which poor people's movements must depend upon for effectiveness. Social Security, they maintain, met the moral demands of the movement without giving the members anything. Seven years would elapse before Townsend members could be eligible and they would have had to have amassed working time to provide adequate pensions. (Piven and Cloward, 1979, p. 31.)

A closer look at social security, even though cursory here, suggests another way of seeing the act and its origins, somewhat different from the emphasis of the historians, political scientists and sociologists above. These focus on the specific movement of the moment and its organized program. In the same fashion Gamson attributes to the activities of protest organizations the success or failure of their aims. But the Act has a history and a context. Whatever criticisms of the Act at the time for failure to insure a wider segment of the population or for not effecting greater income redistribution, it was nevertheless a remarkable break with a dominant operating assumption about the dependence of the aged on the market and on individual resources. (Lubove, 1968.) It provided old age insurance on a compulsory basis and with government support where this had not occurred in the past. It laid a base for later widening of provisions and coverage, including Medicare. Whether or not it aided the Townsend supporters, it cannot be dismissed lightly as a minor change in American political or social structure.

> For all the defects of the Act, it still meant a tremendous break with the inhibitions of the past. The federal government was at last charged with obligation to provide its citizens a measure of protection from the hazards and vicissitudes of life. (Schlesinger, 1959, p. 315.)

What role did social movements and social movement organizations play in producing a social change of such significance? In the absence of a more thorough study I can only hint at one possible approach which sees the organized efforts as *an* element but only *an* and not *the*.

One significant thread in the cloth of the Social Security legislation came from the circle of advisors and assistants whom Franklin Roosevelt brought with him into power. In such people as Harry Hopkins, assistant to the President, and Frances Perkins, Secretary of Labor, he tapped into groups of people who had been active for many years in various phases of the social insurance movements. For two decades before the New Deal the social insurance movement had been growing in the United States, manifested in a small corps of people in fields such as social work, labor organizations, and academic life who had been active in programs for old age assistance, health insurance, pension plans and aid for dependent mothers. The movement in federal and state programs remained relatively subordinate to the dominant American theme of voluntary, private action. (Lubove, 1968.) Only one prominent American political leader, Franklin Delano Roosevelt (as New York State governor) had been a strong advocate. He named his State Industrial Commissioner, Frances Perkins, to be Secretary of Labor when he assumed the Presidency. In June of 1934, before the Townsend Movement gained momentum, he named a cabinet Committee on Economic Security, with Perkins as Chair. They formulated a program for Unemployment Compensation and for Social Security and in January, 1935, the legislation was introduced into the Senate. (Schlesinger, 1959, Ch. 18.)

The Townsend Movement may have been an important element in getting Congress to accept the legislation, and the Great Depression, of course, a major important context. Even with amendments, it was a change of significant proportions both in effects and in the traditional conceptions of American governmental obligations to the aged. Yet it is hardly attributable to specific protest actions or to the activities of specific movement organizations. The Townsend Movement was not engaged in violent or overt protest. Nor did it make a general Social Security program its major aim. It sought to do something "then and now" for the aged.

The social insurance movement formed a backdrop from which emerged a corps of people, a set of programs (including the influential plan previously adopted by Wisconsin) and a familiarity with ideas. These became more operational in the context of Depression. I do not mean to imply that specific movements never play a significant role in social change or that protest and mass agitation are necessary. But these need to be seen as problematic and situational and their relation to more fluid, less directed aspects of movements needs to be examined and recognized.

2. *The Alcoholism and Prevention Movements: The Nesting of Movements*

The relation between specific and general movements, between several specific movements or between "cultural drifts" and both types of movements is an important problem for the delineation of how meanings, associations and activities interrelated. Such relationships may be structural, in the sense of drawing on similar groups in the social structure, or cultural in the sense of a logical, symbolic or meaningful relation. The movement for the Equal Rights Amendment is clearly both in its relation to the larger and more encompassing Woman's Movement. Both, in turn, may have affinities to the generalized equalitarian impulse found in many ethnic, racial, minority, deviant groups. The Gay Rights movement might be traced to new orientations toward sexual expressiveness as well as the egalitarian impulses. Finding and delineating the nests of movements at differing levels is another avenue along which to investigate how changes are happening.

The analysis of policies and programs connected with alcohol issues since Repeal (1933) provides a good illustration of how such nestings may and may not occur.[5] The Temperance movement and Prohibition conceived alcohol problems as matters of drinking and drunkenness, as well as chronic inebriety. By 1900 direct controls over the availability of alcohol had come to be the major policy for minimizing and/or eradicating the alcohol problem. With Repeal of the Prohibition Amendment, that policy was discredited. A long period of American history during which church groups had played a dominant role in addressing the public question of alcohol had come to an end. In the wake of that era the problem of alcohol was defined in different fashion by emerging groups espousing new policies.

Chief among the new public opinion leaders and shapers were academic science, in the form of such groups as the Yale School of Alcohol Studies; a corps of self-labelled ''alcoholics,'' especially in Alcoholics Anonymous; and a newly emergent group of profesional and quasi-professional workers drawn from medicine, social work and clinical psychology. What was common to this otherwise often conflicting association was a focus on the chronic inebriate and the etiology of his problems in a disease called ''alcoholism.'' Removing the stigma against the alcoholic into a definition of his problem as ''sickness'' and providing for his treatment as a medical problem were the key aims of this movement.

During the period 1933-1970 the various associations and programs that were part of what has come to be called ''the Alcoholism movement'' were active in gaining a widened commitment of American states for financial support of treatment of alcoholism. In 1970 they played a major role in bringing about the National Institute on Alcohol Abuse and Alcoholism. (Again, as with Social Security, there are several other threads in that cloth.) The NIAAA brought a much enhanced program of financial support for the treatment of alcoholics.

In attempting to explain the movement toward a redefinition of the alcohol issue into the alcoholism issue and the move to inculcate the disease concept of alcoholism in the American population, it is difficult to relate it clearly to other movements at the same or differing levels in American life during this histori-cal period. The role of psychological counseling and therapy and its growth bears some relation to the development of a corps of professionals and quasi-professionals committed to treatment as a policy. However, it cannot account for the self-motivated associations of recovered alcoholics and AA nor for the origin and proliferation of the disease concept nor for the absence of a wider definition of alcohol problems or of social control measures. In an era of increasing governmental intervention in the economy, the Alcoholism movement was going in an opposite direction.

The Alcoholism movement has been considered in terms of the vacuum created by the sudden discrediting of the dominant religious groups associated with Prohibition and their definition of alcohol questions. It is hard to find a larger movement of ideas or of associations in which the Alcoholism movement clearly nested. To be sure, the general direction toward medicalization of social and other problems bears some relationship but this is by no means clear or direct. Medicalization has been under way for a long time in mental "illness."

Currently, however, the nesting of alcohol movements with other medical movements seems clearer. This is especially the case in its relation to the current movement toward Prevention and away from treatment in medicine.

Since the early 1970s alcohol studies and alcohol policy has been subject to a new impulse toward prevention of alcohol problems rather than their resolution through treatment and medicalization. Policies aimed at controlling the availability of alcoholic beverages and controlling their use have come to be seriously considered, discussed and debated in academic, organizational and governmental circles. Policies of taxation, minimum-age laws, drinking-driving legislation and other environmental changes have gained a corps of adherents as alternative to alcoholism as the prime problem and to treatment as the major policy. From the dominance of alcoholism and its medicalization, the public issues of alcohol problems now demonstrate a conflict sparked by a new movement critical of the disease concept of alcoholism and oriented toward the prevention of alcohol problems.

The movement toward prevention in the area of alcohol problems coincides with a more general movement away from treatment-oriented medicine and toward public health and prevention as policy models in health in the United States. The general movement has a number of elements in its makeup. The criticism of treatment-oriented medicine is, in part, a response to the growing costs of hospitals and physicians, the commitment of a welfare-committed government to health insurance, and the high proportion of medical expenditures as a part of the gross national product. But it is also more than that. It is also part of the egalitarian wave of distrust of experts and of doctors, itself another piece of the widened conception of citizen rights and egalitarian values. It is also a heightened awareness of environmental elements in health.

At still another level, the increased interest in health as a matter of public policy and private action, independent of professional medical practitioners, represents a redefinition of how health is achievable. An emphasis on appropriate life styles shifts the burden of illness responsibility from external agents, such as bacteria and constitutional genetic characteristics toward the public provision of information and environment and the citizen's responsibility to live appropriately. It is noteworthy that the model of the effective public prevention program is found, in government prevention papers and in other circles, in the campaign against cigarette smoking and the movement toward exercise and care to avoid heart attacks.

The preventive movement in alcohol problems is thus nested in a general prevention movement in the field of health in which government public health officials have led. That is in turn nested in a larger movement toward redefinition of medicine and the responsibility for resolving illness.[6] To study alcohol movements in isolation from such changes is to tell only a piece of the story.

How the nesting occurs and how the specific and general movements relate to each other is a matter of much greater study. In the case of the "new Temperance movement" (as I call it) the linkage would appear to have much to do with the inclusion of alcohol issues in the Federal government with the establishment of the National Institute on Alcohol Abuse and Alcoholism in 1970. As a part of the National Institutes of Health and the Public Health Service it became more open to general movements in health.

3. The Natural Foods Movement: The "Deep Structure" of Movements

An emphasis on the fluidity of movements leads also to the recognition that a change in meaning on one level can also be viewed as change in meaning at other levels. Foods, being an aspect of everyday life in its most mundane fashion, offer a clue to the general paradigms of existence. They can serve as instances in which is revealed the underlying, "deep structure" by which events are given order and made understandable. Levi-Strauss has made the distinction between the raw and the cooked a basic device by which to make sense of a wide variety of primitive mythes. (Levi-Strauss, 1969.) Others, such as Mary Douglas and Roland Barthes, also call attention to the signification used in the consumption of foods. (Douglas, 1971; Barthes, 1979.) Thus Barthes writes:

> Sugar is not just a foodstuff, even when it is used in conjunction with other foods; it is, if you will, an "attitude" . . . I remember an American hit song *Sugar Time*. Sugar is a time, a category of the world. (Barthes, 1979, pp. 166-67.)

The shifts in food usages and the movements for and against the use of certain foods or drink may then be clues to wider changes in thought and meaning. The symbolic properties projected onto foods constitutes part of a system for understanding and evaluating that may be found in other areas and in other movements.

The concept of "natural foods" contains in its very naming a contrast with artificial, human-made food. The alternative term "health food"carries with it the conception that non-natural forms of food are unhealthy. Processed foods, foods using preservatives, foods to which chemicals have been added—all qualify as other than food as found in nature. The products of food technology are thus derogated and placed in the category of harmful. The standardized, the mass-produced and mass-consumed items are, by virtue of their departure from the natural, *ipso facto* unhealthy and unaesthetic. Perhaps no food is as symbolic of the unnatural as processed and pre-sliced white bread.

The opposite has, of course, also been the case. The quest for the new and the modern has taken supremacy over the traditional food. The rise of middle classes in many underdeveloped countries has been accompanied by shifting food habits away from the native, the peasant, the traditional foods toward those of Western origins. The products of modern technology take on social status from their users but they also carry meanings about the virtues of the artificial and the vices of the natural. Even the shift from breast feeding to formula milk for babies in parts of Africa has had this set of meanings. (Uchendu, 1970.)

I am just beginning the study of natural food movements but they are by no means confined to the present period in history. Certainly in the late nineteenth century in the United States such a movement was rife. It lives on in the legacy of corn flakes. The humble morning cereal had its origins in health food missionaries, Kellogg and Post, who invented the common flake as a natural food to replace meat. (Carson, 1957.)

The movement toward the use of natural foods may then be seen in the context of paradigms concerning the values of nature vs. culture; of the natural against the artificial; human nature against civilization. It is an old theme, but one that all cultures have developd some meaning about. Henry Nasby Smith, in his analysis of American literature about the frontier, suggests that American writers saw the frontier as overcoming the natural side of human beings—their impulsive, destructive and anti-social humanness. It was civilization—the artificial control of the human—that made the frontier livable. (Smith, 1956; also see Wright, 1975.) The transformation was to be appreciated, not lamented. Against this Hobbesian and Freudian theme, there has also been the Rousseauistic glorification of the noble savage and the regret that culture and civilization create an artificial and dessicated human being, devoid of the innocent virtues that are inherent but covered over by society.

While the theme of nature and culture and the resulting tension between the two is by no means new, just how and when one or the other side of the conflict becomes dominant and in what parts of the society is a theme which the study of social movements can find significant. The paradigm of thought is linked to the anti-modern, the anti-technological, the anti-science movements which appear and disappear and reappear. These cannot easily be explained as responses to industrialism since they occurred again well after industrialism was enthroned. The communes movement of the 1960s contained a glorification of the simple, the natural and nontechnological; preferring natural food to artificial, human energy to motors, feelings to reasons. (Berger, forth.)

An analysis of natural foods movements, from this fluid perspective, would attempt to find the ''deep structure'' that makes the symbolism of natural and artificial food convincing and understandable. It would be a cultural search, in is efforts to construct the categories of logical understanding in use in the symbolism of foods. It would be social structural in attempting to find which parts of the social structure were carriers of the movement and the congruent mental structures.

For each of these movements discussed above, I posit the hypothesis of dual action and reaction; the specific influences the general by providing the reflective realization that change is happening at several levels. The more general movements in turn strengthen and support the specific ones; make them more understandable and acceptable.

What this programmatic paper calls for is less attention to change as defined in the program of the movement and less attention to movements as organized demands for change. What I have in mind is a greater role for the observer, the sociologist, in finding and naming the presence of a movement and in telling the reader or the listener what is happening from as wide a perspective as he or she, the observer, concludes is relevant.

ACKNOWLEDGMENTS

This paper was stimulated by a seminar on The Impact of the '60s on the '80s which I conducted in Winter, 1980. I am grateful to the following participants for their impact on my thought: Bennett Berger, Jay Coplin, Fred Davis, Tanice Foltz, Robin Franck, Henry Johnston, June Lowenberg, Kristin Luker, Jerzy Michalowicz, Ashley Phillips, Mireille Rajah and James Skelly.

NOTES

1.   Two outstanding exceptions to this generalization are Ash (1972) and Gamson (1975). Both of these are greatly concerned with effects of movements, although within a linear model (especially Gamson).

2.   I am indebted to Jerzy Michalowicz for my knowledge of the movement and its leadership composition.

3.   Henry Johnson is currently studying this problem in analyzing the waxing and waning of Catalan Regional Nationalism in Spain.

4.   I have presented this theory before in *Symblic Crusade* (1963), Ch. 6. The Civil Rights Movement and ethnic renaissance of recent years represents an important qualification. Yet, as Wilson's study indicates, even race is receding as a superimposed category. (Wilson, 1978)

5.   I have examined the alcohol movements discussed here more carefully in a forthcoming paper. Bibliographical references are contained here. (Gusfield, forth.)

6. In a personal communication, Jerzy Michalowicz has suggested that the movement toward greater concern for health has roots in a new glorification of the body as an object.

REFERENCES

Aaron, Paul and David Musto
    1980   ''Temperance and Prohibition in America,'' (Draft paper prepared for the Panel of the National Academy of Sciences on ALTERNATIVE POLICIES AFFECTING THE PREVENTION OF ALCOHOL ABUSE AND ALCOHOLISM.

Ash, Roberta
    1972   Social Movements in America. Chicago: Markham Publishing Co.

Banks, J.A.
    1972   The Sociology of Social Movements. London: Macmillan.

Barthes, Roland
    1979   ''Toward a psychosociology of contemporary food consumption.'' In R. Forster and O. Ranum (eds.), Food and Drink in History. Baltimore: The Johns Hopkins University Press.

Berger, Bennett
    Forthcoming
        The Survival of a Counter-Culture. Berkeley: University of California Press.

Blumer, Herbert
    1939   ''Collective behavior.'' In Robert Park (ed.), An Outline of the Principles of Sociology. New York: Barnes and Noble, Inc.

Burke, Kenneth
    1965   Permanence and Change. Indianapolis: the Bobbs-Merrill Co., Inc.

Carson, Gerald
    1957   Cornflake Crusade. New York: Rinehart.

Cross, Whitney
    1950   The Burned-Over District. Ithaca, NY: Cornell University Press.

Currie, Eliot and Jerome Skolnick
    1970   ''A critical note on conceptions of collective behavior.'' Annals of the American Academy of Political and Social Science 391(September): 34-45.

Denisoff, R.S.
    1974   The Sociology of Dissent. New York: Harcourt Brace Jovanovich.

Douglas, Mary
    1971   ''Deciphering a meal.'' In C. Geertz (ed.), Mythes, Symbols and Culture. New York: W.W. Norton and Co.

Foucault, Michel
    1973   The Order of Things. New York; Vintage Books.
    1975   The Birth of the Clinic. New York: Vintage Books.

Gamson, William
    1975   The Strategy of Social Protest. Homewood, IL: Dorsey Press.

Gerth, Hans and C. Wright Mills
    1942   ''A Marx for the managers.'' Ethics 52(January).

Gitlin, Todd
    1980   The Whole World is Watching. Berkeley: University of California Press.

Green, Arnold and Eleanor Melnick
    1950   ''What has happened to the feminist movement?'' In A.W. Gouldner (ed.), Studies in Leadership. New York: Harper and Row.

Gusfield, Joseph
    1963   Symbolic Crusade. Urbana, IL: University of Illinois Press.

1968   ''Prohibition: the impact of political utopianism.'' In John Braeman, Robert Bremner and David Brody (eds.), Change and Continuity in Twentieth-Century America, The 1920's. Columbus, OH: Ohio State University Press.

1978a   ''Historical problematics and sociological fields: American liberalism and the study of social movements.'' In Robert A. Jones (ed.), Research in Sociology of Knowledge, Sciences and Art, Vol. 1. Greenwich, CT: JAI Press Inc.

1978b   ''The sociological reality of America: an essay on mass culture.'' In H. Gans. N. Glazer, J. Gusfield and C. Jencks (eds.), On the Making of Americans. Philadelphia: University of Pennsylvania Press.

1980   ''The modernity of social movements: public roles and private parts.'' In Amos Hawle (ed.), Societal Growth. New York: Free Press.

1981   The Culture of Public Problems: Drinking-Driving and the Symbolic Order. Chicago: University of Chicago Press.

Forthcoming
            ''Prevention: rise, decline and renaissance.'' In T. Coffey and E. Gomberg (eds.), Alcohol, Science and Society Revisited. New Brunswick, NJ: Rutgers University Center of Alcohol Studies.

Handler, Joel
1980   Social Movements and the Law. New York: Academic Press.

Hechter, Michael
1975   Internal Colonialism. Berkeley: University of California Press.

Hofstadter, Richard
1965   The Paranoid Style in American Politics and Other Essays. New York: Alfred A. Knopf.

Holtzman, Abraham
1963   The Townsend Movement: A Political Study. New York: Bookman Associates, Inc.

Levi-Strauss, Claude
1968   The Raw and the Cooked. New York: Harper Torchbooks.

Lubove, Roy
1968   The Struggle for Social Security, 1900-1935. Cambridge, MA: Harvard University Press.

McCarthy, John and Mayer Zald
1973   The Trend of Social Movements in America: Professionalization and Resource Mobilization. Morristown, NJ: General Learning Corp.

Oberschall, Anthony
1978   ''The decline of the 1960s social movements.'' In Louis Kriesberg (ed.), Research in Social Movements, Conflicts and Change, Vol. 1. Greenwich, CT: JAI Press Inc.

Perrow, Charles
1978   ''The sixties observed.'' In Mayer Zald and John McCarthy (eds.), the Dynamics of Social Movements. Cambridge, MA: Winthrop Publishers.

Piven, Frances Fox and Richard Cloward
1979   Poor People's Movements. New York: Vintage Books.

Rothman, David
1971   The Discovery of the Asylum. Boston: Little, Brown and Company.

Sanders, Daniel
1973   The Impact of Reform Movements on Social Policy Change: The Case of Social Insurance. Fair Lawn, NJ: R.E. Burdick, Inc.

Schlesinger, Arthur M., Jr.
1959   The Coming of the New Deal. Boston: Houghton Mifflin Co.

Sennett, Richard
1978   The Fall of Public Man. New York: Vintage Books.

Shorter, Edward and Charles Tilly
  1974   Strikes in France, 1830-1968. Cambridge University Press.
Smelser, Neil
  1963   The Theory of Collective Behavior. New York: The Free Press.
Smith, Henry Nash
  1950   Virgin Land: The American West as Symbol and Myth. Cambridge, MA: Harvard
            University Press.
Snyder, David and William Kelly
  1979   "Strategies for investigating violence and social change." In Mayer Zald and John
            McCarthy (eds.), The Dynamics of Social Movements. Cambridge, MA: Winthrop
            Publishers.
Spinrad, William
  1970   Civil Liberties. Chicago: Quadrangle Books.
Taylor, Carl
  1953   The Farmers Movement 1620-1920. New York: American Book Co.
Thompson, E.A.
  1963   The Making of the English Working Class. New York: Vintage Books.
Thompson, W.I.
  1967   The Imagination of an Insurrection: Dublin, Easter 1916. New York: Harper Colo-
            phon Books.
Tilly, Charles, Louise Tilly and Richard Tilly
  1975   The Rebellious Century: 1830-1930. Cambridge, MA: Harvard University Press.
Tilly, Charles
  1978   From Mobiization to Revolution. Reading, MA: Addison-Wesley.
Trilling, Lionel
  1972   Sincerity and Authenticity. Cambridge, MA: Harvad University Press.
Turner, Ralph
  1969   "The theme of contemporary social movements." British Journal of Sociology 20
            (December): 390-405.
  1976   "The real self: from institution to impluse." American Journal of Sociology 21
            (March): 989-1016.
Tyler, Alice
  1962   Freedom's Ferment. New York: Harper Torchbooks.
Uchendu, Victor
  1970   "Cultural and economic factors influencing food habit patterns in Sub-Saharan
            Africa." 3rd International Congress of Food and Science Technology, Washington,
            DC, August 9-14, pp. 160-68.
Wilson, William J.
  1978   The Declining Significance of Race. Chicago: University of Chicago Press.
Wright, Will
  1975   Six Guns and Society. Berkeley: University of California Press.
Zald, Mayer and Roberta Ash
  1966   "Social movement organizations: growth, decay and change." Social Forces 44
            (March): 327-41.

AUTHOR INDEX

SUBJECT INDEX

351

Indices prepared by Richard Stempien
and Suzanne Stempien